# A Guide to St John's Gospel

SPCK International Study Guide 51

# A Guide to St John's Gospel

Fergus J. King

First published in Great Britain in 2015

Society for Promoting Christian Knowledge
36 Causton Street
London SW1P 4ST
www.spckpublishing.co.uk

*British Library Cataloguing-in-Publication Data*
A catalogue record for this book is available from the British Library.

SPCK ISBN 978–0–281–06730–5
eBook ISBN 978–0–281–06731–2

Originated by The Manila Typesetting Company
First printed in Great Britain by Ashford Colour Press
Subsequently digitally printed in Great Britain

eBook by Graphicraft Limited, Hong Kong

Produced on paper from sustainable forests

# Contents

Contributors                                                viii
The SPCK International Study Guides                          x
Acknowledgements                                            xi
Using this Guide                                            xii
Works consulted and further reading                         xv

Introduction                                                1
  The location of the Gospel                      2
  The identity of John                            4
  The date of the Gospel                          5
  The context of the Gospel                       5
  John and the Synoptic Gospels                   6
  The good news according to John                 7

**Part 1  The Book of Signs**

1.1—2.12: Jesus: in heaven and on earth                     13
  1.1–18: The Prologue                            13
  1.19–51: Jesus' earthly context                 19
  2.1–12: The miracle at Cana                      26

2.13—4.54: The first Passover                               31
  2.13–22: Jesus cleanses the Temple              31
  2.23–25: Signs and trust                        35
  3.1–21: Jesus and Nicodemus                     37
  3.22–36: The Baptist, Jesus and the Messiah     44
  4.1–42: Jesus at the Well of Jacob              47
  4.43–54: Jesus returns to Galilee               54

5.1–47: The first Sabbath controversy                       58
  5.1–47: Jesus heals a sick man                  58

Theological essay 1: Sonship in John's Gospel               66
S. Robertson

6.1–71: The second Passover                                 74
  6.1–15: A miraculous meal                       74

6.16–21: A miracle at sea   77

6.22–50: Jesus and the crowd   79

6.51–59: Jesus and the Jews   84

6.60–71: Jesus and the disciples   87

*Excursus: John 6 and the Eucharist*   90

7.1—8.59: The Festival of Booths   93

7.1–13: Family matters   93

7.14–31: The first *Sukkoth* dialogue   96

7.32–36: The second attempt to arrest Jesus   99

7.37–52: The second *Sukkoth* dialogue   100

7.53—8.11: A very late addition to the Gospel   104

8.12–20: The third *Sukkoth* dialogue   107

8.21–30: Jesus speaks of a mysterious journey   109

8.31–38: Jesus describes his disciples   112

8.39–59: A violent debate about ancestry   115

9.1—10.21: The second Sabbath controversy   121

9.1–12: Jesus the magician?   121

9.13–34: The blind man, his parents and the Pharisees   124

9.35–39: Jesus finds the blind man   128

9.40—10.21: Jesus, the Pharisees and the Good Shepherd   130

10.22—11.54: The Festival of Dedication   138

10.22–42: Rejection and blasphemy   138

11.1–54: Acting as the Good Shepherd – Martha, Mary and Lazarus   142

11.55—12.50: Jesus' last Passover   152

11.55—12.11: Events at Bethany   152

12.12–19: The entry to Jerusalem   155

12.20–36a: Remarks about death   157

12.36b–50: Peroration   162

*Theological essay 2: Signs in John's Gospel*   165
Voon Choon Khing

**Part 2   The Book of Glory**

13.1—17.26: The Last Meal and farewell speeches   175

13.1–20: Washing the disciples' feet   175

13.21–38: Predictions to the disciples   182

14.1–31: Farewell Speech 1   186

15.1—16.33: Farewell Speech 2   193

17.1–26: Farewell Speech 3 – the prayer of Jesus   203

*Theological essay 3: The 'I am' sayings of Jesus in*
*John's Gospel*                                                         209
Samuel Otieno Sudhe

18.1—19.42: From Jesus' arrest to his death and burial        217
    18.1–11: The arrest of Jesus                        217
    18.12–27: At the house of the high priest           220
    18.28—19.16a: At the headquarters of Pilate         224
    19.16b–42: The crucifixion and death of Jesus       233

20.1–31: The resurrection appearances                         244
    20.1–10: Mary Magdalene and the two disciples       244
    20.11–18: Mary Magdalene and Jesus                   249
    20.19–23: The disciples and Jesus                    252
    20.24–29: Thomas and Jesus                          256
    20.30–31: Concluding remarks                        258

**Part 3 The Epilogue**

21.1–14: Jesus at the Sea of Tiberias                          263
21.15–23: Jesus, Peter and the Beloved Disciple               268
21.24–25: The Afterword                                       273
*Theological essay 4: Discipleship in John's Gospel*          274
Kwa Kiem-Kiok

*Appendices*                                                  281
*Index*                                                       289

# Contributors

**The Revd Dr Fergus J. King** is Conjoint Senior Lecturer in Theology and Religious Studies at the University of Newcastle, Australia, and Rector of the Parish of the Good Shepherd in the Anglican Diocese of Newcastle. He is also an honorary Canon and the Canon Theologian of the Diocese of Tanga, Tanzania. He holds a DTh from the University of South Africa, published in revised form as *More Than a Passover: Inculturation in the Supper Narratives of the New Testament* (Frankfurt: Peter Lang, 2007). He has taught in Tanzania, and is the author of several articles on missiological and New Testament themes.

Life has been an adventure with God for **Voon Choon Khing** ever since her conversion from traditional Chinese beliefs in 1966. God's primary call on her as God's beloved has found varying expressions: as a trained nurse and midwife (UK), Christian ministry among overseas students and nurses (UK), Christian social work with mentally ill women (Malaysia), and theological education as librarian (1986–2001), counsellor and lecturer with Seminari Theoloji Malaysia (1992–). Her academic training includes an MA in Library and Information Studies (London University), MTh (Duke University) and DMin in Spiritual Direction (Graduate Theological Foundation, Indiana).

**Dr Kwa Kiem-Kiok** teaches at the East Asia School of Theology in Singapore. From 1999 to 2003 she was involved in training, curriculum development, discipleship and mentoring at Trinity Methodist Church, Singapore. While pursuing her doctoral studies she also worked at the International Office at Asbury Theological Seminary. She has worked with the Graduates' Christian Fellowship, an affiliate of Fellowship of Evangelical Students, equipping graduates for witness and ministry in the marketplace. She and her husband Ivan Tan enjoy walking and listening to classical music.

**Dr S. Robertson** specializes in the field of Indian religion, particularly Hinduism, and has published widely. He has MAs in Public Administration and in Sanskrit. His 1994 MTh thesis analysed an almost atheist ideology of a local political movement. His doctoral studies, completed in 2003, explored a local *bhakti* (devotion) tradition in India. Presently he is researching the 'freedom of religion in India as a human rights issue'. Since 2005, he has been Principal of Bethel Bible College, affiliated to the Senate of Serampore College (University). He is married to S. R. Selin Rani and they have a son, Ayush Robertson.

**The Revd Samuel Otieno Sudhe** is a priest in the Diocese of Bondo in the Anglican Church of Kenya. He is currently working as the deputy principal at Bishop Okullu College of Theology and Development, which is a constituent College of the Great Lakes University of Kisumu, Kenya. The Revd Samuel Sudhe undertook his theological training at St Paul's United Theological College, Limuru, and at Virginia Theological Seminary, Alexandria, USA. He is currently a PhD candidate at Maseno University, Kenya.

# The SPCK International Study Guides

For over 40 years, SPCK Worldwide's International Study Guides have provided resources for students training for service across a wide range of church traditions. The series contains biblical commentaries, books on pastoral care, church history and theology, as well as those on contemporary issues such as HIV and AIDS, and each title includes resources for discussion and further reading. Primarily aimed at those for whom English is an alternative language, the Study Guides are clear and accessible resources designed to enable students to explore their own theologies and discern God's mission in their own context. Many other Christians will also find the ISGs useful.

Today, with such plurality within the Church of God, the Study Guides draw upon the breadth of Christian experience across the globe. The contributors come from different countries and from a variety of church backgrounds. Most of them are theological educators. They bring their particular perspectives to bear as they demonstrate the influence of their contexts on the subjects they address. They provide a practical emphasis alongside contemporary scholarly reflection.

*David Craig*
*Editor, International Study Guides*

# Acknowledgements

It is impossible to approach a work like John's Gospel without being aware that 'we are standing on the shoulders of giants'. Some of these appear in the list of works consulted and suggestions for further reading, others in the more subtle shaping of a scholarly approach in the classroom. Both students and teachers join in this process, so I must acknowledge my debts to those with whom I have been privileged to read at St Andrews, Edinburgh, St Mark's Dar es Salaam, the universities of South Africa and Newcastle (NSW), and the Anglican Diocese here. I also record my thanks to David Craig, Lauren Zimmerman, and those at SPCK who saw the draft script into its final format, including the commissioning editor Angus Crichton, editorial manager Louise Clairmonte and copy editor Mollie Barker. Thanks, too, to Scott Kirkland for the index.

Not all learning is confined to the academy, so thank you, too, to Irene, the boys, my parents and brother, and the parishioners at Kotara South.

As I worked on the Guide, my father died, on All Souls' Day 2011. The following was part of a longer reading at his funeral:

*Man cannot exist without a philosophy of some kind. However he may try to keep awake he must always find something to lay his muddled head upon. Civilised life is too complex, too full of superficialities and false doctrines. The philosophy of the hills is a simple one. On them we approach a little nearer to the ends of the earth and the beginnings of Heaven. Over the hills the spirit of Man passes towards his Maker.*

(Frank Smythe, *Climbs and Ski Runs*,
Blackwood, 1929)

As I worked on this Guide, the words of the Gospel provided a counter-balance to such a spirituality: 'Jesus went up the mountain and sat down there with his disciples' (John 6.3).

Rest in peace, John Abercromby King.

*Fergus J. King*
*Newcastle, New South Wales*
*Australia*

# Using this Guide

The plan of this Guide follows much the same pattern as that of other biblical Guides in the series.

In the **Introduction** the author sets the scene for our study of the biblical book that is selected by providing a brief note on its background. Its relationship with other biblical books may also be explored.

The study of the biblical book itself has been divided into short sections according to natural breaks in the text. But before beginning their work, readers may find it helpful to consider how they can make the best use of this Guide.

Each section consists of:

 1    A **summary** of the passage, briefly indicating the subject-matter it contains. Of course the summary is not intended as a substitute for the words of the Bible itself, which need to be read very carefully at each stage of our study.

 2    **Notes and commentary** on particular words and points of possible difficulty, especially as relating to the purpose of the writing, and to the situation which gave rise to the writing.

 3    An **interpretation** of the passage and the teaching it contains, both as it applied to those to whom it was addressed, and as we should understand and apply it to our own situation today.

 ## Theological essays

Topics that warrant extended attention because of their implications for theology and the current situation of many churches today are covered in 'Theological essays'. The authors of these essays show one way in which a theme, a biblical text and a particular context can be read together to discern God's will in our world today.

Readers will note that the essays sometimes reach different conclusions from the main text of the Guide. They are encouraged to compare the different views reached, and work out which they think is better and why. This step is vital for readers to learn to engage critically with literature of this type. Placing different views within a single volume is considered a part of acknowledging the variety of theological views which are possible, and the need for students to develop skills in comparing and criticizing them.

# **?** Study suggestions

Suggestions for further study and review are included at the end of each section. Besides enabling students working alone to check their own progress, they provide subjects for individual and group research, and topics for discussion. They are of three main sorts:

1 **Word study,** to help readers check and deepen their understanding of important words and phrases.

2 **Review of content,** to help readers check the work they have done, and make sure they have fully grasped the ideas and points of teaching given.

3 **Discussion and application,** to help readers think out the practical significance of the passage being studied, both to those to whom the biblical author was writing, and for the life and work of the churches and of individual Christians in the modern situation. Many of these are suitable for use in a group as well as for students working alone.

The best way to use these study suggestions is:

- to reread the Bible passage;

- to read the appropriate section of the Guide once or twice;

- to do the work suggested, either in writing or in group discussion, without looking at the Guide again unless instructed to do so.

Please note that all these are only **suggestions.** Some readers may not wish to use them. Some teachers may wish to select only those most relevant to the needs of their particular students, or may wish to substitute questions of their own.

A list of **works consulted** and suggestions for **further reading** is provided on p. xv, and a **map** of the countries around the eastern Mediterranean in New Testament times may be found on p. 3.

## Index

The Index includes only the more important names of people and places and the main subjects treated in John's Gospel or discussed in the Guide.

## Bible versions

John's Gospel was originally written in Greek, and many handwritten manuscripts of it survive. The text used in this Guide is the New Revised Standard Version (NRSV), which has been worked on by scholars from many religious traditions. Sometimes translations may reflect a particular denominational or confessional view; the NRSV has been produced with all traditions in mind. Sometimes, though, it may be suggested that an alternative translation might bring out better the meaning of the original Greek (e.g. Notes and commentary, 1.5).

# Works consulted and further reading

Barker, Margaret (1992). *The Great Angel: A Study of Israel's Second God*, Louisville: Westminster John Knox Press.

Barrett, Charles K. (1978). *The Gospel According to St John* (2nd edn), Philadelphia: Westminster.

Barrett, Charles K. (1982). *Essays on John*, London: SPCK.

Barrett, Charles K. (1983). *The Gospel of John and Judaism*, London: SPCK.

Bauckham, Richard (2007). *The Testimony of the Beloved Disciple: Narrative, History and Theology in the Gospel of John*, Grand Rapids: Baker.

Bekken, Per Jarle (2008). 'The Controversy on Self-Testimony According to John 5:31–40; 8:12–20 and Philo, *Legum Allegoriae* III. 205–08'. Pages 19–42 in B. Holmberg and M. Winninge (eds), *Identity Formation in the New Testament* (WUNT 227), Tübingen: Mohr Siebeck.

Bennema, Cornelis (2005). 'The Sword of the Messiah and the Concept of Liberation in the Fourth Gospel', *Biblica* 86/1, 35–58.

Blomberg, Craig L. (2001). *The Historical Reliability of John's Gospel*, Leicester: Apollos (IVP).

Boyarin, Daniel (2012). *The Jewish Gospels: The Story of the Jewish Christ*, New York: The New Press.

Brant, Jo-Ann A. (2011). *John* (Paideia Commentaries on the New Testament), Grand Rapids: Baker.

Brodie, Thomas L. (1993). *The Gospel According to John: A Literary and Theological Commentary*, Oxford: Oxford University Press.

Brown, Raymond E. (1988). *The Gospel According to John 1—2* (Anchor Bible Commentary 29), London: Geoffrey Chapman.

Brown, Raymond E. (1994). *The Death of the Messiah, From Gethsemane to the Grave: A Commentary on the Passion Narratives in the Four Gospels* (Anchor Yale Bible Reference Library), 2 vols, London: Geoffrey Chapman.

Bultmann, Rudolf (1971). *The Gospel of John: A Commentary* (trans. G. R. Beasley-Murray with R. W. N. Hoare and J. K. Riches), Oxford: Blackwell.

Burchard, Christoph (1987). 'The Importance of *Joseph and Aseneth* for a Study of the New Testament: A General Survey and a Fresh Look at the Lord's Supper', *New Testament Studies* 33/1, 102–34.

Burridge, Richard A. (2008). *John* (The People's Bible Commentary: 2008 Lambeth Conference Edition), Abingdon: Bible Reading Fellowship.

Carter, Warren (2006). *John: Storyteller, Interpreter, Evangelist*, Peabody: Hendrickson.

Dodd, Charles H. (1978). *The Interpretation of the Fourth Gospel*, Cambridge: Cambridge University Press.

Donovan, Vincent J. (2003). *Christianity Rediscovered*, Maryknoll: Orbis.

Dover, Kenneth J. (1989). *Greek Homosexuality*, Cambridge, MA: Harvard University Press.

Engberg-Pedersen, Troels (2001). *Paul beyond the Judaism/Hellenism Divide*, Louisville: Westminster John Knox Press.

Fenton, John (1991). 'Eating People', *Theology* 94/762, 414–23.

Foucault, Michel (2001). *Fearless Speech* (ed. Joseph Pearson), Los Angeles: Semiotext(e).

George, Archimandrite (2006). *Theosis: The True Purpose of Human Life*, Mt Athos: Holy Monastery of St Gregorios <http://orthodoxinfo.com/general/theosis-english.pdf>.

Gerhardsson, Birger (1998). *Memory and Manuscript: Oral Tradition and Written Transmission in Rabbinic Judaism and Early Christianity; with, Tradition and Transmission in Early Christianity*, Grand Rapids: Eerdmans.

Hengel, Martin (1986). *The Cross of the Son of God*, London: SCM.

Hengel, Martin (1990). *The Johannine Question*, London: SCM.

Hengel, Martin (1995). *Studies in Early Christology*, Edinburgh: T&T Clark.

Johnson, Luke T. (1989). 'The New Testament's Anti-Jewish Slander and the Conventions of Ancient Polemic', *Journal of Biblical Literature* 108/3, 419–41.

Keener, Craig S. (2003). *The Gospel of John: A Commentary*, vols 1–2, Peabody: Hendrickson.

Kilpatrick, George D. (1983). *The Eucharist in Bible and Liturgy*, Cambridge: Cambridge University Press.

King, Fergus J. (2007). *More Than a Passover: Inculturation in the Supper Narratives of the New Testament* (New Testament Studies in Contextual Exegesis 3), Frankfurt am Main: Peter Lang.

King, Fergus J. (2010). '"Father, forgive them, for they know not what they do": Reflections on Luke 23:34a, Kol Nidre and the Atonement', *Australian Journal of Jewish Studies* 24, 134–60.

Klawans, Jonathan (2002). 'Interpreting the Last Supper: Sacrifice, Spiritualization, and Anti-Sacrifice', *New Testament Studies* 48/1, 1–17.

Knohl, Israel (2009). *Messiahs and Resurrection in 'The Gabriel Revelation'*, London: Continuum.

Köstenberger, Andreas J. (2007). 'John'. Pages 415–512 in G. K. Beale and D. A. Carson (eds), *Commentary on the New Testament Use of the Old Testament*, Grand Rapids: Baker.

Lee, Aquila H. I. (2005). *From Messiah to Pre-existent Son* (WUNT 2/192), Tübingen: Mohr Siebeck.

Lindars, Barnabas (1972). *The Gospel of John* (New Century Bible), London: Marshall, Morgan & Scott.

Malina, Bruce A. and Richard L. Rohrbaugh (1998). *Social-Science Commentary on the Gospel of John*, Minneapolis: Fortress.

Marshall, I. H., A. R. Millard, J. I. Packer and D. J. Wiseman (2010). *The New Bible Dictionary* (3rd edn), Downers Grove and Nottingham: Inter-Varsity Press.

Matson, Mark A. Matson (no date), 'Current Approaches to the Priority of John' <http://www.milligan.edu/administrative/mmatson/JohnPriority2.pdf>.

McKnight, Scot and Joseph Modica (2008), *Who Do My Opponents Say That I Am?: An Investigation of the Accusations against Jesus*, London: T&T Clark.

Meiser, Martin (2010). 'Some Facets of Pauline Anthropology: How Would a Greco-Roman Reader Understand It?'. Pages 55–85 in M. Labahn and M. Lehtipuu (eds), *Anthropology in the New Testament and Its Ancient Context: Papers from the EABS-Meeting in Piliscsaba/Budapest*, Leuven: Peeters.

Moffatt, James (1913). *The New Testament: A New Translation*, New York: Hodder & Stoughton.

Moloney, Francis J. (1998a). *The Gospel of John* (Sacra Pagina 4), Collegeville: Liturgical Press.

Moloney, Francis J. (1998b). *Glory Not Dishonor: Reading John 13—21*, Minneapolis: Fortress.

Moule, Charles F. D. (1953). *An Idiom-Book of New Testament Greek*, Cambridge: Cambridge University Press.

Newsom, Carol A. (2001). 'Apocalyptic Subjects: Social Construction of the Self in the Qumran Hodayot', *Journal for the Study of the Pseudepigrapha* 12, 3–35.

Neyrey, Jerome H. (2009). *The Gospel of John in Cultural and Rhetorical Perspective*, Grand Rapids: Eerdmans.

Nürnberger, Klaus (2007). *The Living Dead and the Living God: Christ and the Ancestors in Changing Africa*, Pietermaritzburg: Cluster.

Page, Sydney H. T. (1995). *Powers of Evil: A Biblical Study of Satan and Demons*, Grand Rapids: Baker/Apollos.

Painter, John (1991). *The Quest for the Messiah: The History, Literature and Theology of the Johannine Community*, Edinburgh: T&T Clark.

Robinson, John A. T. (1976). *Re-dating the New Testament*, London: SCM.

Robinson, John A. T. (2011). *The Priority of John* (ed. J. F. Coakley), Eugene: Wipf & Stock.

Sandmel, Samuel (1962). 'Parallelomania', *Journal of Biblical Literature* 81/1, 1–13.

Schnackenburg, Rudolf (1980–2). *The Gospel According to St John 1—3* (trans. K. Smyth), London: Burns & Oates.

Schnelle, Udo (1992). *Antidocetic Christology in the Gospel of John*, Minneapolis: Fortress.

Temple, William (1939–40). *Readings in St John's Gospel*, 2 vols, London: Macmillan.

Thomson, John B. (2004). *Church on Edge?: Practising Ministry Today*, London: Darton, Longman & Todd.

Vacek, Edward Collins (1996). 'Love, Christian and Diverse: A Response to Colin Grant', *Journal of Religious Ethics* 24/1, 29–34.

Viviano, Benedict T. and Justin Taylor (1992). 'Sadducees, Angels and Resurrection', *Journal of Biblical Literature* 111/3, 49–98.

von Wahlde, Urban C. (2010). *The Gospel and Letters of John, vol. 2: Commentary on the Gospel of John* (Eerdmans Critical Commentary), Grand Rapids: Eerdmans.

Winter, Paul (1974). *On the Trial of Jesus* (Studia Judaica: Forschungen zur Wissenschaft des Judentums: Band 1; 2nd edn, rev. and ed. T. A. Burkill and Geza Vermes), Berlin/New York: Walter de Gruyter.

Zinkuratire, Victor, Angelo Colacrai et al. (1999). *The African Bible*, Nairobi: Paulines Publications Africa.

# Introduction

The Gospel according to John is a very important writing for Christian tradition. It has a character all its own, and presents a picture of Jesus of Nazareth which is both similar to the other Gospels and yet very different from them.

John's Gospel has had a mixed reception. Many people have enjoyed and valued it as a straightforward account of Jesus' life, death and purpose, while others have seen it as rich in complex spiritual understanding – what one writer calls its 'exalted mysticism'. Yet many who hold different views about Jesus have also claimed that this Gospel supports their views, among them the Docetics (those who believed that Jesus did not really become human, but only seemed to), the Gnostics (who believed that they had secret knowledge enabling them to enter heaven), the Montanists (who believed they had a special new revelation from God which surpassed that of other Christians) and the Quartodecimans (who believed Easter should be celebrated on the fourteenth day of the Jewish month of Nisan). Even in our time, groups like the Jehovah's Witnesses, who do not believe God became human in Jesus, base their beliefs on an interpretation of verses from John's Gospel.

Given this history, one of the things that a Guide like this should do is to take us back to the text itself, to try to understand what it says in its own right.

This is a difficult task because John's world was very different from ours and we often do not have a complete picture of it. In recent years, biblical scholars, especially those from what is called the Global South, have reminded us that this is really only part of the whole work of reading the Bible. They tell us that the Bible is not simply a collection of ancient texts with an historical meaning, but *texts for transformation*. By this, they mean that reading the Bible should have an effect on how the readers live: reading the books of the Bible means applying the text to our own life and context. This is not actually very different from what ancient Jewish interpreters believed. They talked of something called 'correspondence in history', meaning that we have never finished reading a text until we explore what it means for us in our time and place. It's also very close to John 20.31, with the hope that the Gospel becomes a source of life.

A useful way of summarizing this way of reading, and these two linked stages of reading, is 'letting the Bible in its context speak to us in our context'. In this Guide, we try to do this with the following method:

- We learn about the culture and context which shaped the Gospel.

- With this information we try to work out what messages the first readers might have drawn from their reading: what the text meant then.

- We then should look at what this might make the text mean for us. Because this book is written in the hopes that people from all over the world living in different cultures will read it, we cannot answer all these questions in a book like this. So there are 'Discussion and application' questions at the end of each section, which you may wish to explore in personal or group reflections.

Studies of John's Gospel from the first half of the twentieth century share a consensus that the Gospel was written comparatively late (from 90 CE onwards) and came from a Graeco-Roman context.

The discovery of the Dead Sea Scrolls in 1947 above Qumran near the Dead Sea has changed this view. These scrolls have greatly increased our knowledge of Second Temple Judaism, the Judaism of Jesus' time, and show that many ideas which scholars said had to come from Graeco-Roman sources were already part and parcel of Judaic thought; for example, the dualism of light and dark, prominent in the Dead Sea Scrolls (Appendix B), and pre-existence (Appendix F).

Scholars have sometimes suggested that the Gospel was written over a long period of time and written to make theological points rather than report history accurately. Recent detailed research has shown that the Gospels most closely resemble writings called *Bioi* (lives) – the accounts written of the great figures of the ancient world, designed to give good examples and role models. This suggests that the Gospel was written with a view to provide an account of Jesus.

## The location of the Gospel

Three places have been suggested as locations for the Gospel: Antioch or Syria, Alexandria in Egypt, and Ephesus in Asia Minor (see the map on p. 3).

Alexandria in Egypt has been suggested because a fragment of the Gospel, named Papyrus 52, was found there. This ancient papyrus contains the text of John 18.31, 38 and is dated by most scholars between 100 and 150 CE, and by many to between 117 and 138 CE by the style of writing. However, this manuscript need not have been written where it was found.

Other evidence suggested includes the cosmopolitan nature of the city (which included Greek, Jewish and even Samaritan communities) and its strong philosophical tradition, exemplified by Philo, a first-century Jewish philosopher. The Gospel also became very important in later Alexandrian theological disputes. However, earlier debates from Alexandria refer more to Paul than John: Valentinus (roughly 100–155 CE) said that Paul, not John, taught his own teacher, Theudas. John's Gospel became important later in Alexandria.

Antioch and Syria have been suggested because there are some links between the Gospel and the writings of Ignatius of Antioch (born between 35 and 50 CE, died between 98 and 117). His letter *To the Ephesians* 20

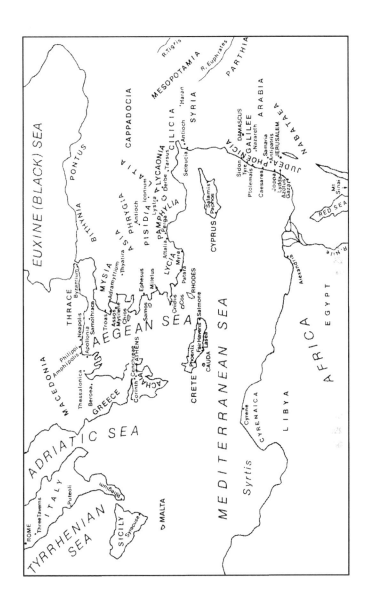

**The eastern Mediterranean in New Testament times**
*Source:* Kim Huat Tan ISG 40: *A Guide to Galatians and Philippians*, p. xv.

seems influenced by John 6, but is not identical with it. While tradition sometimes claims Ignatius as a pupil of John (*The Martyrdom of Ignatius* 1), links to Antioch are more difficult.

The connection of Ignatius, John and *To the Ephesians* has led to the suggestion that the Gospel might be better associated with Ephesus. Furthermore, the writings of Polycarp, who was martyred by 168 CE, mention a significant church figure called John of Ephesus. Scholars who view these traditions as basically reliable suggest that John of Ephesus might be the writer of the Gospel.

None of this evidence is conclusive, and different writers continue to argue for all these locations: Alexandria because of physical evidence, Antioch or Syria because of Ignatius, and Ephesus because of the historical records and traditions of the Church in Asia Minor.

## The identity of John

The New Testament contains five books which claim John as the author: the Gospel, three letters and Revelation. Traditionally these have been grouped together as the 'Johannine corpus' and have been attributed to John the son of Zebedee, one of the twelve disciples. Many have questioned whether or not the whole Johannine corpus could be attributed to one person. One particular problem is the language and style of the book of Revelation: its Greek is very different in quality from the other writings. Compared to mainstream Greek of the period, Revelation reads like the Greek of someone for whom it is a second language, or as though it has been translated in a quite literal fashion from Hebrew or Aramaic.

Let us focus only on who might have written the Gospel.

The traditional identification of 'John' with John, son of Zebedee and brother of James, has been queried because:

1 Papias (roughly 60–135 CE), a church historian and bishop of Hierapolis, a town near Colossae and Laodicea in Asia Minor or modern-day Turkey, tells of John's early death – and this would seem to rule him out as a potential writer of the Gospel.

2 John the son of Zebedee would have been a Galilean, but the Gospel, unlike the Synoptic Gospels, does not dwell in detail on Jesus' ministry in Galilee, preferring to focus on his activities in and around Jerusalem.

3 Scholars then have asked whether or not there was some other John who might be the author. A number point to John of Ephesus, a church elder or leader, as a potential writer. Others think the writer might be a character who appears in the Gospel; Lazarus, Mary and/ or Martha, and Matthias have all been suggested. The most likely candidate is the Beloved Disciple (13.23–26; 19.25–27; 20.2–8; 21.7; 21.20–23, 24).

Scholars have identified the Beloved Disciple with the 'other disciple': a follower of Jesus based in Jerusalem, known to the high priest (18.15: able to get Peter admitted to the house where Jesus is being questioned). It is even suggested that he may be the 'unknown disciple' of John the Baptist who accompanies Andrew (1.35–42). This person, it is suggested, becomes an authoritative source about Jesus, whose witness is equivalent to that of Peter, with whom he is often linked and compared, for example in 20.2–10; 21.20–25. He becomes an exile from Jerusalem in the persecutions of the emerging Christian community, flees to Syria, and eventually settles in Asia Minor. The Gospel as we have it becomes the final version of a story which he has taken with him, finally shaped amid a number of controversies within the community about who Jesus was.

## The date of the Gospel

It is easiest to start by looking at the latest date for the Gospel. Papyrus 52 (see 'The location of the Gospel', p. 2) shows that the Gospel must have been written before 150 CE. The fact that Ignatius seems to know the Gospel makes the last date earlier, as he died by 117 CE. Some would date the book even earlier. The majority now see the Gospel written before 100 CE when John died. This fits with use of the Gospel by Ignatius; it was a work in circulation by the time he passed through Asia Minor.

Let us now look at the earliest date. Some scholars argue that the Gospel was written very early, maybe even by 65 CE. There is nothing which demands a long period of writing, or forces a late date.

In conclusion, the broadest window for the date of the Gospel is between 65 and about 110 CE; most scholars think it dates to 90–100 CE, but a significant minority would date it earlier.

## The context of the Gospel

In order to understand the context in which the Gospel was written, we need more information than just the identity of the writer, the location of the Gospel and its date. It is very important to know about the ideas, values and behaviours of the people who wrote and first used the Gospel.

Graeco-Roman society was very varied, and tended to blend different cultures together. Greeks and Romans worshipped many gods. Their different religious practices had different meanings: the state and imperial cults were about political loyalty; if people felt a need for personal salvation they turned to mystery religions; and both ancient myths and philosophical schools helped people to develop a worldview – an understanding about how the world functions.

Jewish culture was essentially monotheistic; people worshipped a single god. It too had many different religious traditions, which shared the same three interests as Graeco-Roman religion: politics, personal salvation, worldview. There was a great interest in purity, which meant living

5

life in a way which was pleasing to God; the key elements of purity are found in the books of the Torah.

All these ancient cultures had some distinctive features which shaped how people lived. Their values were affected by the structure of the societies. Networks of relationships were based on kinship and power; also important was people's attitude to honour and shame in areas such as health, beauty, place of birth, citizenship, social strata (slave, freed or free), class, and ancestry. In Judaic society, maintaining a degree of ritual purity was also significant. A number of these issues appear in the Gospel in discussions about Jesus' origins and authority (for example, 1.46).

## John and the Synoptic Gospels

Scholars have also explored the similarities between John and the Synoptic Gospels (the collective name for Mark, Matthew and Luke). John is quite different from them. He does not use narrative parables like those in the Synoptics. Nor does he include exorcisms or pronouncement stories (short questions and answers like Mark 2.13–17, 18–22, 23–28), although he may record similar material in longer dialogues. John does not know the long sermons like the Sermon on the Mount (Matthew 5—7) or the Sermon on the Plain (Luke 6.17–49).

Despite these differences, scholars still try to connect John and the Synoptics. Many have made great efforts recently to find links between John and Mark. These include incidental details as well as sayings or specific events. Thus, John occasionally seems to be familiar with events told in Mark, but does not include them in his own narrative. For example, he mentions the imprisonment of John the Baptist (3.24; see Mark 6.14–29) to distinguish the events in chapter 3 from those of chapter 5, which seem to be dated after the Baptist's imprisonment. There are also echoes of Mark's story in characters and events that are not introduced clearly, but seem to be familiar to his readers: Mary (11.1–2; cf. Mark 14.9), the trial before Caiaphas (18.24; see Mark 14.53–65), John the Baptist, Simon Peter, the 'twelve', Judas Iscariot and Pontius Pilate. None of this, however, proves that John knew the Gospel according to Mark. It shows that both writer and audience *might* have known Mark's Gospel, or, failing that, he knew the sources and traditions which it used.

Scholars often assume that differences mean that John is less historically accurate than the other Gospels. There are two kinds of problem passages: the first, like the cleansing of the Temple (2.13–22), is where an event is described by the various Gospels but there are differences in how John tells it; the second, like the raising of Lazarus (11.1–44), is where an event is found only in John.

We must be careful not to jump to premature conclusions about which Gospel is more or less accurate, especially when we do not know the sources for the different versions of events, and have no way of retrieving the events themselves separately from the written versions we have. To assume that the Synoptics always are right, and John wrong, would be like listening to two witnesses to an incident and treating all that one said as wrong, and the other as right.

Care also needs to be taken when the Gospel is compared to other ancient texts. When we compare passages, we must look at both the similarities and differences between the passages. A comparison should consider:

- language (style, grammar and vocabulary);
- ideology (religious ideas, ethical parallels);
- social and historical parallels.

Sometimes writers share these features, but that does not mean that one can be explained by showing what the other has said. Examples of such comparisons can be seen in 2.10; 20.7.

## The good news according to John

In 20.31, John outlines the purpose of writing his Gospel. A summary of the main themes might look like this:

- God is love;
- This love drives a creative process;
- The Creation currently does not know God the Father;
- God sends the Logos, in the person of Jesus of Nazareth, into the world;
- Jesus reveals who God is, and allows the Creation to know God;
- Knowing God creates unity with God;
- Knowing God demands that we do the will of God;
- Doing the will of God separates us from the values of 'the world' (those who do not know God);
- Doing the will of God brings eternal life;
- God has sent both Jesus and the Holy Spirit to help believers do the will of God;
- This Gospel is a reliable authority when it reveals these truths.

Warren Carter says this about John's 'good news' (Gospel) about Jesus:

> *The good news according to John is that Jesus is the definitive revealer of God's life-giving purposes and that his mission continues in and through the alternative community, the church, an antisociety that is sustained by the Spirit, or Paraclete, in a hostile world until God's purposes are established in full.*
>
> (*John: Storyteller, Interpreter, Evangelist*, p. 197)

This is a complex sentence which sums up beautifully what John is attempting to do, and it is worth working out what it means in less technical language:

- 'definitive revealer of God's life-giving purposes' – Jesus is the best guide to God's plan;
- 'his mission' – the way in which God makes his plan happen;
- 'continues' – it is still work in progress, but not yet perfected;
- 'in and through' – God enlists the help of others;
- 'an alternative community' – God sets up a new group of people committed to helping in his work; this alternative community follows Jesus' example;
- 'the church' – a group of God's people;
- 'antisociety' – the values of this group are very different from those of the world around them;
- 'sustained by the Spirit, or Paraclete' – the group is given additional help by the Spirit;
- 'in a hostile world' – the wider society does not like the work which this alternative community is doing and reacts violently to it;
- 'until God's purposes are established in full' – God's work is not yet completed.

The Gospel does this by:

1 giving information about Jesus, his life and teaching;

2 challenging the reader to accept what it teaches about Jesus.

 STUDY SUGGESTIONS

### Review of content

1 What do we know of the world in which John was written?

2 How similar is John to the other canonical Gospels?

3 What are the key features of John's theological style?

### Discussion and application

4 How do the values of the Church differ from the values of the wider society in which you live?

5 Are there any points at which Christian faith and behaviour clashes with how your wider community, family or workplace expects you to behave?

6 Do we use 'churchy' or theological language which is not understood by the people we are talking to?

# Part 1

## The Book of Signs

Scholars have identified the first part of the Gospel as the 'Book of Signs' (Appendix C). It includes a formal Prologue (1.1–18) and an introduction to Jesus' earthly ministry (1.19—2.12). Within the Book of Signs, most sections begin with references to the Temple and festivals of the Jewish calendar. These sections share a pattern in which a work Jesus performed becomes the catalyst for dialogues and teaching. These break the text into smaller units. The Book of Signs ends with a peroration (a formal conclusion) (12.36b–50). The last feast mentioned (the Passover, 11.55) serves as a bridge which will mark the end of Jesus' public ministry (12.36) in the run-up to the festival and lead into the 'Book of Glory' (chapters 13—20).

# John 1.1—2.12

## Jesus: in heaven and on earth

 Summary

The Book of Signs begins with a Prologue (1.1–18) which summarizes the whole theme of the Gospel. After this the story of Jesus' earthly life begins when John the Baptist identifies him as the Lamb of God (1.19–34). His disciples begin to follow Jesus and bring their colleagues to him (1.35–51). The section finishes with the first of Jesus' signs: the changing of water into wine at Cana (2.1–12).

## 1.1–18: The Prologue

 Introduction

John starts his Gospel with a hymn or poem that sums up God's plan for the world, from its creation to its end. The hymn also shows that people need to make a choice to be with God (1.18).

The story continues with episodes in which John the Baptist bears witness to Jesus (1.19–34), and the first disciples begin to follow Jesus (1.35–51). The section concludes with Jesus' first sign: the wine of Cana (2.1–12).

 Notes and commentary

**1.1a. In the beginning was the Word, and the Word was with God:** John starts with a clear reference to Genesis 1.1, stressing the role of the Logos in creation. The Greek word *logos* literally means 'Word' but also refers to God's speech (Psalm 19.1–4), which is able to create (Genesis 1.3, 9, 11, 15, 24, 29–30). Sometimes this comes near to talking about the Word as a person (Psalms 33.6; 107.20; Isaiah 55.1–11), but Old Testament (OT) writers never name a specific figure; John, however, identifies the Word with an historical person (1.14).

Similar ideas were also found in Greek philosophy. For example, the Stoics, a philosophical school originally founded in Athens in the fourth century BCE, which had become popular and influential in early imperial Rome, referred to the divine power or principle that shapes the world as the Logos. The word *logos* was used because it stresses the idea of order: that the world is created with some order, purpose and meaning which may be understood if one thinks rightly about such matters. John differs from two different views of God in Greek theology: the idea that God would not touch matter and that the world is a corrupt place created by an inferior deity, and the idea that the gods could not touch matter and were not involved in creating this world at all.

**1.1b. And the Word was God:** John describes the Logos as 'divine' or 'God'. While some have taken this to mean that the Word is not God, this imports 'degrees of deity', as if the Logos is divine but not fully God, which are not part of the text. The words translated as 'the Word was God' can also be translated as 'What God was, so was the Word', which has the advantage of stressing that the Word has the same nature, rank or status as God, but is not exactly the same as God; he is a different 'person', as later Christian thinking would put it.

**1.3. Without him not one thing came into being:** Echoing Genesis, the Logos is shown to be God by his creative power. Further, the verse also stresses that the Logos is not a creature, or made as part of Creation, but exists before the world is created (1.2).

**1.4. In him was life, and the life was the light of all people:** The verse links the Logos with 'life' and 'light', two images which will be linked to Jesus throughout the Gospel. 'Life' and 'light' are not separate, but are linked: as Jesus brings light, he also brings life. The creation of life, sometimes linked with light, is also in Genesis 1.20–31; 2.7; 3.20. This verse introduces the dualism (Appendix B) of light–dark, which also echoes Genesis 1.3–5, 17–18.

**1.5a. The light shines in the darkness:** The world is described as a dark place, and the light is visible in it. It contrasts the Logos and Creation, again stressing that the Logos is not part of the world. Light is a symbol of what is good, and, even in the OT prophets, is a symbol of the Messiah (Isaiah 9.2; 42.6–7; 49.6; 60.1–5; Malachi 4.2).

**1.5b. And the darkness did not overcome it:** An alternative translation, 'the darkness did not master it' (Moffatt, *The New Testament*), implies that the dark can neither overwhelm nor understand the light. This verse anticipates the way in which the powers of this world will not understand or beat Jesus. In this context, the verse may refer to the presence of the Word in the world before the Incarnation, during the OT period. The language of light and dark might mean that the world is the place of a war between good and evil, or that there was some kind of light superior to natural light (Wisdom 7.29–30), or refer to a choice between good and evil.

**1.6–8. There was a man sent from God, whose name was John. He came as a witness to testify to the light . . . He himself was not the light, but he came to testify to the light:** This section introduces John the Baptist. It carefully records that he is a man, sent by God; he is not the light, but was sent to testify to the light. The Baptist, while a special person, is not as important as the Logos.

**1.9. The true light, which enlightens everyone, was coming into the world:** This comment stresses that John the Baptist is not the 'true light'.

**1.10. He was in the world . . . yet the world did not know him:** This verse continues to describe the Word (1.5). 'Did not know him' suggests that a contrast is being drawn between the Word as life and light and the world as darkness. This has an additional irony (1.11): the Word made the world, and the world does not recognize him, or accept him.

**1.11. He came to what was his own:** This may refer either to the Jewish people or the whole of humanity. Note that both Jews and Romans will be involved in the rejection of Jesus later in the Gospel.

**1.12a. But to all who received him, who believed in his name:** While the world as a whole rejects the Word who made it, there is a group of people who do recognize him, and believe in his name. The 'name' was a way of talking about God and may show that the Word is God. In the New Testament, 'believe' means 'believe in' and 'trust'.

**1.12b. He gave power to become children of God:** In the OT, the people of Israel are God's children, but there is a change here. These 'children' are people who may trace the origins of their belief and trust in God not to human birth, or any natural process, but to some intervention by God. Individuals cannot claim to receive the Word because of where they were born or who their parents were, but only because of God's action. See further, 8.39–48.

**1.14a. And the Word became flesh:** This verse marks a distinct phase in the existence of the Word, who 'became flesh': a contrast from what he is in the earlier part of the hymn. This short phrase stresses that the Word really becomes a part of this world, and does not pretend to do so. It seems that John had to deal with opponents who argued that Jesus was never a real person, but only pretended to be human and pretended to die (a belief known as Docetism). The statement also clashes head-on with ancient philosophical and religious traditions which held that spirit and matter could never mix, or that deities might come to earth, but never become truly human.

**1.14b. And lived among us:** The Greek literally means 'pitched his tent among us' and refers to the exodus story in which God's presence with his people is described using the image of the tabernacle (or 'tent', Exodus 25.8–9; 33.7).

**1.14c. We have seen his glory, the glory as of a father's only son, full of grace and truth:** The phrases 'glory' (Exodus 33.22; Numbers 14.10; Deuteronomy 5.24) and 'grace and truth' (Exodus 34.6) allude to the *Shekinah*, God's presence with his people and faithfulness to the covenant he made with them. As the *Shekinah* might be linked to the Temple (Jeremiah 17.12; Ezekiel 10.4; Psalm 102.16) or the Torah (Exodus 3.18; 34.28), this statement may further be seen as a claim that Jesus replaced either or both of these. Grace is associated with the ideas of gift and thanksgiving. Rather than imagine grace as a kind of force, it is well translated as generosity. For 'truth', see Appendix E.

The phrase 'only son' (NRSV) is sometimes translated 'only begotten', which may mean 'only' or 'one of a kind'. This second meaning is used of an only child in the OT (Judges 11.34; Tobit 3.15; 8.17). It may be replaced by 'beloved' (Genesis 22.2, 12, 16), also used directly about Jesus in Mark 1.11; 9.7 and in the parable of Mark 12.6. Hebrews 11.17 describes Isaac as 'only', and this may be what the word meant at the time. 'Only begotten' may be a translation which was influenced by later Christian thinking about the nature of Christ and the Trinity.

**1.15. He who comes after me ranks ahead of me because he was before me:** Mark 1.4 makes a similar point, using the image of John not seeing himself as worthy to untie Jesus' sandals. Jesus is superior to the Baptist, a remark made more significant by being placed on the Baptist's own lips.

**1.16–17. Grace upon grace . . . grace and truth:** These verses contrast the law, which was given by Moses, with grace and truth which were revealed in the person of Jesus. The Gospel will explore this in detail, showing Jesus as superior to Moses, and as the definitive revelation of God's love.

**1.18a. No one has ever seen God:** Making Jesus superior to Moses may explain the strange beginning to verse 18. While a number of OT traditions state the commonly held view that humans cannot look at the face of God and live (Genesis 16.13; Exodus 33.20), Exodus 24.9–11 describes Moses and the elders of Israel not only looking at God, but also eating and drinking with him. Exodus 33.11 uses face-to-face encounters to indicate the closeness of Moses' friendship with God (see also Appendix I), as does Deuteronomy 34.10. John overlooks such traditions to stress the superior revelation given by Jesus, and stresses this by describing him as 'close to the Father's heart', a figure of speech indicating intimacy. In John 1.50–51, Jesus will promise the disciples visions of heaven.

**1.18b. It is God the only Son, who is close to the Father's heart, who has made him known:** Both testaments use 'Father' to tell of God's close bond to his people when he entered into partnership with them through covenants. It reflects the patriarchal nature of most ancient societies, in which the father was the head of the household. As such, the designation 'Father' signifies a social role and status, not the gender of God. We must be careful not to use the word 'Father' in a way that limits God to the functions of a human male. Nor should we use it to claim that men are superior to women: Genesis 1.27 shows that men and women are all made in the image of God without any further distinction of rank. The fatherhood of God (in its fullest developed forms) includes the following elements:

1 the Father as Creator: this role is part of the Creation mandate or covenant (Genesis 9.1–17);

2 the Father of the people of God (theocratic fatherhood, Malachi 1.6) through the covenant of faith (Genesis 15.1–6; 17.1–22);

3 generative fatherhood – used only for the Father–Son relationship in the New Testament (NT);

4 adoptive fatherhood: believers become children of God through his gift, not by their nature (1.12–13; NT only).

 ## Interpretation

The Gospel starts by setting the context for Jesus' earthly life: it sets both a theological and a historical context.

The theological comes first: in 1.1–18 a hymn, often called the Prologue (Foreword or Introduction), sets Jesus in relation to God. The letter 1 John starts just like this too: with a hymn that refers to the Logos. The Johannine writings show us how important hymns like this were for passing on the Christian message or building up faith in the early Christian communities: Revelation, in particular, makes extensive use of hymns. Perhaps the most famous example is found in Philippians 2.5–11, a piece of writing which shows that hymns were written very early and that such early writing could be highly complex and profound; it is very dangerous for scholars to assume that complicated ideas must be late in origin.

Scholars debate the origins of the hymn which makes up the Prologue, and also the date when it became part of the Gospel. In terms of origins, the debate is between whether it is a hymn from Jewish or Graeco-Roman traditions. Various scholars have suggested that the hymn may have come from Gnostic writing, Jewish wisdom literature, and even Jewish philosophical writing like that of Philo. They suggest that it owes much to those schools of thought which include philosophical reflection on the nature of the world and its relation to God. We can make too much of the issue of whether it is Jewish *or* Greek, as both traditions had sometimes become mixed, as in Philo's writing, and even in Jewish wisdom literature that had already been influenced by ideas from Greek philosophy.

One thing is more certain, that John has not slavishly copied a hymn and simply placed it at the beginning of the Gospel. Wherever the hymn might have come from, John appears to have edited and added to it; scholars suggest that verses 6–9, 13, 15 and 17–18 may have been added to the original hymn. As John is a highly original and creative thinker, we should be wary of claims which suggest that he remains trapped by earlier writing or ideas which he adopts and uses within his writing. John uses nothing which cannot be reshaped to suit his purposes. He has thus ensured that the section which describes how the Logos had a role in creation, and was made flesh (1.14), is clearly linked to the historical Jesus through references to Scripture and the Baptist. While he shares the term Logos with Greek philosophy, he is not limited by the Greek philosophical usage; he gives the term his own particular meaning.

The hymn has a poetic shape which some critics describe as a *chiasmus*, meaning that there is an idea A which leads to B; B is repeated and then followed by A again (A-B-B-A); others say it is an example of parallelism, a common practice in Hebrew poetry, notably the Psalms, in which verses repeat the same theme. Neither of these really holds up all the way through. A further way of looking at the hymn is to describe it as like a stepladder, in which the idea which finishes one section begins the next. Thus: the Word as God (1.1–2), the Word in creation (1.3–5), the Word in the world (1.10–12) and the Word and the community (1.14–16).

John starts his Gospel with the claim that the Logos is God and is intimately connected with the creation of the world, giving it some kind of purpose. Such a purpose will demand a response from the audience, and will be filled out as the Gospel progresses when we hear and see what Jesus does and teaches. The contrast between light and dark leaves no doubt as to what kind of choice the audience should make. The way in which it refers to the great story of Israel's origins in Genesis and Exodus reveals that this is the beginning of John's great story about Jesus, who will come to be seen as more important than Moses and the patriarchs (the key historical figures of Israel's earliest history), and as the one who gives the clearest revelation of God and his love for humanity.

Because the hymn comes right at the beginning of the Gospel, it can be tempting to use it as a key to understand all that follows. However, the hymn may have been added to the Gospel just before it was completed. This means it is better to see it as a summary of the whole Gospel. It is useful to return to the hymn and see how much clearer it has become as a result of reading the whole Gospel.

Importantly, the hymn claims for Jesus status and honour superior to that of both Moses and John the Baptist, both highly revered leaders.

 ## STUDY SUGGESTIONS

### Word study

1 Explain 'the Logos'. Is John using this term in a new way? How?

### Review of content

2 What does the Prologue tell us about John's view of creation?

**3** What does light and dark tell us about John's view of the world?

**4** Describe the role played by John the Baptist.

### Discussion and application

**5** Does the Prologue, which stresses that God has a plan for the world, challenge how people think about the world and the meaning of life in your context?

**6** What is the traditional understanding of how the world was made in your culture? How does the Prologue challenge that view?

**7** When we use terms and ideas from our contexts, do we remain trapped by their original meanings, or, like John, do we adapt them for our own purposes?

## 1.19–51: Jesus' earthly context

 Introduction

John introduces Jesus as an adult: there are no accounts of his birth, or youth. The stage is set by introducing a well-respected leader, John the Baptist (1.34), who will direct people's attentions to Jesus. His followers provide Jesus' first disciples (1.35–40). A journey to Galilee produces a further disciple, Philip (1.43), and leads to conversations with Nathanael (1.45–51). The section finishes with the first miracle: the changing of water into wine at Cana (2.1–12).

 Notes and commentary

**1.19. The Jews sent priests and Levites from Jerusalem to ask him, 'Who are you?':** The verse suggests that some people viewed the Baptist with suspicion. The term 'the Jews' is used here for those who are hostile to Jesus; they seem to be figures in authority. Note that here they are sufficiently influential to send 'priests and Levites' to question the Baptist. These were the official figures who controlled the cult worship at the Temple in Jerusalem. See Appendix L.

**1.21. Are you Elijah? . . . Are you the prophet?:** The Baptist may have been asked if he was Elijah because of beliefs that this prophet, who did not experience death and burial (2 Kings 2.11), was expected to return before the appearance of the Messiah (Matthew 16.14; 17.3–4). John's appearance resembled that of Elijah (Matthew 3.4; 2 Kings 1.8), as did his preaching (Matthew 3.7–12; Luke 3.7–17), and both Jesus (Matthew 11.14; 17.12; Mark 9.13) and the angel of the Lord called him Elijah (Luke 1.17, which draws on Malachi 4.5). Some bystanders at the foot of the cross think that the dying Jesus is calling for Elijah (Mark 15.35; Matthew 27.47). The 'prophet' is a reference to Moses (Deuteronomy 18.15, 18; 1 Maccabees 4.46). The Baptist denies that he is either of these expected characters, and again plays down his own importance.

**1.23. I am the voice of one crying out in the wilderness, 'Make straight the way of the Lord':** The Baptist defines himself using a quotation from Isaiah 40.3, which is meant to give comfort to God's people and suggest that they should prepare themselves for his coming. Compare Mark 1.2–3, where the Gospel writer makes a prophecy from Isaiah 40.3 and Malachi 3.1.

**1.24. Now they had been sent from the Pharisees:** The Baptist's questioners are described as coming from 'the Pharisees', a sect whose members thought that all people should maintain the ideals of purity demanded of the priesthood. This may suggest either a further description of the first group (1.19), or the introduction of a second group of questioners.

**1.25–27. 'Why then are you baptizing . . .?' John answered them, 'I baptize with water. Among you stands one whom you do not know, the one who is coming after me; I am not worthy to untie the thong of his sandal':** The Baptist does not really answer the Jews' question, but replies that he is the inferior of the one who is to come (compare 1.15). To untie sandals was the lowliest task to be performed by a slave.

**1.28. Bethany across the Jordan:** This was a different town from the Bethany near Jerusalem (John 12.1; Mark 14.3–9). Some ancient commentators identified it with Bethabara. If so, Jesus, like Joshua, starts outside Israel (Joshua 1.1–2) and leads his people into the Promised Land.

**1.29a. The next day he saw Jesus:** The references to days only indicate different days in the narrative. While it is tempting to view these as parallel to the six days of creation or the revelation at Sinai (Exodus 24.16), they simply do not add up accurately or report a time frame; nor do they explain the jump to 'the third day' (see further in 2.1).

**1.29b. Lamb of God:** This title has three possible layers of meaning:

1 *An apocalyptic lamb*: This figure will conquer evil in the world (Revelation 17.14). Some object that the idea of taking away sin does not fit well with this image.

2 *The lamb as the Suffering Servant* (Isaiah 42.1–4; 49.1–6; 52.13–53): Although these verses may originally have referred to Israel as a nation, they become increasingly used to describe an individual, even the Messiah, in Christian writing. Other references suggest that John may have Isaiah

in mind (John 1.23, 32–34; Isaiah 42.1; 53.1; 61.1; John 10.38). This idea may also draw from Jeremiah 9.19.

3 *The paschal lamb*: While it may be argued that people did not think of the paschal lamb (the Passover lamb) as a sacrifice, consider 1 Corinthians 5.7. There is also a chance that 'lamb' might refer to other sacrifices offered in the Temple, especially the daily sin-offering (Exodus 29.38–46; Leviticus 4.32). John will later connect the Passover explicitly with the timing of Jesus' death (18.28; 19.31, 42).

We do not need to choose between these: it is possible that the title may refer to more than one of them.

**1.29c. Who takes away the sin of the world:** 'Sin' refers to activity which is contrary to the will or command of God.

**1.30. After me comes a man who ranks ahead of me because he was before me:** The phrase 'he was before me' echoes 1.1–2. The Baptist is talking of the pre-existence of Jesus (the Word), although he may have originally been referring to a figure like Elijah.

**1.31. I myself did not know him; but I came baptizing with water for this reason, that he might be revealed to Israel:** The Baptist finally answers the question from 1.26 clearly. He baptizes with water in order to reveal Jesus. This may be genuine, or a reason supplied by the Gospel writer.

**1.32. I saw the Spirit descending from heaven like a dove, and it remained on him:** Unlike the prophets who were often only temporarily given the Spirit (Numbers 11.25–26; Judges 3.10; 1 Samuel 10.6), the Spirit will remain with Jesus until his death, and, by implication, with the community which will come to receive it (19.30). The fact that Jesus permanently possesses the Spirit gives him a higher status.

Some have argued that this verse supports an adoptionist Christology (that Jesus is not divine until the time he is given the Spirit at baptism) but this is rejected in both the Prologue (1.1–18) and the Baptist's previous words (1.30–31).

The Spirit may be 'like a dove' because of the creation story (Genesis 1.2). The dove was also a symbol of Israel (*4 Ezra* 5.26) and the new Creation after the Noah story (Genesis 8.8–12).

**1.33. I myself did not know him, but the one who sent me to baptize with water said to me, 'He on whom you see the Spirit descend and remain is the one who baptizes with the Holy Spirit':** John never says that Jesus was baptized by the Baptist (unlike Mark 1.9; Matthew 3.13; Luke 3.21), perhaps to avoid the claim that the Baptist is superior to Jesus. Here, only the Baptist sees the Spirit and is told what it means.

**1.34. Son of God:** The phrase is most likely drawn from Psalm 2.7, an enthronement psalm which was later used for Jesus' exaltation (Acts 13.32–33). It looks forward to the time when Jesus is raised up by God. In a wider

Graeco-Roman context, it means Jesus has 'the quality of God', specifically the power to create and to control. In the OT, the phrase 'son of God' is used in two different ways:

1 *the heavenly sons of Elohim* (Genesis 6.2, 4; Deuteronomy 32.8; Job 1.6; 38.7; Psalms 29.1; 82.1, 6; 89.6; Daniel 3.25): angelic figures manifested in heavenly form;

2 *the sons of Yahweh*: individual human beings identified with God (Psalm 2.7; 89.26; 1 Chronicles 28.6), or the people of Israel (Exodus 4.22; Hosea 1.10).

In the NT, the term 'son of God' may also be used to describe heroic or faithful humans (Matthew 5.9; Luke 20.36; see also 5.1–47). Acts 14.8–18 reports the Graeco-Roman belief that gods might come down from heaven.

**1.35a. The next day:** On the third day in the narrative, the Baptist, presumably still at Bethany, identifies Jesus to two of his followers as the Lamb of God (1.29). The two follow Jesus.

**1.35b. John . . . was standing with two of his disciples:** The writer uses the word 'disciples' for those who accept the teaching of the Baptist, and will also use it for followers of Jesus. John does not limit disciples to the twelve (6.66).

**1.38. Rabbi:** The disciples give Jesus an honorific Judaic title, which also means they accept Jesus' authority as a teacher. John translates Semitic terms like this, suggesting that some of his audience are not familiar with Hebrew or Aramaic: they speak Greek.

**1.39a. Come and see:** Jesus' invitation gives a definite guarantee or promise.

**1.39b. They came and saw where he was staying, and they remained with him:** The two words 'stay' and 'remain' are synonyms throughout the Gospel. John uses them 40 times, compared to 12 in the Synoptic Gospels. They indicate loyalty, as does 'follow' (1.37). The disciples leave the circle around the Baptist for a new fellowship with Jesus. Following has dimensions that are both spiritual (learning from and copying a leader) and physical (accompanying someone).

**1.40. One of the two . . . was Andrew:** Andrew (Gk, *Andreas*, 'manly') is described differently in Mark 1.1–18. He is identified here as a follower of the Baptist rather than a fisherman, and in a different place (Bethany, 1.28; rather than the Sea of Galilee). Andrew fetches Simon Peter and brings him to Jesus (1.41–42). He and Peter come from Bethsaida (a town on the north shore of the Sea of Galilee, near the Jordan river), like Philip (1.44). He will appear again in 6.8–9; 12.21–22. For more on Peter, see 21.2, 3. This pattern of meeting Jesus and bringing others to him will occur again (1.45; 4.28–29).

**1.41. The Messiah:** For this term, see 1.38; 4.4, 19; 6.14–15; Appendix K.

**1.42. Cephas (which is translated Peter):** Cephas, or Peter (1.38), means 'Rocky', implying someone firm or stable. The nickname is ironic as Peter will prove to be unreliable (18.15–27).

**1.43a. The next day:** On the fourth day in the narrative Jesus plans to travel to Galilee, where the miracle at Cana (2.1–12) will take place.

**1.43b. He found Philip and said to him, 'Follow me':** Jesus finds Philip and asks him to 'follow' (1.38–39). Philip is a Greek name, like Andrew and Simon. These names might mean the people are Greeks (12.20–21), but many Jewish people had Greek names, even those who would be considered strong Jewish nationalists (1 Maccabees 5.55; 11.60).

**1.45a. Nathanael:** His name means 'God has given'. He is also a Galilean, from Cana (2.1).

**1.45b. We have found him:** Philip identifies Jesus as the one who has been described by Moses and the prophets. His claim that they have found him is puzzling: disciples are called by Jesus – they do not choose him through their own insights – and, as the following dialogue will show, Philip has not really understood whom he has found.

**1.45c. Jesus son of Joseph from Nazareth:** Jesus is identified in conventional terms using his father's name and town of origin. Place and genealogy were important indicators of status.

**1.46. Can anything good come out of Nazareth?:** The question indicates the popular view that Nazareth was a place of no importance.

**1.47. An Israelite in whom there is no deceit:** Jesus considers that Nathanael is someone genuinely worthy to see what Scripture has promised (1.45), an honest person (compare Jacob in Genesis 27.35–36) who does not lie (Psalm 32.2; Isaiah 53.9) and is not an idolater (Revelation 14.5).

**1.48a. Where did you come to know me?** This is a common expression in both Semitic and Greek languages, meaning 'How do you know me?'

**1.48b. I saw you under the fig tree before Philip called you:** Jesus' answer gives a sense that something miraculous is happening to Nathanael: he is in the presence of someone who has an uncanny knowledge of him. A number of explanations for the mention of the fig tree have been offered, but none is completely convincing. Fig trees are thought to represent:

- *peace and prosperity* (1 Kings 5.5), sometimes associated with the Messiah (Micah 4.4; Zechariah 3.10);

- *the study of the law* (*Midrash Rabbah on Ecclesiastes* 5.11), suggesting that Nathanael is a scribe or rabbi;

- *a way of revealing accurate knowledge,* based on the Susanna story in Daniel 13 (in the Greek version of the OT known as the Septuagint (LXX));

- *one's own home* (Isaiah 36.16; Micah 4.4; Zechariah 3.10), suggesting that Nathanael knows all he needs to know;

- *shade or darkness*, meaning a lack of understanding from which Nathanael will pass to knowledge or enlightenment;

- *an ideal or blissful location*, described in Graeco-Roman poetry and philosophical traditions.

**1.49. Rabbi, you are the Son of God! You are the King of Israel:** Nathanael's initial scepticism is replaced by a number of strong confessions of faith (1.38, 32–33). 'King of Israel' also suggests the Messiah (1.41), and a text like Psalm 2.6–7 might provide a link to make it and 'Son of God' both messianic.

**1.50. Do you believe because I told you that I saw you under the fig tree? You will see greater things than these:** Jesus promises Nathanael that his knowledge of him is nothing really special.

**1.51. Very truly, I tell you, you will see heaven opened and the angels of God ascending and descending upon the Son of Man:** For emphasis, Jesus uses the phrase 'Very truly', an emphatic statement like 'I say to you' or 'Amen, I say to you' in the Synoptic Gospels (Appendix I). Jesus is giving his word to Nathanael that he will be privileged to see revelations which equal those given to Jacob (Genesis 28.10–12). The visions share the image of angels ascending and descending, but here the angels minister around the Son of Man.

'Son of Man' is a Semitic saying, and many scholars believe it is very likely that Jesus used it. The fact that it is not good Greek makes it unlikely that later writers invented or inserted it: it most likely comes from early traditions about Jesus. The phrase can be used in any of three ways:

1  as a way of saying 'I';

2  as a way of talking about the average person, like the English phrase 'the man in the street';

3  as a title (based on Daniel 7.13–14).

This made it a good phrase for Jesus to use to describe himself as it is ambiguous and would make people think for themselves about who he was, rather than simply believe what they heard. When John uses the phrase, he describes Jesus' suffering and his glory (as in the above points 2 and 3), and gives further layers of meaning to the title (3.13–14; 5.27; 6.62; 8.28).

By Jesus' time, the phrase 'Son of Man' blended together two elements:

1  a pre-existent, transcendent Messiah;

2  the idea that a human being would embody that Messiah.

The title is thus used of Jesus because he fitted these hopes. In other ways, he will be different from what people expected (6.15).

 ## Interpretation

In 1.19—2.12, a series of earthly encounters gives a preview of the nature and purpose of Jesus' earthly life. Jesus is linked to known characters such as John the Baptist and the disciples, and to places like Cana.

Was John the Baptist an historical figure? Our main sources for him lie within the Gospels, but crucially Josephus, a first-century CE Jewish writer, refers to him in one of his works (Josephus, *Antiquities* 18.116).

How accurate is John's picture of the Baptist? John has a very clear agenda: he wants to show the superiority of Jesus. There is always a chance that the Baptist did not mean exactly what John makes him say. For example, it is possible that when the Baptist expects the 'one who is to come' he means Elijah (1.30–31), and that the Gospel writer has made him refer to Jesus. We might sum up this line of argument as John saying: 'You thought the Baptist was talking about Elijah [the hidden Messiah], but he was really talking about this man, Jesus [the hidden Messiah now revealed].'

In 1.35–42, two of the Baptist's disciples are shown as leaving him to follow Jesus, fulfilling 1.23. The Baptist raises no objections to their leaving, and even seems to urge them to follow Jesus. This again shows the significance and superiority of Jesus to the Baptist.

In 1.43–51, Philip and Nathanael are introduced. The dialogues which take place show John's use of misunderstanding to reveal Jesus' identity (Appendix H). The first of these shows that Philip's claim, 'We have found', is rash. Unlike the Baptist, he appears completely unaware of Jesus' being the Word and related to God (1.32–33). Both Philip and Nathanael think they know who Jesus is, but Philip's quotations of Scripture, and Nathanael's concerns with Jesus' parentage and home town, really show that they still do not understand whom they have met. In terms of honour and shame, Jesus scores highly for having a status which is far above his supposed origins.

John reveals an important feature of discipleship here: often new converts are very excited, and may be tempted to think they know everything. John shows that such enthusiasm is not enough, and may even be a sign of overconfidence, arrogance or weakness. Nathanael's sarcastic response to the mention of Nazareth shows how even wise people may instinctively speak from prejudice. In this Gospel, the disciples learn and grow in faith by their misunderstandings and corrections.

Jesus' greeting puzzles Nathanael. It is also deeply ironic: Nathanael is praised extravagantly by the one he has ridiculed (1.46). In response, Nathanael replies with a series of titles which reaches a climax when he describes Jesus as 'King of Israel', a messianic title. These titles are typical of the hopes people had at this time about the Messiah. Jesus ignores the titles and tells Nathanael that he will see more wonderful things: visions of the heavenly nature of Jesus. This will be revealed by the end of the Gospel: Jesus will have been raised and revealed in all his glory, and Nathanael will be a witness to the risen Lord (21.2).

 ## STUDY SUGGESTIONS

### Word studies

**1** What does 'Jews' mean? Why is this a problematic word when we interpret John?

**2** Which Aramaic or Hebrew words does John translate for his readers? Why?

**3** Give a definition of 'Son of Man'. How does John use it?

### Review of content

**4** What role is played by John the Baptist?

**5** Compare this version of the calling of the disciples with those in the Synoptics (Mark 1.16–20; Matthew 4.18–22; Luke 5.2–11). What differences in detail can you see?

**6** Is there a pattern to the way the disciples first meet Jesus?

### Discussion and application

**7** The difficult word often translated 'Jews' has been used by Christians to stir up racial hatred. Does our use of language like this ever deliberately or accidentally lead to others being persecuted or treated badly? Is this appropriate behaviour for us?

**8** The Gospel writers' treatment of John the Baptist shows a great respect for religious experience seen in their own context. Are we as generous as they are in our attitudes? Do we show respect for religious experience in our contexts? If we are not as generous, why is this so?

# 2.1–12: The miracle at Cana

 ## Introduction

Jesus continues to travel in Galilee. An invitation to a wedding leads to a request to assist the bridegroom, and the first of Jesus' signs.

# Notes and commentary

**2.1a. On the third day:** The previous sequence has four days (1.19), followed by three next days (1.29, 35, 43), so this may be the third day after 1.53. This could be either the sixth or seventh day if counted exclusively or inclusively. Yet another possibility is that 1.40–42 implies a further day, making this the eighth day. Six days might draw parallels to the days taken by God to make the world (Genesis 1.7), seven to the Sabbath, or eight to the resurrection. Constructing an exact sequence may be irrelevant: this may simply be a temporal reference showing that the events at Cana take place two days after the previous action.

**2.1b. There was a wedding:** Palestinian weddings of the time involved a procession in which the bride was taken from her father's house to her new husband's home. A contract and the act of living together (cohabitation) formed the marriage. The marriage was accompanied by feasting, which might last for up to two weeks. The wedding may have a symbolic meaning: signifying the 'end times' (Hosea 2.19–20; Isaiah 25.6–8; Jeremiah 2.2; Song of Solomon), the time of the Messiah (Isaiah 44.4–8; 62.4–5; Matthew 8.11; 22.1–4; Luke 22.16–18; Revelation 19.9) or, in Graeco-Roman literature, of death. The setting at a wedding may point to Jesus' death.

**2.1c. Cana of Galilee:** The setting was Khirbet-Qanah, nine miles north of Nazareth in the Beth Notafah valley. See also 4.46; 21.2.

**2.3. The mother of Jesus:** Mary is not mentioned by name, but identified as 'the mother of . . .'. This naming practice may give honour by showing her status as a mother (19.26–27).

**2.4a. Jesus said to her, 'Woman':** Jesus' use of 'woman' is not as abrupt as we might think, and is used elsewhere (4.21; 20.15).

**2.4b. What concern is that to you and to me?:** Jesus has no reason to fulfil the request.

**2.4c. My hour has not yet come:** Jesus explains the lack of obligation: it is not yet the appropriate time for him to act. The phrase suggests a divine plan which includes Jesus' public ministry, glorification, salvation, the testing of the disciples, and their eventual enlightenment and understanding. At other times, it seems to refer more precisely to Jesus' Passion, thus including the idea of 'hour' connected to death commonly found in Judaic and Graeco-Roman writing. See also 4.21; 7.6, 8, 30; 12.23; 13.1; 17.1.

**2.5. Do whatever he tells you:** Mary does not argue further with Jesus, but simply tells the servants to do what he wants. She leaves the decision to Jesus himself.

**2.6a. There were six stone water-jars:** Stone water-jars were used to guarantee freedom from impurity from either people or objects (Leviticus 11.33).

Some writers suggest that the number six implies imperfection, and so suggests that the Jewish legal system was imperfect. Care should be taken here: regrettably, in later times, Christians rejected Judaic practice outright rather than seeing Jesus as one who accepted Judaic values and considered himself a reformer. The number, which is very large for a domestic situation, may simply function to show the extravagance of Jesus' actions.

**2.6b. For the Jewish rites of purification:** The word 'Jewish' here is descriptive and does not imply any hostility or opposition to Jesus. The water is described as being used for purification. Purification is not a major theme in John (unlike Mark 7). This seems to be a descriptive detail rather than a point of theological controversy (11.55; 18.28).

**2.6c. Each holding twenty or thirty gallons:** An imperial gallon is the equivalent of about 4.5 litres.

**2.8. The chief steward:** This individual was a guest who was chosen to ensure that the ceremonies ran smoothly.

**2.9. The bridegroom:** Perhaps this man was a relative of Jesus, or of Nathanael. While some have suggested that Jesus draws attention away from the wedding, the narrative makes clear that he actually saves the bridegroom's honour (since it is he, not Jesus, who is praised for the wine, 2.10) and fulfils his own social responsibilities. Later esoteric claims that Jesus himself was the bridegroom ignore the flow of the story.

**2.11. The first of his signs:** Jesus has already revealed his powers in his dealings with Nathanael (1.43–51). This verse refers to his first sign performed openly or in public. 'First' is the same as 'beginning' (1.1), so this may imply the start of Jesus' public ministry (Appendix C).

**2.12a. He went down to Capernaum:** Jesus returned to a town by the Sea of Galilee (also in 4.46–54; 6.17–59).

**2.12b. His brothers:** The writer suggests that Jesus is part of a larger family; Mark 6.3 names Jesus' brothers. These need not be brothers with the same mother and father. The term 'brothers' included half-brothers, cousins or brothers-in-law. It does not mean 'believers' here (7.5).

 ## Interpretation

Jesus and the disciples are invited to a wedding, showing that he still belongs to a world in which they have social duties and responsibilities. The disciples are present, but take no part in the story which unfolds. They witness both the social contract of a wedding, and Jesus' glory. The episode contains a puzzling dialogue between Jesus and his mother. It includes a misunderstanding (Appendix H). Mary believes that her request to Jesus is legitimate. Her words imply that Jesus may assist with a social problem: the hosts have

run out of wine (2.3). His reply suggests that he has more important concerns.

This pattern of reluctance and then compliance is found elsewhere (4.46–
54; 7.2–14; 11.1–16). The pattern has four stages: request (2.3), reluctance
(2.4), agreement to the request (2.7) and conflict (2.13–14). In all of these
Jesus eventually helps people who might be categorized as family or friends
within his own circle. In all four instances, the pattern concludes with a story
of conflict with outsiders which follows, but is not caused by, the request
story.

The miracle at Cana is the first of Jesus' signs. It is not just a miraculous
event: the symbolism of the wedding, and the talk of the hour, indicate
the divine plan of which Jesus is a part, and anticipate his death and the
continued role of his followers as witnesses and believers.

This is worth close study: John will not always associate miracles with
seeing and believing. First, this story points out that it is the disciples who
believe, not all those who are present, thus marking a difference between
those who follow Jesus and the world at large. Second, the verse tells us
that the sign took place *and* the disciples believed. Note that the Greek
never says '*so that* the disciples believed'. Belief does not follow automatically from seeing the sign. This lack of direct connection between sign
and belief will become even clearer in later passages when people see or
experience Jesus' signs, but refuse to believe in him (chapter 6). Here,
John is warning that seeing signs is not the foundation of true belief. This
reaches its climax in John's claim that it is better to believe without seeing
(20.29).

The sign is connected to glory, a term which has been used earlier to describe the Word (1.14). It may echo traditions which show God's glory being revealed to his people (Exodus 16.7; Numbers 14.22). The setting of the
wedding suggests that glory is linked to messianic times. It may also show
a new dispensation which reforms or replaces current practices. The use of
wine may further indicate new teaching or reform. There is an interesting
parallel that Mark 2.19 starts Jesus' ministry with a discussion of new wine,
comparing his teaching to that of the Pharisees, just as John here describes
Jesus giving a better-quality wine (2.10) as he starts his ministry. Again we
need to be careful: we may note a parallel, but should not say that this must
be so because of Mark. To do that would actually be a mistake: to make the
meaning of John depend on Mark.

The presence of wine has sometimes led readers to think that this may
be a symbolic story about the Eucharist or sacraments. This is at best a
minor theme. People who want to read a eucharistic meaning point to
the Passover season, which links Cana (2.13) to the feeding miracle (6.4)
and the Last Supper (13.1). Additionally, 19.34 links Mary, blood and the
death of Jesus with wine; others see a link through the phrase 'blood of
grapes' (Genesis 49.11; Deuteronomy 32.14; Sirach 1.15). However, for
John the identity and person of Jesus (who he is) and the coming of the
messianic age matter more than sacraments or the Eucharist.

STUDY SUGGESTIONS

**Word study**

1  Why is 'brothers' (2.12) difficult to interpret?

**Review of content**

2  In John's opinion, are signs a good basis for faith or belief?

3  How does John show that Jesus is a highly regarded spiritual leader?

4  Did Jesus have brothers and sisters? Does this matter?

**Discussion and application**

5  Do John's views raise any issues about the way we usually think about miracles and belief?

6  Have traditional beliefs and practices become so much a part of our faith practice over time that they no longer corrupt our worship or beliefs?

# John 2.13—4.54

# The first Passover

 ## Summary

In this section John uses Jesus' visit to Jerusalem to frame the cleansing of the Temple (2.13–22), a summary about the nature of belief (2.23–25) and a debate with Nicodemus (3.1–21). From Jerusalem Jesus heads to the countryside, which prompts a second set of material about John the Baptist (3.22–36), before he returns to Galilee via Samaritan territory (4.1–6). On this journey he engages in two dialogues: one with the Samaritan woman, the other with the disciples (4.31–38). On his return to Galilee, a third conversation leads to the healing of a royal official's son (4.43–54).

## 2.13–22: Jesus cleanses the Temple

 ## Introduction

This marks Jesus' first visit to Jerusalem in the Gospel story. His actions in the Temple are used to predict his resurrection.

 ## Notes and commentary

**2.13. The Passover:** OT prescriptions for the Passover are found in Exodus 12.43–49; Leviticus 23.4–8; Numbers 9.1–5; Deuteronomy 16.1–8. There are a number of differences in the details. Later, the Passover was combined with the Festival of Unleavened Bread. The festival seems to have been first celebrated in households, but by the time of Jesus, the feast was celebrated in Jerusalem on 14/15 of the month of Nisan. Until the destruction of the Temple in 70 CE, the lambs were slaughtered in its precincts, and then the *Seder* meal (the Passover meal), with its complex rituals and *Haggadah* (literally, 'telling') in which the significance of the feast was recalled, was held in houses throughout the city by families or fellowship groups. The Samaritans held their own version of the Passover, separate from the Festival of Unleavened Bread and, perhaps, on Mount Gerizim (4.4, 19).

**2.14a. People selling cattle, sheep, and doves:** Temple regulations specified that only animals in good condition could be sacrificed, so pilgrims might choose to buy animals at the Temple rather than risk travelling with them.

**2.14b. Money-changers seated at their tables:** The commandment against idols (Exodus 20.4; 34.17; Deuteronomy 5.8) meant that Roman currency, which was marked with letters and often the head of the emperor, was not used in the Temple. Pilgrims changed their imperial currency for blank Temple coins.

**2.15–16. Making a whip of cords, he drove all of them out of the temple . . . 'Take these things out of here! Stop making my Father's house a marketplace!':** Mark, Matthew and Luke share the basic details (Mark 11.15; Matthew 21.12). John adds the whip of cords.

Jesus' words vary. In John the concern is with 'my Father's house', which has been turned into a marketplace. In the Synoptics, a different prophecy is quoted (Mark 11.17; Matthew 21.13; Luke 19.45, combining Isaiah 56.7 and Jeremiah 7.11). All give a positive value to the Temple: Jesus is rejecting only those who exploit the Temple rituals and its worshippers for their own gain.

**2.17. Zeal for your house will consume me:** John uses Psalm 69.9 to focus on Jesus and his mission. Zeal is a strong spiritual impulse, not anger. The psalm helps the disciples to remember that Jesus was previously identified as 'Messiah' (1.41) and 'King of Israel' (1.49), and Jesus fulfils a conventional understanding of the Messiah: reforming the Temple. This hope has an historical precedent: the rededication of the Temple (2 Maccabees 10.1–8).

**2.18. The Jews then said to him,** 'What sign can you show us for doing this?': The complex term 'Jews' (Appendix L) reappears, best understood here as those in dispute with Jesus (1.19). They question Jesus' authority.

**2.19a. Destroy this temple:** The people who are questioning Jesus assume he is talking of the Temple. His reply must be confusing (Appendix H) as Jesus seems to say that his opponents are planning to destroy the Temple buildings.

**2.19b. I will raise it up:** The verb 'raise up' is deliberately ambiguous: it may mean either to erect a building or to resurrect a dead body.

**2.20. This temple has been under construction for forty-six years, and will you raise it up in three days?:** Jesus' opponents ask for clarification: they remind Jesus of the impossibility of rebuilding in three days a building which had taken so long to erect. Josephus notes that construction of the Temple was begun by Herod in 20/19 BCE (*Antiquities* 15.11.1). If 46 years were taken up to the time of the events described, this would give a date of 28 CE. Some later commentators suggested that the 'three days' referred to Jesus' resurrection (Jonah 1.17). The phrase had come to signify the resurrection of Israel in the end times (Hosea 6.2). It may just mean a short time, not a literal three-day period (thus, Exodus 19.11; Hosea 6.2; Luke 13.32). The hope of the world to come should be focused on Jesus rather than the Temple. It also raises the possibility that this may be a prophetic use of OT traditions.

The dialogue is incomplete: Jesus never answers the question.

**2.21. But he was speaking of the temple of his body:** John offers clarification: Jesus is talking about his body, not the Temple. The misunderstanding is resolved only for the reader, not for Jesus' opponents.

**2.22. After he was raised from the dead, his disciples remembered that he had said this; and they believed the scripture and the word that Jesus had spoken:** John explains the source of this interpretation. It comes from the later reflections of the disciples, after Jesus was raised from the dead (2.19). It was based on their memories of what he had said, and their acceptance of this as true. This truth, in turn, comes from two authoritative sources: the Jewish Scriptures, and Jesus himself.

 ## Interpretation

Unlike the Synoptic Gospels, John places the cleansing of the Temple at the beginning of Jesus' ministry. John has made this first public action the manifesto for his portrayal of Jesus: claims for Jesus as a fuller manifestation of the Temple and its festivals recur throughout chapters 3—12. Yet this replacement is not a rejection of the Temple, but a claim to embody all it stands for.

This timing has led some to question whether John is a reliable historian. A few conservative scholars, keen to argue that neither the Synoptics nor John has made a mistake, have suggested that Jesus cleansed the Temple twice. This is unbelievable: can we really imagine that the Temple authorities would allow the same person to cause such trouble twice? Comparing the different accounts shows us that the details of the story are similar, that the OT verses quoted are similar, and even that all the Gospel writers place the event near the feast of the Passover.

The main difference is that the Synoptics make the cleansing of the Temple the main cause of Jesus' death. But is this really different from John?

1 John's wording suggests that it is Jesus' zeal which will be the cause of his death: a passion for the things of God exemplified by the cleansing.
2 Reading any of the Gospels reveals a number of reasons for Jesus' death (see below, 11.1–44). To explain Jesus' death as linked to one

single event seems too simplistic, and, as such, makes the date of the other less of a problem. The Synoptics and John share a tradition that what Jesus did in the Temple caused a lot of upset, but not enough to see him banned from entering it: Jesus is still free to return to the Temple (Mark 11.27; 12.35; 13.1; Matthew 21.23; 24.1; Luke 19.47; 20.1; John 5.14; 7.14; 10.23).

3 John links the cleansing to pronouncements about the destruction of the Temple. Similar remarks are found in the Synoptics after this episode (Mark 13.1–2; Matthew 24.1–2; Luke 21.5–6). They link it to apocalyptic passages which anticipate destruction and terror before the coming of the Son of Man. John completely avoids this apocalyptic scene. He develops a metaphor: the Temple is not the Jerusalem building, but Jesus. The Temple in Jerusalem is not important. What matters is that Jesus is raised from the dead (2.21–22), is not guilty of speaking badly of the Temple, and has no interest in the apocalyptic timetable. In John's view, everything will be accomplished by Jesus' death and resurrection. Events which are separated by time in the Synoptics all occur in the Passion and the resurrection in John's Gospel (19.30, 34).

Jesus' actions do not mean he rejected the Temple and its cult. The words of 2.16 suggest that bad practice is corrupting what is essentially good: Jesus is a reformer rather than a revolutionary. Sometimes when scholars say that Jesus completely rejected any value for the Temple or its cult, they are transferring the arguments from the Reformation – between Roman Catholics and the Reformers about worship and festivals – back into the texts of the Gospels where they really do not belong.

The dialogue between Jesus and his interlocutors is never completed. Instead, John inserts an interpretation made by the disciples. This makes a number of important theological points:

1 It stresses the significance of the resurrection as an event in shaping theological reflection.

2 It stresses the value of what Jesus said and did: such traditions were important.

3 It considers that the Jewish Scriptures also provide a witness to the truth.

As such, this affirms the ability of the disciples to think theologically, and also the importance they placed in passing on the story of Jesus. It is a reminder of how important the Scriptures and Jesus himself are – they provide the solid authority on which faith must be anchored. We note here another point of status: Jesus is presented as equal or superior to the Temple and its cult.

## STUDY SUGGESTIONS

### Word study

**1** 'Three days'. Why did Christian interpreters think that Jonah 1.17 was a good symbol of the resurrection? If 'three days' means 'a short time', how does this change the way the verse refers to Jesus' resurrection?

### Review of content

**2** Read the stories of the cleansing of the Temple in the Synoptics (Mark 11.15–19; Matthew 21.12–17; Luke 19.45–47). Compare these accounts with the one in John. What differences and similarities do you see?

**3** Does Jesus present a threat to the Temple in John's view?

### Discussion and application

**4** What does Jesus' attitude to the Temple tell us about replacing religious traditions and practice which are already found in a society?

**5** What should Christians do when they see people using religious practice as a way of exploiting others?

## 2.23–25: Signs and trust

## Introduction

John adds a short explanatory note about the relationship between signs and faith.

## Notes and commentary

**2.23. Many believed . . . because they saw the signs he was doing:** This refers to the ancient convention of taking miracles as a basis of faith (2.11).

**2.24. Jesus . . . would not entrust himself to them:** The Greek verb word translated 'entrust' here is the same word used for 'believe' and 'trust' (Appendix B).

**2.25. [Jesus] needed no one to testify about anyone; for he himself knew what was in everyone:** This statement suggests that Jesus had some supernatural power to judge people, but it does not necessarily mean this. It might simply show that Jesus is an astute judge of character.

 ## Interpretation

This short interlude explores the nature of belief. It notes and questions the tendency to believe on account of signs or miracles: what we might call 'gee-whizz' theology. Belief is as much about the quality of a relationship as what one believes. 'Gee-whizz' theology may turn heads, but does not build deep relationships and is unlikely to last long. We know the truth of this from our own experience: we may have had 'friends' who deserted us when more exciting company came along, and may even have realized they were going to do just that. To use John's language, such 'friends' are more interested in 'signs' than 'belief'. They are not the kind of disciples whom Jesus seeks. The passage thus raises more questions about 'true belief' (2.11). Jesus does not have confidence in people who believe because of signs alone; disciples need more. The previous section has given some clues about what may be needed: awareness of traditions about Jesus and the Jewish Scriptures as they relate to him.

 ## STUDY SUGGESTIONS

### Word study

1 Are faith and trust related?

### Review of content

2 What is John teaching about faith in this section?

### Discussion and application

3 Does our Christian faith practice need to include signs and miracles?

4 Do we often think theologically, and yet sometimes still rely on the sort of witnesses whom the disciples relied on? Have we allowed other 'authorities' (cultural, philosophical, ideological) to divert our attention away from theology?

5 What is our belief really based on?

## 3.1–21: Jesus and Nicodemus

 Introduction

An encounter with Nicodemus gives an opportunity for Jesus to show his skills as a teacher and debater. The dialogue allows Jesus to explain the plan which God has for the world.

 Notes and commentary

**3.1. A Pharisee named Nicodemus, a leader of the Jews:** Nicodemus is introduced as a significant person: he is identifiable both as a member of the school of the Pharisees (1.24) and a figure of authority. Nicodemus appears here and in 7.50–52 and 19.39, but is otherwise unknown. A number of legends appear about him in later Christian writing. The term 'Jews' is used of the nation or people here, not in the sense of opposing Jesus.

**3.2a. He came by night:** The use of light–dark (Appendix B) may imply that Nicodemus is in need of enlightenment.

**3.2b. Rabbi, we know that you are a teacher who has come from God; for no one can do these signs . . . apart from the presence of God:** Nicodemus is respectful of Jesus' teaching and abilities. His greeting recognizes Jesus as an equal, but also makes a claim about his own status – that he knows what makes a good teacher. Nicodemus stresses the place of signs in identifying what is true and of God.

**3.3. Very truly . . . no one can see the kingdom of God without being born from above:** See 1.51; Appendix I. Jesus does not reply in the usual polite way by praising Nicodemus. Instead he suggests that the one who knows God must be born from above. He thus questions the authority with which Nicodemus claims to speak. For the term 'kingdom of God, see Appendix M.

The metaphor of birth is used for a significant act. The phrase translated 'from above' has two possible meanings: 'from above' and 'again'. This double meaning is found only in Greek, and would not have worked in Aramaic. Scholars who argue that this story is genuinely from Jesus suggest that he knew Greek. This is not impossible: Greek was a lingua franca in the ancient Mediterranean, just as English, French, Kiswahili and Spanish are in the modern world. John will later imply that Jesus knew Greek by showing him interacting with both Greeks (7.35–36; 12.20–26) and Pilate (18.28–38).

**3.4. Born . . . a second time:** Nicodemus thinks that Jesus has used 'from above' to mean 'a second time' (again) and thinks that his statement is meaningless. The dialogue follows a familiar pattern (Appendix H).

**3.5. Born of water and Spirit:** These words do not mean a second literal birth. Water is used in the OT as a symbol of God's blessing and spiritual refreshment (Psalm 23.2; Isaiah 32.2). Ezekiel connects water, seen as a blessing, with the Temple cult (Ezekiel 47.1–11). Water is associated with the Spirit in the Last Days (Gk, *eschaton*) (Ezekiel 36.25–27).

In the OT, 'spirit' has a number of meanings: wind or breath as a mysterious force (Genesis 8.1) which has life-giving power (Genesis 6.17) and divine power (Judges 3.10). These meanings often overlap: they identify the divine energy which gives life. Being born of the Spirit means receiving the Spirit; being born of water and Spirit suggests a ritual use of water during which one receives the Spirit. Even if baptism is not explicitly mentioned, it appears to be implied by this phrase.

**3.6. What is born of the flesh is flesh, and what is born of the Spirit is spirit:** Jesus emphasizes that he is not talking of a literal birth by clearly distinguishing what is flesh and what is spirit: these are discrete or separate categories (Appendix B).

**3.7. Do not be astonished that I said . . . 'You must be born from above':** Jesus corrects Nicodemus: he meant birth from above, not a second time.

**3.8. The wind blows . . . and you hear the sound of it:** Jesus continues to talk about the mystery of the Spirit, comparing it to the wind. This plays on the multiple meanings of 'spirit'. 'Sound' suggests the need to listen to God through the Spirit and Jesus.

**3.9. How can these things be?:** Nicodemus' difficulty in understanding allows Jesus to question his earlier claims (3.2). Nicodemus is a teacher, but he does not understand. The speeches which follow show that Jesus does know, and therefore he is a superior teacher to Nicodemus.

**3.11. We . . . testify to what we have seen:** The first proof of Jesus' superior knowledge is based on what he has seen, and he therefore implies that he has seen the things of heaven.

**3.12. If I have told you about earthly things and you do not believe . . . how can you believe . . . about heavenly things?:** Jesus is using a rabbinic argument called *qal-wahômer* (light and heavy): if Nicodemus does not understand what is light (earthly), how will he understand what is heavy (heavenly)? See also 7.23; 10.34.

**3.13. No one has ascended into heaven except the one who descended from heaven, the Son of Man:** Jesus claims that his knowledge is based on a lived experience of the heavenly (he ascended into heaven) and that he has come from there. This claim also identifies Jesus with the Son of Man (1.51).

**3.14. Moses lifted up the serpent in the wilderness:** This statement is based on the account in Numbers 21.4–9 (see also 2 Kings 18.4). It serves as a second proof for Jesus' claims: an analogy. An analogy works by a stress on a shared detail. In this case, it is being 'raised up': Moses raised the serpent, and Jesus will be raised on the cross. The passage thus hints at Jesus' death on the cross, and is only clear if the reader of the Gospel already knows what is going to happen. Without such knowledge, Jesus' words would be obscure. Some commentators see a further layer of meaning: looking either at the bronze serpent or at Jesus means that death is put to an end. There may be a second word-play: Hebrew *seraph* means 'messenger' as well as 'serpent' (Isaiah 6.1–6).

**3.15. Whoever believes in him may have eternal life:** Death is conquered because those who believe in Jesus are given eternal life. This is the first time the phrase 'eternal life' is used: it occurs 36 times in this Gospel. It does not refer to natural life, since eternal life cannot be ended by death (11.26). Natural life came when God breathed life into the dust of the earth (Genesis 2.7). Eternal life comes when Jesus gives his Spirit to the disciples (20.22) through the living waters of baptism (3.5; 4.10, 14; 7.37–39) and the Eucharist (6.51–58). Eternal life is different in quality from natural life; it is not simply such a life without an end. Yet this lack of limits gives an indication of what is meant: natural life is finite, whereas eternal life is limitless; it is a full, not a limited, existence, in which life is lived to its full potential. For John, life of this kind is gained by living in Jesus. Finally, we may note that, in many ways, John's eternal life is very similar to the kingdom (Appendix M). If we think in terms of the timing of the kingdom, John leans towards a more realized eschatology, since Jesus has already started this process.

**3.16. For God so loved the world that he gave his only Son:** This provides a third proof for Jesus' claims by telling his motives. The verb 'love' here is the Greek *agapaō*, which is used for love throughout the Gospels; for exceptions, see 5.21.

**3.17. God did not send the Son . . . to condemn the world:** This verse says what God is *not* doing. He is not coming to look for the guilty, but saving the world, not just individuals (Romans 8.18–22). 'Condemn' (NRSV) may be translated 'judge', which often means 'to find a verdict' in English. If we return to the language of realized eschatology (3.3), it means that one is condemned when one rejects Jesus, but there is also a future sense when God will judge all people by their words and behaviour. Essentially, judgement comes from rejecting Jesus, who prompts people to judge themselves.

**3.18. Those who believe in him are not condemned:** There is no condemnation for believers. Their belief means they are not condemned.

**3.19. The light has come into the world:** See 1.7.

**3.20a. All who do evil hate the light:** Personal behaviour is important in judging good and evil (7.7; 17.5). This is the first time that the word 'hate' is used in the Gospel.

**3.20b. And do not come to the light, so that their deeds may not be exposed:** People reject Jesus because he reveals the true nature of their actions.

 ## Interpretation

The signs have made people ask questions about Jesus (2.23). As a result, Nicodemus comes to Jesus, and positively identifies him as a teacher, but not as either Messiah or the Son of God. In reply, Jesus questions the thinking that has led Nicodemus to his conclusions. To paraphrase C. S. Lewis, it is all well and good to think of Jesus as a teacher, but really the claims he makes demand much more. Jesus goes on to provide three proofs which imply that he is more than a teacher. We might recognize these from detective stories in which the police look for three things: means, motive and opportunity. Jesus offers three proofs to suggest that Nicodemus has not yet understood: means (the Spirit, 3.5–8), motive (God's love, 3.16–17) and opportunity (the cross, 3.14–15).

Not all of Jesus' encounters with either those in authority or the Pharisees were hostile. This meeting with Nicodemus resembles passages in the Synoptic Gospels where Jesus is the guest of Pharisees (Luke 7.36). Jesus' relationships with other sectarians were complex, and we need to be careful that we do not oversimplify them, always presenting those who talk to Jesus in a bad light. When we fail to read carefully, we increase the chance of making anti-Judaic readings which are not part of the text. This dialogue is not marked by hostility; indeed, we see later that Nicodemus grows into a follower of Jesus. However, the first conversation is immediately challenging: Jesus questions how Nicodemus and his colleagues identify right teaching.

Nicodemus emerges as a character who is an influential member of society. This prevents us from thinking that Jesus' followers came only from among the poor and marginalized. It is easy to romanticize Jesus, to view him as a social revolutionary, and see his message as part of a straightforward 'rich versus poor' class struggle. George Orwell, in his famous novel *Animal Farm*, showed the danger of some revolutionary political movements: they do not eventually solve major social injustices, but simply exchange the types of people who benefit and suffer. In recent political upheavals in Africa this has sometimes been called 'It's our turn to eat'. Such changes fall far short of Jesus' kingdom. In his vision and teaching, there is a promise that social wrongs will be set right, in such a way that the rich and powerful are converted or changed, not simply removed. It is a programme which demands a radical change to the whole ordering of society. Many societies have complex structures and hierarchies shaped by different factors (people's gender, age, wealth, marital standing, and status as free individuals or slaves). Jesus envisions a kingdom in which these factors are irrelevant, and all are equal in the eyes of God. Yet this equality exists not to preserve injustice or a pecking order, but to end discrimination and persecution. Jesus replaces 'Our turn to eat' with 'There is enough for everyone'.

The dialogue raises questions about how we can have correct knowledge. Nicodemus is sure of his status as a teacher, but Jesus quickly shows him that he knows nothing, even getting confused over simple phrases like 'from above'. Jesus also offers an alternative: whatever Nicodemus considers important, such as signs, needs to be replaced: he needs to receive the Spirit, the life-giving dynamic force associated with God. While this may seem mysterious to Nicodemus, the Gospel will subsequently show that Jesus, through his lived experience, is an authority on the Spirit, and therefore is uniquely qualified to be teacher and guide. Nicodemus is here challenged to set aside the conventional wisdom of his tradition, and live by a new set of standards, and Jesus is portrayed as superior to Nicodemus and his Pharisaic tradition.

Modern thinkers sometimes talk about 'paradigm shifts', by which they mean radical changes in how we look at the world. One example was the change which came about at the time of Copernicus: people began to reject a medieval cosmology which included God, angels and the like, and replaced it with modern scientific explanations. All societies and cultures have a world-view, and the claims that Jesus makes when he challenges Nicodemus are claims that he makes to everyone: are we ready to give up our conventional philosophies and worldviews and replace them with Jesus' teaching?

The passage throws up a number of questions about the worldviews which might have shaped it. Some suggest that it draws on Greek ideas of reincarnation (that human beings have a cycle of lives), but this does not fit at all well with John's eschatology, which presents a 'one-off' set of choices. Others think that the language of rebirth is based on the Greek 'mystery' religions in which people participated in rituals designed to guarantee their own salvation, but this type of initiation primarily set them free from fate, not from moral evil. There is much stronger evidence to suggest that John is drawing on Judaic ideas of rebirth: converts were compared to newborn children because they had been saved from the consequences of sin.

This passage implies that baptism is important, but does not treat it as a major theme. Yet John brings up or anticipates a theme to which he will return later on. It is also ironic that while the phrase 'born again' is very important in some contemporary church traditions, it is never actually used or approved by Jesus, who talks of 'being born from above'. Only Nicodemus, in his confusion, talks of being 'born again'.

Verse 14 reveals three tools which John uses to support the analogy of the serpent:

1 *Typology*: An OT passage anticipates and reveals a truth which will be used to say something about God and Jesus (examples include Abraham

and Isaac (Genesis 22.1–18) and Melchizedek (Genesis 14.18–20; Psalm 110; Hebrews 7).

2 *Correspondence in history* (see the Introduction).

3 *Word-play*: the word *seraphim* may allow John to apply a verse about serpents to the one sent by God.

Verse 16 is one of the most famous verses in the Bible, yet it is worth asking whether we have really grasped its significance. It is a sad fact that the Church and Christians are often perceived as hard and judgmental. Yet John says that God's prime motive is not judgement, but love. Judgement appears second to love. It is worth thinking about how differently the Church and Christians might behave if they based their actions on love, rather than judgement. We have recently seen what this might look like. When HIV and AIDS first appeared, many talked of it as God's judgement, but, in the course of time, attitudes changed: more and more people began to see that those living with HIV and AIDS should be treated primarily with love, not judgement, even if behaviour that caused the transmission of the virus was not approved.

This verse and those like it in the Gospel which stress God's love and sending have helped shape modern mission theology; this bases the Church's missionary task on the fact that to be 'missionary' is to live in the world just like God. (Some prefer to use the more recently adopted adjective 'missional', which has less historical baggage.) As God loved and sent Jesus, so it is vital for the Church to love and send Jesus, in word and sacrament, into the world.

A number of theologians over the centuries have argued that God's plan for salvation is universal, meaning everyone is automatically saved by the actions of Jesus. John does not agree. It is true that God's aim is primarily to save, and not to condemn, but it does not follow that salvation is automatic. Salvation depends on belief, and belief involves both knowing about and trusting in Jesus. While this may seem harsh, it does mean that we are prompted to think seriously about matters of good and evil, or knowledge and ignorance. John uses the image of darkness to talk of both evil and ignorance (1.5), and so prompts us to choose what is good and wise. This a serious business: a matter of eternal life or death. The great danger of universalism is that it can make such choices seem irrelevant, and, in so doing, leaves those most at risk of abuse by the powerful even more vulnerable.

John thus presents a scenario in which a God motivated by love, not by judgement, offers eternal life to all, but all do not take it. Why do people reject God's offer? God's offer in Jesus demands that people have to be honest about themselves, for the relationship of love offered by God depends on truth and respect. But many people do not like what they see, and would rather live in darkness or ignorance rather than face the true horror of their lives and choices and do something to change. This echoes T. S. Eliot's remark in his poem 'Burnt Norton', that humankind cannot bear too much reality. We still see this in our world. Psychologists talk about 'denial' when people refuse to face the truth of their lives and choices, and instead prefer to pretend everything is all right. While theologians traditionally have often talked about sin, we may also see the truth of this by using instead the language of addiction. We know that people can become addicted to sex, power, drugs, gambling, and all sorts of damaging behaviour. Such addicted individuals often deny the damage the addiction is doing, or its power over them. How many times do addicts say that they can 'give up whenever they want', but never do? We may have many tricks to hide our negative and damaging behaviour, but here Jesus reveals how useless these really are. He both reveals the nature and extent of sin and addiction, and reminds us of our need to face up to reality and reject whatever has a hold over us.

 STUDY SUGGESTIONS

### Word study

1 Should Christians describe themselves as 'born again'?

2 Write a short note describing the Spirit in the language of Scripture.

3 What does John mean by 'eternal life'?

### Review of content

4 What do we learn about Nicodemus? Is he more or less significant than Jesus according to John?

5 What does this dialogue teach us about the nature of God?

6 Do you think that universalism fits John's description of God's love?

### Discussion and application

7 What is the basic motivation for your church: love or judgement? Does its behaviour mirror the nature of God?

8 Why do people continue to reject God's gift of eternal life?

## 3.22–36: The Baptist, Jesus and the Messiah

 Introduction

The narrative continues with a move from Jerusalem (2.23) to Judaea (3.22), and develops two themes seen in the last section. The first returns to the theme: who is Jesus? Now he will be identified as superior to another significant religious figure: John the Baptist. The second explores the link between water and the Spirit, specifically the ritual use of water. The significance of such rituals, including ceremonial washings and baptism (3.25–26), is now raised.

 Notes and commentary

**3.22. Jesus and his disciples went into the Judean countryside . . . and baptized:** Baptism is mentioned as part of the public ministry of Jesus and the disciples. In the Synoptics, neither Jesus, the twelve nor the seventy (seventy-two) disciples are described as baptizing (Mark 6.6–13; Matthew 10.1–4; Luke 9.1–6; 10.1–12).

**3.23. John also was baptizing at Aenon near Salim:** Aenon is identified with three possible sites: (1) in Perea, the Transjordan (1.22); (2) in the north Jordan, near Bethabara; (3) in Samaria. This last is preferred, and provides a geographical link with chapter 4, echoing Jesus' relative openness to Samaritans (Luke 10.33; 17.16).

Aenon (spring) and Salim (salvation) may be invented symbolic names, but it would be odd to associate salvation with John the Baptist.

**3.24. John . . . had not yet been thrown into prison:** Only John describes this period of Jesus' ministry before the arrest of the Baptist (Mark 6.17–29; Matthew 14.1–12).

**3.25. Now a discussion . . . arose between John's disciples and a Jew:** The Greek offers a number of readings: 'a Jew', 'Jews', or even 'Jesus', although there is no textual support for this last suggestion. The substance of the dispute is unclear, but probably suggests criticism or rejection of the way John the Baptist baptized (compare Luke 7.30).

**3.26. They came to John and said to him, 'Rabbi':** The Baptist, like Jesus, is identified as a teacher (rabbi) with respect (3.2). It is not clear who is talking to the Baptist: his disciples alone, or his disciples and their opponents (3.25).

**3.28. You yourselves are my witnesses that I said, 'I am not the Messiah':** The Baptist reminds his correspondents of an earlier discussion (1.19–28). The discussion now shifts to the identity of the Messiah.

**3.29a. He who has the bride is the bridegroom:** A common biblical image of God's relationship with Israel is that of a bridegroom with his bride (Song of Solomon; Isaiah 54.6; Jeremiah 2.2; 3.20; Ezekiel 16.8; 23.4; Hosea 2.6). In the NT, it is used of the relationship between Christ and the Church (2 Corinthians 11.2; Ephesians 5.25–27; Revelation 19.7–9; 21.2; 22.17). At some points in the Synoptic Gospels, bridegroom imagery seems to be used to describe the Messiah (Mark 2.19–20; Matthew 9.15; Luke 5.34–35) and the kingdom (Matthew 22.1; 25.1).

**3.29b. The friend of the bridegroom . . . rejoices . . . For this reason my joy has been fulfilled:** Classical philosophers gave a high value to joy: Plato related it to true pleasure (*Philebus* 63e–64a). The Stoics, however, distinguished pleasure from joy.

**3.30. He must increase, but I must decrease:** Social commentators remind us that people in the ancient world considered honour to be a limited good. Here the Baptist voluntarily gives up his honour so that Jesus may have more.

**3.31. The one who comes from above is above all:** The verse implies that Jesus, who is from heaven, is superior to other teachers, who are of the earth (Appendix B).

Verses 3.31–36 (see below) may be part of a speech by the Baptist, or a commentary by the Gospel writer, or words which really belong to Jesus at the end of the Nicodemus passage. Whoever said it makes no difference to its interpretation. It does, however, show that it is very difficult on grounds of style to separate the 'voices' of Jesus, the Baptist and the Gospel writer.

**3.32. He testifies to what he has seen and heard:** See also 1.5, 11.

**3.33. Whoever has accepted his testimony has certified this, that God is true:** Truth is associated with the Spirit (3.6–8) as a gift of God. It is 'certified', that is, sealed: a seal was a mark in wax made with a signet ring to show the authority of the giver. A common modern equivalent is the marking of currency by a government.

**3.34. For he gives the Spirit without measure:** This statement rejects the idea of limited good (3.30). It may be contrasted with the limited gifts of the Spirit found in rabbinic literature (*Midrash Rabbah on Leviticus* 15.2). If so, like Hebrews 1.1, it claims the superiority of Jesus. It may also suggest that this is the final, definitive outpouring of the Spirit, which is only given in all its fullness in the Last Days. This repeats John's claim that, when Jesus became flesh, the final phase of God's plan had begun.

**3.35. The Father loves the Son:** This repeats 3.16, that God is primarily identified by love. For 'Son', see 1.14–15.

**3.36. Whoever believes in the Son has eternal life; whoever disobeys the Son will not see life, but must endure God's wrath:** This repeats the

45

theme that judgement depends on whether one receives or denies Jesus (3.19–21). Belief is rewarded with eternal life (3.16), denial with God's 'wrath'. A similar phrase, common from the OT (e.g. Isaiah 34.2; Judith 9.9) and intertestamental writing (Dead Sea Scrolls, 1QS 4.12; Esdras 8.21; *1 Enoch* 62.12; *Sibylline Oracles* 5.75–77), is given to the Baptist (Matthew 3.7; Luke 3.7). This might indicate that this section belongs properly in the Baptist's speech. It was common to describe God's anger as a response to injustice. Those who reject Christ and so also reject God are liable to feel God's anger because they deny that God is true (3.33).

 ## Interpretation

This passage enters a wider debate within Judaism about ceremonial washings or rites of purification. Presumably the tactic is to suggest that, if Jesus is baptizing, John must therefore be in error. The Baptist ignores the question of ritual, and focuses on the nature of authority. The Baptist, like Jesus in the dialogue with Nicodemus, stresses that true teaching has a heavenly origin. He thus supports the comments made by Jesus. Yet, while the Baptist is used as an authoritative witness to support what Jesus has said, he also affirms the description of himself as a witness in the Prologue (1.8). The Baptist describes Jesus as his better because Jesus is the bridegroom, and he is only the friend of the bridegroom (3.29). The Baptist's voluntary surrender of his own honour and status makes a very strong statement about Jesus' identity: a known and respected teacher is voluntarily deferring to him.

This final passage draws together the threads of the longer section, which we might summarize as:

- truth comes from heaven, not from signs;

- truth is related to the Spirit;

- truth is associated with God;

- Jesus' authority as one who knows the truth is revealed by (1) his heavenly connections and (2) authoritative witnesses respected within contemporary Judaism, notably the Baptist (3.25–30) and Scripture (by analogy, 3.14–15).

The Baptist's answer affirms what Jesus is doing as it is based on a revelation from heaven. The words in verses 31–36, whoever said them, make clear that the truth of Jesus' teaching, ministry and identity has its origins in God. The section concludes by identifying Jesus as a source of truth and knowledge about God. Listening to him gives the benefit of eternal life.

# STUDY SUGGESTIONS

## Word study

**1** Write a note about the symbolism of the 'bridegroom'.

## Review of content

**2** What did the Baptist's questioners think about him?

**3** What does the Baptist teach us about giving due honour to Jesus?

## Discussion and application

**4** Do Christians in your context seek honour for themselves rather than Jesus?

---

# 4.1–42: Jesus at the Well of Jacob

## Introduction

A break in Jesus' journey prompts two dialogues (Appendix H): one with a Samaritan woman (4.7–26), the other with his disciples (4.27–38).

## Notes and commentary

**4.1. Jesus learned that the Pharisees had heard, 'Jesus is making and baptizing more disciples than John':** There is no dispute between Jesus and the Pharisees, only a report of what they are saying.

**4.2. It was not Jesus himself but his disciples who baptized:** This verse appears to contradict 3.22. The problem may come from the Greek. An alternative translation may read: 'It was not just Jesus himself but also his disciples who baptized.' This would mean that Jesus and his disciples all baptized, and would also explain the greater numbers.

**4.4. But he had to go through Samaria:** The journey from Jerusalem to Galilee is through Samaritan territory.

**4.5. He came to a Samaritan city called Sychar, near the plot of ground that Jacob had given to his son Joseph:** The town is often identified with Askar, on the eastern slopes of Mount Ebal. For Jacob, see Genesis 48.21–22; Joshua 24.32. We should not directly identify the Samaritans of Jesus' time with those of 2 Kings 17.29. Their origins go back to the fourth century BCE and the rebuilding of Shechem. The Samaritans formed a religious community with a temple at Mount Gerizim, and were separate from the Jews (Ezra 4.1–6, 8–24; Sirach 50.26). Little, however, is known about their religious practices: they were monotheists, held Moses as a prophet, kept to the law as written in the Pentateuch, had a sacrificial cult at Mount Gerizim, and believed in a day of judgement and the return of a figure whom they called the *Taheb* (literally, 'one who returns/restores'), hailed as a prophet-king like Moses (Appendix K; 6.14).

**4.6a. Jesus, tired out by his journey, was sitting by the well:** Jesus' feelings show his true humanity (see the Introduction and 1.14).

**4.6b. It was about noon:** It was unusual to fetch water at this time: it was usually done in the evening (Genesis 24.11). Any woman approaching the well at this time must be an outcast from her community, coming to draw water when no one else is there.

**4.7. A Samaritan woman came to draw water:** Jesus upsets contemporary protocols by talking to (a) a Samaritan, (b) a woman, and (c) one on the margins of her society. Common Jewish opinion regarded Samaritan women as always unclean. While the OT has stories of encounters at wells that result in marriages (Genesis 24.10–21; Exodus 2.16–23), this narrative is really about Jesus being more important than Jacob. The idea that the Samaritan woman mirrors Rebekah as the founder of a community in faith is debatable: the Samaritans will believe for themselves and not solely because of her (4.39–42), and there is no evidence of a lasting community at Sychar.

**4.8. Jesus said to her, 'Give me a drink.' (His disciples had gone to the city to buy food):** The disciples do not fetch water for Jesus because they have been sent to perform a different task.

**4.9a. How is it that you, a Jew, ask a drink of me, a woman of Samaria?:** The woman is puzzled by Jesus' request and voices the usual conventions. She also breaks them by speaking to him: it was not normal for women to speak to unrelated males in public. Calling Jesus 'a Jew' confirms the difficulty of translating the word. Here it is used in an ethnic sense. The woman also thinks Jesus is claiming to be spiritually superior: her words are a polemic device to mock such claims (see also Revelation 2.9). It is also ironic: Jesus will claim to offer worship superior to both Judaic and Samaritan tradition (4.21).

**4.9b. Jews do not share things in common with Samaritans:** The conventions are further explained in an editorial note to the readers (1.38, 41, 42). Jesus will be classified as impure if he drinks from the woman's water jar (4.7).

**4.10a. If you knew the gift of God, and who it is that is saying to you, 'Give me a drink':** Jesus implies that the woman is not wise in the things of God. Just as he questioned Nicodemus' credentials (3.3), so he questions hers. She has two shortcomings: not knowing about God, and not knowing who Jesus really is.

**4.10b. He would have given you living water:** The phrase 'living water' usually means water from a spring rather than a cistern (Jeremiah 2.13). The OT also uses water as a metaphor for the Spirit, especially related to wisdom (Psalms 36.9; 51.2, 9–14; Sirach 15.3; 24.5; Isaiah 32.15; 44.3; 55.1–3; Ezekiel 36.25–27; 39.29). John uses 'living water' when referring to the Spirit (7.37–39). Jesus does not identify himself with the water (compare John 6), but offers the Spirit as the source of life. Later it is seen that Jesus and the Spirit are related (14.16).

**4.11. Sir, you have no bucket, and the well is deep. Where do you get that living water?:** In a typical conversation (Appendix H), the woman thinks Jesus is speaking about water from the well. Her greeting, 'Sir', is polite: the Greek word is capable of meaning a title (Lord), and can be used for God, though it is not used in that sense here.

**4.12. Are you greater than our ancestor Jacob, who gave us this well?:** Her reply is forthright – even socially unacceptable: she answers back, accusing Jesus of thinking himself better than Jacob. She also defends her religious heritage by stressing that they share the same common ancestor ('our ancestor Jacob'; see also 8.53).

**4.13. Everyone who drinks of this water will be thirsty again:** The quality of the water Jesus will give implies that he is superior to Jacob: it will give eternal life (3.15), not just quench thirst.

**4.14. Those who drink of the water that I will give them will never be thirsty:** The phrase for 'never' is used here for the first time (also in 8.35, 51, 52; 10.28; 11.26; 14.16 where it means 'for ever') in a negative sense ('not for ever'). Never being thirsty includes what happens after physical death (Revelation 21.5) and so this verse is about eternal life (3.15). The Spirit is the source of eternal life.

**4.15. Sir, give me this water, so that I may never be thirsty:** The woman replies politely again (4.11), but has yet to understand what Jesus is offering her.

**4.18. You have had five husbands:** The number shows that the woman has had a very irregular life (4.6). No explanation is given of how Jesus knows her past.

**4.19. Sir, I see that you are a prophet:** The woman is possibly making a reference to the *Taheb* (6.14).

**4.20. Our ancestors worshipped on this mountain**: See 4.5.

**4.21. The hour is coming:** Although this usually refers to the Passion in John, here it tells when the gift of the Spirit is made available. However,

John thinks the gift of the Spirit is linked to the Passion (19.30; also 2.4; 7.6, 8, 30; 12.23; 13.1; 17.1).

**4.22. You worship what you do not know; we worship what we know, for salvation is from the Jews:** This verse suggests that the Jews had a superior knowledge to the Samaritans, and knew what is needed for salvation. This may arise because John uses prophetic texts to make claims for Jesus' identity: Samaritans did not view prophetic texts as valuable or authoritative.

**4.23. The true worshippers will worship the Father in spirit and truth, for the Father seeks such as these to worship him:** Any pride based on the previous verse is now rejected. All rituals (Jewish or Samaritan) are less important than 'worship . . . in spirit and truth'. Spirit and truth imply that such worship is truly related to God; other worship risks being inferior or a human invention.

**4.25. I know that Messiah is coming:** Some have argued that John's use of 'Messiah' rather than '*Taheb*' by the woman makes the episode unhistorical. This, however, need not be so. For the sake of his readers, John may have simplified his text, using words that he considered synonyms (6.14–15).

**4.26. I am he:** The Greek word *eimi* bears a number of meanings (6.35). Often in the Bible it is used for the Hebrew yhwh, the holiest name for God (Exodus 3.14; John 8.58). Here it is an affirmative ('Yes') as Jesus reveals himself as the Messiah. The openness with which Jesus talks about himself in John is very different from the Synoptic Gospels.

**4.27. His disciples . . . were astonished that he was speaking with a woman:** The verse echoes conventions already seen in 4.9.

**4.28–29a. The woman . . . went back to the city. She said to the people, 'Come and see a man who told me everything I have ever done':** The woman again breaks conventions by speaking publicly about Jesus to the people in her city.

**4.29b. He cannot be the Messiah, can he?:** The woman voices her hope. The question also suggests that her dialogue with Jesus has not given a complete answer; she remains unsure, but it has made her think. Her excitement is based on what she has heard (a possible sign), and so is based on weak foundations (John 2; 3). Nevertheless, Jesus' words have challenged her previous beliefs.

**4.31. The disciples were urging him, 'Rabbi, eat something':** The return of the disciples prompts a discussion about food. For 'rabbi' see 1.38. The title may indicate that the disciples also do not understand fully who Jesus is.

**4.34. My food is to do the will of him who sent me and to complete his work:** The food of which Jesus speaks is doing the will of the one who sent him. The word 'work' in the OT often refers to God's work of creation, but here is likely to refer to Jesus' ministry (5.36). To 'complete' means to finish or bring to perfection. Jesus will utter this same word from the cross (19.30).

**4.35. Four months more, then comes the harvest:** Jesus quotes a proverb, which places four months between sowing and reaping, so introducing the imagery of 4.36. Harvest was a common symbol of the end times (Gk, *eschaton*) and final judgement (Isaiah 27.12; Jeremiah 51.33; Joel 4.13; 2 Esdras 4.29–39; *2 Baruch* 70.1–2; Mark 4.26–29; Matthew 9.37).

**4.36. The reaper is already receiving wages and is gathering fruit for eternal life, so that sower and reaper may rejoice together:** Jesus implies that the process of reward and blessing has already started, indicating an inaugurated eschatology (3.3, 15).

**4.37. One sows and another reaps:** This second proverb is a commonplace about economic life: the new reapers are in a place of privilege. A number of possible identifications are given for the sowers and the reaper, but none is certain. They include: Jesus and the disciples, the apostles and the generations which followed them, possibly John's readers, or John the Baptist and Jesus (based on 3.22–30).

**4.39. Many Samaritans from that city believed in him because of the woman's testimony:** The woman's testimony is not rejected immediately even though she is speaking inappropriately, that is, in public and to men as well as women. The preaching of the good news transcends conventional boundaries.

**4.42. Saviour of the world:** This title goes beyond the *Taheb* and Messiah: Jesus is providing a new hope which exceeds previous traditions. 'Saviour' in the OT was used of the Father (Isaiah 43.3, 11; 63.8–9). In secular life, Greek kings such as Ptolemy I Soter (Gk, *sōtēr*, 'saviour', 'deliverer') used it to describe their role in providing political and economic security for the state, as did philosophers like Epicurus (341–270 BCE). It was a title which could be understood by Jews and non-Jews: the Saviour can save human beings from evil of all kinds – spiritual, moral, physical and/or political.

 ## Interpretation

If we translate 4.2 as we suggested above: 'It was not just Jesus himself but also his disciples who baptized', the verse shows Jesus sharing the tasks of ministry with the disciples, and echoes the sending out of the twelve and the seventy (Mark 6.7–13; Matthew 10.5–47; Luke 9.1–6; 10.1–12). It might indicate that at an early stage Jesus was setting up a ministry which would survive him and share his pattern of leadership. This is a critical leadership issue: many plans and organizations that are centred on a charismatic leader fail when that leader leaves or dies. This question of ministry resurfaces in the dialogue between Jesus and the disciples (4.31–38). Ministry is a team effort which transcends different generations of ministers: no generation of Christians, including John's audience, can say that ministry is not their business. The proverb 'One sows and another reaps' also warns that some generations will be rewarded for the ministry done by others, and that some will not themselves see any reward for their work, but later generations will.

The second dialogue presents the outcast Samaritan woman in a positive light. The parable of the Good Samaritan (Luke 10.25–12), the washing of Jesus' feet (Luke 7.36–50) and the robust dialogue with the Syrophoenician woman (Mark 7.24–30) all show how Jesus challenges contemporary conventions and brings fresh hope and transformation to those considered impure, unclean or outcasts; this is common to all four Gospels. The Samaritan woman is brought back into society, with her former behaviour forgiven, and a new beginning (4.29–30, 39–42). The way Jesus treated the woman does not simply make her acceptable, but also ushers in a new way of living for the community.

Is it harsh of Jesus to criticize the woman for not knowing him? Perhaps – but it might indicate the all-too-human tendency to be too quick to judge people based on appearances. The woman has recognized him as a Jew or Judaean, and prejudged him, instead of bothering to find out who he really is. The debate between the two of them breaks almost every convention of their cultures. Such frank speaking (Appendix I) transforms the woman: no longer an outcast, but welcomed by Jesus, she becomes one of the first to proclaim the good news (4.29). The change in how she is accepted indicates the new way of living which Jesus institutes: traditional conventions governing the behaviour of women and men are changed. The barrier which separated women and men has been broken down: both are able to proclaim the good news publicly. Because of this, others hear the good news, and come to believe in Jesus, not because of what they have been told, but by what they have experienced for themselves. The Greek philosopher Plato, in the famous metaphor of the Cave (*Republic* 514a–520a), says that human beings are usually content to accept unthinkingly the opinions which others pass on to them. Those who are truly wise do not do this but struggle to find out the real truth for themselves. The Samaritans are like Plato's wise people, not just believing because of what the woman says, but because of what they find out and assess for themselves.

The encounter with Jesus leads the Samaritans to proclaim him 'Saviour of the world'. This title implies that Jesus will do far more than save individual humans and bring them life after death. It suggests that he will end every form of evil which damages God's Creation.

This section raises the claims being made about Jesus: he is now identified both as superior to one of the patriarchs (4.12) and as the Saviour of the world (4.42). Both have been suggested beforehand. The dialogue with Nathanael seemed to compare Jesus and Jacob (1.51). The dialogue with the woman at the well now shows that Jesus is superior to Jacob within both Judaic and Samaritan tradition, and that he even expands the role of the Messiah. While some of the disciples have already recognized Jesus as the Messiah (1.41), here they call him 'Rabbi' (4.31). Their earlier recognition makes it unlikely that we should now think of them as inferior to the Samaritans. The role of the Samaritans might make us reflect that sometimes new believers may reinvigorate the faith of the established community.

 STUDY SUGGESTIONS

### Word study

1 Explain 'living water'.

2 Explain 'eternal life'.

3 What does *eimi* mean?

4 What does Jesus mean by 'food'?

5 What would John's audience understand by 'Saviour of the world'?

### Review of content

6 How does the dialogue between Jesus and the Samaritan woman break social conventions? What does this say about Jesus' views of these conventions?

7 What is this section saying about the status of Jesus?

8 What is 'worship in spirit and truth'?

9 What does meeting Jesus do for the Samaritan woman? How does it change her?

10 What do we learn about John's eschatology from this section (especially verses 31–38)?

### Discussion and application

11 Do churches plan their ministry structures for the future, or do they fail when gifted leaders move on or die?

12 Do we prejudge people in our encounters or do we really try to get to know them? Do we let stereotypes and prejudices shape the way we relate to others?

13 Meeting Jesus causes the Samaritan woman to rethink her beliefs and hopes. When we 'meet Jesus', as we pray, read Scripture, worship and serve others, do we allow him to influence our hopes and beliefs, or do we cling to what is familiar to us?

14 Do we explore faith and truth for ourselves, or do we simply believe because of what others have told us? Is this good enough?

**15** Is our understanding of salvation as broad as that of the Samaritans, or have we set false limits on the work of God, for example by talking only of the salvation of individuals?

## 4.43–54: Jesus returns to Galilee

 Introduction

After a stay in Samaria, Jesus continues his journey back to Galilee. At Cana he is met by a royal official who has travelled from Capernaum to see him.

 Notes and commentary

**4.43. When the two days were over, he went from that place to Galilee:** This verse repeats 4.40, referring to Jesus' stay with the Samaritans.

**4.44. A prophet has no honour in the prophet's own country:** John reports indirectly a statement placed elsewhere on Jesus' lips (Mark 6.4; Matthew 13.57; Luke 4.24; see also 7.5).

**4.45. The Galileans welcomed him, since they had seen all that he had done in Jerusalem at the festival:** Jesus' reputation is based on what he has done in Jerusalem (2.23) rather than the miracle at Cana (2.1–11).

**4.46a. Now there was a royal official:** Returning to Cana (2.1), Jesus meets a royal official from Capernaum (2.12). 'Royal' implies either a relative or employee of the king. He might well have been a soldier (Josephus, *Antiquities* 10.7.6; 15.8.4; 17.10, 3, 4, 7). The centurion in the Synoptic versions (Matthew 8.5–13; Luke 7.1–10) would not be described as royal since (a) a centurion was a Roman military rank and (b) the Romans avoided royal language, using either military (imperial) or republican (political) ranks of office.

**4.46b. Whose son lay ill in Capernaum:** In Matthew and Luke, his servant is ill.

**4.47. He . . . begged him to come down and heal his son, for he was at the point of death:** This verse stresses the seriousness of the illness (Luke 7.2).

**4.48. Signs and wonders:** This expression also appears elsewhere in the NT (Mark 13.22; Matthew 24.24; Acts 2.43; 4.30; 5.12; 6.8; 7.36; 14.3; 15.12). In the Septuagint (LXX), the Greek text of the OT, it is commonly used to describe miracles (Exodus 7.3; Isaiah 8.18; Daniel 4.2; 6.27), but Mark and Matthew use the phrase to describe signs by false messiahs. Jesus here repeats his concern that faith is being wrongly based on signs (2.23–25).

**4.49. Sir, come down before my little boy dies:** The official politely (using the same term as 4.11) requests Jesus to come to Capernaum.

**4.50a. Go; your son will live:** Jesus tells the man to return. This may be read as an inversion of their status, as the official might be expected to be senior to Jesus. 'Your son will live' might be paraphrased: 'Your son has recovered [or is healed].' The words are identical to 1 Kings 17.23.

**4.50b. The man believed the word that Jesus spoke:** The response in faith is not based on a sign, but on Jesus' word.

**4.50c. And started on his way:** The man left with no proof that his request had been answered.

**4.52a. Yesterday at one in the afternoon:** This stresses the distance the man has had to travel: 20 miles or 32 kilometres between Capernaum and Cana. It also shows when he met with Jesus. 'One in the afternoon' is literally 'the seventh hour': hours were recorded from dawn with 7 a.m. as the first hour, and so on.

**4.52b. The fever left him:** The illness is identified now as a fever (compare Matthew 8.5, where it is paralysis; see also Mark 1.29–31 for fever).

**4.53a. The father realized that this was the hour when Jesus had said to him, 'Your son will live':** The official connects the healing to his meeting with Jesus.

**4.53b. So he himself believed, along with his whole household:** In a client–patron society, people who were dependent on an authority figure might well follow their patron's lead.

**4.54. The second sign:** The meaning is ambiguous. The first sign might be the changing of the water into wine (2.1–11) and part of a series in which the appearance at the Sea of Tiberias (21.14) is the third Galilean sign. However, this goes against the natural sense of the Greek which would make this the second sign after coming back from Judaea; the first sign would thus be Jesus' knowledge of the Samaritan woman's past.

 Interpretation

This passage concludes the journey from Judaea to Galilee. It resembles in many ways the Synoptic miracle of the centurion's servant (4.46). It performs several functions:

1 It makes Jesus superior to the official. The man might normally be expected to give commands to Jesus, but here he does what he was told. If previous episodes have shown that Jesus has superior spiritual or teaching authority, this one shows that he also has a high political profile. Politics was not separated from spirituality and religion in the

55

ancient world. Religion was used for political purposes, for example as a gauge of loyalty to the state. It even raises questions about the way modern politicians may pay lip-service to religious traditions and ethics, while engaging in cruelty and corruption. This encounter suggests that politics should also be separate from moral or spiritual concerns. We might prefer to put this differently: politics should be part of a wider morality, and not exempt from ethical or moral considerations. In many countries this is taken for granted, but people who live under brutal totalitarian or dictatorial regimes know what it means when politicians and leaders think they are above morality or law.

2 It asks: what is the basis for faith? It includes a criticism of signs and wonders which becomes even more significant if we remember that Jesus, in the Synoptics, is quoted as using this phrase to talk about false messiahs (4.48). This criticism of signs and wonders is advanced when the official is praised for (a) doing what Jesus tells him, and (b) believing before he has even seen his healed son. Part of John's strategy here is to build up hope for those generations of Christians who could never live in the presence of the earthly Jesus. It is part of a longer argument which stretches through the Gospel and will end in the risen Jesus' words: 'Blessed are those who have not seen and yet have come to believe' (20.29).

3 It raises questions about belief. We may struggle with the idea that the members of a household would believe on the strength of what their master did. This difficulty is acute for those who come from traditions which have been strongly shaped by individualism: the philosophy that we stand alone, make our own decisions, and so forth. Such individualism became a strong part of many Christian traditions after the Reformation, particularly those which stress personal conversion and the place of the individual. If anything, this philosophical view has become even stronger through the modern period: where John Donne could write that 'no man is an island' in the seventeenth century, Paul Simon could write, 'I am a rock, I am an island' in the late twentieth.

Individualism has also shaped many mission strategies, and made Christians scornful of historical mass conversions like those of the Frankish people, prompted by the conversion of their king, Clovis (465–511 CE). It is worth noting, then, that one of the most significant books on Christian mission of the last 50 years took a more positive view of the social factors behind mass conversions. In *Christianity Rediscovered*, Vincent Donovan described his experience among the Maasai. Individual conversions did not work, because strong social bonds linked men and women together in age-groups. It was better, he concluded, to share faith with a group and then receive the whole group into the Church. Donovan's remarks should make us examine the ways in which social links and networks may affect mission and evangelization.

STUDY SUGGESTIONS

## Word study

**1** Write a note about 'signs and wonders'.

## Review of content

**2** Compare this episode with Matthew 8.5–13 and Luke 7.1–10. Look at how they differ in detail, and how they are similar: can we say that one version is 'right' and the others 'wrong'? Why might we prefer one to the other? Do the differences actually matter?

**3** Does this version of the story give a different picture of who Jesus is or what he does from the Synoptic versions?

## Discussion and application

**4** In your experience, do politicians use religion to do the right thing or to look as if they are doing the right thing?

**5** Are mass conversions ever good mission practice?

**6** Do we consider how societies are shaped when we make plans for evangelization, or do we assume that our mission pattern fits every situation?

# John 5.1–47

## The first Sabbath controversy

 ## Summary

Jesus' healing of a sick man (5.1–9) leads to dialogues between the sick man and the Jews (5.10–13), Jesus and the man (5.14), and Jesus and the Jews (5.17–47). The controversy centres on the Sabbath (5.9) and Jesus' claim that he is not breaking any laws.

### 5.1–47: Jesus heals a sick man

 ## Introduction

The next section focuses on a single series of events which take place in Jerusalem at an unnamed festival. The events which follow centre not on a feast, but on the keeping of the Sabbath, the day of rest. Jesus will defend himself from the charge that he has broken the fourth of the Ten Commandments (Exodus 20.8–11; Deuteronomy 5.12–15).

 ## Notes and commentary

**5.1. There was a festival of the Jews:** The festival remains unidentified, and gives a reason for Jesus to be in Jerusalem. It presumably falls in the year between the first (2.13) and second Passovers (6.4). In John's chronology, it marks Jesus' second visit to the city.

**5.2a. By the Sheep Gate there is a pool, called in Hebrew Bethzatha:** Many scholars connect the location to Nehemiah 3.1, 32; 12.39. The description includes the 'Hebrew' (actually Aramaic) name; 'Bethesda' is a better transliteration of the Hebrew version of the name.

**5.2b. Which has five porticoes:** Scholars thought this was a symbolic description, representing the five books of Moses. However, archaeological discoveries from the 1960s onward have revealed a pool complex with five covered colonnades near the Sheep Gate. One of the pools also has steps down into it. Therefore, this appears to be a historically accurate description.

**5.3. In these lay many invalids – blind, lame, and paralysed:** These three groups would be excluded from Temple worship as they were considered impure (Leviticus 21.17–23). Healings in the Synoptics often involve the people healed showing themselves to a priest to confirm they are better (Luke 5.12–16) and allow participation in worship again. The story does not tell whether Jesus' patient is lame (Matthew 15.30) or paralysed (Mark 2.1–12; Matthew 9.2–8; Luke 5.17–26).

In the NRSV a long explanation (5.3b–4) about an angel stirring up the waters of the pool has been removed. It is a later addition not found in any of the earliest and most reliable manuscripts.

**5.5. One man was there who had been ill for thirty-eight years:** This information stresses the chronic nature of the illness and highlights the significance of the miracle (Acts 4.22). The number of years may symbolize the years that Israel spent in the wilderness (Deuteronomy 2.14), suggesting a new deliverance.

**5.7a. Sir, I have no one to put me into the pool:** The patient misunderstands Jesus' question as an offer to help him into the water.

**5.7b. When the water is stirred up:** The water was considered to have healing properties when stirred up. Stirring up occurred because water moved between the pools to replenish or purify it.

**5.8. Jesus said to him, 'Stand up, take your mat and walk':** Jesus heals without using the properties of the water. The word used for 'stand up' will also be used for raising the dead (5.21).

**5.9. Now that day was a sabbath:** The seventh day of the week was claimed as a day of rest in imitation of God, who rested after creation (Genesis 2.1–3). To break the Sabbath was an offence punishable by death (Numbers 15.32–36). Keeping or breaking the Sabbath was surrounded by a vast amount of regulations, both in the OT (Exodus 16.29–30; 34.21; 35.3; 15.32–36), and later writing and oral tradition. The Synoptics record several disputes about the Sabbath (Mark 2.23–28; 3.1–6; Matthew 12.1–14; Luke 4.31–39; 6.1–11; 13.10–17).

**5.10a. So the Jews said to the man who had been cured:** In this episode the term 'Jews' points to a clash between the leaders or authorities with Jesus. The Synoptics identify similar critics as scribes (Mark 2.6; Matthew 9.3) or scribes and Pharisees (Luke 5.21).

**5.10b. It is the sabbath; it is not lawful for you to carry your mat:** The initial cause of dispute is the man carrying his mat: rabbinic literature specifically banned the moving of a pallet or bed on the Sabbath (Mishnah, *Shabbat*).

**5.11. The man who made me well said to me, 'Take up your mat and walk':** Unlike the Baptist, this man does not witness to Jesus, but appears moved by shame or fear.

**5.12. Who is the man who said to you, 'Take it up and walk'?:** The questioners are more interested in finding out who has encouraged him than punishing the man himself.

**5.13. Now the man who had been healed did not know who it was:** Because the man cannot identify Jesus, he does not function as a model of belief. Some commentators suggest a difference here from the Synoptics, where healing and belief are closely linked.

**5.14a. See, you have been made well! Do not sin any more:** Jesus meets the man and tells him not to sin. The healing of the paralytic (Mark 2.5–12; Matthew 9.2–8; Luke 5.17–26) is followed by teaching that sin is forgiven, but not by an instruction to sin no more. Sin and illness were often linked together.

**5.14b. So that nothing worse happens to you:** Jesus' warning might imply a worse illness, but more likely refers to some final judgement. If so, Jesus is departing from popular opinion by talking of judgement rather than illness as the consequence for sin (9.2–3).

**5.15. The man . . . told the Jews that it was Jesus who had made him well:** The patient points Jesus out to his questioners. Perhaps to avoid 'nothing worse', he now tells what Jesus has done.

**5.16. Therefore the Jews started persecuting Jesus:** To 'persecute' may mean 'bring a charge against'. The following exchange is like a legal defence. The charge of breaking the Sabbath now shifts to Jesus, for causing a breach of Sabbath regulations.

**5.17. My Father is still working:** This is the first argument given by Jesus: he is able to work on the Sabbath because God does. While Genesis 2.3 and Exodus 20.11 claimed that God rested, they prompted a debate about whether God could work on the Sabbath. A number of later thinkers, including Philo (*On the Cherubim* 86–90; *Allegorical Interpretation of Genesis 2* 1.5–7), *Letter of Aristeas* 210; *Jubilees* 2.21, 30, and rabbinic texts (*Exodus Rabbah* 30.9; Babylonian Talmud, *Ta'an* 2a; *Genesis Rabbah* 11.10) argued that he could.

**15.18a. The Jews were seeking all the more to kill him:** The penalty prescribed by Scripture for blasphemy was death by stoning (Leviticus 24.10–16; see also 8.59; 10.31–33; 11.8). His opponents seek the full penalty of the law. The legal situation is complicated: it is highly debatable whether the Jewish authorities retained the legal right or power to make and carry out such a sentence under Roman rule (18.28—19.16). It may refer to illicit action: sometimes disputes within Judaism could turn violent.

**5.18b. He was not only breaking the sabbath, but was also calling God his own Father:** Jesus' first defence (that God can work on the Sabbath) is accepted, but it provokes a second, more serious charge: Jesus has identified himself with God.

**5.18c. Making himself equal to God:** A central part of such a charge would be that Jesus was making such a claim himself. God is the one who should make such revelations. The charge may have a scriptural origin in the sin of Adam (Genesis 3.5–6).

**5.19a. Very truly:** This phrase is also used in 5.24, 25; see 1.51. The repetition emphasizes the seriousness of Jesus' words.

**5.19b. The Son can do nothing on his own:** See 1.14, 18. This statement stresses the unity of the Father and the Son.

**5.20. The Father loves the Son and shows him all that he himself is doing; and he will show him greater works than these:** Heredity is Jesus' first defence for his actions: the relationship between the Father and the Son is based in love (3.16), and promises greater revelations than have been seen already. Here Greek *phileō* is used for 'love' (11.3; 13.23; 16.27; 19.26; 21.7, 20). Scholars have often argued that *agapaō* (3.16) means a higher, self-giving love, but it is unlikely that John makes such a distinction (21.15–17).

**5.21. Just as the Father raises the dead and gives them life, so also the Son gives life to whomsoever he wishes:** The greater revelation of 5.20 is linked to God's power over life and death. In the OT, the phrase 'raise the dead' was used before there were beliefs in bodily resurrection (1 Samuel 2.6; Tobit 13.2; Wisdom 16.13). In Second Temple Judaism, resurrection was seen as transformation rather than resuscitation (a return to this mode of existence; see also 11.38–44). The verse also limits who 'the Jews' (5.18) might be: they are from those groups who believe in some form of life after death (like the Pharisees, Acts 23.8), otherwise the argument is redundant.

**5.22–23a. The Father judges no one but has given all judgement to the Son, so that all may honour the Son just as they honour the Father:** Imitating the Father's actions makes Jesus' second argument: he performs the same actions as the Father so that he will be honoured like the Father. According to Jewish legal principles, a designated representative (like the Son) was entitled to the same honour as the one represented. The Father has delegated the task of judgement (3.17) to the Son, to ensure again that honour is given properly to the Son.

**5.23b. Anyone who does not honour the Son does not honour the Father who sent him:** Failure to honour the Son implies a failure to honour the Father. The Father and the one who sends are clearly shown to be the same.

**5.24. Very truly, I tell you, anyone who hears my word and believes him who sent me has eternal life, and does not come under judgement, but has passed from death to life:** Jesus' third argument defines the work given by the Father. It echoes traditional belief (Daniel 12.2). He repeats the claim that right belief brings eternal life (3.16). Note here that belief is directed towards the Father, not Jesus (12.44). Jesus is now the agent by whom God's will is to be done. The trumpet which announces the resurrection (1 Corinthians 15.52; 1 Thessalonians 4.16) is replaced by 'my word'. Here the call is both to the living and the dead: all who hear will pass from death to life.

**5.25. Very truly, I tell you, the hour is coming, and is now here, when the dead will hear the voice of the Son of God, and those who hear will live:** This repeats 5.24, and focuses on the dead. We should avoid simply comparing this with 1 Peter 3.18–20; 4.6 as these verses are notoriously difficult to interpret. The title 'Son of God' has been used already (1.34).

**5.27. Son of Man:** See 1.51. This term (Daniel 7.13) makes clear the earlier identification with Daniel 12.2, and suggests a messianic claim.

**5.28. All who are in their graves will hear his voice:** Here is a second reference to belief in the general resurrection.

**5.29. And will come out – those who have done good, to the resurrection of life, and those who have done evil, to the resurrection of condemnation:** The final judgement determines the post-resurrection life of the individual. The judgements made by people about themselves (3.17) have consequences for the future.

**5.30. I can do nothing on my own. As I hear, I judge; and my judgement is just, because I seek to do not my own will but the will of him who sent me:** Jesus' fourth argument is that he is doing the will of him who sent him – he shares a unity of purpose with the Father (5.23) and, indeed, the very presence of the one who sent him. He is not independent; he can only judge what he hears.

**5.31. If I testify about myself, my testimony is not true:** Jesus agrees with the Jewish legal principle that self-testimony is inadequate. Two or more witnesses were needed to make a legally strong claim (Numbers 35.30; Deuteronomy 17.6; 19.15; Daniel 13 (LXX) – Susanna and the Elders). See also 8.12–20.

**5.32–33. There is another who testifies on my behalf, and I know that his testimony to me is true. You sent messengers to John, and he testified to the truth:** Jesus reminds his questioners of the Baptist's witness. 'You sent . . . he testified' suggests a past action which still has binding effect: the Baptist witnessed – and his witness is still valid (1.19–28; 3.25–30).

**5.34. Not that I accept such human testimony, but I say these things so that you may be saved:** Jesus now rejects the witness of the Baptist, who would have been a respected authority, claiming better witnesses. Jesus' defence will benefit his opponents – they may be saved (4.42) – rather than just make a point.

**5.35. He was a burning and shining lamp, and you were willing to rejoice for a while in his light:** Compare 1.6–10. 'You were willing' shows how Jesus' opponents took a positive view of the Baptist.

**5.36. But I have a testimony greater than John's. The works that the Father has given me to complete, the very works that I am doing, testify on my behalf that the Father has sent me:** Jesus' first witness is his works: he does not base his witness on signs (Appendix C; 2.11). The works refer to the many tasks which Jesus performs to complete the work of his mission and reveal his glory (2.11; 11.4, 40).

**5.37–38. And the Father who sent me has himself testified on my behalf. You have never heard his voice or seen his form:** Jesus' second witness is the Father. His argument claims that it is ignorance of the Father which stops his questioners from recognizing the truth of his claims.

**5.39. You search the scriptures because you think that in them you have eternal life; and it is they that testify on my behalf:** Jesus continues to attack his opponents: they have failed to read Scripture properly, and do not see how it witnesses to him.

**5.40. Yet you refuse to come to me to have life:** If Jesus' opponents understood Scripture, they would come to him to have life (Appendix D; 3.15 for life as eternal life). This effectively makes Scripture a third witness to Jesus.

**5.42. I know that you do not have the love of God in you:** Jesus accuses his opponents of a second failing. They do not understand what is fundamental to the nature of God – love (3.16).

**5.43. I have come in my Father's name, and you do not accept me; if another comes in his own name, you will accept him:** Instead of following God, his opponents follow another who comes in his own name. This makes two points:

1 They follow one who is not the Father.

2 Such witness is inadequate. 'In his own name' means he bears witness to himself without the legal requirement of two witnesses (5.31). Ironically, they follow someone who does exactly what they have claimed Jesus is doing.

**5.44. How can you believe when you accept glory from one another and do not seek the glory that comes from the one who alone is God?:** Jesus' opponents are more interested in getting glory from one another than God; glory is something to be received rightly from God alone (Matthew 6.27).

**5.45. Do not think that I will accuse you before the Father; your accuser is Moses, on whom you have set your hope:** It is not Jesus who presents himself as their accuser, but Moses (Exodus 18.13–27). Again, Jesus suggests that his opponents are unqualified to accuse or judge him. They do not believe in Moses, and have no understanding of the law; this failure implies that they are unable to believe him. Moses, too, becomes a witness to Jesus. But, like the witness of Scripture, this is not as important as the works (5.36) and the Father (5.37).

 ## Interpretation

This episode starts with a healing (5.9) which seems to break Sabbath regulations (5.10–12). Jesus is revealed as an agent of healing far superior to the waters of the pool. He heals a man who has been waiting for healing for a long time, but he does this by his own authority, not even by using the pool itself.

The passage bears similarities to a number of Synoptic passages which relate both to healing and the Sabbath regulations. Although location and precise details vary, we may note the following broader correspondences:

1 All involve claims that Jesus heals people.

2 Healings point to the forgiveness of sin, which includes a warning not to sin any more (5.14), and to the authority which Jesus bears.

3 All involve confrontations with authorities within Judaism.

4 Jesus is accused of blasphemy. When Jesus is identified as the source of healing, attention turns to his breaking Sabbath regulations (5.16). His defence, that the Father is still working (5.17), leads to a further charge: that he is identifying himself with God. This provokes an interesting parallel to the Synoptics. In their accounts of the healing of the paralytic, Jesus is accused of blasphemy because he says something which properly belongs to God: that sins are forgiven (Mark 2.7; Matthew 9.3; Luke 5.21). Blasphemy is a difficult term to define. For us, it often means 'taking the name of the Lord in vain' or insulting God. At the time of Jesus, it also included idolatry, disrespect for God, insulting his leaders, and a wide range of insulting speech and activity. Claiming to do what was God's prerogative fits into such a definition – and this provides the grounds for the subsequent charges against Jesus: making himself equal to God.

When we talk of Jesus being equal with God, our thinking is often shaped by the later Trinitarian debates which focus on ontology (the nature of being). These arguments come from a very different time and period from John. Later on, John will remind his audience of Jewish beliefs that human beings can be called gods (10.31–39; see also 1.32–33) because of right behaviour, not nature. However, the NT writers also move beyond the language of behaviour. Paul talks of adoption (Romans 8.15, 19–23; Ephesians 1.5). Where Paul uses adoption, John uses social status and authority. The status of a father is handed down to a son, unless some misbehaviour cancels out the inheritance, but, while the father still lives, this will involve a hierarchy in which the father is superior. Their status (i.e. being) is the same, but the son still submits to the father in a hierarchy. This is subtly different from the later heresy of subordinationism, which argued that the Son was not equal in being to the Father. In this Gospel, John shows that Jesus does what the Father does and so is equal with him: he gives eternal life and judges. These shared tasks mean that an equivalent honour and worship is due to him – even his very being is equivalent – and that his 'submission' in no way makes him an inferior deity.

As the notes show, Jesus' defence is based on four separate arguments which present him as a genuine agent of God. They raise a question of timing: when will this happen? The answer shows why we should not think of John's eschatology as realized, or futuristic, but as inaugurated (3.3): the work has already been started, since Jesus' voice is being heard, but equally there are indications that the work is not completed. The timing will unfold as the work of the Spirit is revealed, but it does not cancel out the fact that inaugurated eschatology involves a call to new life on this side of the grave. The UK charity Christian Aid summed up this aspect in a slogan: 'We believe in life before death.'

It is worth noting the arguments which Jesus brings in the final section (5.30–42). They need to be interpreted carefully. They never involve a rejection of Judaism. Jesus upholds:

1  legal principles about witnesses and self-testimony;

2  the value of Scripture;

3  the value of the Father;

4  the value of Moses.

This last section is essentially an attack on the qualifications of his accusers. Jesus attacks their credentials, not the Jewish faith, its traditions or its key figures. Rather, he shows that his opponents do not know what they claim to know. It is important to make this point, because without it, we are more likely to make a false anti-Judaic reading of the Gospel. This is especially true if the debate is turned into an anachronistic 'Jew versus Christian' scenario. This is a dispute *within* Judaism, between competing interpretations. Such debates were often marked by a strong rhetorical polemic in which attacks were made on the opponent's abilities or character – what philosophers call *ad hominem* arguments (literally, 'to the man'). It must always be remembered that these are not literally true descriptions of Jesus' opponents (many of whom, like Nicodemus and Nathanael, would be well educated and well versed in Scripture) but are made for effect: winning an argument. This kind of argument will be seen in an even more savage form (8.39–59).

By the end of this section, Jesus is shown to be equal to the Father, using notions of sending and status familiar from ancient ideas about honour and shame. While Jesus holds the authorities of Judaism (the Father, Scripture and Moses) in high regard, he thinks little of his opponents' calibre as teachers.

 STUDY SUGGESTIONS

**Word study**

1 Write a note about the 'Sabbath'.

**Review of content**

2 Read Mark 2.1–11 and 7.24–30. Compare them with John 5.1–9. Do all stories of healing fit into a single pattern in which the person healed needs to have faith? (Clue: look very carefully at who is described as having faith in each story.)

3 Read the Sabbath controversies in Mark 2.23–28; 3.1–6; Matthew 12.1–14; Luke 4.31–39; 6.1–11; 13.10–17. What points in common do they have with John 5? Do John and the Synoptics make different points from them?

**Discussion and application**

4 Do we still treat people with disabilities badly? What do Jesus' actions tell us we should do?

5 Should we use *ad hominem* arguments in our debates?

 Theological essay 1
## Sonship in John's Gospel

S. ROBERTSON

### Introduction

John uses two important titles for Jesus, 'Son of Man' and 'Son of God', to explain the unique relationship between God and Jesus. The theme 'sonship' in John is very relevant in the context of plurality of identity. Plurality of identity implies, here, different religions and ideologies (including political ideologies). It also includes religions which do not require belief in the existence of a Creator God. I group religions and ideologies together to suggest the view that religions alone cannot be instruments of transformation in some contexts. My own country of India is one such context in which there are many ideologies and religions that often seem to be in competition with one another. However, those people who belong to religions and ideologies committed to the salvation of God's Creation need to work together.

Human beings have always attempted to understand ultimate reality in many different ways, as their intellect and cultural context permitted. Thus, plurality of religion and ideology is as old as human history. But the world is no longer a place where different religions and ideologies merely exist alongside one another; people from different religions and ideologies are now trying to co-operate and work together towards the salvation of the entire universe. This is not a call for uniformity but a call for uniting, without losing our individuality, to bring about the liberation of the world.

## Unity between Son and Father

When we look at sonship in John's Gospel, we see that a unique relation-ship exists between Jesus and God on the one hand, and between Jesus and people on the other. The unity of the Son with the Father is the basis of unity between the believer and God, as well as of unity between the believer and other believers.

This unique relation is based on love. The love the Father had for the Son before the foundation of the world (17.24) is working in the life, death and resurrection of Jesus. The same love brings all Creation into that unity of which the Father–Son relationship is the eternal model. John also makes a distinction between the love between Jesus and God, and the love between God and the rest of Creation. That is why John presents Jesus as the only, unique 'Son of God' who is begotten by God. Others may become children of God, but Jesus' sonship stands apart from that of all others. Jesus never speaks of God as 'our Father' in a way that would place him in the same relationship to God as his disciples. On the contrary, he sets his sonship apart when he says to Mary Magdalene, 'I am ascending to my Father and your Father, to my God and your God' (20.17).

In this relationship, we also see the unique revelation that Jesus brought. As the only Son, Jesus claims to possess an exclusive knowledge of the Father. No one has seen the Father except him who is from God (6.46). As the Father knows the Son, so the Son knows the Father (10.15). Jesus declares to the world what he has heard from the Father (8.26); he speaks only what the Father has taught him (8.28). The reason God sent Jesus is to communicate that unique knowledge which is the eternal plan of God for the salvation of the entire Creation.

The relationship between the Father and the Son is woven through the entire fabric of the Gospel to show that Jesus' whole ministry is domin-ated by a consciousness that he has been divinely commissioned.

We can have an intimate relationship with God based on the love of God. The relationship has the purpose of revealing God with a view to mission. This is an important belief in India where most branches of Christian theology affirm the personal nature of God revealed in the person of Jesus for the purpose of mission. Worshipping an impersonal God has not appealed greatly to Indian Christians.

In the context of many religions and ideologies, the possibility of an intimate relationship with a loving God, who reveals his plan and the purpose of his plan and the purpose of his mission to his people, is meaningful. It is meaningful because human beings are constantly searching for God's love. Also, God's knowledge and God's plan are for everyone. Above all, in a pluralistic context the relationship between one individual and another needs to be patterned after the relationship between an individual and God.

## Connecting the transcendental and the immanent

According to John, Christ brought salvation by coming down from heaven but at the same time living among people in order to link the world with the eternal divine plan of God. The transcendental God who loves the world presents himself immanently through the life and work of Jesus Christ.

In a religiously pluralistic context, the ultimate reality is often considered as the Mystery (the Father) because it manifests in many forms. It is beyond the comprehension of ordinary human beings. Hence religions are recognized as having responded differently to the mystery of the ultimate. This sense of mystery provides a point of unity to the plurality of religions, together with a common purpose – salvation.

In John, Jesus reveals the Father and makes the claim to be the exclusive revelation of the Father. He alone has seen the Father (6.46). He therefore is the sole medium by which men and women may come to know him. When the Pharisees asked, 'Where is your Father?' Jesus pointed out, 'If you knew me, you would know my Father also' (8.19). A similar response was given to Philip's request, 'Show us the Father.' Jesus puts the question, 'Have I been with you all this time, Philip, and you still do not know me?' (14.8–9). It was as clear as it could be.

Closely parallel to this point is the fact that the Son speaks the words of the Father. Not only works but words are vehicles of the Father's activity. Jesus had received a charge from the Father (10.18). He calls his disciples 'friends' and then adds, 'because I have made known to you everything that I have heard from my Father' (15.15).

In India, where there is a marked difference between the personal and impersonal philosophical notion of God, the principle of Jesus revealing the Father in his earthly form becomes a bridge-builder or a middle path between the transcendent and immanent aspects of God. It also makes it possible to think that the transcendental God can be revealed and one can have personal communion with him. In other words, here, the distance between the transcendence and immanence is removed.

## Personal religion

John's presentation of sonship is a hope for people who are familiar with personal religions, particularly the way of devotion in Hinduism and Islam. It satisfies those with philosophical minds who seek supreme ideals in an abstract way, and at the same time it satisfies the ordinary seeker of God who enjoys the immanent presence of God as found in Jesus.

Perhaps the most impressive of all John's 'Son of Man' sayings comes in 1.51 where the disciples are promised an opened heaven and the angels ascending and descending on the ladder of the 'Son of Man'. This means that Jesus as the 'Son of Man' has come to establish communication between heaven and earth. The 'Son of Man' is the entrance to heaven and he is God's presence on earth. It signifies that, at present, Jesus the visible, historical person is the place of revelation, and the place over which heaven has been opened for others as well.

The presentation of the personal dimension of Jesus ensures that his followers are not excluded from the reality that Jesus represents. Jesus incorporates his disciples into union with himself in God. He gives them power to become children of God. Jesus ascends to heaven (3.13) and so will his disciples (14.12). Jesus testifies to what he has seen and heard from God (3.32) and the disciples will also (20.23). Jesus does the works of God, and his followers do so as well (6.28–29; 9.4) and they will do even greater works (14.12). Jesus is God's Son, and his followers are 'children of the Most High' (see John 10.34–35). Where Jesus is, his disciples will be also (14.3). Jesus is the vine, his disciples are the branches, and the Father is the vinedresser (15.1–11). Nothing could express more completely the collective, corporate nature of the Johannine view of sonship than 14.20: 'you will know that I am in my Father, and you in me, and I in you.' John not only preserved the collective aspect of the Son of Man, but also brings this aspect to the forefront by distinctly connecting God, Jesus and the believers.

## Ascent and descent

John presents Jesus not as an ordinary person, but as 'Son of Man' and 'Son of God' who was existing eternally with the Father and came down to voluntarily lay down his life for the salvation of others. The idea of descent is integral to John's whole approach to Jesus as the connecting link between earth and heaven. It at once differentiates Jesus from the pre-Christian Jewish idea of 'Son of Man', where the idea of descent is wholly absent. The concept of 'descent' is a vivid expression of the breaking in of the 'Son of Man' from the spiritual world of God to the material world.

The corresponding idea of ascent is important because it makes clear that the real sphere of the Son of Man is in heaven and not on earth. Once his earthly mission is accomplished he returns to God. As the Son of Man, Jesus is the one who descended from heaven and who ascends into heaven (3.13). As such, he can establish a decisive link between heaven and earth, between God and his Creation.

The principle of descent and ascent is very much in tune with the notion of *avatara* (incarnation) in Hinduism and in other religions where there is a belief that God descends to the earth to set the world right through his righteousness and to destroy wickedness. The Johannine idea of incarnation is completely different from that in other religions as it is a once-for-all act. Nevertheless, the belief that God is concerned with the right order of things on the earth can be an encouraging principle, allowing religions and ideologies to work together to establish a just and righteous order of life on the earth.

## Love of God

'Sonship' in John explains the real love of God, which is freely available to all who accept him. Building upon the love of God for his Creation is vital in religiously plural contexts, where love, not strength, is the main operating principle. Where Christianity is in a minority status, it cannot boast about its numerical strength. Yet the strength it derives from the love of God for humanity can inspire it to engage in the struggles of life, not as the strongest force, but as a community with a simple and substantial message.

The love of God can also motivate believers to engage in God's mission so that it is accomplished in co-operation with different ideologies and religions committed to the cause of salvation for all. Christians cannot use their numerical weakness as an excuse to avoid participation in mission. We need to work alongside other religions and ideologies in the spirit of love to serve others. People may be unwilling to accept other ideologies and religions, but few can dislike mission pursued from the perspective of love of God. That is the lesson we learn in a pluralistic context, and John's expression of sonship is also justified in this context.

The love of God and the love for God bring people of all religions and ideologies closer to God and closer to liberation.

This method is found in Jesus Christ. All through his life, Jesus was dedicated to empowering and emancipating the lives of others, particularly the marginalized. His concern for the value of life was the result of his commitment to his Father, who is understood as Mystery in the Indian pluralistic context. He was conscious of his responsibility to the Father and acknowledged the people involved in such responsibility as his brothers, sisters and mother, irrespective of their backgrounds.

Religions are to protect and strengthen life in all possible ways. Jesus did not want forms of religious observance – Sabbath, offerings, law and so on – to become a hindrance to life-giving or life-saving acts. Such a conviction is possible only because of God's love. In this persuasion the struggles and concerns of people take precedence.

In many parts of the world the crying evil is not a lack of religion or ideology, but a lack of bread. Love of God helps us to see God in humanity and helps us to be involved in the struggles of the poor. It affirms that God can be worshipped by serving other people. Mahatma Gandhi appealed to the religion of humanity underlying all religions. Here is the crucial need for engaging with other religions and ideologies as well for the purpose of saving life.

In a multi-religious context, people of other faiths often categorize the mission of the Church based on God's love as an indirect way to convert them. This misconception needs urgent correction. If Christian mission is pursued on the basis of love of God, it can convey the message that Christian initiatives are not for mere conversion but to create awareness among people about the need for co-operative action among religions and ideologies to serve humanity with love. Conversion from one religion to another is the choice of individuals.

The most frequently reiterated element in Jesus' mission is to mediate life to men and women. Faith in Jesus as the Son of God issues in the possession of eternal life (3.36; 6.40, 47; 10.10) as well.

Jesus' mission of salvation involves his death, which was an event over which Jesus had full control. Jesus says, 'No one takes [my life] from me, but I lay it down of my own accord' (10.18). The life-giving mission of Jesus which is the result of the love of God can be a source of great encouragement to people to engage themselves in salvific activities even in co-operation with other religions and ideologies.

## Voluntary and sacrificial suffering

The voluntary suffering of Jesus is the first visible expression of God's love. God sent his only begotten Son to the world to establish a unique relationship between humanity and God. This unique relationship required voluntary suffering – a suffering oriented towards the salvation of others. Jesus demands that kind of suffering from everyone who accepts him. This voluntary suffering leads to greater fellowship with God and humanity. Jesus declares that people must eat the flesh and drink the blood of the 'Son of Man' to experience this life (6.35). This unique relationship guarantees the experience of a new life.

John's portrayal of the Son's suffering as sovereignty, and the cross as his glory, has great relevance as we seek to understand the implication for Christianity in pluralistic contexts. Existing in a place where other religions and ideologies are powerful *is* the suffering of Christianity. The Church cannot proclaim itself as a victorious champion but instead needs to fulfil its mission, despite all the constraints, because that is the glory envisaged in John's Gospel. Christianity needs to exist in the midst of other faiths without failing in its role as bearer of truth, light and life.

In the normal affairs of life, each individual, irrespective of his or her religious or ideological affiliation, is earnestly engaged in the daily struggles of life. The world lacks genuine and strong spiritual life which emits God's love for others through suffering. But this kind of spiritual life is possible if we consider that loving suffering for others is the means to bring about salvation for the universe. Those who are called to serve God are also called to suffer and called to engage those from other religions and ideologies in similar suffering for the sake of the world's salvation. In the midst of many ideologies and religions, we need to be prepared to undergo suffering of this type for the sake of the salvation of others.

Participation in the struggles of people and commitment to the love of God are two sides of the same coin. Mission pursued from the perspective of suffering is committed to friendship and co-operation among religions and to a pooling of resources to empower all life.

## Suffering and exaltation

According to John, the 'Son of Man' is one who suffers and is then exalted. This includes the two ideas of humiliation and honour. For John, the 'Son of Man' must be 'lifted up' in crucifixion (John 3.14; 12.34). There are three passages in which a lifting up is mentioned in John (3.14; 8.28; 12:32–34). The term 'lifted up' seems to encompass resurrection and exaltation as well as crucifixion (3.14; 12.23, 34; 13.31). This is equally clear from the analogy of Moses' lifting up of the serpent (3.14) and of Jesus' statement to the Jews that they would lift him up (8.28). His death will not be a mere human tragedy but will be the means by which he will re-enter the glory from which he had come.

The glorification of Jesus begins on earth (through the cross), but continues beyond (he will come again as judge). John claims in his Prologue that 'we have seen his glory, the glory as of the Father's only Son' (1.14). The glory was more important to Jesus than the shame. This is an encouraging aspect of God's mission, that our voluntary and sacrificial sufferings are not unrewarded, but rather we will be glorified. This voluntary suffering leads to greater fellowship with God and humanity. Such a stupendous insight strengthens Christian ministers who undergo difficulty in ministry as well.

## Conclusions

The sonship of Jesus as presented in John's Gospel is relevant for fulfilling God's mission, initiated through Jesus, in a pluralistic context. John reveals the possibility that believers in Jesus can have a special relationship with God and fellow believers. This inspires us in God's mission of co-operation with other religions and ideologies. God's sending of his only begotten Son has bridged the gap between the transcendental and immanent understanding about God. It helps people who are uncomfortable with abstract religious principles and therefore seek a personal relationship with a personal God.

John's sonship has much appeal to pluralistic contexts where many religions and ideologies exist and function side by side. Particularly the notion of Jesus descending from heaven and ascending to heaven has helped people from different walks of life to see God's concern for the world. It is more striking because the entire process of empowerment and liberation is the result of God's love. That love demands voluntary and sacrificial suffering, to the extent of ignoring personal identities, from all who are committed to the salvation of the world. Finally, confidence that suffering leads to final glory gives hope as we continue our faith pilgrimage.

# John 6.1–71

# The second Passover

## Summary

This section takes place in Galilee. A similar sequence is found in Mark 6.30–57 and Matthew 14.13–35: a miraculous meal (6.1–15), a miracle at sea (6.16–21), an encounter after a sea journey (6.22–71). This raises questions about either a remembered sequence of events or common sources (see the Introduction, 'John and the Synoptic Gospels', p. 6). The third event is the most different. It splits into three shorter dialogues: Jesus and the crowd (6.25–50), Jesus and the Jews (6.51–59), Jesus and the disciples (6.60–71).

## 6.1–15: A miraculous meal

## Introduction

At the second Passover in John's account of the public ministry of Jesus, a miraculous meal takes place by the Sea of Galilee.

## Notes and commentary

**6.1. After this Jesus went to the other side of the Sea of Galilee, also called the Sea of Tiberias:** No information is given about Jesus' journey from Jerusalem to Galilee. The 'other side' is not a clear location, but the reference to 'Tiberias' may suggest the western area. The 'Sea' of Galilee, also known as the Sea of Chinnereth in the OT (Numbers 34.11; Joshua 12.3), is really a freshwater lake. It is about 21 kilometres long, 11 kilometres wide, and lies at 211 metres below sea level. Several of the towns built on its shores were the sites of Jesus' public ministry in Galilee.

**6.2. A large crowd kept following him, because they saw the signs that he was doing for the sick:** The crowd is still following Jesus because of signs. This anticipates a challenge to their belief (Appendix C). The verse implies that a number of healings have happened, but gives no details.

**6.3. Jesus went up the mountain:** The location may suggest a messianic meal on Mount Zion (Isaiah 25.6–7; Matthew 15.29–31). Mountains were locations for significant meetings with God (Exodus 24.9–11; 1 Kings 19.11–17; Mark 9.2; Matthew 17.1; Luke 9.28) and for learning (Matthew 5.1).

**6.4. The Passover . . . was near:** This second Passover implies a second year of Jesus' public ministry; the first Passover is recorded in 2.13.

**6.5–7. Jesus said to Philip, 'Where are we to buy bread for these people to eat?' . . . Philip answered him, 'Six months' wages would not buy enough bread for each of them to get a little':** The dialogue tells of the scale of the crowd and, presumably, the impossibility of getting enough food from conventional sources. Only Jesus knows what will happen; he knows more than everyone else who is there. The remark also shows Jesus' superiority to Moses (Numbers 11.13).

**6.8–9. Andrew . . . said to him, 'There is a boy here who has five barley loaves and two fish. But what are they among so many people?':** Andrew's (1.40) remark repeats the scale of the problem, with only a small amount of food available. The loaves and fish provide the 'seed' of the miracle.

**6.10a. Make the people sit down:** The people become dependent on Jesus.

**6.10b. Now there was a great deal of grass in the place:** Normal conventions about food handling and preparation could not be observed in a location outside. It may indicate that Jesus takes an independent view of the laws of purity.

**6.10c. So they sat down, about five thousand in all:** This may not be an exact number, and it is used to count only adult males. It indicates a huge crowd.

**6.11a. Jesus took the loaves, and when he had given thanks, he distributed them:** Jesus performs these actions: the food comes from his work, and everyone else receives from his actions. Jewish law prescribed a prayer of thanksgiving for any foodstuff larger than an olive.

**6.11b. As much as they wanted:** This indicates the quantity of food provided and the scale of the miracle.

**6.12. Gather up the fragments left over, so that nothing may be lost:** There is food left over – a sign of the generosity of God. The command may also imply that what has been given out has a holy character, and deserves special care.

**6.13. From the fragments . . . they filled twelve baskets:** Twelve is both a large amount and a symbolic number. Twelve was the number of the tribes of Israel, and remained important in the early Church; there were twelve disciples. Twelve and its multiples were important in apocalyptic and eschatological writing (Revelation 21.9–21), signifying wholeness and perfection.

**6.14a. When the people saw the sign that he had done:** The people believe because of the sign (2.13; Appendix B).

**6.14b. They began to say, 'This is indeed the prophet':** Jesus is thought to be the Messiah (6.32; Appendix K).

**6.15a. Jesus realized that they were about to come and take him by force:** John always portrays Jesus in control of what happens to him (18.1–8).

**6.15b. To make him king:** Again, this suggests a messianic reading. It is also reflects secular thinking. The Roman imperial regime was in part based on the expectations that the ruler would both feed and entertain the people (from which we get the English expression, 'bread and circuses'). The acclamation of Jesus arises from a similar action.

 ## Interpretation

There are a striking number of correspondences in detail between the Synoptic accounts and John, even in seemingly incidental details: the number of loaves and fishes, the size of the crowds, the location, the actions performed by Jesus, and even the amount of food left over. It is possible that either a well-remembered event or a shared tradition lies behind all these versions of the miracle.

Modern biblical studies have sometimes struggled with the miraculous. As European scholarship took on the defining characteristics of the Enlightenment, confidence in the literal truth of miracles was shaken. Scholars struggled to find rationalistic explanations for the miracles. Some argued that, in this case, the boy's selflessness and generosity encouraged everyone to bring out food they had secretly stashed in their clothes. The text gives no evidence for this at all, but this interpretation seemed reasonable in the intellectual climate of the time.

John and the Synoptic writers have no interest in explaining how the miracle happened. They are interested in what it signifies. For John, this is straightforward: verses 14 and 15 show the desire of the people to identify Jesus with a prophetic or royal character, the Messiah. The location on a mountain, so often ignored in the quest to explain how the miracle happened, is crucial. Isaiah 25.6–7 describes a meal at which all God's people, Jewish and non-Jewish, are gathered together on Mount Zion in the presence of God. This miracle performed by Jesus fulfils this hope in the present (3.3). Jesus will not simply subscribe to the messianic hopes of those around him. He will not allow what he knows to be the truth about the Messiah to be hijacked by popular expectations. What Jesus means by the miracle, and thus what he understands about the nature of the Messiah, will be spelled out in 6.25–71.

# STUDY SUGGESTIONS

## Word study

**1** What is the symbolic meaning of 'twelve'?

## Review of content

**2** What details does John share with the feeding miracles in the Synoptic Gospels (Mark 6.34–44; 8.1–9; Matthew 14.13–21; 15.32–39; Luke 9.10–17)?

**3** What does reading Isaiah add to the meaning of this miracle?

## Discussion and application

**4** Are we more concerned with how miracles occur than why they are important? Is this interest helpful or damaging to the reading of Scripture and evangelism?

# 6.16–21: A miracle at sea

 Introduction

John has the same sequence of events as Mark and Matthew: a miraculous walking on the sea follows the feeding miracle.

 Notes and commentary

**6.16. When evening came, his disciples went down to the lake:** The sea (NRSV: 'lake') has a symbolic meaning as well as providing a geographical location. It represents the power of chaos and evil. According to Semitic cosmology, the waters under the earth were in danger of breaking out and flooding the world. God's covenant with Noah (Genesis 8) was seen as preventing that. Some suggest that the Temple rituals were thought of as a way of reinforcing this covenant and preserving the world from destruction and chaos.

**6.17. It was now dark:** Darkness usually indicates some kind of threat or evil (Appendix B).

**6.18. The lake became rough because a strong wind was blowing:** Storms on the sea/lake were a real and frequent threat.

**6.19a. When they had rowed about three or four miles:** The distance is given literally as '25–30 stadia', a third of the distance to Capernaum. This is about six or seven kilometres.

**6.19b. They saw Jesus walking on the lake:** Some read the phrase as 'by the lakeshore', but the story would be pointless without the miraculous element given by 'on'.

**6.20. He said to them, 'It is I':** See 'I am he' (4.26). This may imply a *theophany* (1.50–51). Jesus' 'I am' confirms the divine action he has performed. Some see a reference here to the exodus story as told in Psalm 77.18–19.

**6.21. Immediately the boat reached the land towards which they were going:** These words may echo Psalm 107.23–32: God's promise to bring his people to their rightful place.

 ## Interpretation

It is hard to see what the miracle at sea contributes to the main flow of John 6, which is mainly concerned with food. John has retained it, showing that he respects and values his sources so much that he does not edit this detail out.

The miraculous element should be retained (6.19). The tone of the passage is meant to convey an impression of awe and wonder which would be absent from a walk along the shore. The miracle contains a claim about Jesus. In walking on the water, Jesus reveals that he has the power of God. This is nothing less than a claim that Jesus has power over the sea, the most powerful embodiment of evil and chaos. With such power, he can block evil's powers to damage and disrupt, and its capacity for fear. The disciples are brought to safety: God's promises are available to his disciples here and now.

 ## STUDY SUGGESTIONS

### Word study

1 Write a note about the symbolic meaning of 'sea'.

### Review of content

2 Compare the accounts of the miracle at sea in Mark, Matthew and John. What differences can you see in detail?

3 Does John give the story a different meaning from Mark and Matthew?

**Discussion and application**

**4** Can we still use this story to illustrate Jesus' power over evil today, or do the miraculous elements make this difficult?

## 6.22–50: Jesus and the crowd

 Introduction

The meal (6.1–15) provokes a discussion between Jesus and the crowd about how he got to Capernaum, the nature of signs, and how he compares to Moses. The end of this section shifts attention from the crowd to Jesus' opponents (6.41–51).

 Notes and commentary

**6.22. The next day the crowd . . . saw that Jesus had not got into the boat with his disciples:** The miracle leads to a question: how did Jesus get to Capernaum? This starts the longer conversations.

**6.23. Some boats from Tiberias came near the place where they had eaten the bread after the Lord had given thanks:** The meal took place near Tiberias (6.1), but its precise location remains unknown. The terms used to refer to the miracle (6.1–14) – 'bread' (singular), 'Lord' (a title, 4.11) and giving thanks – may hint at the Eucharist.

**6.24. The crowd . . . went to Capernaum looking for Jesus:** The crowd meets Jesus in Capernaum, a town of about 1,500 people on the northern shore of the Sea of Galilee.

**6.25. Rabbi, when did you come here?:** Despite the talk of Jesus being the 'prophet' and the attempt to make him king (6.14–15), the people in the crowd still only address Jesus as 'Rabbi' (1.38).

**6.26. You are looking for me, not because you saw signs, but because you ate your fill of the loaves:** Jesus does not speak about his journey, but criticizes the people's motives. They have not even believed because of signs (2.24), but because their physical hunger was satisfied.

**6.27a. Do not work for the food that perishes, but for the food that endures for eternal life:** 'Your fill' is now described as 'food that perishes', unfavourably compared to food that endures for eternal life (3.15): a contrast between the temporal and the eternal, this world and heaven.

**6.27b. Which the Son of Man will give you. For it is on him that God the Father has set his seal:** The lack of references to Daniel or judgement may mean that the phrase 'Son of Man' (1.51) only means 'I' in this verse. However the following phrase, 'it is on him', may hint at the title. The dialogue seems to play on the phrase 'set his seal', referring to a wax seal or signet (3.34).

**6.28. What must we do to perform the works of God?:** The people ask Jesus what they need to do, not where they may find the Son of Man. Their question echoes the common hope that the law of Moses allowed direct access to God.

**6.29. This is the work of God, that you believe in him whom he has sent:** Jesus suggests there is one key action: believe in him. Belief includes following Jesus (6.66).

**6.30. What sign are you going to give us then, so that we may see it and believe you?:** The demand for a new sign suggests that the crowd is still immature. The people seem to be hoping for something more spectacular.

**6.31a. Our ancestors ate the manna in the wilderness:** Those in the crowd challenge Jesus by referring to Moses: if Moses could and did feed his people, what more are you going to do? For 'manna', see Exodus 16.13–15. Later Jewish traditions and *midrash* (interpretation of the Torah) identified manna with the gift of the law. The crowd is asking how Jesus is superior to the law. Some Jewish groups at the time of Jesus used manna to signify a ritual meal.

**6.31b. He gave them bread from heaven to eat:** This not a direct quotation from the OT, but composed from Exodus 16.4, 15; Psalm 78.24; Nehemiah 9.15. Wisdom 16.20 anticipates a time when God will again feed his people.

**6.32. It was not Moses who gave you the bread from heaven, but it is my Father who gives you the true bread from heaven:** Jesus' reply corrects their thinking: the Father, not Moses, is the source of the bread from heaven. The Father's *true* bread from heaven is better than manna (bread from heaven).

**6.33a. That which comes down:** This phrase could also be translated 'the one who comes down' – a possible reference to Jesus.

**6.33b. Gives life to the whole world:** This bread is better than the bread of Moses which fed only Israel. 'The whole world' may refer to the gathering of the nations to be fed by God (6.1–5; Isaiah 25.6–10). Life is more than physical existence; it is eternal life (3.15).

**6.34. Sir, give us this bread always:** The crowd persists in asking for bread, while John's audience will have identified the bread with Jesus.

**6.35a. I am the bread of life:** 'I am' (4.26) is joined to a predicate, 'bread of life'. This pattern will be seen again in 8.12, 18, 23; 10.7, 9, 11, 14; 11.25; 14.6; 15.1, 5). 'I am' is used in the OT when God reveals himself and gives commands (Exodus 3.6, 14; 20.2; Isaiah 51.12). Some argue that its origins may also be seen in language used of Isis (an Egyptian deity absorbed into the Graeco-Roman pantheon), which has shaped earlier wisdom traditions.

Jesus is identified, like the law (word) as bread: God's word feeds humanity, and Jesus is that Word. For 'life', see 6.33.

**6.35b. Whoever comes to me will never be hungry, and whoever believes in me will never be thirsty:** The benefits are placed in the future ('will never') – an inaugurated rather than a realized eschatology (3.3). For 'hungry' and 'thirsty' as eschatological terms, see 4.14; 6.27. Sirach 24.21 describes hunger and thirst for wisdom. Jesus can satisfy the hunger for wisdom (6.48).

**6.36. I said to you that you have seen me and yet do not believe:** Jesus reminds the crowd that they have not done what is necessary to receive the promised blessings because they do not believe what they have seen or heard.

**6.37a. Everything that the Father gives me will come to me:** This statement repeats Jesus' solidarity with the Father (1.14, 18; 3.16–17; 5.19).

**6.37b. Anyone who comes to me I will never drive away:** Here is a possible comparison with Genesis 3.24 (see also 6.50–51). The bread of life may echo the fruit desired by early humanity, but without the dire consequences.

**6.39. The last day:** This is a further indication of a future eschatology.

**6.40a. All who see the Son and believe in him may have eternal life:** See 3.15. This makes clear the quality of life offered by Jesus.

**6.40b. I will raise them up on the last day:** See 2.19–22; 5.21.

**6.41a. Then the Jews began to complain about him:** See 1.19. This different set of questioners suggests a new phase in the dialogue. It also implies that not all the members of the crowd were complaining about Jesus' previous remarks. It is an important indication that the term 'Jews' should not be given a universal interpretation. The argument will repeat points already made, suggesting that these opponents have been in the crowd.

**6.41b. I am the bread that came down from heaven:** Jesus has not used these words, but they are a logical summary of the previous dialogue.

**6.42. Is this not Jesus, the son of Joseph, whose father and mother we know?:** See 1.45. Jesus' opponents claim to know his parentage, and so dispute his claims in terms of honour and status. They are arguing that he cannot have a status which exceeds his parents', and so his heavenly claims are false.

**6.43. Do not complain:** See Exodus 16.8; 17.3; Numbers 11.1; 14.27, 29. Jesus appears to be comparing his opponents to those who complained against God in the wilderness.

**6.44. No one can come to me unless drawn by the Father:** An early rabbinical work uses similar language to describe conversion and an increased knowledge of God (*Pirke Abot* 1.2). Some commentators suggest echoes of Jeremiah 38.3 (LXX). The theme will return in 12.32.

**6.45a. It is written in the prophets:** This plural might be a generalization, or a reference to some collection of prophecies.

**6.45b. And they shall all be taught by God:** See Isaiah 54.13, also Isaiah 50.4. The quotation defends the assertion that belief in Jesus originates with the Father, not human learning. The universal 'all' applied in Isaiah to the whole of Israel is here restricted to those who believe in Jesus as Messiah.

**6.45c. Everyone who has heard:** Hearing becomes the dominant sense for relating to God, given the problems of seeing (6.46). It is a part of the experience at Sinai (Deuteronomy 4.12; 5.24; 18.16; Sirach 17.13; 45.5).

**6.46. Not that anyone has seen the Father except the one who is from God:** The argument here seems to support the view (1.18) that Moses did not see the face of God. Jesus, the one who is from God, is therefore superior to Moses.

**6.47. Very truly, I tell you:** See 1.51.

**6.48. I am the bread of life:** This verse repeats 6.35.

**6.49. Your ancestors ate the manna in the wilderness, and they died:** The argument now begins to explore claims that one must eat the bread of life. The ancestors who ate the manna experienced physical death.

**6.50. This is the bread that comes down from heaven, so that one may eat of it and not die:** Those who eat the bread of heaven will not experience spiritual death, but will rather live for ever and experience eternal life (3.15). Some compare this gift of eternal life with the death brought by the fruit in the Garden of Eden (Genesis 2.17; 3.3).

 Interpretation

The crowd which follows Jesus to Capernaum is moved to follow him by two concerns: the bread consumed and the mystery of his disappearance. When the people meet up with him, there is a dialogue characterized by misunderstandings (Appendix H). Chief among these is the misunderstanding about bread: Jesus challenges their hopes for bread that simply serves to stop hunger, and directs their attention to bread as a metaphor for the law and doing the will of God: the sapiential (wisdom) tradition. In so doing, he further corrects their interpretation of Moses. The net result is that Jesus is claiming to offer something superior to both Moses and the Mosaic law. He also resists their demand to provide a bigger and better sign of what he claims, so reinforcing John's repeated theme about the inadequacy of signs. Jesus' teaching, not signs, contains what is needed to reveal the basis of faith.

The shape of this argument (which continues into the next section) bears close comparison to the pattern of interpretation found in Jewish commentaries like the Palestinian Midrashim and Philo:

- an initial citation of Scripture (6.31);

- a paraphrase (6.32);

- exegesis – 'bread of heaven' (6.33–36);

- exegesis – 'Father gives' (6.37–40);

- objection to 'coming down' (6.41–44);

- subordinate support from Scripture (6.45–47);

- exegesis – 'to eat' (6.48–50).

In the dialogue, Jesus introduces an 'I am' saying which identifies him as the Bread of Life. Sayings like these perform two functions:

- They demand responses from their hearers similar to the 'I say to you' sayings often found in Matthew (5.22, 28, 32). Like them, they claim superiority to the letter of the law and its associated traditions.

- They function like parables in the Synoptic tradition: they offer a commentary on what Jesus is doing.

This section may also have an application to our modern life. Many societies today are increasingly materialistic: people are concerned with this world and its problems, and have no place for the heavenly or supernatural. Jesus, according to John, disagrees violently with such views: he constantly reminds the crowd not to dwell simply on physical phenomena, like hunger. When he uses these terms, Jesus invests them with a further spiritual or ethical quality: they demand a lifestyle in which the believer does what is pleasing to God. This means that life is not just about the physical, but about the relational. This relational aspect goes far beyond mere physicality: it involves qualities which are described as 'eternal' – 'eternal' because the one to whom the believer relates is pursuing a relationship with them that is far beyond this physical life, because he (God) is more than physical.

This section raises the question of pre-existence (Appendix F) because of the references to coming down from heaven. Earlier interpretation of the story might have focused on the imagery of bread. In *2 Baruch* 29.8 and *Ecclesiastes Rabbah* 1.9, manna, associated with the end times, comes down from heaven. So contemporary usage does not demand talk of pre-existence. Here, Jesus is identified as both the bread of heaven and the eschatological bread. That said, Jesus' statement 'I have come down from heaven' (6.38) provides the strongest evidence for claims of physical pre-existence. However, these verses may be a later addition in one of the last re-editings of the text before it reached this final form. So it is possible that early forms of this tradition and story were not about pre-existence, but later editing of the Gospel included it.

By the end of this section, John has presented us with a picture of Jesus who surpasses the law and Moses. He is the best witness to the wisdom tradition, of how to live as God wants. He is identified as the bread of heaven, the bread of the Last Days, and, because of 6.38–39, a pre-existent being.

 STUDY SUGGESTIONS

### Word study

1 What was 'manna' in the exodus story and later traditions? How does John engage with these traditions?

### Review of content

2 How does John show that Jesus is better than Moses? Clue: think about where he comes from and the effects given by the bread.

3 What does this section finally describe Jesus as?

### Discussion and application

4 Could we use the pattern of interpretation seen in this section in preaching and teaching today?

## 6.51–59: Jesus and the Jews

 Introduction

Attention now shifts from Jesus as a heavenly being to the question of how he might give his flesh as food. Bread and eating provide the link between this and the previous section.

Notes and commentary

**6.51. I am the living bread that came down from heaven. Whoever eats of this bread will live for ever; and the bread that I will give for the life of the world is my flesh:** This verse really marks the beginning of a new section and adds a new emphasis, focusing on flesh rather than bread.

The Church Fathers saw a reference to Genesis 3.22, comparing forbidden fruit with the Eucharist. This theme may reflect the readings for the Passover, which sets the scene for the discourse (6.4). If John is thinking in this way, and we cannot be sure of this, he may be using the 'bread of life' material to contrast Jesus with the Passover (see 1 Corinthians 5.7–8).

**6.52. The Jews then disputed among themselves, saying, 'How can this man give us his flesh to eat?':** The Jews (1.18; 6.41) take a literal physical reading of 'flesh'. Anthropophagy or cannibalism was rejected by all who counted themselves civilized: Greek, Roman or Jew. The use of 'Jews' in this verse is unique: those who are usually united in their opposition to Jesus are arguing among themselves. Again this warns against the tendency to universalize. It may also indicate differences between Jewish sects of how eating might be interpreted symbolically, given the unlikelihood of a literal reading.

**6.53a. Unless you eat the flesh of the Son of Man:** Jesus gives a symbolic or spiritual understanding of flesh. If the Son of Man (1.51) is a heavenly figure, his flesh will also be heavenly. It will not be physical meat or flesh. The Greek word used in this verse for 'eat' literally means 'munch' or 'chew'. Arguments that these words stress the physical nature of eating (perhaps to reject Docetic teaching that Jesus did not become a true physical human being) contradict the previous verse. 'Eat' may not have any such significance; it can be swapped with the other word for 'eat' used in 6.31. The Greek text (LXX) of Psalm 40.9 uses both as synonyms.

**6.53b. And drink his blood:** The addition of 'drink' is seen by many commentators as a sign that the Eucharist is meant: the original miracle was only about eating. However, flesh and blood may simply be a Hebrew expression meaning 'the whole person'. To drink blood, even of a creature, was prohibited by Jewish law (Leviticus 3.17; Deuteronomy 12.23; Acts 15.20). The story of David suggests interesting precedents (2 Samuel 23.17; 1 Chronicles 11.19). David refused to drink water, because it would be the same as drinking his men's blood. Stories about David are sometimes used to reveal truths about Jesus. The story of the water can be compared to the Eucharist. Where David rejects his men's water/blood and is not responsible for their risk/deaths, Jesus makes his disciples drink his wine/blood and so tells them that they are responsible for his death.

**6.53c. You have no life:** Eating and drinking, however interpreted, are necessary for having eternal life.

**6.54a. Those who eat my flesh and drink my blood have eternal life:** This statement identifies Jesus with the Son of Man (6.53). The identification marks a radical departure from contemporary thinking about the Son of Man.

**6.54b. Raise them up on the last day:** The phrase refers to resurrection in the end times (2.19; 6.39, 40).

**6.55. My flesh is true food and my blood is true drink:** The food and drink associated with Jesus as Son of Man is superior to both the food of the miracle, and wisdom.

**6.56. Abide in me:** The same verb is used in 1.38–39; 15.4–7. It also refers to mutual indwelling or maintaining a relationship (Appendix B).

**6.57. Just as the living Father sent me, and I live because of the Father, so whoever eats me will live because of me:** Jesus' relationship with his Father provides the basis for believing what he says.

**6.58. The one who eats this bread will live for ever:** The act of eating is now associated with food that brings life or death, like the bread of 6.54.

 ## Interpretation

The issue of blood/wine is particularly contentious in John. It is a problem that John in particular had to address, perhaps either as the community became more distant from mainstream Judaism or was threatened by an internal conflict.

Scholars agree that this section adds in the element of eating (an action) which surpasses the acquiring of knowledge. They differ on whether it belongs to a different layer of tradition or not. In the sapiential (wisdom) tradition (6.35–50), life was centred on the nature of the bread of heaven identified with Jesus. The argument now demands eating the bread as a necessity for eternal life. This raises the question of what eating entails. Theological commentators tend to argue for a sacramental understanding, while socio-historical research talks rather of ritual. Most scholars, even some from traditions which have no sacramental bias, suggest that this section imports the idea of sacramental eating into the life of disciples (see the following Excursus).

 ## STUDY SUGGESTIONS

### Word study

1 Does 'eat' (6.51) demand a very strong physical action?

## Review of content

**2** What did people in Jesus' time think of eating flesh?

## Discussion and application

**3** A seven-year-old once said, 'Yuck, eating Jesus' flesh and drinking his blood – I'm never going to do that!' What answer would you give to this child about the Eucharist?

---

# 6.60–71: Jesus and the disciples

 Introduction

The discussions which follow the meal finish with one between Jesus and his disciples. The discussion shows that even those who claim to follow Jesus may find his teaching puzzling or hard to accept.

 Notes and commentary

**6.60. When many of his disciples heard it, they said, 'This teaching is difficult; who can accept it?':** The disciples are not presented in a favourable light. Ancient traditions distinguished two types of disciples: 'gentle' ones who could accept correction and 'hard' who could not accept criticism and resisted frank speech.

**6.61. Aware that they were complaining:** Jesus has foreknowledge of who is faithful and who is not, but does not explain how (6.64).

**6.62. Then what if you were to see the Son of Man ascending to where he was before?:** This verse refers to both the pre-existence of Jesus (as do 6.38–39) and his Passion. It is a rhetorical question (it is not meant to be answered) which shows his disappointment or indignation.

**6.63a. The flesh is useless:** This does not refer to the flesh of 6.50–58 which has been identified with heavenly, spiritual bread. The flesh of Jesus is useful (1.14, 18), gives true understanding, and is essential for (eternal) life (6.51–58). The verse means the flesh of human beings, or from 'below' (1.13; 3.6; 8.23) – limited as a source of knowledge (7.24; 8.15) and with no saving power.

**6.63b. The words that I have spoken to you are spirit and life:** The Spirit both gives and is the source of life. The words of Jesus are to be closely identified with the Spirit, but they are not identical (11.25; 14.6). Jesus' words witness to the Spirit, and trigger belief. Belief will lead people to receive the Spirit when Jesus goes to the Father.

**6.64. Jesus knew from the first who were the ones that did not believe, and who was the one that would betray him:** 'From the first' repeats the same idea as in 6.61. The Greek word translated 'betray' may mean 'hand over', but when used of two people, one 'handing over' the other, it often has the sense of betraying.

**6.65. No one can come to me unless it is granted by the Father:** The true disciple is the one who has been given the opportunity by God, who is the agent of salvation.

**6.66a. Because of this many of his disciples turned back:** They leave either because they have not been chosen by the Father (6.65) or because of their inability to accept Jesus' teaching (6.35–58).

**6.66b. And no longer went about with him:** 'Went about' has the sense of 'walked around with', and is often used with symbolic language (8.25; 12.35). Here it means 'continued to be disciples'.

**6.67. Jesus asked the twelve:** The phrase 'the twelve' is only used in this section and in 20.24. John never lists the full group of disciples – only seven are named throughout the Gospel (1.35–51; 6.71; 11.16; 13.23; 14.22; 18.15; 21.2).

**6.68a. Simon Peter:** See 1.40, 42; 21.2, 3.

**6.68b. The words of eternal life:** See 3.15.

**6.69a. We have come to believe and know:** This is a process which started in the past and still continues. 'Believe' and 'know' are almost identical in meaning.

**6.69b. That you are the Holy One of God:** See Mark 1.24. Jesus is God's agent, who has been sent into the world (6.27, 29).

**6.70a. Did I not choose you, the twelve?:** Jesus, not the Father, is here presented as the one who chooses. Although Jesus submits to the Father, he also has initiative to make some of his own decisions: he is no automaton or robot.

**6.70b. Yet one of you is a devil:** For 'devil', see Appendix J.

**6.71. Judas son of Simon Iscariot:** The name Judas must not be used to represent the whole Jewish nation, nor even the whole tribe of Judah. It refers to one person further identified as Iscariot, most likely referring to the town he came from: 'the man from Kerioth'. This is also a reminder that even 'perfect believers' may not persevere.

Interpretation

This episode finishes with the reaction of the disciples to Jesus' words. Some of those who had joined his circle drop out, and so the narrative contains the warning that not all disciples are true disciples. John notes that this is true even of the twelve, one of whom will betray Jesus (6.71). It is possible that this reflects John's own experience within his own community, but it is spelled out in reference to what was known to have happened to Jesus and his disciples.

Verse 61 suggests that some part company from Jesus because his teaching is too hard for them. This is very different from saying that other Christians have driven them away, and we need to be aware that church discipline may actually obscure or hide the teaching of Jesus. We must always be on guard that we do not take our own preferences and prejudices and present them as the teaching of Jesus. Paul knew the difference (1 Corinthians 7.12) and so should we.

Why do people turn away from Jesus? Is it simply their own choice? Verse 65 suggests something slightly different: that it is God who gives his blessing to true apostles. Some later traditions used verses like this to preach a doctrine of the elect, an offer made only to a select few. John does not know this kind of thinking: he sees Jesus as sent to the whole world (3.16–17). The verse stresses that following Jesus is not simply a matter of our own choosing, something that we do on our own. It is rather a matter of accepting a gift already given by God. A simple example may show the difference. We might see a wad of money lying in the street; we can choose to pick it up or leave it alone. That represents the idea that we choose to be disciples. John gives a different picture: the wad of money is placed firmly in our hands by God; we choose to either keep it or throw it away. It is God's initiative to call disciples, to 'put the money' in everyone's hands, but this is no guarantee that people will keep it.

 STUDY SUGGESTIONS

### Word study

1 Why is 'betray' an accurate translation of 'hand over' in 6.64, 71?

### Review of content

2 What does this passage say about being a disciple?

3 Does God's offer of salvation extend to all, or some?

## Discussion and application

**4** Do we avoid the hard teaching of the gospel rather than speak the truth openly? Are we more worried about losing disciples, or how we look, than being faithful to Jesus' difficult teaching?

---

 Excursus

## John 6 and the Eucharist

In John 6, a miraculous meal with messianic significance becomes the launching-off point for a discussion of Jesus as a living embodiment of the wisdom tradition, a claim for Jesus' superiority to Moses and the law, and, most controversially, an explanation of the Eucharist.

The flow of argument goes through the following stages:

- Jesus feeds the people.

- He is the Messiah, but on his own terms.

- The meal is not just to stop hunger.

- The food given by Jesus is bread – a common metaphor for the wisdom of God.

- The food given by Jesus is better than Moses' manna: Jesus is superior to Moses.

- Food is more than a metaphor.

- An act of eating becomes necessary.

- This physical act is not a literal eating of flesh and blood.

- The act of eating is a ritual event. As such, it is not meant to be a literal eating of flesh and blood. This ritual is also John's answer to how the miracle works: a ritual activity has replaced a miraculous activity.

- The ritual event imparts spiritual blessings.

- The ritual event echoes sacramental traditions found in Second Temple Judaism.

The connection of John 6 with the Eucharist is marked by a wide number of Greek words which appear here and in the context of the Last Supper: 'lie down' (6.9), 'bread' (6.11, 33, 41, etc.), 'give thanks' (6.11), 'fragments' (6.12), 'drink', 'blood' (6.56). The inclusion of 'drink' and 'blood' are reckoned to be particularly important (6.53), otherwise interpretation of the miracle would be concerned solely with eating. The inclusion of drinking raises the question: where was drinking significant for the first Christians? The only context found for this action is the ritual meal (1 Corinthians 11.23–30). Some have argued that the shape of the Supper Narratives further supports such a ritual identification. However, caution is needed, because the tendency is to compare John 6 with the Supper Narratives in the Synoptics (Mark 14.22–25; Matthew 26.26–29; Luke 22.14–23), and doing so locates meaning outside John's context.

Dualism has often been considered an important element in shaping the flow of arguments in John. There is a danger that the physical and the spiritual are viewed as mutually exclusive: something may be physical or spiritual, but not both. However, in John's symbolism, there is no necessary distinction between the spiritual and the physical. We might sum this up crudely: the earthly participates in the heavenly. It is worth considering whether any practices from the time echo such a scenario. Sacraments are sometimes suggested as possible candidates. The common description of a sacrament as 'an outward and visible sign of an inward and spiritual grace' really dates from Augustine of Hippo (354–430 CE): it does not fit with John's context. It is better to explore the context of Second Temple Judaism.

Ritual meals were known elsewhere within Judaism of the time. The Dead Sea sectarians viewed their meal practice as prefiguring their places or roles in the messianic rule (Dead Sea Scrolls, 1QS 6.4–6; 1QSa 2.17–21). There were also *sacramentals* in Jewish thinking contemporary with the Gospels: ordinary items blessed and performing a spiritual function which they ordinarily did not possess. *Joseph and Aseneth*, a Jewish text written about the same time as the Gospels in the late first century CE mentions a ritual meal (*Joseph and Aseneth* 8.5, 11; 15.5; 16.15–16; 19.5; 21.21). It depicts Aseneth being given a piece of honeycomb as part of her ritual purification and conversion from paganism (*Joseph and Aseneth* 16.15–16; 19.5). The honeycomb is identified as both manna and the 'bread of life', as in the wisdom tradition (6.36). Such sacramental patterns may explain how the emerging Christian movement ended up with a ritual meal focused on bread and a cup, drawing on ideas already familiar from the Judaic context.

There were ideas present within Second Temple Judaism which would have allowed the first Christians to develop a ritual meal theology using everyday materials and wisdom traditions. To that extent, John resonates with the culture of the time. Sacramental or symbolic eating is not the point at issue.

The radical departure is the language about blood. Even if we are able to modify or explain the interpretation given (6.53), it still remains hard teaching. Thomas Brodie argues that such revolting imagery about blood is demanded by the real subject matter: death. Such language is necessarily grim, but contributes to a transformation: the horror of death is swallowed up by the Eucharist. It is brutally open speech, clearly viewed as absolute truth by the speaker (Appendix I): Jesus does not sugar-coat his message with rhetorical pleasantries. The text itself admits as much: 'This teaching is difficult: who can accept it?' John answers, 'We can', implied in an identification with the disciples who remain faithful, praising members of his own community for their right belief and dependence on Jesus.

 ## STUDY SUGGESTIONS

### Word study

**1** Which words found in this section are also used of the Eucharist in other early Christian writings? Do you think this is just a coincidence, or is John using them to talk about the Eucharist?

### Review of content

**2** Is it right to base theories about the Eucharist on this section? Give reasons.

**3** What characterized *sacramentals* in Judaism? How does this differ from our teaching about sacraments?

### Discussion and application

**4** If the ritual of the Eucharist is, for John, an expression of the feeding miracle (6.1–15), why can Christians from traditions with miracles not accept the rituals of other Christians as signs of God's work? Why do those who prefer rituals distrust the miracles seen in other churches?

# John 7.1—8.59

# The Festival of Booths

 Summary

The next section takes place at the Festival of Booths held in Jerusalem, and continues after the end of the festival. After a discussion with his family, Jesus goes to Jerusalem in secret (7.1–13). Despite his previous actions (2.13–16), he is able to preach publicly (7.14–31). An attempt to arrest him fails (7.32–36). On the last day of the festival, he preaches again in the Temple and there is a second attempt to arrest him (7.37–52). The initial focus on the Sabbath (7.21–24; see 5.1–9) will lead into dialogues which reflect the festival (7.37–52; 8.12–20). A later addition to the text (7.53—8.11) interrupts the flow of the narrative, which continues with a dialogue about the light of the world (8.12–20), leads to a puzzling dialogue about a journey (8.21–30), and finishes with a discussion of discipleship (8.31–38) which turns into an argument about ancestry (8.39–58). Jesus escapes from the angry crowd (8.59).

## 7.1–13: Family matters

 Introduction

A discussion between Jesus and his brothers is prompted by the fact that his opponents now want to kill him. They discuss whether he should attend the Festival of Booths in Jerusalem. Jesus tells them he will not attend, but goes later in secret.

 Notes and commentary

**7.1. The Jews were looking for an opportunity to kill him:** This is the second mention of plans to kill Jesus (5.18).

**7.2. The Jewish festival of Booths:** This autumn harvest festival (Heb. *Sukkoth*, 'booths') was held outside: huts from tree branches were made in the vineyards. The feast was associated with the wandering of the people of Israel in the wilderness. Leviticus 23.33–43 describes a feast lasting seven days, which began on 15 Tishri (September–October), and included a day of complete rest. Deuteronomy 16.13 omits the rest-day. All Jewish males were expected to celebrate the feast in Jerusalem. On the eighth day, the pilgrims remembered God's care for his people, and asked for his continued favour. The daily rituals of the feast included:

1 a water libation at the Water Gate, both as a request for rain and for the fulfilment of eschatological hopes (Ezekiel 47.1–5; Zechariah 14);

2 a ceremony of light – a reminder of the pillar of fire (Exodus 13.21) expected in the end times (Isaiah 4.5; Zechariah 14.6–8; Baruch 5.8–9).

3 a ritual at sunrise each day when the priests faced the Temple sanctuary, rejecting sun worship (Ezekiel 8.16).

**7.3a. So his brothers said to him:** The term 'brothers' here most likely includes family or relatives (2.12).

**7.3b. Leave here and go to Judea so that your disciples:** Jesus has disciples in Judaea, presumably from his earlier visits (2.13–25; 5.1–47).

**7.3c. May see the works you are doing:** 'Works' is the same word as in 5.36, used rather than 'signs'. While his brothers show a degree of understanding by talking of works, Jesus rejects their view that he needs to show himself to the world.

**7.4. Be widely known:** The same word is used for 'speak frankly'. It includes the idea of integrity and a serious purpose (Appendix I).

**7.5. Not even his brothers believed in him:** Their request for works may be either a demand to prove himself or flattery. Because the brothers do not believe, they should not be confused with the disciples. Rejection of Jesus by his family is in the Synoptics (Mark 3.21). It is possible that the brothers are even trying to get Jesus into trouble: seeking fame was considered dangerous, attracting the attention of rivals or enemies.

**7.6. My time has not yet come, but your time is always here:** Jesus shows wisdom: he is not tempted by fame. He will set his own agenda, and not be adversely influenced by others. It also shows that he is superior to his brothers. 'Time' here means 'opportunity, the right moment', rather than 'time' in a general sense. Jesus is waiting for the right moment to act.

**7.7. The world cannot hate you, but it hates me because I testify . . . that its works are evil:** The world is described as evil (3.19). Jesus' brothers do not inspire hatred because, unlike Jesus (3.19–21), they do not reveal evil (Appendix I).

**7.8. I am not going to this festival, for my time has not yet fully come:** 'Going to' is literally 'going up'. There is a pun here: Jesus will go up to the festival, but will not go up, or ascend, to the Father (20.17), because the time is not right (10.18).

**7.11. The Jews were looking for him:** 'The Jews' (1.19; 7.13) suggests 'those who stand in opposition to Jesus'.

**7.12. There was considerable complaining about him . . . some were saying, 'He is a good man':** It is better to translate 'complaining' as 'whispering' or 'discussion' as some are praising Jesus, and others are critical: not all Jewish people reject Jesus.

**7.13. No one would speak openly about him for fear of the Jews:** 'The Jews' are a group who have power to intimidate others.

# Interpretation

In many cultures, family is important. Duties, hopes and expectations are set by family concerns. Jesus is subject to pressure from his family telling him what they think is right and what he ought to do. However, he does not give into this pressure. Sometimes, being a Christian may clash with family traditions and duties. Jesus shows his allegiance to a different set of priorities from those expected by his family. Christian discipleship is not an excuse to shirk all family responsibilities, but does show that faith, and its demands, may sometimes have a higher priority than those family concerns, even when these are strong commitments (Matthew 8.18–22; Luke 9.57–62). In some ways the Church functions as a 'fictive family' led by God (Matthew 23.9) and Jesus (Mark 14.22–25; Matthew 26.26–29; Luke 22.14–23). Belief, not heredity, makes a family member (Mark 3.31–35; Matthew 12.46–50).

*Sukkoth*, a festival which anticipates the presence of the Messiah, is a powerful background for John's claim that Jesus is the Messiah: the expected Messiah has actually appeared at the feast. The shape of the feast is mirrored in teaching about Jesus as the Messiah (7.25–31, 40–42), the living water (7.37–39) and the light of the world (8.12–20): he embodies the feast. John is not rejecting the meaning of the festival, but rather showing how it is better revealed in Jesus.

# STUDY SUGGESTIONS

## Word study

**1** Write a description of the Festival of Booths.

### Review of content

**2** Why did Jesus' brothers try to influence what he was doing? Were their motives good?

### Discussion and application

**3** How can family or cultural commitments clash with the gospel in your context?

---

## 7.14–31: The first Sukkoth dialogue

 Introduction

The first dialogue at the festival involves Jesus' opponents and deals with the authority of his teaching, and whether the law is being interpreted properly. It concludes with questions from the people of Jerusalem about whether Jesus might be the Messiah.

 Notes and commentary

**7.14. About the middle of the festival:** This means about the fourth day of the festival.

**7.15. How does this man have such learning, when he has never been taught?:** His opponents query how Jesus had gained a specialist knowledge, when he is not connected to a recognized teacher. Most teachers would be able to show from whom they had learned.

**7.16. My teaching is not mine but his who sent me:** See 5.37. Jesus claims God (the Father) as his teacher. This implies an education superior to that given by any earthly teacher.

**7.17. Anyone who resolves to do the will:** Those who know the will of God will recognize the truth of Jesus' claims.

**7.18. Those who speak on their own seek their own glory; but the one who seeks the glory of him who sent him is true:** Jesus distinguishes himself from other teachers who seek their own glory while he seeks the glory of the one who sent him (5.41–47).

**7.19. Did not Moses give you the law? Yet none of you keeps the law. Why are you looking for an opportunity to kill me?:** 'Keeps the law' is a Semitic expression. The argument makes three points:

1 The law is given by Moses.

2 Jesus' opponents do not keep it (Exodus 20.13), since

3 They are trying to kill Jesus.

**7.20. The crowd answered, 'You have a demon!':** The crowd denies the claim that people are trying to kill Jesus. Although possession in the ancient world might be seen as a good thing, it depended on the possessing deity or spirit (8.48–49; Mark 3.22; Matthew 12.24; Luke 11.15).

**7.21. I performed one work:** See 5.1–9. This ties the discussion of the law to Sabbath regulations.

**7.22. Moses gave you circumcision (it is, of course, not from Moses, but from the patriarchs), and you circumcise a man on the sabbath:** Jesus defends his earlier action. His argument is twofold. First, his opponents' knowledge of the origins of the law is faulty: circumcision comes from the patriarchs (Genesis 17.9–14), not just Moses (Exodus 12.44, 48–49; Leviticus 12.3). As an older requirement, it may take priority over the Sabbath regulations given by Moses. While the OT gives no record that circumcision may be performed on the Sabbath, such views appear to reflect later practice (Mishnah, *Shabbat* 19.1, 3).

**7.23. If a man receives circumcision on the sabbath in order that the law of Moses may not be broken, are you angry with me because I healed a man's whole body on the sabbath?:** Second, Jesus uses a *qal-waḥômer* argument (3.12; 10.34). In philosophy, this is also known as an *ab minore ad maiorem* argument (literally, 'from the lesser to the greater'). It roughly means: if something smaller or more insignificant may occur, there is no reason to prohibit something more important. Here, to save life (important) is more important than to perform circumcision (less important). If the lesser action may be done on the Sabbath, so may the important one. The logic of his opponents' own argument absolves Jesus of any wrongdoing.

When he asks, 'Are you angry?' Jesus means that his opponents are reacting emotionally, not rationally. This strengthens his position: he has healed on the Sabbath as a balanced reaction to God's commands.

**7.24. Do not judge by appearances, but judge with right judgement:** Superficial judgement (Leviticus 19.15) is not the mark of the Messiah: right judgement is (Isaiah 11.3; Zechariah 7.9; Deuteronomy 16.19–20). Jesus may here be claiming to be the Messiah, as well as saying he has better judgement.

**7.25. Some of the people of Jerusalem were saying, 'Is not this the man whom they are trying to kill?':** The people of Jerusalem appear aware of a plot against Jesus, unlike the earlier crowd (7.20).

**7.28. You know me, and you know where I am from:** The people know that Jesus comes from Nazareth (1.45). While some argued that no one would know the origins of the Messiah until he was anointed by Elijah

(Justin Martyr, *Dialogue with Trypho* 8.4; 90.1), others thought a Davidic Messiah might come from Bethlehem (7.42; Micah 5.2).

**7.29. I know him, because I am from him, and he sent me:** Jesus rejects the crowd's interest in where he is from: what matters is who sent him. 'I am from him' may imply pre-existence, but does not have to. It may simply mean 'I have been taught by him'. A similar phrase is used in 1.40: 'heard John speak' (NRSV), literally 'heard from John'; here there is no reference to pre-existence.

**7.30. His hour had not yet come:** This repeats the statement made in 7.8. The people cannot change what has been set in motion by the Father.

 Interpretation

This section is typical of the kind of confrontation known as an *agōn* (contest), which included formal battles in epic poetry between heroes, and political debates. Here Jesus takes on his opponents in a public confrontation. He defends his earlier action and shows weaknesses in his opponents' understanding of tradition (7.22) and logic (they are angry, 7.23; they judge by appearances, 7.24). Jesus uses the *qal-wahômer* argument (7.23) to clear himself of an accusation of past wrongdoing (5.1–9). The 'uneducated' teacher overcomes his supposedly superior opponents.

The crowd's reaction suggests that 'right judgement' is a messianic claim. The debate about origins is a classic example of misunderstanding (Appendix H) in which Jesus' claims about origins centre on the teaching he has received from the Father (and, perhaps, a claim about pre-existence) as opposed to the Jerusalemites' concern about his place of birth and family. Jesus' connection with the Father far outweighs his opponents' interests in lineage and birthplace. The section closes with uncertainty about whether Jesus is the Messiah (7.31) which betrays two abiding weaknesses:

1 a continued dependence on signs;

2 a focus on the future and who might come, not on the one who has already come (Jesus).

The setting of the scene makes for a greater irony: this all unfolds during *Sukkoth*, a festival that anticipated the Messiah's coming (7.2). The worshippers have failed to recognize the one they are waiting for.

 STUDY SUGGESTIONS

**Word study**

1 What is needed for 'right judgement'?

2 What is an *agōn*?

## Review of content

**3** Explain in your own words how a *qal-wahômer* argument works.

**4** What is significant about Jesus' origins?

## Discussion and application

**5** Is it appropriate to call one's opponents demon-possessed?

---

# 7.32–36: The second attempt to arrest Jesus

 Introduction

Jesus' opponents make attempts to arrest him, but these meet with failure, because even the police are confused by Jesus' authority. This short section ends with confusion about where Jesus might be going.

 Notes and commentary

**7.32. The chief priests and Pharisees sent temple police to arrest him:** The chief priests were those involved in the administration of the Temple and the ordering of worship; the Pharisees were a Jewish sect already seen as opposed to John the Baptist (1.24). These two groups were not always in agreement, and had different political and religious interests. The 'police' were attendants or stewards who kept order in the Temple and its precincts under the control of the chief priests.

**7.33. A little while longer:** This phrase implies that soon there will be some change in how people perceive Jesus. It will be repeated several times as the Passion approaches (12.35; 13.33; 14.19; 16.16).

**7.35a. The Jews said to one another:** Here, the difficult word 'Jews' might include the Temple police and some of the crowd among Jesus' opponents.

**7.35b. Where does this man intend to go?:** Jesus' words provoke a misunderstanding (Appendix H). His opponents think he may go travelling, perhaps using the network of synagogues across the Mediterranean which linked the Jews of the Diaspora to Judaea and Jerusalem. This synagogue network became one of the principal foundations of Judaism after the destruction of Jerusalem in 70 CE. Synagogues were the focal points for Judaic worship in Palestine and the Diaspora. They provided a means of communication used by the first Christians (Acts 13.5, 14; 14.1; 17.1; 18.4; 19.8). While scholars traditionally argued that the Council of Jamnia

(86 CE) marked the formal expulsion of the followers of Jesus from Jewish places of worship, this is increasingly questioned. The formal division is now more likely to be dated in the second century CE. Persecutions and expulsion suffered by Christians (like John's audience) in the first century CE would have been informal and local.

**7.35c. To the Dispersion among the Greeks:** The phrase has two possible meanings:

- to Greek-speaking Jews in the Diaspora;
- to pagan Greeks in the Diaspora (like 12.20).

No choice needs to be made. The phrase shows his opponents' confusion, not what Jesus knows will happen.

 ## Interpretation

The second attempt to arrest Jesus fails. In a short dialogue with a misunderstanding (Appendix H), Jesus' remarks about returning to the one who sent him (3.17) are taken as a possible intention to take a journey. He is, of course, talking about the return he will make to the Father. John's audience or readers occupy a privileged position: they understand what Jesus meant in a way that the worshippers at the feast did not.

## 7.37–52: The second Sukkoth *dialogue*

 ## Introduction

In this section, Jesus says that the Messiah has come – the very thing worshippers at the festival were hoping for. However, they reject what he says.

 ## Notes and commentary

**7.37a. On the last day of the festival:** This would be the seventh or eighth day (7:2).

**7.37b. The great day:** This might refer to the seventh day of the festival, or stress the significance of what Jesus will say (a meaning preferred by those who identify this as the eighth day). On the eighth day there were sacrifices, the booths were dismantled and the *Hallel* (Psalms 113—118) was sung.

**7.37c. Let anyone who is thirsty come to me:** Jesus now offers the promised water (4.14; Isaiah 55.1 – but note that 7.38 suggests the water is still to be given).

**7.38. And let the one who believes in me drink. As the scripture has said, 'Out of the believer's heart shall flow rivers of living water':** This verse is difficult to punctuate and interpret. A literal translation reads: 'The one believing in me, as Scripture said, rivers from his belly (or heart) will flow of living water.' While the grammar seems to suggest that water flows from 'the believer', this does not fit other verses which make Jesus the source of the water (4.14; 19.34). The verse is difficult to translate smoothly but might read something like: 'The one believing in me, as Scripture says, "water will flow from his [that is, my] belly (or heart)."' This would mean that Jesus is the source of flowing water for the believer – Scripture says water will flow from Jesus' heart. The Scripture phrase is not a direct quotation, but put together from verses like Isaiah 58.11; Ezekiel 47.1–11; Zechariah 14.8, 16–19; and Psalm 78.16, 20.

The English word 'heart' is the equivalent of the Greek 'belly', which was considered the most important vital organ. There may also be a play on the words for heart and rock (either in the wilderness story of Exodus or the place where the Temple was built). The basic meaning is that Jesus is the source. The phrase 'shall flow' fits with John's inaugurated eschatology and is still able to look to the future.

**7.39a. Now he said this about the Spirit, which believers in him were to receive; for as yet there was no Spirit:** John provides an editorial comment on when the waters will flow: glory and the gift of water will be seen in 19.34. 'Living water' is identified with the Spirit (4.7–26, esp. 14). The Spirit has not yet been given (19.34; 20.22).

**7.39b. Jesus was not yet glorified:** This is a reference to the Passion or death of Jesus. A similar thought is seen in 11.4; 12.28; 17.1, 4; 21.19.

**7.40. This is really the prophet:** The use of 'the' distinguishes the Mosaic prophet-Messiah (1.21, 25; 6.14) from prophets in general (7.52).

**7.41. Surely the Messiah does not come from Galilee:** John makes the connection of Jesus with Galilee a point of honour where many would think it shameful. Nazareth was an unimportant town and no one significant could come from there according to popular opinion. Yet Jesus has high status in spite of being associated with a town of no consequence. This means he has the strength of character to overcome the disadvantage of coming from an unimportant town.

**7.42. Has not the scripture said that the Messiah is descended from David and comes from Bethlehem, the village where David lived?:** The dispute about Jesus' origins in any town is a mark of misunderstanding (7.26–27). This differs from Matthew 2.1–12 and Luke 2.1–7, which show Jesus as the Davidic Messiah who comes from Bethlehem.

**7.43. So there was a division in the crowd because of him:** The debate about origins is inconclusive. The crowd can reach no agreement about Jesus' identity.

**7.47. Surely you have not been deceived too, have you?:** The Pharisees stress the firmness with which they and the chief priests resist Jesus: they claim to be right because they are experts.

**7.48. Has any one of the authorities or of the Pharisees believed in him?:** The claim that no Pharisee believes Jesus will be immediately revealed as a lie. Nicodemus, 'a Pharisee' and 'a leader of the Jews' (3.1), is sympathetic to what Jesus says.

**7.50–51. Nicodemus . . . asked: Our law does not judge people without first giving them a hearing to find out what they are doing, does it?:** Nicodemus, an equal of the Pharisees, now accuses them of not following proper legal protocols (Deuteronomy 1.16–17; 17.4; 19.18) and echoes Jesus' criticism (7.24). His words refute the claims made in 7.48. If John's audience already knows the end of the story, the irony is heightened by Nicodemus' later role (19.39).

**7.52a. Surely you are not also from Galilee, are you?:** The Pharisees insult Nicodemus by suggesting he comes from Galilee (7.41).

**7.52b. No prophet is to arise from Galilee:** A number of scholars argue that the best manuscript tradition would read: 'The Prophet is not to arise from Galilee.' However, one of the other messianic claimants of the period, a Jewish leader called Judas, is said to have come from Galilee, so perhaps the tradition was not rigid (Acts 5.37; Josephus, *Jewish War* 2.433; *Antiquities* 18.1–10, 23). If the phrase refers to prophets in general, Jesus' opponents have overlooked Jonah (2 Kings 14.25), and possibly Elijah (1 Kings 17.1) and Nahum (Nahum 1.1), who all came from Galilee, and their authority as experts is therefore questioned.

 Interpretation

By the end of this second *Sukkoth* dialogue Jesus has been identified both as the Messiah and the source of living water (7.38). At the height of the feast, he proclaims himself the source of living water in the Temple itself. It is as if Jesus is claiming to be what the feast has anticipated. As such, he is not rejecting the Temple or the festival, but embracing them in their entirety: he is the Temple, he is the *Sukkoth*. His claims provoke a diversity of responses. Many ordinary people begin to ask if he might be the Messiah.

This alarms the chief priests and the Pharisees, who are concerned that even their Temple attendants are beginning to waver. Their response is an authoritarian crackdown in which they write off the people as accursed, and stress their own teaching authority. The episode, however, raises questions about their claimed authority, as did 7.15, 22 and

24. John completes this demolition by introducing Nicodemus, one of their own, who is concerned about their lack of rigour (7.51). They have no answer for him but insults.

The arguments in this section show that fewer people are opposing Jesus. This does not mean that the majority have become his followers, but rather that an increasing number are less certain than before that he is making false claims. This section moves away from signs; Jesus' authority is now based on what he has said, and on his learning. What was heard with incredulity at the beginning (7.15) is accepted in the end, at least by some (7.46).

Jesus' opponents become more and more shrill in their condemnation, and resort to arguments which criticize those who do not think like them, not the substance of the arguments. We are all aware of how this happens in our world: opponents of dictatorships and authoritarian regimes are re-educated, or taken away to gulags and concentration camps, or declared psychologically disturbed for not subscribing to the dominant ideology. Church institutions like the Inquisition have resorted to torture and persecution. This tendency is not restricted to extremist ideologies; even liberal and supposedly generous societies can be ruthless in their dealings with those who do not fit in. Within the Church we must ask whether or not our debates have been tainted by similar behaviour. In debates on human sexuality, for example, both liberals and conservatives alike have accused each other of failing to understand Scripture and tradition, or of being unable to understand or love their fellow human beings.

This section reveals important insights into how people argue over truth. Even religious people, focused on all that is good, true and right, risk becoming authoritarian and judgmental when they defend what they believe. It is constructive to learn how not to behave from studying the dialogues between Jesus and his opponents.

 ## STUDY SUGGESTIONS

### Word study

1 Write a note describing 'living water'.

2 How does Nicodemus challenge the claims made by Jesus' opponents?

### Review of content

3 What did people in Jesus' time believe about the origins of the Messiah?

4 Are Jesus' opponents following the correct legal processes of their time?

**5** Is Jesus rejecting what the *Sukkoth* feast represents?

## Discussion and application

**6** Think of contentious debates in your church. Do Christians behave like Jesus' opponents? Should they do this?

# 7.53—8.11: A very late addition to the Gospel

 Introduction

This famous passage is most likely not part of the original Gospel. It interrupts the flow of events which happen at the Festival of *Sukkoth* by adding an extra day (8.2). The passage has been inserted in other places within this Gospel (7.36; 21.25) and at Luke 21.38. In this passage, Jesus' opponents try to catch him out with a legal question about the verdict on a woman caught in adultery.

 Notes and commentary

**8.1. The Mount of Olives:** This stands across the Kidron valley opposite the Temple Mount. It is approximately 1,000 metres high, and has a ridge that is 3 kilometres long with three summits.

**8.2. Early in the morning he came again to the temple:** If this additional day is included, the last dialogue (8.12–20) takes place after the festival, and the structure using the feast is destroyed.

**8.3. The scribes and Pharisees:** This is a common phrase in the Synoptic Gospels (Mark 2.16; 7.1, 5; Matthew 5.20; 12.38; 15.1; 23.2, 13–15; Luke 5.21, 30; 6.7; 11.53; 15.2), but found only here in John.

**8.4a. They said to him, 'Teacher':** See 1.38.

**8.4b. This woman was caught in the very act of committing adultery:** Deuteronomy 19.5 suggests that two witnesses were needed, as well as the husband. Some see echoes of the story of Susanna (Daniel 13 (lxx)).

**8.5a. In the law Moses commanded us to stone such women:** Leviticus 20.10 mentions the death penalty. Deuteronomy 22.21 makes stoning the penalty for a betrothed woman; Ezekiel 16.38–40 describes it as the penalty for all types of adultery.

**8.5b–6a. 'Now what do you say?' They said this to test him:** The narrator interprets this as a trick question. A similar pattern is seen in the Synoptic Gospels (Mark 12.13–17; Matthew 22.15–22; Luke 20.20–26; also 6.6).

**8.6b. Jesus . . . wrote . . . on the ground:** Some suggest this proves that Jesus could write, but the word 'wrote' may also mean 'drew'. The writing remains a mystery, but the following have all been suggested:

- the sins of Jesus' accusers;

- the sentence he would give;

- Jeremiah 17.13, which would pick up the *Sukkoth* theme of living water (7.38) and imply rejection of Jesus;

- Exodus 23.1, suggesting entrapment;

- drawing or doodling to hide his feelings, or gain time to think.

No clear answer has been found.

**8.7. Let anyone among you who is without sin be the first to throw a stone at her:** Jesus challenges the witness to throw the first stone. Proper legal process has not been followed, and no details about formal testimony and due process have been given. Deuteronomy 17.7 places a special burden on the witnesses whose testimony is used to advocate death for the accused, perhaps to test whether or not the charge has been set up by the husband (8.4).

**8.8. Once again he . . . wrote on the ground:** See 8.6. Again the content is unknown. Deuteronomy 23.7 has been suggested (Susanna 53 – Daniel 15.53 (LXX)).

**8.9b–10. Jesus was left alone with the woman . . . 'Has no one condemned you?':** There are no witnesses and no accusers left: the case has collapsed.

**8.11. Do not sin again:** Presumably this means the adultery, but it might be a general command. 'Again' implies that the woman is indeed guilty of some sin.

 ## Interpretation

A strong case has been made for the authenticity of this story. Ancient authorities like Eusebius (*Ecclesiastical History* 3.39.17) and the *Didascalia Apostolorum* 2.24.6 know it. The story might have been rejected by some because it did not fit with the stern discipline practised by the early Church. The narrative, like no other, illustrates the tension between discipline and forgiveness.

The question of its origins raises issues about whether the passage should be considered part of the canon. Some reject it because the author is unknown and it was included at a late date. Others urge that it has earned its place to be in the canon because it was widely preserved and accepted. One thing is certain: it is a passage which fits well with the canonical picture of Jesus, and cannot be excluded on the grounds that it distorts his image.

The text should not be read with an excess of emotion or drama. One recent commentary describes the woman as 'distressed and disheveled' and 'in . . . considerable distress, half-clad, and aware that she is facing death' (Moloney, *The Gospel of John*, p. 263). All of this may be reasonable to infer, but none of it is actually stated.

This passage raises questions about the methods used by Jesus' opponents. It begs the question: where is the man, the woman's co-adulterer (8.4)? In many societies, there are double standards about sex: women are condemned if they are sexually active, but men are praised. The bringing of the woman alone is an indicator of such a pattern, and Jesus rejects it as unjust. Some suggest that this may be a contrived charge: entrapment. The hearing itself is also difficult: no witness testimony is provided, the accused is silent, and the usual court routines are absent. In a world where many suffer injustice, this passage holds out the promise that injustice cannot withstand Jesus, and his followers should not collude in unjust systems. It also reveals a double standard: the woman is not allowed to speak in her own defence. In fact, she is irrelevant, simply an opportunity to test Jesus (8.6). Only Jesus' final remarks (8.10, 11) give her dignity: she is a real person, not a means to an end. Jesus thus gives respect to those, like this woman, who are mere pawns in the games played by the powerful.

 ## STUDY SUGGESTIONS

### Word study

1 Do we need to know what Jesus wrote on the ground?

### Review of content

2 What evidence is there to suggest this is a trap for Jesus rather than a real trial?

3 How does Jesus give the woman dignity?

### Discussion and application

4 Does the treatment of people accused of crimes in your context treat them as less than human? What does this passage say about such dehumanizing systems?

5 The accusers are really out to catch Jesus. Does the use of power in your context ever lead to people being used to trap and make difficulties for others?

# 8.12–20: The third Sukkoth dialogue

 Introduction

This section continues the *Sukkoth* dialogues, which have been interrupted by the insertion of the story about a woman caught in adultery. The theme of light becomes prominent.

 Notes and commentary

**8.12a. I am:** See Appendix G and 6.35 for this kind of grammatical construction.

**8.12b. The light of the world:** Jesus claims to be the manifestation of the presence of God (1.14); he is the glory of God which freed Israel from Egypt and was reckoned to be present in the Temple. God (Psalms 27.1; 36.9) and his word or law (Psalm 119.105; Proverbs 6.23) are identified as light (1.4).

**8.12c. Whoever follows me will never walk in darkness but will have the light:** For the symbolism of light–dark, see Appendix B.

**8.13. You are testifying on your own behalf; your testimony is not valid:** The argument focuses on Jesus' testimony. Jesus here defends self-testimony, although he does not openly admit to doing this (compare 5.31–38). There was one possible exception to the principle that self-testimony was inadequate: only God is able to bear witness to himself, since no one else can (Philo, *Allegorical Interpretation* 3.205–8). When he says that his self-testimony is legitimate, Jesus may be claiming to be God.

**8.14. Even if I testify on my own behalf, my testimony is valid because I know where I have come from and where I am going, but you do not know where I come from or where I am going:** 'Even if' suggests that Jesus is going along with his opponents (even if he does not actually agree with them), but can still justify what has happened. His testimony is valid because he knows the facts: his opponents do not.

**8.15a. You judge by human standards:** Jesus attacks his opponents' methods and practice (7.24), who literally judge 'according to the flesh'. See 3.6; 6.63 for the inadequacy of the flesh.

**8.15b. I judge no one:** See 3.16.

**8.16a. Yet even if I do judge, my judgement is valid:** The reliability of Jesus' judgement is based on his relationship to the Father who sent him (5.21–23; 8.13).

**8.16b. It is not I alone who judge, but I and the Father who sent me:** Literally, this reads: 'I am not alone [or one], but I and the one sending me – the Father.' 'I am' may be a form of the divine name and stress Jesus' solidarity with God (6.35).

**8.17. In your law . . . the testimony of two witnesses is valid:** See 5.31.

**8.18. I testify on my own behalf, and the Father who sent me testifies on my behalf:** The two witnesses are again identified as Jesus himself and the Father (8.16). This is odd: two witnesses usually meant two people other than the one who was being examined. One exception, according to some rabbinic evidence, was that only one parent was needed to witness to the identity of a child. The relationship between the Father and Jesus might allow this. Others suggest that Jesus' situation is unique: therefore 'your law' (8.17) does not apply.

**8.19a. Where is your Father?:** The Pharisees ask for the Father to be brought forward as a witness. This may show they cannot think outside their own legal method. It repeats the issue of origins (1.46; 6.42; 7.27, 42, 52).

**8.19b. You know neither me nor my Father. If you knew me, you would know my Father also:** Jesus accuses his opponents of being ignorant of the Father. The idea that knowing Jesus means knowing the Father will be repeated (14.7; 16.3). It shows the unity between Jesus and the Father (see 6.37–39).

**8.20. In the treasury:** This may mean 'near to the treasury', which was beside the Court of the Women in the Temple (Mark 12.41).

 Interpretation

This third dialogue sees Jesus identified as the presence of God. Given this starting point, it is quite likely that the later remarks about his relationship with the Father will include language which makes claims about being God (8.16).

The dialogue continues the *agōn* of the earlier dialogues. Jesus' comments reveal shortcomings in his opponents' legal method: Jesus questions both their legal abilities and their theological understanding. Whether or not any opponents were convinced by these arguments is uncertain: John's readers would be expected to agree with what Jesus has said.

What are we to make of 8.15, where Jesus says that he judges no one, and 8.16, that his judgement is valid? The answers are found by revisiting 3.17–21 and 5.25–30. The first is a reminder that Jesus does not judge or condemn, but causes people to judge themselves, the second that such judgements are binding in the Last Days at the general resurrection. God will accept our judgement of ourselves. These consequences are valid and binding because Jesus has the support of the Father, and can only exercise whatever judgement God gives to him.

By now, Jesus has effectively declared himself to be the embodiment of all the hopes expressed in the *Sukkoth* rituals: Messiah, living water, and light of the world. The claims about self-testimony further imply divine status.

In the Synoptic Gospels, the confession at Caesarea Philippi marks the moment when Peter identifies Jesus as the Messiah (Mark 8.27–30; 16.13–20; Luke 9.18–20). The same pattern emerges here: Jesus, after declaring that he is the Messiah, speaks of his own death and discipleship (8.21–38; Mark 8.31—9.1; Matthew 16.21–27; Luke 9.21–26).

## STUDY SUGGESTIONS

### Word study

**1** Write a note, using the OT passages cited, about the 'light of the world'.

### Review of content

**2** If Jesus can bear witness to himself (self-testimony), does this mean he is being described as God?

**3** What does the order of events in John's Gospel share with the Synoptics?

### Discussion and application

**4** How does Jesus allow us to become our own judges? (Clue: also read 3.17–21 and 5.25–30.) Does this mean we can do what we like?

# 8.21–30: Jesus speaks of a mysterious journey

 Introduction

The dialogue returns to a theme already raised (7.34): Jesus is going to a place where his opponents cannot follow.

 Notes and commentary

**8.21. Again he said to them, 'I am going away, and you will search for me, but you will die in your sin:** The verse repeats the points made in

7.33–34 and 8.14, but adds that Jesus' opponents will die in their sin (Ezekiel 3.18; Proverbs 24.9).

**8.22a. Then the Jews said:** See 1.19. The difference in opponents (they are named as the Pharisees in 8.12–21) should not be used to separate the flow of the different sections in chapters 7—8.

**8.22b. Is he going to kill himself?:** John's audience will be aware of the irony in this remark. While suicide was forbidden by readings of Genesis 9.5, it was viewed by some Jews as preferable to defeat and slavery. Josephus recounts the mass suicide by besieged Jews at Masada (*Jewish War* 7.389–406). During the Bar-Kochba revolt (132–5 CE), *Sanhedrin* 74a forbade suicide except to avoid murder, worshipping idols or illicit sexual acts. It is possible that this is an *ad hominem* remark to undermine Jesus' character or credibility (7.20). It also draws attentions away from his opponents' failure to understand Jesus (8.19).

**8.23. You are from below, I am from above; you are of this world, I am not of this world:** Jesus distinguishes himself and his opponents by using the contrasts 'above–below' and 'this world–not this world' (Appendix B).

**8.24. You will die in your sins unless you believe that I am he:** Belief in Jesus is the only way to avoid death. For 'I am he', see 4.26; 6.20. The phrase is used here as the divine name (8.28, 58; 13.19; 18.5). The term may have its origins in Exodus 3.14 (LXX), but also appears in Isaiah 43.25; 45.18; 51.12; 52.6 (LXX).

**8.25. Why do I speak to you at all?:** A number of translations are possible, either as a question or a statement:

1  What I have been telling you from the beginning (i.e. an answer to the question 'Who are you?').
2  What is the point of talking to you? This might only show Jesus' frustration.
3  I am what I tell you from the beginning – implying pre-existence.

Option 2 is closest to the NRSV translation, and was preferred by the Greek Fathers. The increasing shrillness of the debate, John's use of a different phrase for 'from the beginning' elsewhere (8.44; 15.27; 16.4), and the short question and answer in 10.24–25 also support this translation.

**8.26. I have much to say about you and much to condemn; but the one who sent me is true:** This contrasts what Jesus might say about his opponents with what he can say about God. For the separation of his opponents from God, see 8.39–58.

**8.27. They did not understand that he was speaking to them about the Father:** John inserts a note to tell his audience about the failure of Jesus' opponents to understand.

**8.28a. When you have lifted up:** The language foreshadows the mixed themes of exaltation and crucifixion (3.14–15). Here, Jesus' death is a direct action done by his opponents ('you').

**8.28b. The Son of Man:** See 1.50–51.

**8.28c. You will realize that I am he, and that I do nothing on my own:** Jesus' opponents will learn two things: that he reveals God ('you will know that I am [the name for God]') and that he does nothing on his own authority (5.19–20).

**8.29a. He has not left me alone:** The verse suggests that somehow the Father is with Jesus during his earthly ministry.

**8.29b. For I always do what is pleasing to him:** Jesus' confidence comes from knowing that he always does what the Father wishes – a further example of their unity (5.19–20).

**8.30. Believed in him:** This phrase may mean true faith rather than a partial faith.

 ## Interpretation

The section continues the misunderstanding (Appendix H) between Jesus and his opponents found in 7.33–36. There the confusion was over geography; here they think Jesus may kill himself (8.22). Such details are irrelevant, because Jesus means neither of these things and thus shows how his opponents fail to understand the world and God. They are now warned that believing in Jesus is, literally, a matter of life and death (see Appendix B; 3.15). The verses which follow stress Jesus' unity with the Father and, surprisingly, lead many to believe.

 ## STUDY SUGGESTIONS

### Word study

**1** What does 'I am' (8.24, 28) tell us about Jesus?

### Review of content

**2** Is Jesus likely to kill himself?

**3** Put in your own words the relationship which Jesus has with the Father according to this section of the Gospel.

**Discussion and application**

4 Jesus' opponents often seem to have fixed opinions which stop them hearing what he is saying. How can we ensure that fixed opinions (even good ones) do not prevent us from understanding others?

---

## 8.31–38: Jesus describes his disciples

 Introduction

In the last section, Jesus said his opponents could not follow him. Here he describes the kind of people who can, and it challenges his opponents' view of why they are true believers. This begins one of the most hostile debates in the New Testament.

 Notes and commentary

**8.31–32a. If you continue in my word, you are truly my disciples; and you will know the truth:** See Appendix E. Here, 'truth' may be:

1 the revelation of God in Jesus;

2 the reality of God.

Option 1 is to be preferred, because it stresses that God is known by knowing Jesus. Option 2 might suggest that one can know God without knowing Jesus. This undermines the unity of the Father and the Son (8.19).

**8.32b. And the truth will make you free:** Judaic tradition saw the law as bringing freedom (*Exodus Rabbah* 12.2; *Sifre Leviticus* 11; *Sifre Numbers* 115.5.1–3; *Pirke Abot* 3.5; 6.2). Jesus is claiming the effective purpose of the law for himself (6.30–40).

**8.33a. We are descendants of Abraham:** Abraham was the patriarch with whom God first makes his covenant about Israel (Genesis 12.1—25.11).

**8.33b. And have never been slaves to anyone:** The Jews viewed themselves as the superior descendants of Abraham by Sarah through Isaac (Genesis 21.1–7). Abraham had other descendants by his slave Hagar through Ishmael (Genesis 16). They also reject the implication, drawn on the conventions of the ancient world, that they are slaves and so of low status. Jesus has thus insulted them by saying that they need to be set free. Given the history of Israel, the Babylonian captivity and the subsequent domination of their territory by the Seleucids and the Romans, the claim that they have never been slaves is simply not true.

**8.33c. What do you mean . . . 'You will be made free'?:** Jesus' audience believe that they already have freedom because they are the descendants of Abraham.

**8.34. Everyone who commits sin is a slave to sin:** It is not ancestry that makes us free or slave, according to Jesus, but the tendency to sin (8.7).

**8.37a. I know that you are descendants of Abraham:** Jesus accepts the claim made by his opponents.

**8.37b. Yet you look for an opportunity to kill me, because there is no place in you for my word:** This charge shows the shallowness of the Jews' belief (irrespective of the phrasing in 8.30). Failure to accept what Jesus says leads to the disordered wish to kill him.

**8.38a. I declare what I have seen in the Father's presence:** What Jesus has heard is better than the Jews' knowledge because he has received it directly from the Father (1.18).

**8.38b. As for you, you should do what you have heard from the Father:** If Jesus' opponents had truly listened to the word of God, they would have seen the continuity between what they had already heard, and what Jesus is saying. Descendants or not, they do not know the will of God.

 ## Interpretation

Jesus now spells out the consequences of believing in him (8.30). Jesus claims to be the one who does what, for Jews, the law was claimed to do: bring freedom. His words produce a sharp response: his hearers do not need the freedom which he offers – they already have it. It is yet another example of a misunderstanding (Appendix H) connected to questions of origins. For Jesus' opponents, freedom comes from their ancestry with Abraham. Jesus, on the other hand, views slavery as based on sin.

The Danish writer Hans Christian Andersen wrote a story, 'The Emperor's New Clothes', about a ruler who gets tricked by two swindlers into buying a set of very expensive clothes, which actually do not exist. When the emperor parades in his new clothes everyone tells him how smart he looks – except for a small child who shouts out, 'But he isn't wearing anything!' Everyone else was too much in the grip of social status and convention to say what was really going on. Jesus here challenges a deeply and popularly held view, and, like the small boy in the story, is criticized. He makes enemies by upsetting the view which people have of themselves and their own identity, and reminds us that truth is more important than flattery or being popular. It is a lesson which Christian preachers and evangelists need to remember when they are courted by unscrupulous or corrupt politicians and leaders who wish to present themselves in a good light.

Jesus does the opposite: he makes his opponents seem less important than they want to be by redefining the household economy and their place in it. Those who viewed themselves as sons are actually slaves. There is only one Son: it is faith in him which brings freedom. Jesus has effectively demoted his opponents in this picture.

Jesus' teaching is closer to the Exodus story than his opponents might wish. The first generation of Hebrews failed to enter the Promised Land because of their constant lack of faith and their testing of God (Psalm 95); their ancestry did not save them. Paul uses their example to warn the Corinthians that they must not assume that they will automatically receive the promises of Christ because they have received the sacraments (1 Corinthians 10—11). Jewish practice linked right faith with right behaviour in a way that much Graeco-Roman religion did not. In many Graeco-Roman cults, taking part in rituals with little or no change in behaviour could still guarantee salvation. For Paul, wrong behaviour could always annul faith and participation in ritual. For John, not continuing in Jesus' word (8.31) cancels out discipleship.

 STUDY SUGGESTIONS

### Word study

**1** Why was Abraham an important figure of faith for Jesus' opponents?

### Review of content

**2** What is the relationship between forgiveness, religious tradition and behaviour?

**3** Read John 8.34–36 and Galatians 4.21–31. What points do they share?

### Discussion and application

**4** Do people today think that they can be forgiven without changing how they behave? What should we say to people who think this way?

## 8.39–59: A violent debate about ancestry

 Introduction

The debate continues and becomes more heated, with insults traded between Jesus and his opponents.

 Notes and commentary

**8.39a. Abraham is our father:** Jesus' opponents repeat their claim to be
descended from Abraham.

**8.39b. If you were Abraham's children you would be doing what Abraham
did:** Jesus offers a new definition of descent. It does not depend on ancestry, but behaviour. Philosophers call this kind of argument a *modus
tollens* (a denial): If A, then B; if not B, then not A. Here: If you were
from Abraham, you would do X: you do not do X, therefore you are not
Abraham's descendants. The argument may be based on Abraham's wel-
coming of visitors (Genesis 18.1–8) or his obedience in general (Genesis
12.1–9; 15.1–6; 22.1–19).

**8.40a. You are trying to kill me:** Here is a specific example of wrong
behaviour – trying to kill Jesus for speaking the truth.

**8.40b. A man:** This term need not deny the divine status of Jesus: it may
just mean 'someone'.

**8.40c. Who has told you the truth I heard from God:** This clause again
stresses the direct nature of what Jesus says (8.38).

**8.40d. This is not what Abraham did:** Compare Genesis 18.1–8.

**8.41a. Doing what your father does:** Children behave the same way as
their ancestors, according to the thought of the time. As Jesus' opponents
do not act like Abraham, they cannot be his descendants. Their father must
be someone else.

**8.41b. We are not illegitimate children:** This may be going back to the
question of origins, and even be a further *ad hominem* argument about
Jesus' own birth and ancestry (1.45). Like 8.39, it suggests that behaviour
is shaped by descent. To be a 'child of fornication' (the literal translation
of the Pharisees' words) implied apostasy (rejection of God) or spiritual
infidelity (Hosea 1.2; 4.12–15; Ezekiel 16.15, 33–34; 23.1–49). Jesus' opponents imply that he has insulted them.

**8.41c. We have one father, God:** The covenant between God and Israel allows Jesus' opponents to claim they are children of God (Exodus 4.22; Deuteronomy 14.1; 32.6; Isaiah 63.16; 64.8; Jeremiah 3.4, 19; 31.9).

**8.42a. I came from God and now I am here:** This statement refers to Jesus' earthly life (8.29).

**8.42b. I did not come on my own, but he sent me:** The verse repeats the themes of unity with the Father (5.19–20), and of Jesus being sent by God (3.17).

**8.43. You cannot accept my word:** This charge is more critical than 'you have no place in you for my word' (8.37); it suggests that Jesus' opponents are *incapable* of hearing what he is revealing.

**8.44a. You are from your father the devil:** Jesus now uses an *ad hominem* argument, mimicking his opponents. For 'the devil', see Appendix J.

**8.44b. You choose to do your father's desires:** Jesus returns to the argument that behaviour is linked to ancestry (8.39, 41).

**8.44c. He was a murderer from the beginning:** The devil robs humanity of immortality (Genesis 3.1–12) and prompts Cain to slay Abel (Genesis 4.1–15).

**8.44d. And does not stand in the truth:** The devil is opposed to God and Jesus, but does not have equal status with them. The devil is not God.

**8.44e. A liar and the father of lies:** Lies are the mechanism by which the devil brings about murder (Genesis 3.4).

**8.46. Which of you convicts me of sin?:** Sin is a consequence of lies and disobedience (1.29); it is alien to Jesus, who speaks the truth (8.44).

**8.47. Whoever is from God hears the words of God. The reason you do not hear them is that you are not from God:** This is another *modus tollens* argument (8.39): if you were from God, you would hear; you do not hear, therefore you cannot be from God.

**8.48. You are a Samaritan and have a demon:** Jesus is again criticized in two status categories: being a Samaritan (an outsider of low status) and possessed (5.20; 7.19). The word 'Samaritan' would have been an insult. It may be based on the positive encounter that Jesus has had with the Samaritans (4.7–40). Some of Jesus' contemporaries combined the two ideas and believed that Samaritan prophets were possessed by demons.

**8.49. I do not have a demon . . . you dishonour me:** Jesus openly admits that the charges are insults to his honour and status.

**8.50. I do not seek my own glory:** Jesus is concerned with the glory of the Father, not his own status (5.18).

**8.51a. Very truly:** The phrase indicates that what Jesus says here is very important (1.50–51).

**8.51b. Whoever keeps my word will never taste death:** This repeats ideas seen in a previous argument (5.24).

**8.52a. We know you have a demon:** In the Synoptics, Jesus was also accused of being possessed (Mark 3.21–22).

**8.52b. Abraham died, and so did the prophets:** The historical fact of Abraham's death (and that of the prophets) is seen as grounds for believing that Jesus is possessed. How could anyone say these people had not died? The argument here is tailored to make Jesus look bad.

**8.53. Are you greater than our father Abraham, who died? The prophets also died:** Jesus is accused of making himself superior to Abraham and the prophets. His opponents expect that anyone who hears this argument will automatically think Jesus is in the wrong.

**8.54. If I glorify myself, my glory is nothing:** Jesus dodges their charge: he is not seeking glory for himself (8.50).

**8.55. You do not know him. But I know him; if I were to say that I do not know him, I would be a liar like you. But I do know him and I keep his word:** Jesus repeats the assertions made in 8.42–47.

**8.56. Your ancestor Abraham rejoiced that he would see my day:** Contemporary Jewish literature connected Abraham's joy to Genesis 17.17 (*Jubilees* 15.17; Philo, *On the Change of Names* 154), or to the birth of Isaac (*Jubilees* 14.21; 15.17; 16.19–20). The Jews also had widespread traditions, based on their interpretations of Genesis 15, that God gave Abraham visions of the future, including revelations of the Messiah and messianic age. Scholars debate whether these visions were given to Abraham in his earthly life (12.41) or whether he is seeing them from heaven (Luke 10.24; Hebrews 11.13; 1 Peter 1.10–12).

**8.57. You are not yet fifty years old, and have you seen Abraham?:** The Jews think that Jesus is claiming to have known Abraham in his earthly existence. Because Jesus is not yet 50 years old and they see him only in earthly terms, they consider his claim impossible. The age of 50 was commonly held to be the end of a person's working life (Numbers 4.2–3, 39; 8.24–25).

**8.58. Before Abraham was, I am:** The verse contrasts the Greek word *ginomai* which has the sense 'come to be' with 'I am' (Gk, *eimi*) (4.26). The verse thus has the sense: 'Before Abraham came into being or was created, I am', and contrasts a creature (Abraham) with 'I am' (God, called 'I am' in the OT). As an answer to the question of 8.57, it implies a claim in which Jesus identifies himself with God. It may also imply timeless pre-existence (since, unlike *ginomai*, *eimi* would have no beginning or starting point; Psalm 90.2). Some commentators suggest it may also imply Jewish belief in the pre-existence of the Messiah.

**8.59. They picked up stones to throw at him:** See 5.18. The *agōn* (8.12–20) is not a proper trial. The reaction could be one of mob justice.

 ## Interpretation

In the time of Jesus, blasphemy did not just mean misuse of the divine name, but also idolatry, disrespect for God, and even insulting his leaders. Some scholars also argue that it could include claiming to be the Messiah or to be the Son of God (1.34; 19.7), since only God could announce and enthrone the Messiah (*Beth ha Midrash* 3.73.14). Thus, the reaction of the people might imply that they have understood Jesus was claiming to be either God or the Messiah.

This section continues the theme of origins, but the language of the debate becomes more and more violent.

Jesus claims that descent should focus on behaviour rather than ancestry: on doing what Abraham did. His opponents claim a place of privilege. They are not just descendants of Abraham; they are the children of God (8.41). The irony of this claim will be noticed by John's audience: they are claiming for themselves a status which uniquely belongs to Jesus. In effect, they are trying to regain the status as sons which Jesus has already denied them in his redefinition of the household of God (8.34–35).

Jesus defends himself by attacking the status of his opponents and argues that their behaviour shows they are not children of God (8.42–43). He then accuses them of being unable to comprehend the truth because their descent comes from the devil (8.44). This must be balanced by 8.37 and 8.56, which both acknowledge a genealogical descent from Abraham and, as such, this assertion is not to be read literally. The key lies in a misunderstanding (Appendix H). Jesus is not really talking of genealogical descent, but behaviour: Abraham and the devil are exemplars. Jesus is arguing that his opponents follow the example of the devil, not Abraham. The recurring *modus tollens* arguments repeat the stress on behaviour: *what you do*. We might sum it up as follows:

1 Sons copy their fathers;

2 You do what the devil does: commit murder;

3 Therefore, the devil is your father.

John's audience may well remember that Jesus shares the behaviour of the Father, which is even superior to Abraham. This claim is repeated at the end of the argument, where Jesus is obviously claiming to be superior to Abraham (8.58). The argument further makes it clear that the categories of behaviour are mutually exclusive: one cannot be in both groups.

The aggressive tone of the *agōn* is difficult, especially in communities trying to deal with an anti-Semitic past. Censoring the text is not an answer: it may only mean that we are forcing the text to conform to our conventions of what is appropriate. Attempts to say that such polemic is historically inaccurate risk replacing the supposed inaccuracy with an equally inaccurate reading; there was certainly confrontation between Jesus and his contemporaries.

In many ways, we do better to see the polemic as the product of an 'in-house' Judaic controversy about the nature of the Messiah. From this perspective, we may note that the kind of insults and slander found in this section were typical of both Jewish and Graeco-Roman controversy, in which philosophers of different schools had, over the years, developed styles of speaking in which it was customary to ridicule or mock the teaching of others. This rhetorical style included standard remarks which would be applied to others whether or not they were accurate. Such remarks serve to show that someone is an opponent – nothing more, nothing less. Remarks of this kind are found in Jewish literature (Josephus, *Against Apion* 2.6.68; 2.8.92–6; 2.14.148; Philo, *The Embassy to Gaius* 18.120; 19.131; 20.132; *Contemplative Life* 1.8–9; 2.10; 14.22–8; Dead Sea Scrolls, 1QS 3.13; 1QS 1.10; 1QM 1.7). The comments about the devil, and being possessed, are typical.

What is the upshot of this? First, it shows that this kind of language should not be taken literally. This can be seen when the opponents are described as both descendants of the devil and of Abraham (8.37, 44, 56). This cannot be literally true. Second, looking at other passages from the time shows that this is a comparatively well-mannered debate; others were even cruder. Third, it really indicates that the abuse shows opposition, but does not describe opponents accurately. This kind of language only shows that the speakers oppose each other – nothing more, nothing less. Above all else, it should show that the words placed on the lips of Jesus are not to be the basis for a demonization of the Jewish people as a whole.

By the end of this section, the following claims have been made:

1 Jesus is the Messiah (7.31, 41).

2 He is the living embodiment of living water (7.37).

3 He is the living embodiment of the light of the world (8.12).

4 These three anticipated things are now present (inaugurated eschatology; see 3.3).

5 He is superior to Abraham (8.53–54).

6 He is either divine or the Messiah (8.58).

 ## STUDY SUGGESTIONS

### Word study

1 What does it mean to be the 'father' of someone? Is this about genealogy and descent, or behaviour?

## Review of content

**2** Compare John 8.51–58 with Mark 12.26–27. What is being said about God and the patriarchs? What does this tell us about the way texts can be used to fit arguments?

**3** What is a *modus tollens* argument?

**4** What makes Jesus and the devil very different from each other? Clue: think of opposites.

## Discussion and application

**5** Think about the language of polemic: does your culture use standard remarks which are not really accurate to describe opponents? How might this behaviour be seen by an outsider? Could it give a wrong impression of what we really think?

# John 9.1—10.21

# The second Sabbath controversy

 Summary

This section revisits a theme already raised in 5.1–18: the Sabbath. It starts with a healing (9.1–12), possibly magical in appearance, which includes a reflection on sin (9.2–3). The healed man is taken before the Pharisees, on the basis that Jesus has healed on the Sabbath (9.16), but the dialogues which follow focus on blindness (9.13–34). Physical blindness becomes a metaphor for spiritual blindness and the inability to see God (9.35–39).

The theme abruptly changes (10.1) to the Good Shepherd. Spiritual blindness is then explored in the imagery of the relationship between the sheep and the Shepherd (10.1–21).

## 9.1–12: Jesus the magician?

 Introduction

This section starts with the healing of a man born blind. The passage includes a reflection on the relationship between healing and illness or disability.

 Notes and commentary

**9.1a. As he walked along:** An interval of time has passed since the end of the previous episode (8.59). The openness with which Jesus moves is very different from hiding and leaving the Temple (8.59).

**9.1b. He saw a man blind from birth:** The man has not become blind by an accident or later illness. He has never seen. The gift of sight will be like a new birth or creation. Blindness made people impure because they could not see that they were breaking purity rules.

**9.2a. His disciples asked him, 'Rabbi':** 'Rabbi' was a title of respect (1.38). 'Disciples' here is not a reference to the twelve (6.67), but may refer to the disciples of 7.3. Calling Jesus 'Rabbi' may show that they have yet to understand fully who he is.

**9.2b. Who sinned?:** Many people believed that illness or suffering was caused by sin (Exodus 20.5; Numbers 14.18; Deuteronomy 5.9; see also Luke 13.2) in spite of criticism in the OT of this view (Job; Jeremiah 31.29–30; Ezekiel 18). Jesus has previously talked on this subject (5.14).

**9.3a. Neither this man nor his parents sinned:** Jesus comments only on this particular case.

**9.3b. He was born blind so that God's works might be revealed:** While some of Jesus' contemporaries taught that those who bore suffering would be rewarded, Jesus is silent on that point, but stresses that this suffering will glorify God (11.4).

**9.4. Work . . . while it is day:** This points to the short time of Jesus' earthly ministry, possibly based on a proverb (11.9–10).

**9.5. I am the light of the world:** Jesus has already revealed himself as the light of the world (1.4–5, 9; 8.12).

**9.6. He spat . . . and made mud:** Mark 7.33; 8.23 also describes Jesus using spittle, which was believed to be a medicine, but also magical (*Tosefta* 12.10 includes spittle with using charms). Mud echoes the theme of creation (Genesis 2.7; Job 10.9). Any criticism of Jesus here relates only to magic. Arguments about the Sabbath will follow later (9.14).

**9.7a. Go, wash:** Naaman was told to act in a similar way by Elisha (2 Kings 5.10–13).

**9.7b. In the pool of Siloam:** This was a pool at the southern end of the eastern hill in Jerusalem. Water from Siloam was used at *Sukkoth* – a link to the previous chapters (7—8), like 'I am the light of the world'. The pool was associated by the rabbis with purification. If this was known to Jesus, the sending for purification resembles Synoptic accounts of healing (Luke 17.12–15). This is about purity and reconciliation, not just restoring sight. Some see an echo of Genesis 49.10, given a messianic interpretation by Jewish and Christian readers.

**9.7c. He went and washed and came back able to see:** The miracle happens at a distance from Jesus; it is not functioning as a sign (4.46–54).

**9.8–9a. The neighbours . . . began to ask, 'Is this not the man who used to sit and beg?' Some were saying, 'It is he.' Others were saying, 'No, but it is someone like him':** The whole passage to verse 12 is full of irony. Those who had seen the blind man are now not sure who they are looking at. Despite their sight, they are effectively blind.

**9.9b. He kept saying, 'I am the man':** In this context the phrase beginning 'I am' means simply 'Yes, I am', not that the blind man is claiming to be God.

**9.11. The man called Jesus:** No indication is given of how the blind man knows Jesus. The gaps in the narrative, as well as the coming and going, give a sense of distance and prevent this being a magical act or a sign (9.7).

Interpretation

This section shows how we may sometimes rush to interpret a passage based on our existing knowledge. The accusation against Jesus about the Sabbath only comes to light in 9.14; before that, his actions have provoked interest, but not hostility. Commentators may read the Sabbath controversy back into the story, by citing 9.14 in their discussion of 9.5. This first section should prompt a reflection on Jesus as a magician, before the Sabbath is considered.

Magic was common in Jesus' time, practised in both Judaism and Graeco-Roman contexts. It is difficult to separate ancient magic and religion because similar rituals were used in both. There was a difference between religion and magic: magic was used to manipulate the world for one's own advantage. As Jesus' words in 9.3 indicate that Jesus works for the Father's glory, his healing action is neither self-centred nor magical. Jesus is not a magician – even if he looks like one.

The first section (9.1–12) also reflects on the question of suffering and evil (theodicy). These verses, especially when combined with 5.14, depart from conventional understandings where suffering was seen as someone's fault. Many thought that the sick person must have sinned or be a victim of ancestral or inherited sin. Jesus rejects that here. In 9.3 he denies that blindness is the result of either the man's actions or those of his ancestors or parents. Jesus' words echo the prophets who wrestled with the problem of why the wicked prosper and the righteous suffer. They also echo the book of Job: Job's comforters run through the stock answers about suffering, and Job tears them to pieces. Job finds the answer to the question of suffering in the mystery of God and an admission of the difference between his Creator and himself. The Gospels take this a step further: God becomes the victim of suffering too. God, in the person of Jesus, takes on human suffering on the cross, and transforms it. To understand the question of suffering, there is much to be said for placing oneself at the foot of the cross and observing the suffering of God for the sake of his Creation.

 STUDY SUGGESTIONS

**Word study**

1 Why does Jesus use 'mud' in this healing?

2 Do phrases containing 'I am' always indicate a claim to be God?

**Review of content**

3 What was the difference between magic and religion in the cultures of Jesus' time?

4 Was Jesus a magician?

123

**Discussion and application**

**5** Are Christians today at risk of using holy items, like rosaries or holy water, in a magical way? What would we say to someone engaged in such actions?

---

# 9.13–34: The blind man, his parents and the Pharisees

 Introduction

The man born blind is now questioned by the Pharisees. The focus shifts to accusations that Jesus has broken the Sabbath. The man's parents are brought for questioning, but they say nothing because they are afraid. In a second set of questions, the man born blind speaks back to the Pharisees, who refuse to listen to his testimony.

 Notes and commentary

**9.13. They brought to the Pharisees the man who had formerly been blind:** The Pharisees belonged to a particular religious tradition or school, and were often counted among Jesus' opponents (1.24; 3.1, 25; 4.1; 7.32, 47–52; 8.13). Some scholars have noted that the Pharisees are often Jesus' opponents in the Synoptics, but he was also admitted to their *chaburah* (table-fellowship meals; possibly, Luke 7.36). For this reason, some see Jesus at the centre of an intra-Pharisaic debate – a dispute between different Pharisees over the interpretation of the law.

**9.14. It was a sabbath day when Jesus made the mud and opened his eyes:** As in 5.9, the controversy is about Sabbath observance. Only now is it said that Jesus has broken Sabbath law. So far, there has been no evidence of wrongdoing. A section from the Talmud (third century CE) says 'fasting spittle' should not be put on the eyes on the Sabbath (Jerusalem Talmud, Sabbath 14.14d.17).

**9.16. Some of the Pharisees said, 'This man is not from God, for he does not observe the sabbath.' But others said, 'How can a man who is a sinner perform such signs?':** The Pharisees are divided over Jesus' actions. This suggests that his actions break oral interpretations of the law rather than the law itself: there would be no such division if he had clearly broken the written letter of the law. Scripture describes people opposed to God who were still able to work miracles (Exodus 7.11; Matthew 24.24).

This may be part of John's longer critique of signs: even unrighteous people may perform them. It may also imply that the Pharisees have not read Scripture properly, and thus questions their logic.

**9.17. 'He is a prophet':** This may refer to Elisha or Elijah: both worked miracles. If 'prophet' has a capital letter – the Prophet – this verse implies that Jesus is being identified as the Messiah (6.14–15). The man's faith in Jesus is now superior to that of the disciples who addressed him as 'Rabbi' (9.2).

**9.21a. We do not know . . . Ask him; he is of age:** The man is old enough to be legally responsible for his own actions. His parents do not need to defend him as if he were a minor.

**9.21b. He will speak for himself:** The man's parents refuse to speak on his behalf. If this were any kind of official hearing, it would leave him without a defence. It was unusual for someone to give self-testimony (5.31).

**9.22a. His parents . . . said this because they were afraid of the Jews:** The 'Jews' (1.19) use power to interfere with the legal process. This verse would seem to link Jews with Pharisees (9.13; 15).

**9.22b. Anyone who confessed Jesus to be the Messiah would be put out of the synagogue:** Synagogues were focal points of Jewish communities in the Diaspora (7.35). The verse may reflect the experience of John's audience rather than what happened to Jesus in his own ministry.

**9.24a. So . . . they said to him, 'Give glory to God!':** This was a formula used before making a testimony or a confession (Joshua 7.19; *1 Ezra* 9.8). Here, the man born blind will give glory to God by confessing his belief in Jesus.

**9.24b. We know that this man is a sinner:** Jesus' opponents claim to have knowledge (3.2), but it will prove to be false.

**9.25. I do not know whether he is a sinner. One thing I do know:** The healed man rejects the wisdom of his questioners because of his own experience. He neither denies nor agrees that Jesus is a sinner. As in 9.21, the speaker is careful to admit what he does or does not know.

**9.26–27. 'How did he open your eyes?' He answered them, 'I have told you already . . . Why do you want to hear it again? Do you also want to become his disciples?':** The blind man does not answer the Pharisees' question, but tells them that they have not listened to what he has said. He finishes with a taunt. Such figures of speech were part of the current debating style (8.39–59).

**9.28. We are disciples of Moses:** The Pharisees respond that they are followers of Moses, the archetypal lawgiver and patriarch.

**9.29a. We know that God has spoken to Moses:** The Pharisees reinforce their argument by citing the tradition that Moses spoke with God (Exodus 33.11; Numbers 12.2–8).

**9.29b. As for this man, we do not know where he comes from:** This contradicts what earlier opponents have said, when they talked about Jesus' descent and lineage (1.45; 7.40–52). They question the claim that Jesus comes from God, by contrasting him with Moses. They imply he is inferior to Moses.

**9.30. You do not know where he comes from, and yet he opened my eyes:** The blind man ignores their claims, suggesting that the facts (his blindness has been cured) outweigh their theology.

**9.31–33. We know that God does not listen to sinners, but he does listen to one who worships him and obeys his will . . . If this man were not from God, he could do nothing:** The blind man argues (9.16) that Jesus is on the side of God. God has heard Jesus, who is therefore righteous (Psalms 34.15; 66.19; 145.19; Proverbs 15.29) and not a sinner (Job 27.9; Psalm 66.18; Isaiah 1.15; 59.2; Ezekiel 8.18; Micah 3.4; Zechariah 7.13).

**9.34. You were born entirely in sins:** In this *ad hominem* argument (5.1–47) the Pharisees reject the man, based on a view that Jesus has already rejected (9.3). The events of this chapter have had no impact on them.

 ## Interpretation

The healed man is interrogated by the Pharisees in the absence of Jesus (9.35). There are several stages to the argument: the setting up of a charge of breaking the Sabbath (9.13–17), a cross-examination (9.18–23) and a final questioning (9.24–33).

The debate with the Pharisees again challenges their methods and knowledge of Scripture. Their understanding of signs is contradicted by Exodus (see 9.16). Their exercise of authority means that fear has replaced justice: the blind man's parents will not enter into the discussion, which puts their son in danger (9.19–23). This criticizes people who use power for their own ends, and not for justice. In recent years, churches have had an admirable record in standing up against injustices in society, but their record is always open to betrayal by their own behaviour. In addition, some African politicians pointed out that bishops appointed for life were telling secular leaders to leave public office after completing limited terms. If the Church is truly to speak about issues of justice it must first set its own house in order: churches which play favourites with the rich and powerful, engage in shady deals and are not transparent end up compromising the gospel. Often such practice has been done, it is said, for the good of the Church, to protect its name and reputation. Cover-ups of sexual abuse within the Church have occurred in many different churches. These cover-ups always end up being more damaging in the long run. The episode warns about excluding people as a method of exercising power and control. John is not the only critic of the abuse of power. In 1 and 2 Corinthians, Paul sees the exercise of leadership and the use of discipline as serving one end: reconciliation. Any exercising of discipline and power which does not heal divisions is inadequate.

The caution with which the blind man speaks about Jesus echoes his parents' words (9.21). Their reluctance to speak may come from fear, but it also makes the Pharisees appear arrogant and over-eager to judge Jesus. They claim to speak with knowledge and certainty, but do not. In contrast, both the man and his parents are much more circumspect, and clearly state what they know to be true, and what is uncertain. This is an important philosophical point. Much of the philosophical quest depends on knowing what can be stated with certainty and what cannot. Here, the Pharisees, the experts of their time, are shown to make mistakes (9.24), and be muddled (9.16). In contrast, the ordinary folk, the blind man and his parents, who admit what they do not know, reveal themselves as wiser.

The second dialogue shows the blind man gaining confidence. At points he appears impatient with the Pharisees, even to the point of taunting them (9.27, 30). He knows more and will not allow himself to be bullied or threatened. Furthermore, unlike the Pharisees, whose reading of the Scriptures is open to question (9.16), his remarks about precedent match the Old Testament. John is using this to give his audience a message: believers are given wisdom and confidence to bear witness to the truth. An ordinary man is able to challenge experts and to win the argument, even if he is driven out. Even if John's audience are being driven out of the synagogues, they still have the best of the argument and the truth (16.2).

Unable to refute his words, the Pharisees accuse the blind man of being unfit to speak. We see similar behaviour when political regimes label their critics as psychologically disturbed, and send them off to gulags or concentration camps.

This also has been true of Christians. Such behaviour is not confined to the past; when proponents of a particular viewpoint, either liberal or traditional, label their critics as 'heretics' or '— phobic', they are using this method of winning a debate. When this happens, Christians should try to see the other side of the argument. Part of the theological task must involve respect for the integrity, abilities and humanity of those who hold other views and a desire to take them seriously, even when disagreeing with their conclusions. It also involves growing through reflection and discussion, not closing the mind and clinging to entrenched viewpoints. Holding the same conclusion after reflection is very different from never exploring contrary views: the first shows growth and maturity; the second, stagnation and death.

 ## STUDY SUGGESTIONS

### Word study

**1** What is a synagogue?

**2** Why do some think Jesus might have been closely linked to the Pharisees?

## Review of content

**3** Why do the blind man's parents not take part in questioning?

**4** How does the blind man grow in confidence in this section?

## Discussion and application

**5** In your context, have Christians, and especially Christian leaders, exercised power in a way that has either been unjust or compromised the values of the gospel?

**6** Has faith in Jesus enabled people in your community to stand up to those who are powerful or unjust?

---

# 9.35–39: Jesus finds the blind man

 Introduction

Jesus finds the man born blind, and reveals himself as the Son of Man. The man born blind worships him.

 Notes and commentary

**9.35a. Jesus heard that they had driven him out:** Jesus now looks for the blind man.

**9.35b. Son of Man:** For the variety of meanings of this phrase, see 1.50–51. It is only used as a confession of faith here in John (compare Matthew 8.20). It is unlikely here to mean 'I, me' given what follows.

**9.36. Who is he?:** The healed man does not recognize Jesus as the Son of Man.

**9.37. Jesus said to him, 'You have seen him, and the one speaking with you is he':** Jesus identifies himself as the Son of Man. This is characteristic of John's Gospel, but not of the Synoptics, where Jesus tends to avoid direct assertions about his status.

**9.38. And he worshipped him:** The Greek word translated 'worship' literally means 'bend the knee'. The man's actions show that he gives Jesus divine status. Jesus, in not stopping him, obviously agrees with this.

**9.39. I came into this world . . . so that those who do not see may see, and those who do see may become blind:** Jesus states a reversal of the world order. The blind man has now become the one who sees and understands, in contrast to the Pharisees, who are revealed as blind (Matthew 23.16) and ignorant (12.40).

 ## Interpretation

The man born blind is healed from blindness and ignorance. He has gained confidence in knowledge and courage, able to resist the pressure put on him by the Pharisees to deny Jesus. He both confesses and worships Jesus as God.

This is a highpoint of the Gospel – the first time that Jesus has been accepted and worshipped as God. A blind man, not the disciples, has become a new creation. His transformation sends a positive message to John's audience: those who seem blind, ignorant and insignificant are transformed by Jesus and become the superiors of those seen as expert in matters of faith and religion. This passage could have had an additional shock value for John's audience, who might well have been accustomed to think of the Pharisees as experts and role-models (not the demonized and highly criticized figures that decades of Christian interpretation has made them), and of the disciples as spiritually superior. The world has been turned upside down.

John's audience are shown that they have the potential to imitate the blind man in their knowledge of faith. They can also gain the confidence to resist those who would put pressure on them to deny Jesus.

 # STUDY SUGGESTIONS

### Word study

**1** What does 'worship' mean?

### Review of content

**2** Is it enough to believe that Jesus was a wise man or teacher?

### Discussion and application

**3** Bowing the knee was a form of worship or showing respect in Jesus' time. What are the kinds of worship found in your culture? Can we adapt these actions and gestures to show our faith that Jesus is God?

## 9.40—10.21: Jesus, the Pharisees and the Good Shepherd

 Introduction

Jesus begins to speak to some Pharisees who have seen and heard his conversation with the man born blind. There is a very brief discussion of sin, which leads into Jesus' teaching about the Good Shepherd.

 Notes and commentary

**9.40. Some of the Pharisees . . . said to him, 'Surely we are not blind, are we?':** Jesus' words to the blind man prompt a question from some Pharisees. Blindness and seeing remain metaphors for spiritual ignorance and awareness.

**9.41. If you were blind, you would not have sin. But now that you say, 'We see', your sin remains:** In 3.17, Jesus becomes the means by which people judge themselves. In this verse, the Pharisees have become their own judges (15.1—16.33, esp. 15.21).

**10.1a. Very truly, I tell you:** What Jesus says here is to be treated as very important (1.50–51).

**10.1b. Anyone who does not enter the sheepfold:** There were several types of sheepfolds. They could be stone enclosures on a hillside, or a walled yard in front of a house.

**10.1c. A thief and a bandit:** The word 'bandit' is also used of political revolutionaries (Luke 23.19). Some of these movements were also messianic, so it may include people who are raising false messianic hopes (10.12; Mark 11.17; Luke 10.30).

**10.2a. The one who enters by the gate:** The 'gate' is the entrance to the sheepfold (10.7).

**10.2b. The shepherd:** The image of a shepherd is used in three ways in the OT, to represent:

1 unrighteous leaders of Israel (Isaiah 11.4–17; Jeremiah 23.1–8; Ezekiel 34.1–10);

2 God as the Shepherd who will save his flock (Genesis 48.15; 49.24; Psalm 23.1; 28.9; 77.20; 78.52; 80.1; Isaiah 40.11; 49.9–10; Jeremiah 23.3; 31.9–10; Ezekiel 34.11–16; Micah 2.12; Sirach 18.13);

3 the Davidic messianic figure (Jeremiah 3.15; Ezekiel 34.23–24; 37.24; Micah 5.3–4; Zechariah 13.7–9).

**10.2c. Of the sheep:** These represent the people who belong to God (Psalms 74.1; 78.52; 79.13; 95.7; 100.3; Ezekiel 34.31). This may be referring to his people in the end times (Micah 2.12–13). The Romans would sometimes use similar imagery to describe subjects or those under authority. The emperor Tiberius is said to have criticized governors who demanded excessive taxes from their subjects: 'A good shepherd shears his flock; he does not skin them' (Suetonius, *Tiberius* 32).

**10.3a. The gatekeeper opens the gate for him:** The character of the gatekeeper remains unidentified. There is no need for a precise identification because this is not an allegory in which every detail represents something. Sometimes details in parables simply tell the story, without a symbolic meaning.

**10.3b. The sheep hear his voice:** To hear Jesus' voice (hear and respond to him) describes the relationship between Jesus and his followers (5.24, 28).

**10.3c. He calls his own sheep by name:** This suggests a strong familiarity between the shepherd and the sheep (see Revelation 1.17; 3.5, 12 for the degree of intimacy implied by knowing names). The risen Jesus will greet Mary Magdalene (20.16) and Peter (21.15–17) by name.

**10.4. He goes ahead:** The shepherd leads the animals rather than drives them from behind. Some see a reference to Numbers 27.15–18 about the Messiah (Appendix K).

**10.6. Figure of speech:** Jesus often used figures of speech such as proverbs or parables – stories with a hidden meaning. Hebrew parables included proverbs, riddles, allegories and figurative stories. In the Synoptics, as here, Jesus' parables sometimes need further explanation (Mark 4.1–10, 13–20).

**10.7a. Very truly, I tell you:** This phrase (10.1, 7) also suggests frank speaking (Appendix I), so plain and figurative speech may overlap.

**10.7b. I am the gate for the sheep:** Traditions from the Near East, but no literary sources, suggest that the shepherd might lie in the gateway of the sheepfold, and so act as the gate or door. 'Door' might suggest a heavenly door (Psalms 78.23; 118.20) or the traditions about entering the kingdom of God (Mark 9.43, 45, 47; Matthew 7.7, 13; 25.10; Luke 11.9; 13.24–25). The only way to make such an entry is through Jesus (10.9).

**10.8. All who came before me are thieves and bandits:** This is unlikely to be a blanket condemnation of all the patriarchs and prophets: some traditions omit 'all' to avoid such an interpretation. More likely, this statement refers to those who were leaders in Israel at the time of Jesus.

**10.9. Come in and go out:** This language may echo any or all of the following:

- a blessing for obedience (Deuteronomy 28.6; Psalm 121.8);
- the entrance to the Promised Land (Numbers 27.16–18);
- the restoration of Israel (Isaiah 49.9–10);
- the saving of Israel from the nations (Ezekiel 34.12–15).

There is no need to choose one of these rather than the others.

**10.10. I came that they may have life:** 'Life' here means eternal life (3.15; 6.68).

**10.11a. I am the good shepherd:** This is a construction similar to the one used in 6.35 and 9.5. The adjective 'good' implies an absolute difference in quality from the other shepherds – even suggesting that Jesus, as he speaks, is the only good shepherd. It is an expression which may be used of God or the Messiah (Psalm 23.1).

**10.11b. Lays down his life:** Some think that 1 Samuel 17.34–37 may add more detail to this phrase. It also anticipates Jesus' death (18.28–30).

**10.12a. The hired hand:** Such people have no real interest in those they are meant to be caring for (10.14).

**10.12b. Leaves the sheep and runs away:** While this might be a reflection on weak or poor leaders (Jeremiah 10.21; 12.10; 23.1–4; Ezekiel 34; Zephaniah 3.3; Zechariah 10.2–3; 11.17), it may also be referring to a specific historical event: by 70 CE the Jewish leadership had relocated from Jerusalem to Jamnia. If so, the references here include the Jewish leadership when the Gospel was written, not just in Jesus' time.

**10.12c. The wolf snatches them:** The term 'wolves' is often used of false officials (Ezekiel 22.27; Zechariah 10.3), judges (Zephaniah 3.3) and prophets (Matthew 7.15; 10.16; Luke 10.3); 'sheep' is used for Israel, or the people of God (Ezekiel 34.2–4; Zechariah 10.3).

**10.14–15. I know my own and my own know me, just as the Father knows me and I know the Father:** Jesus and the Father provide the model for the relationship between Jesus and his followers (6.37–39; 8.19).

**10.16a. I have other sheep:** This is a reminder of inclusive Old Testament traditions which saw God's love and salvation extended to some non-Jews (Isaiah 56.6–8). This might appeal to John's audience if they were non-Jewish (6.1–15, 33).

**10.16b. One flock, one shepherd:** See Ezekiel 34.23; 37.24. While these OT references mainly speak of a united Israel, here the inclusion of Jews and non-Jews is meant (as in Isaiah 56.6–8; Ezekiel 37.15–28; Micah 2.12).

**10.17. I lay down my life:** This repeats and thus stresses the importance of the shepherd laying down his life (10.11).

**10.18a. No one takes it from me:** This repeats the theme of Jesus (and God's) ultimate control over events which are taking place (7.8).

**10.18b. I have power to take it up again:** This claims a power over death, and anticipates the resurrection. Such power over death will be seen when Lazarus is raised (11.38–44).

**10.19. The Jews were divided:** Again, Jesus' words reveal divisions among those who oppose him (9.16).

**10.20a. Many of them were saying:** The majority still do not believe Jesus.

**10.20b. He has a demon and is out of his mind:** See 7.19. Possession is linked to madness (Luke 7.35).

**10.21. Can a demon open the eyes of the blind?:** Some OT passages suggest blindness is cured by God (Exodus 4.11; Psalm 146.8).

 ## Interpretation

Jesus' short answer to the Pharisees introduces the famous teaching about the Good Shepherd. The way in which John has been broken into chapters and verses gives the impression that the Good Shepherd material stands on its own. However, it is linked to the end of chapter 9, and will contrast Jesus with the Pharisees. Imagery of the shepherd was a component of the Festival of Dedication (10.22). The festivals of Booths and Dedication were several months apart, making this unlikely to be a literal timetable. However, the Shepherd material provides a theme which bridges the gap. It allows a critical reflection on leadership in response to the Pharisees, and leads into the material which will follow about the Dedication.

The passage draws on imagery relevant to both the rural society of Jesus' time and its spiritual and political traditions. The image of the shepherd had been widely used in the Old Testament (10.2), often describing how leaders failed to care for the nation. It also contrasted the way in which God cared for his people with their leaders' negligence or selfishness. It even described the Messiah. John uses all these traditions to describe how Jesus the Messiah cares for his people and exemplifies the love of God for them.

It is also imagery which resonates with the picture of Jesus given in the Synoptics. The imagery is not used identically: where the Synoptics attribute harm directly to the wolves, John focuses on the hired hands (10.12–13) who leave the sheep at the mercy of others. Jesus is the shepherd who replaces the unjust shepherds, the 'thieves and bandits' (10.2, 8) who have failed to lead properly.

The first section identifies Jesus with the shepherd (10.1–6), drawing on a theme which John has already explored at length: hearing and knowing his voice. This stresses the relationship of knowledge and trust which characterizes Jesus' intimacy with his followers. It indicates a criticism of the Pharisees (9.40), which is not obvious: Jesus will spell it out (10.7–10, 11–18).

The second section (10.7–10) gives another role to Jesus: the gate of the sheep. However, the practice of the shepherd blocking the entrance to the pen with his own body (literally making himself the gate) adds a new dimension to care. This is compared to the care taken by other shepherds. They bring death and destruction while Jesus brings 'life . . . abundantly' (10.10). If we take this passage to be John's way of writing a parable, and parables as commentaries on the narrative (Appendix G), this anticipates the way Jesus gives himself on the cross. He puts himself between his flock and danger for their preservation and salvation.

The addition of 'good' (10.11–18) stresses the superior quality of Jesus' care for his people, and also anticipates his death (10.11, 17–18). The inclusive nature of Jesus' leadership (10.16) is not new: it stands within traditions found in the Old Testament which viewed Israel as having a pivotal role in the work of salvation, but not the only nation to be saved. The parable foreshadows Jesus' later prayer for the unity of his people (17.11, 20–24). It also challenges many more exclusive views which had sprung up within the Judaism of his time, based on exclusivist works like Ezra and Nehemiah.

Just as the meeting at Caesarea Philippi contrasts a claim of high status with predictions of death (Mark 8.27–33; Matthew 16.13–20; Luke 9.18–22), so Jesus' identification of himself as the Good Shepherd is mixed with warnings about his death. Some scholars call the Caesarea Philippi incident the moment of *anagnōrisis* (recognition), a term used in Greek tragedy to describe the moment when a previously concealed identity is revealed. It is also a *peripeteia* (change of fortune, reversal). In Mark, Caesarea Philippi is 'the beginning of the end'. In John, both elements have surfaced already: Jesus has made claims about his own identity (for example, 4.26; 6.35; 8.12, 58), but not at this length. So far, the desire to kill Jesus has been mentioned (5.18; 8.59), but here, Jesus himself is warning of his own death. This, too, marks a change in tone.

The section finishes with a division about who Jesus is: a minority of his opponents appear to believe what he says. The majority accuse him of being mad and demon-possessed.

In some cultures the language of possession and the binding by spirits and powers is very potent; in others, such language is looked on as old-fashioned or redundant, and the language of psychology (or mental illness) is preferred. A recent film, *The Exorcism of Emily Rose*, based on the true story of Anneliese Michel, shows how closely the two may be linked. Anneliese's failure to respond to psychiatric treatment led to her condition being treated by an exorcism. Unfortunately, Anneliese died. However, the court case brought against the exorcists for manslaughter resulted in a 'not guilty' verdict. What might be learned from this? Possibly that there is a validity to both approaches, but those who engage in such practices must undertake a thorough diagnosis and process of discernment to ensure that conditions are being treated appropriately, in consultation with experts from all possible related disciplines. Also to be avoided is an outright rejection of the reasons given in an alien culture. It is more important that the sufferer receives healing than the healer wins an intellectual war about cosmology or psychology.

Jesus' words in 10.10 have been used by the leaders of 'prosperity churches' who preach that faith brings riches and material blessings; this, they contend, is having life 'abundantly'. Such a message is obviously appealing, not least to many looking to escape poverty. But it is problematic. First, some church leaders have used it to justify their own lavish and expensive lifestyles, and so to justify corruption and selfishness. Second, it makes a simple connection between faith and material blessings: if you believe, you will receive. But the world does not work this way. The wicked often seem to prosper while the noble suffer. As a result, this approach can make for a very cruel gospel, for it tells the believer who does not receive material blessings that his or her faith is not good enough. This may lead to despair, not hope. It may even give a very strange picture of God. Many prosperity churches stress the importance of tithing, and say that failure to tithe results in disaster and misfortune. This can make God seem little more than a gangster running a protection racket: if you don't pay, bad things happen. It is difficult to reconcile this with a loving God.

Critics of the prosperity gospel make a different claim. They say that 'abundance' is about spiritual and ethical qualities: virtues such as 'being at peace'. This is all very well, but it risks spiritualizing the gospel and making the teaching and actions of Jesus which addressed the needs of the poor seem irrelevant. Often these interpretations come from those who have not experienced real poverty and despair. People who think like this may be no less selfish than those who would justify their own excesses.

Both interpretations come from privilege and may ignore the plight of the poor. There is much truth in the old saying that 'If you cannot sleep well and eat well, you cannot pray well': the spiritual and physical go together. Preaching and living the gospel must involve both the physical and the spiritual. Some theologians of mission stress this by saying that the mission of the Church must include a 'creation mandate' (health, poverty, education, political liberation, etc.; Genesis 1—2; Exodus 20.1–17; Jeremiah 29.7; Micah 6.8; Romans 13; Galatians 6.10; 1 Peter 2.13–14) and a 'gospel mandate' (salvation and spirituality; Matthew 28.19–20; Acts 1.8; Ephesians 2) because the Church shares in the mission work of a God who is both Creator and Saviour (4.42).

The answer, as so often, lies between the two extremes. Discipleship must involve engagement with the material. In all things disciples are called to be imitators of Christ, and can neither ignore poverty nor condone self-indulgence. Tithing is a useful discipline, not because we are paying God off, but because it focuses our priorities. Where a person's heart really lies can be seen by how he or she uses money. But there is more to life than material prosperity: riches do not necessarily give peace of mind or happiness. Discipleship includes the material to move disciples beyond self-centredness to care for others. God becomes human to make this very point. Both those who would use the prosperity gospel to justify their own excess, and those who would counter with a spiritualized message, need to review their actions against the benchmarks given by Jesus.

By the end of this section Jesus has identified himself as a model leader in the image of God and the Messiah. The parable of the shepherd foreshadows the last days of Jesus' life in Jerusalem: at his Passion Jesus will lay down his life for his sheep.

 # STUDY SUGGESTIONS

## Word study

**1** Write a note to explain the 'Good Shepherd'.

**2** How do you understand 'life' and 'abundantly' (10.10)? Does this study raise questions about your current view? Clue: reflect on how John's understanding of (eternal) life (3.15) matches the one used in your tradition.

## Review of content

**3** Why do the Pharisees remain unforgiven (their 'sin remains')?

**4** Look up the passages cited in the notes on 10.2, and try to work out which details John has used, and which he has omitted in his depiction of the Good Shepherd.

**5** What separates Tiberius' and Jesus' views of people under their authority?

**6** Compare Isaiah 25.6–10 and Ruth with Ezra and Nehemiah. Can these different viewpoints be reconciled? Has your church or tradition a preference for one or the other? Might lessons be learned from the other?

## Discussion and application

**7** Jesus the Good Shepherd suggests a very intimate and close relationship with Jesus based on trust. Does your tradition stress trust and relationship with Jesus, or believing the right things?

**8** Read the passages about the Creation and gospel mandates. Write a 'Mission Manifesto' dealing with your issues which includes them both.

**9** Can the discipline of tithing be abused?

**10** Do modern political and social systems resemble the thinking either of Tiberius or of Jesus?

**11** Does your culture tend to demonize or psychologize health issues? Do you think it is possible to learn from the other tendency, or do you have all the answers already?

# John 10.22—11.54

# The Festival of Dedication

 Summary

John now uses the Festival of Dedication as the starting point for a reflection on Jesus and his claims. The section starts with a dialogue about rejection and blasphemy (10.22–42). The focus then shifts to Bethany and the raising of Lazarus (11.1–54).

## 10.22–42: Rejection and blasphemy

 Introduction

After *Sukkoth* (September–October) and the Sabbath controversy (9.1—10.21), the scene shifts to the Festival of Dedication (November–December). Jesus is again present in the Temple, and is asked to admit that he is the Messiah. A direct answer might make him guilty of blasphemy, so he answers indirectly. His answer still offends his questioners.

 Notes and commentary

**10.22a. The festival of the Dedication:** The Dedication was celebrated to mark the rededication of the Jerusalem Temple after it was desecrated by Antiochus Epiphanes in 167 BCE (1 Maccabees 1.59; Daniel 11.31; used as prophecy, Mark 13.14). The Temple was rededicated on 25 Chislev 164 BCE (1 Maccabees 4.52–59; 2 Maccabees 10.5–8). The feast was a reminder of God's presence, and warned against apostasy and idolatry.

**10.22b. It was winter:** Chislev is the ninth month of the Jewish year: November–December, or early winter in the northern hemisphere.

**10.23. The portico of Solomon:** This was on the eastern side of the Temple (Josephus, *Jewish War* 5.184–5; *Antiquities* 15.396–401; 20.220–1). The reference to Solomon, the son of David, may indicate allusions to the Messiah King.

**10.24. If you are the Messiah, tell us plainly:** See Appendix I. Jesus' questioners wish to receive a clear explanation rather than a parable. They do not think he has yet spoken plainly (10.6), and may have misunderstood him (Appendix H).

**10.25. The works that I do:** For 'works', see 5.36.

**10.26. You do not belong to my sheep:** See 10.2. Belief, rather than descent or genealogy, is considered the mark of belonging (7.3).

**10.27. My sheep hear my voice. I know them, and they follow me:** This verse repeats the description of the Good Shepherd in 10.3–4.

**10.28. I give them eternal life, and they will never perish. No one will snatch them out of my hand:** This repeats the work of the Good Shepherd in 10.10.

**10.29a. What my Father has given me:** Jesus repeats the assertion that life ultimately belongs to the Father (6.65).

**10.29b. No one can snatch it:** 'Snatching' implies stealing or taking what does not belong to you. This repeats the description of other shepherds (10.8).

**10.30. The Father and I are one:** For unity between God and Jesus, see 5.19, 31; 6.37–39; 8.19, 29, 31, 42.

**10.31. The Jews took up stones again to stone him:** Stoning was the penalty for blasphemy (5.18; 8.59).

**10.32. I have shown you many good works:** If this refers to 5.36 and 9.1–12, it implies that any good value in Jesus' actions is cancelled out by what he has said.

**10.33. We are going to stone you . . . for blasphemy:** Jesus has already been accused of blasphemy, and the charge is repeated (5.18; 8.59).

**10.34. Is it not written in your law, 'I said, you are gods'?:** Jesus again uses a *qal-waḥômer* argument (3.12; 7.23): if Israel can be called 'god', it is even more appropriate for Jesus.

'Your law' implies that Jesus is opposed to the Pharisees' position and will challenge them using Scripture. In so doing, he questions whether they are aware of the verse, or know how to interpret it. There may be an additional irony: the charge against Jesus might also apply to those who previously claimed God as their Father (8.41).

'I said, you are gods' is taken from Psalm 82.6. Originally, the verse may have been applied to corrupt judges or Israel under the law. However, the exact identification is unimportant. The point is to show that Jesus is a stronger claimant to be 'god' that either of those. The citation not only provides a proof text for Jesus' claims, but also rejects the charge of blasphemy since it shows that:

- God's representatives in the OT can be called 'god'. This gives a precedent: Jesus can rightly be called 'god' because he is God's representative;

- this Scripture shows human beings could be called 'gods';

- it is possible for someone to be both human and god.

The argument here might reflect a confusion caused by the two different OT terms: sons of Elohim and sons of Yahweh (1.34).

**10.36. God's Son:** The term has already been used for Jesus ('Son of God', 1.34).

**10.37. The works of my Father:** 'Works' is John's preferred term for Jesus' miraculous actions (5.36).

**10.40. He went away again across the Jordan to the place where John had been baptizing earlier:** The location is uncertain. It may be one of the places mentioned in 1.28 or 3.22.

**10.41. Many . . . were saying, 'John performed no sign, but everything that John said about this man was true':** These are popular reasons for Jesus' superiority to the Baptist. The verse follows the popular tradition that the Baptist performed no miracles. Note that a 'sign' could also be an inadequate basis for faith (Appendix C; 2.11, 23; 3.1–20; 4.48–54; 6.2, 14, 26; 7.3).

The Baptist's role as a reliable witness is repeated (5.33).

 Interpretation

This dialogue repeats a number of themes explored earlier, including the reliability of previous testimony about Jesus, based both on his works and on statements from the Baptist. The charge of blasphemy is brought again, and the way Jesus quotes Scripture when defending his position shows his skill as an interpreter. His defence against the charge of 'making himself God' is based on scriptural precedent, and criticizes his opponents' legal knowledge and method (10.34; see also 7.14–31; 9.13–34). This is a further reminder of the Judaic nature of John's claims about Jesus: Jesus fits with scriptural hopes. John takes care to maintain the strongly Judaic pedigree of the claims made about Jesus. Historically, this is perhaps evidence that John saw himself not just as a follower of Christ, but also still Jewish. Theologically, his method shows that Christian theologians from different cultural backgrounds need to consider Judaism and the Old Testament when shaping Christian theology in their contexts.

The early Church found this out very quickly when it reacted to Marcion, a second-century CE theologian who believed that most of the OT and what we call the NT was theologically redundant. The Church formulated a canon of Scripture to protect significant writings. Christians still face this issue when theologians argue about whether portions of Scripture should be included in debates about contentious issues.

The argument raises a number of theological issues about Incarnation (10.34). First, it suggests that Jesus surpasses the other people identified as 'gods' in the OT (1.1; 5.1–47; 8.13; 9.38). This argument suggests that in ontological terms (that is, related to the nature of being) one could be both human and divine.

An examination of the Psalms and their use is helpful: psalms about the enthronement of God (Psalm 9) could also be used for the enthronement of the Messiah King (Acts 17.31; Revelation 19.11), and the enthroned Messiah could be called God (Psalm 45.6–7; Hebrews 1.8), and share both God's powers (Psalms 72.8; 89.25; 91.13) and righteousness (Psalms 35.27; 63.11). Such lines of thinking allow the possibility that Incarnation is not foreign to OT thought, but may be extracted from it.

Such thinking continues into the Second Temple period. Arguably, there are references to an incarnate Messiah in texts such as the *Testaments of the Twelve Patriarchs* (*Testament of Dan* 5.10–13; *Testament of Levi* 18.6–7; *Testament of Simeon* 6.5—7.2; *Testament of Judah* 22.2–3; *Testament of Zebulun* 9.8–9; *Testament of Naphtali* 8.2–3; *Testament of Asher* 7.2–3; *Testament of Benjamin* 10.5–10), *Jubilees* 1.27–28, 31; 20, Pseudo-Philo, *Biblical Antiquities*; 2 Esdras 1—2; Philo, *On Husbandry* 51; see also Wisdom 18.14–16. Care is needed: scholars debate whether all these texts are genuinely Judaic, or include later Christian interpolations (additions).

If this evidence is correct, Judaism in this period could have included ideas about Incarnation (10.34), even if this was not accepted universally. This means that ideas about Incarnation do not need to be imported from Graeco-Roman traditions (gods visiting the earth in human guise, or divine-man theologies). This is not, however, the whole story: verses in John which talk about pre-existence (Appendix F) add to the claims that Jesus is truly God made flesh, not just by status, but by the nature of his being. John makes this claim, but never gives a detailed proof of how this might occur; he is content simply to make the point, without any complex philosophical explanation.

If the Festival of Dedication represented a new beginning for the Temple, it represents similar claims for Jesus: he represents a new beginning. It suggests that he is the sign of the presence of God in a way which is superior to the Temple. This claim has already been anticipated (2.13–25): here it is *inaugurated* (3.3).

The passage continues to identify Jesus as the true Shepherd of Israel, a character who could be identified as both divine and messianic. This section tightens the link between those two elements by claiming that Jesus may legitimately claim to be called God and not be guilty of blasphemy. When we explore the question of when or how a human could be called god in Judaic tradition, we find that God and Messiah King might be merged together, and that such a claim is being made for Jesus: he is both Messiah and God, and he is present. Thus, the dialogue at the Dedication summarizes and draws together claims made before.

## STUDY SUGGESTIONS

### Word study

**1** Who could be called 'gods' in the OT?

### Review of content

**2** Explain how Jesus' arguments reject the charge of blasphemy.

### Discussion and application

**3** Is the understanding of blasphemy used in this passage the same as the term 'blasphemy' if used in your context? Explain the differences.

## 11.1–54: Acting as the Good Shepherd – Martha, Mary and Lazarus

 Introduction

This episode, commonly identified as the raising of Lazarus, introduces new characters to the narrative (11.1–6). It is followed by a dialogue between Jesus and his disciples (11.7–10), and a discussion in which the disciples misinterpret (Appendix H) Jesus' words about the purpose of their journey (11.11–16). Two further dialogues follow: with Martha about the resurrection (11.17–27), and Mary about what has happened to Lazarus (11.28–33). This includes an apparent criticism of Jesus (11.32), which is picked up by the onlookers (11.37). Frustrated by their reaction (11.38), Jesus orders them to open the tomb, and Lazarus comes out when commanded (11.38–44). This will illustrate that Jesus has the power over life which belongs to the Father (10.28–29). The section concludes with a meeting of Jesus' adversaries in which the raising of Lazarus is made a justification for condemning him to death (11.45–54).

Notes and commentary

**11.1a. Lazarus of Bethany:** 'Lazarus' is a shortened form of the name Eleazar, meaning 'God helps'. The town is not the Bethany mentioned in 1.28. Bethany near Jerusalem to the east is associated with Jesus in the Synoptics (Mark 9.11; 14.3).

**11.1b. Mary and her sister Martha:** These two people are also named in Luke 10.38. The way in which women are named shows that the movement around Jesus may have broken with contemporary protocols which separated men and women (but see 11.3 for a different view).

**11.2a. Mary was the one who anointed the Lord with perfume and wiped his feet with her hair:** This description looks forward to 12.1–8.

**11.2b. Her brother:** This might mean a member of an extended family group rather than an immediate brother (2.12).

**11.3. He whom you love:** This phrase, used only with Lazarus, makes some commentators identify him with the Beloved Disciple (see 'The identity of John', p. 4). The intimacy implied between Jesus and this household through his love for Lazarus may explain the freedom with which Jesus talks to Mary and Martha.

**11.4a. This illness does not lead to death:** This suggests that Lazarus will die, but death is not the end. The illness glorifies God and is not caused by sin (9.4).

**11.4b. The Son of God may be glorified:** The glorifying of the Son has been anticipated (7.39; 8.54–59), but is now coming closer.

**11.8a. The disciples said to him, 'Rabbi':** For this title, see 1.35. Its use suggests the disciples have yet to understand fully who Jesus is.

**11.8b. Trying to stone you:** Stoning was the penalty for blasphemy (5.18; 8.59; 10.31).

**11.9a. Twelve hours of daylight:** See also 9.4–5.

**11.9b. Those who walk during the day do not stumble, because they see the light of this world:** The presence of light gives the disciples the opportunity to be guided, not to 'stumble' like those who reject Jesus. For the contrast between light and dark, see Appendix B.

**11.11a. Our friend . . . has fallen asleep:** Sleep was a widely used euphemism for death in the ancient world (1 Kings 1.21; Daniel 12.2; 2 Maccabees 12.45; Acts 7.60; 1 Thessalonians 4.13; Revelation 14.13); it was also used in inscriptions on Jewish tombs.

**11.11b. I am going . . . to awaken him:** Sleep was considered to be a cure or relief from pain or suffering. Both sleep and dreams figure in the cult of Asklepios, a Greek god of healing.

**11.12. He will be all right:** This expression means 'he will be safe, or saved'. The disciples only think Lazarus will get better; however, the story will address his salvation.

**11.13. Jesus, however, had been speaking about his death:** John adds an interpretative verse to explain the disciples' misunderstanding.

**11.14. Then Jesus told them plainly:** Jesus tries to clear up any possible confusion or misunderstanding (Appendix I).

**11.15. For your sake:** What will happen is significant for all who will witness it.

**11.16a. Thomas, who was called the Twin:** The name Thomas means 'twin'; John has translated the name as 'Didymus' for his Greek-speaking audience (1.38; 20.24). It is a nickname; later writings say that Thomas' given name was Judas.

**11.16b. We may die with him:** The grammar is ambiguous but the sense is: in order to die with Jesus. See 10.8 for fears about Jesus' safety.

**11.17. In the tomb for four days:** This is also mentioned in 11.39. The number four may signify that the body has reached the stage of decomposing (that is, Lazarus really is dead), or contemporary beliefs that the soul lingered near the body for three days after death.

**11.18. Bethany was . . . two miles away:** The text says literally '15 stades' or about 2.75 kilometres (11.1).

**11.19a. Many of the Jews had come to Martha and Mary:** For 'Jews', see 1.19. The verse indicates the complex relationship between Jesus and his opponents; they appear to share either friendship for Lazarus, Martha and Mary, or have mutual social obligations.

**11.19b. To console them:** The Jews' support for the sisters appears genuine, and they undertake the mourning rituals for the family.

**11.20. When Martha heard that Jesus was coming, she went and met him, while Mary stayed at home:** Martha, unlike Mary (11.28), goes to Jesus, rather than waiting to be called.

**11.21–22. If you had been here, my brother would not have died. But even now I know that God will give you whatever you ask of him:** Martha seems to criticize Jesus, but hopes that he can do something because God will give him what he asks.

**11.24. I know that he will rise again in the resurrection on the last day:** Many, but not all, Jews believed in a resurrection on the last day (Isaiah 2.2; Micah 4.1). Acts 23.8 reads well as suggesting that the Sadducees did not believe in resurrection, but that the Pharisees did, although they debated whether a person was resurrected as an angel or a spirit. Martha shares the conventional beliefs of the time.

**11.25. Jesus said to her, 'I am the resurrection and the life':** For the kind of construction that uses 'I am', see 6.35. Some texts omit 'and the life' (11.26). In a familiar pattern, Jesus now claims that belief should be focused on himself.

**11.26. Everyone who lives and believes in me will never die:** For 'life', see 3.15; 5.21–26; also 10.10. Jesus is talking of a spiritual life which may be experienced both now and after death. Here Jesus makes himself equal with God: both can give life (1.1; 5.1–47).

**11.27. Yes, Lord, I believe:** Martha's words imply a high degree of belief and trust. However, 11.39 questions how strong her faith really is.

**11.28a. She . . . called her sister:** The same verb is used of the Good Shepherd, so here Jesus, the Good Shepherd, calls Mary (10.3).

**11.28b. And told her privately:** There is possible hostility from others in the house.

**11.28c. The Teacher is here:** The use of a lower-status title in a whispered conversation may indicate that Martha's faith is weak.

**11.29. When she heard:** The same word is used when the sheep 'hear' the shepherd in 10.3, 16.

**11.31. The Jews . . . saw Mary get up quickly and go out. They followed her:** The visitors assume that Mary is going to the tomb. Their reaction to seeing Jesus is not recorded.

**11.32a. Mary . . . knelt at his feet:** The action is the same as in 9.38. It indicates a high level of faith.

**11.32b. Lord, if you had been here, my brother would not have died:** Mary's response is the same as Martha's (11.21), but omits the words of 11.22. Mary trusts Jesus himself, not just that God will do what Jesus asks.

**11.33a. Jesus saw her weeping, and the Jews . . . also weeping:** Both Mary and the Jews are weeping: Mary, too, has reverted to conventional patterns of mourning.

**11.33b. Greatly disturbed in spirit:** While the phrase is often taken to mean that Jesus is affected by grief, this does not make sense (11.15). Rather, it indicates a deep frustration, possibly even anger, with the lack of faith he has encountered, which now includes Mary.

**11.33c. Deeply moved:** This means that Jesus has lost his emotional balance, or cannot contain himself (12.27). A failure to acknowledge the reality of death (11.12, 21, 32, 37) may be the source of his frustration.

**11.35. Jesus began to weep:** This may indicate the depth of Jesus' feeling and experience (Hebrews 5.7). Jesus' frustration at the others' lack of faith moves him to tears. John appears to use emotions to emphasize the humanity of Jesus, perhaps as a rejection of Docetic (see the Introduction) claims.

**11.36. See how he loved him!:** The onlookers take Jesus' tears as a sign of his love for Lazarus.

**11.37. Could not he who opened the eyes of the blind man have kept this man from dying?:** The onlookers know of the events of 9.1–12, and criticize Jesus for helping a stranger but not his own friend, as conventional codes of honour demanded.

**11.38a. Again greatly disturbed:** See 11.35. This repetition again suggests that Jesus is reacting to the bystanders and their criticism, not the fate of Lazarus.

**11.38b. The tomb was a cave:** Caves were common burial sites (20.1).

**11.39. There is a stench:** Martha's faith is weak; she thinks only in physical terms about Lazarus' condition. 'Stench' implies that physical decay has set in.

**11.40a. Did I not tell you that if you believed:** The Greek word for 'you' here is singular: Jesus' reply is addressed only to Martha, not the whole crowd.

**11.40b. You would see the glory of God:** The glory of God will now be focused on the person of Jesus.

**11.42. I knew that you always hear me, but I have said this for the sake of the crowd standing here, so that they may believe that you sent me:** While this resembles Martha's earlier claim (11.22), Jesus' remarks include a reference to his relationship with the Father ('that you sent me'). His relationship to the Father determines what he will do; he does not act simply because God hears him. This repeated identification with God (5.18) may be the reason for the plot to kill him (11.46).

**11.44a. The dead man came out:** This action fulfils the words of Jesus in 5.21 and 10.27–29.

**11.44b. His hands and feet bound with strips of cloth, and his face wrapped in a cloth:** The fact that the cloth is still around Lazarus' face may indicate a difference from Jesus' resurrection (20.5–7).

**11.45. Many of the Jews believed in him:** More of Jesus' opponents come to some measure of belief in him. For the first time it looks as if those who believe are the majority.

**11.46. But some of them went to the Pharisees:** The Pharisees were a Jewish sect, school or group (1.24; 3.1; 7.47), but not officially a political grouping, although they had considerable influence.

**11.47. So the chief priests and the Pharisees called a meeting of the council:** The Sanhedrin **was** the governing council and court of the Jewish nation. There are historical difficulties in putting the Sanhedrin in an alliance with the Pharisees as they were often opposed to each other, despite some Pharisaic membership of the Sanhedrin. John seems to suggest that opponents of Jesus might put aside traditional differences in order to deal with him.

**11.48. If we let him go on like this, everyone will believe in him, and the Romans will come and destroy both our holy place and our nation:** The fears of Jesus' opponents now have a political dimension – possible Roman intervention. Those who favour a later date for the Gospel think the reference here is to the destruction of the Temple in 70 CE. Those who favour an earlier date think it anticipates such a state of affairs, given the Romans' previous history.

**11.49. Caiaphas who was high priest that year:** The high priest was appointed for life. The phrase means 'who was the high priest during that year', not 'who was the high priest [only] that year'. 'That year' is significant because it is the year of Jesus' death, not a year of office.

**11.50. You do not understand that it is better for you to have one man die for the people than to have the whole nation destroyed:** These words have been interpreted in a number of different ways, as:

1 *A genuine prophecy:* This is based on the popular understanding that the high priest could predict the future (11.51).

2 *An ironic statement:* The high priest speaks, but is unaware of how relevant his words really are. While some think there were Jewish traditions that the death of a righteous person had a saving power (2 Samuel 20.22; Jonah 1.12–15; 2 Maccabees 7.38; 4 Maccabees 18.4), there is a world of difference between saying this if you are willing to give up your own life, and saying it when you are offering another's life.

3 *A utilitarian or expedient political statement:* Jesus' death is simply the lesser of two evils.

No decision needs to be made about which is correct.

**11.51. He did not say this on his own, but being high priest that year he prophesied that Jesus was about to die for the nation:** For priests predicting the future, see Numbers 27.21; Philo, *Special Laws* 4.192; Josephus, *Jewish War* 3.352. Caiaphas is not aware of any such revelation or power.

**11.52. To gather into one the dispersed people of God:** John's interpretation of Caiaphas' words includes humanity outside Judaism. Such an interpretation will link Jesus' death to both the OT prophets (Isaiah 11.10–12; Jeremiah 3.17–18) and the Good Shepherd (10.16).

**11.54a. Jesus therefore no longer walked about openly among the Jews:**
John suggests that Jesus is aware of the plot to kill him.

**11.54b. A town called Ephraim in the region near the wilderness:** The
exact location is unknown.

 Interpretation

If the Good Shepherd (10.1–22) is a parable about the narrative, the events
at Bethany show Jesus acting as the Good Shepherd. He risks his life by
returning to Judaea (10.11–15; 11.8, 15–16) to find Lazarus, whom he will
call by name (10.3; 11.43) and restore to life (10.10; 11.44).

While Mary and Martha are known in the Synoptics, Lazarus is absent. This has prompted some commentators to suggest that this story
is fictitious: the meaning of his name may point to a symbolic person
(11.1). If this was a symbolic name, we would expect John to translate
it for the benefit of his readers (1.8, 40, 41), but he does not. This
may therefore indicate a real person. Many critics simply assume that
Lazarus was a real person: some suggest that the discovery of a tomb
near Bethany with the names Mary, Martha and Eleazar is an indication
of historical accuracy. Others use the parable of Lazarus and the rich
man (Luke 16.9–31), but to base history on a parable is a very weak
argument.

Supporters of the idea that Lazarus is fictional also argue that it is unthink-
able that someone who would have been as famous as Lazarus in Christian
circles should be absent from other writings of the early Church. However,
the Synoptic Gospels also record a number of recoveries from death in
which those healed are not named (Mark 5.21–43; Matthew 9.23–26;
Luke 7.11–17), and these people do not appear in later traditions either. There is good reason for this. If people who were raised could be
readily seen, it might make critics of emerging Christianity ask why the
risen Jesus could not be shown to them. To avoid such criticism, the
early Church might have played down the importance or identities of
those who were raised in this way. John may also avoid further mention of Lazarus to stop people concentrating on a sign: a foundation
for belief which he distrusts.

In many ways, this is a story more about the sisters than Lazarus.
The bulk of the episode centres on the responses of Martha and Mary
to Jesus – they are indicators of different stages of faith. Mary is the
strongest role-model and will appear again (12.1–8; 20.1–18). We do
not even hear of Lazarus' subsequent faith or fate: he may simply vanish
from sight because of fear for his life (12.9–11). This makes his response
in faith weaker than that of the man born blind (9.38). Lazarus is not
presented as a role model or exemplar; he may even be a distraction
(12.9). John does not mention him again because he serves no further
purpose.

The section moves through a number of misunderstandings (Appendix H):

1 Jesus' delay (11.5, 21, 32);

2 outcome of the journey (belief, not death, 11.8, 15–16);

3 sleep and death (11.11–13);

4 resurrection (Jesus replaces the general resurrection, 11.24–25);

5 titles of Jesus (11.27–28);

6 life and death (11.25, 39).

Number 1 involves both Martha and Mary, who think that Jesus' delay has meant he is no longer able to assist Lazarus; the audience is shown that they confuse human thinking with the purposes of God (11.4). Numbers 2–3 show that the disciples think of Jesus as being at the mercy of his opponents rather than master of his own destiny (7.7), and that they are heading to martyrdom with him, when in fact they will be led not to death, but belief (11.15–16). Numbers 4 and 5 involve Martha. Number 6 shows that Jesus has the power he has previously claimed (10.28–29).

Martha is not a positive model of faith, but rather is someone who tries to shape faith in her own terms:

- She makes her own way to Jesus rather than being called (11.20).

- She criticizes Jesus for his delay (11.21).

- She fails to see Jesus himself as the source of faith, but views him only as one who may ask favours from God (11.22).

- She presumes to teach Jesus about the general resurrection, failing to recognize him and his power (11.25).

- She addresses him using titles, but, like others before her (1.41, 49, 50–51; 3.1–11; 4.25–26, 29, 42), is muttering pious phrases rather than truly believing. She slips back to calling him the Teacher (11.28), despite her claim that she has long believed in him (11.27). Her behaviour is reminiscent of Peter at Caesarea Philippi: at one moment seemingly gifted with a vision, the next hopelessly confused (Mark 8.27–33; Matthew 16.13–23; Luke 9.18–25).

- She still believes that Lazarus has died (11.39).

Mary provides a better example, but she too is yet to become a model of faith. In her favour:

- she responds to Jesus' calling her (11.29; see 10.4);

- her greeting of Jesus shows a better understanding of his status (11.32; see 9.38);

- her faith is based on Jesus himself (11.32; compare Martha in 11.22).

However, she is yet to become a model of faith because:

- her mourning betrays her lack of confidence (11.32);

- her mourning may show that her attitude is still shaped by peer pressure (11.33);

- she does not fully trust Jesus, whereas the audience know that the miracle will happen (11.2; 12.3; see further Moloney, *The Gospel of John*, pp. 327–330 on Martha and Mary).

The raising of Lazarus (11.38–44) shows Jesus' power over death, and also fulfils the promises of 5.21. It does not indicate the nature of the resurrection. Technically, it is a resuscitation: Lazarus is returned to this life, this level of existence, not resurrection life or eternal life (3.15). Lazarus has been resuscitated, but will die again (some see this indicated by the binding cloths, which he still wears, but which Jesus will leave behind, 20.5–7). The story may function like a *qal-wahômer* argument (3.12; 7.23; 10.34): if Jesus has power over physical death, he also has power over spiritual death. The nature of resurrection life will be explored in the post-Easter stories (20.1—21.23).

Is Lazarus' raising really the reason that Jesus' opponents now try to kill him? If Lazarus is fictional, it is also fictional that he was raised from the dead, and this cannot be an historical reason for the death of Jesus. If it is historical, there are further complications. Raising the dead broke no laws. Indeed, raising the dead was an approved action when performed by the prophets (1 Kings 17.17–24; 2 Kings 4.18–37).

If Jesus' actions provoke the plan to kill him, it is because they identify his acts with 'the glory of God' (11.40). He has moved from claiming to be the Good Shepherd to doing what the Good Shepherd does. This combination of claim and action makes the heightened atmosphere possible: the charge would be blasphemy, particularly the claim that 'you sent me' (11.42). This is not new. The claim has been made before (5.36), but the words and actions are more explicit than ever.

No single action may, however, provoke the charges against Jesus. Scot McKnight and Joseph Modica have edited a collection of essays which enumerates seven different reasons for Jesus' fate (*Who Do My Opponents Say That I Am?: An Investigation of the Accusations against Jesus*): he was a law-breaker, someone who was demon-possessed, a glutton and drunkard, blasphemer, false prophet, king of the Jews, and illegitimate son.

Furthermore, John adds even more reasons, which are not primarily concerned with either blasphemy or purely religious matters. Politics matters; here the concern is that the response to Jesus is in danger of upsetting the status quo, and causing Roman intervention. Politics, as much as religion, causes the death of Jesus; this is made explicit by the role of the Romans in the Passion (18.28—19.38). Anyone who does not see how politics and religion are mixed together has failed to understand the death of Jesus. As Archbishop Desmond Tutu has said, 'Those who say that politics and religion should not mix do not read the same Bible as I do.'

Jesus' emotions are also important in this episode. Whether his reactions (11.33, 35, 38) express either frustration or grief, they reveal his depth of feeling. In contrast to images of impassive and emotionless deities far removed from human affairs, John shows a god whose love for his people is very emotional.

This is not simply a story in which Lazarus is raised from the dead: it addresses issues of faith through the example of the disciples, Martha and Mary. Jesus acts out his identity as the Good Shepherd. This will contribute to his own death (10.11–15; 11.50), but will bring life to others.

 STUDY SUGGESTIONS

## Word study

**1** If 11.33, 38 means that Jesus was deeply angry or frustrated, does it change your understanding of this passage?

## Review of content

**2** Compare the accounts of Jesus raising the dead (Mark 5.21–43; Matthew 9.23–26; Luke 7.11–17; John 11.38–44). Make one list of the similarities, and another of the differences between the stories. Do the accounts make the same point about Jesus?

**3** Is it right to describe Lazarus as a supporting character in this episode?

**4** Explain the difference between resuscitation and resurrection.

**5** List all the points which the story of Martha, Mary and Lazarus shares with the Good Shepherd parable.

**6** Look at McKnight's and Modica's list of possible complaints about Jesus. How many of them can you find in John's Gospel?

## Discussion and application

**7** Consider Jesus' relationships with Martha and Mary. Do they challenge the conventions in your context?

**8** Do Christians in your context deny that the Bible has anything to do with politics? Are they right? How could we change their views?

# John 11.55—12.50

## Jesus' last Passover

 Summary

The Passover of 11.55 sets the scene for the last feast which Jesus will spend with his followers before his death.

### 11.55—12.11: Events at Bethany

 Introduction

Mary's actions at dinner provoke Judas to start his betrayal of Jesus, and signify that Jesus will die soon.

 Notes and commentary

**11.55a. The Passover of the Jews was near:** The approach of the Passover is mentioned three times, twice here and in 12.1. The repetition may signify the importance of the coming feast.

**11.55b. Many went . . . to purify themselves:** Pilgrims for the feast had to be ritually pure (Numbers 9.10; 2 Chronicles 30.17–18; Acts 21.24–27).

**11.57. The chief priests and the Pharisees:** Opposition to Jesus unites rivals (7.45, 48; 11.47).

**12.2a. There they gave a dinner:** This was an evening meal. The narrative does not make clear whether this happens soon after the raising of Lazarus. There may well have been a considerable gap between the two visits to Bethany.

**12.2b. For him:** Jesus is in a privileged place as guest of honour.

**12.2c. Martha served:** Martha's actions are inferior to those of Mary (Luke 10.38–39).

**12.3a. Pure nard:** This is a sweet-scented, light oil (Song of Solomon 1.3, 12).

**12.3b. Anointed Jesus' feet and wiped them with her hair:** It was customary for feet to be washed on arrival at the beginning of the meal. Mary's actions exceed conventional hospitality and show a shocking degree of intimacy.

**12.4. Judas Iscariot:** Judas has already been introduced as the one who will 'betray' Jesus (6.64, 6.71).

**12.5. Why was this perfume not sold for three hundred denarii?:** Judas gives the most expensive pricing of the perfume to support his claim about waste and extravagance (Mark 14.5).

**12.6. He said this . . . because he was a thief:** John gives the most negative reading of Judas' motives. Mark 14.4 has a number of those present complaining; in Matthew 26.8, the disciples complain.

**12.7. She bought it . . . for the day of my burial:** Mary's anointing of Jesus anticipates his burial. Mary may have kept some nard for the burial, but Nicodemus will tend to Jesus' corpse (19.39–40).

**12.9. They came . . . also to see Lazarus:** This is the last appearance of Lazarus.

**12.10. The chief priests planned to put Lazarus to death as well:** There is a plot to kill Lazarus, but no mention is made of Lazarus' future or fate. This second plot shows that Caiaphas' words in 11.50 are untrue.

 Interpretation

The events in this section keep the same order as Mark 14.1–11 and Matthew 26.1–14: the plot to arrest Jesus, the anointing at Bethany, Judas' decision, and the anticipation of Jesus' burial. Only John identifies the woman as Mary. His account has a particular resonance, shaped by the preceding events. Mary, who has responded to the Good Shepherd (11.29–33), now shows the depth of her faith and understanding, anointing him in recognition of his imminent death for his sheep (10.15).

John differs from the Synoptics in how he assesses Judas' motives. In Luke's portrayal of Judas, Satan is the motivating force (Luke 22.3). Mark and Matthew give a more positive view of Judas' motives: a sense of injustice at the apparent neglect of the poor and their needs. Indeed, it has not been unknown for Christians to use this verse as a justification for their own conspicuous consumption. However, to do this means ignoring the considerable amount of Gospel teaching which prompts concern and action on behalf of the poor and even says it is a way of serving God (Matthew 25.31–46). Indeed, the three Gospels seem to imply that the woman's actions are the exception rather than the norm, and that such behaviour is only appropriate as an anticipation of Jesus' burial (Mark 14.8; Matthew 26.12; John 12.7). This is a far cry from justifying extravagance.

Lazarus is mentioned, but does not appear again. We can only speculate about his fate. He may vanish from the narrative because he takes away attention and faith from Jesus, and turns the focus on the miraculous rather than Jesus himself. Signs have been rejected as a firm basis for faith (2.24; 6.26): to believe because one has seen the risen Lazarus rather than trusting in Jesus would be a backwards step.

The plot to kill Lazarus (12.10) shows that Caiaphas' optimistic hope (10.50) is ill-founded. If people still believed the high priest had the ability to predict the future, he is shown to be a false prophet. Already a second death is deemed necessary. His hopes that violence might be minimalized to one death are already gone. The first small steps to control opposition are considered effective and deemed an acceptable price to pay, but gradually violence begets more violence. Those who trust violence to solve their problems find that violence comes to control them. Our world is sadly all too familiar with this reality. John lays bare the false hope that violence and expediency can be limited.

 STUDY SUGGESTIONS

### Word study

**1** Is 'betray' the right word to describe Judas' actions?

### Review of content

**2** Why did Lazarus vanish from the history of the early Church, or from John's narrative?

**3** Compare John's treatment of Judas with that of the other Gospel writers. Is it right to blame Judas for betraying Jesus?

### Discussion and application

**4** Has the use of violence to maintain power ever spiralled out of control in your context?

**5** Do you find the intimacy shown by Mary embarrassing? Why? How might this challenge our attitude to intimacy with Jesus and God?

## 12.12–19: The entry to Jerusalem

## Introduction

Jesus enters Jerusalem for the last time. The reaction of bystanders raises questions about his identity.

## Notes and commentary

**12.12a. The next day:** This was the fifth day before the Passover (12.1).

**12.12b. Coming to Jerusalem:** Although the Passover had originally been celebrated by households, it had become a pilgrimage feast celebrated in Jerusalem (2.13).

**12.13a. They took branches of palm trees:** Willow, palm and myrtle branches were waved by the singers at festivals.

**12.13b. And went out . . . shouting, 'Hosanna!':** The Hebrew word means literally 'Give salvation now!' – a common praise word used at festivals.

**12.13c. Blessed is the one who comes in the name of the Lord – the King of Israel:** The quotation comes from Psalm 118.26. In this period, it was sung at the Festival of Booths and in the *Hallel* psalms (Psalms 113—118) at Passover. The psalm possibly had an eschatological dimension, anticipating a new exodus to be led by the Messiah. Such a meaning is intended by John, who has placed it after the messianic Good Shepherd parable and the Bethany narrative.

**12.14. Jesus found a young donkey:** Mark 11.7 and Luke 19.35 place Jesus on a colt (a young animal). Matthew 21.7 has him on a colt and a donkey. John omits the finding of the animal (Mark 11.1–6; Matthew 21.1–3; Luke 19.29–34).

**12.15. Do not be afraid, daughter of Zion. Look, your king is coming, sitting on a donkey's colt:** John and Matthew 21.5 both quote Zechariah 9.9, but use different versions of the verse. Matthew's is closer to the OT texts than John's. The verse is used of the Messiah in later rabbinic Judaism.

**12.16. His disciples did not understand these things at first; but when Jesus was glorified, then they remembered that these things had been written of him and had been done to him:** John sees Jesus' death and glorification as key to understanding his full significance (2.22; 6.39).

**12.17. The crowd that had been with him when he called Lazarus out of the tomb . . . continued to testify:** This verse exists in a longer version which says that their testimony is only about the raising of Lazarus. They do not believe properly in Jesus (12.37–41).

**12.18. It was also because they heard that he had performed this sign that the crowd went to meet him:** Witnesses to the raising of Lazarus (11.38–44) have caused the crowd to come.

**12.19a. The Pharisees then said to one another:** The Pharisees were a significant Jewish school or sect (1.24; 3.1; 7.45; 8.13; 9.13; 11.46).

**12.19b. The world has gone after him:** The strength of popular feeling is repeated (12.11). Ironically, this anticipates 12.20 (11.50, 52).

 ## Interpretation

John's version of the entry to Jerusalem shares features with the accounts in the Synoptic Gospels (Mark 11.1–11; Matthew 21.1–11; Luke 19.29–40), but is placed after the meal in which Jesus is anointed for burial, not before. The event shares features of the triumphs of ancient Rome reserved for military victors as well as royal processions. There are warnings that this is not a typical triumph, as the crowd will soon drift away (12.37).

The word 'humble' is often used in interpretations of the event, but what sort of humility would put Jesus at the centre of such a scene as this? It is hard to see a model of humility here, especially since, for John, Jesus deserves the glory appropriate to God and the respect due to the Messiah. The symbolism of the donkey spurns conventional hopes (1 Kings 4.26; Isaiah 31.1–3) for a triumphant nationalistic warrior-king Messiah: it is a beast of burden, not a warhorse (Zechariah 9.10; Sirach 33.24; Proverbs 26.3), and the Messiahship of Jesus is not restricted to one nation (12.20).

The passage makes it clear, in John's view, that Jesus thought he was the Messiah. To suggest that Jesus was not aware of what he was doing as he entered Jerusalem, and how others might perceive them, suggests a lack of knowledge which does not fit with his portrayal as a skilled teacher (rabbi). This leads to the conclusion that he knew what he was doing. Although John describes Jesus as speaking openly (Appendix I), his actions are not always clearly understood (2.22; 12.16; 13.7). Thus, John resembles the Synoptics: Jesus acts ambiguously, so that people have to make up their own minds about him. They are not given simple, direct information which forces them to believe in him, but ambiguous statements and actions to help them make a choice about believing in him or not. The following different views of Jesus need to be kept separate:

1 Jesus' own understanding of his actions: he is the Messiah (this assumes a basis in history);

2 who the crowd thinks he is: he might or might not be the Messiah;

3 John's understanding: Jesus is the Messiah.

A note needs to be added about responsibility for Jesus' death. John never says that the crowd, and by implication, the whole Jewish people are responsible for this. In his version, it is not the crowd that is involved in the condemnation of Jesus, but only a few powerful people (18.31, 38; 19.6, 7, 12, 14). This makes John very different from Matthew 27.26 in which the crowd takes responsibility for the death of Jesus. Matthew's version has been used to justify the persecution of the whole Jewish people throughout Christian history – even today. John's Gospel, so often blamed for inciting anti-Semitism, in fact limits historical responsibility for Jesus' death to some opponents within Judaism and the Roman authorities, not the whole people.

 STUDY SUGGESTIONS

**Word study**

1 Compare 12.15, Zechariah 9.9 and Matthew 21.5. Write the verses out in parallel columns and see which words or phrases are shared or different.

**Review of content**

2 Did Jesus believe he was the Messiah?

**Discussion and application**

3 Read Matthew 27.24–26. Is there any reason why people should uphold anti-Semitism based on that passage, in light of John's alternative?

4 Do we make generalized statements which blame whole peoples for what has gone wrong? Should we do this, based on John's treatment of the crowd?

## 12.20–36a: Remarks about death

 Introduction

Jesus follows the excitement of the entry into Jerusalem with unsettling remarks about his death.

 Notes and commentary

**12.20. At the festival were some Greeks:** This could mean Greeks (non-Jews) or Greek-speaking Jews (7.35). Here the phrase is more likely to

157

mean Greeks than Greek-speaking Jews. Their inclusion is a sign of the hour (12.23), the world (12.19), and the gathering in of the nations (11.52) – the signs of the Last Days in the prophetic traditions.

**12.22. Philip . . . and . . . Andrew:** Both were among the first to follow Jesus (1.40, 43).

**12.23a. Jesus answered them:** 'Them' is most likely Andrew and Philip. The Greek text does not make clear whether Jesus is speaking to the disciples or the Greeks (12.20).

**12.23b. The hour:** This term is used often to talk of the time of Jesus' Passion and death (2.4; 4.21; 7.6, 8, 30; 13.1; 17.1).

**12.23c. The Son of Man:** This is a complicated Aramaic phrase which may refer to the Messiah (1.50–51).

**12.24. A grain of wheat:** Grain is used as a symbol of the resurrection (1 Corinthians 15.36–37, 42–45) and as an action which produces good results (Mark 4.8; Matthew 13.9; Luke 8.7).

**12.25a. Those who love their life lose it, and those who hate their life . . . will keep it:** 'Life' here means physical life, although the word is used commonly for 'soul' – a Greek rather than Jewish understanding. The verse is an antithesis contrasting 'love' and 'lose' with 'hate' and 'keep'.

**12.25b. Eternal life:** This is a favourite phrase in John for the results of faith (3.15).

**12.26a. Whoever serves me must follow me, and where I am, there will my servant be also:** Discipleship (the meaning of 'follow', 1.37–39) is linked to service (13.12–15) and guarantees continual presence with Jesus.

**12.26b. Whoever serves me, the Father will honour:** Honour is due to the Father (5.23; 8.49), but here we see that God will give it in return (Mark 8.34–35).

**12.27. My soul is troubled:** The word 'soul' here suggests an emotional element. 'Troubled' can also be translated 'disturbed'. Epicurean philosophers used this word to describe being affected by stress, worry or distress. This may underline the humanity of Jesus over against Docetic theology (1.14).

This verse performs a similar function to the Gethsemane episodes (Mark 14.35; Matthew 26.38–39; Luke 22.42) and resembles Psalm 42.5. Jesus' distress appears short-lived, and is quelled by remembering the purpose of his mission, and submitting to the Father's will. Doing the Father's will is the way to be free from distress (13.21).

**12.28a. Glorify your name:** Jesus makes a request for God to glorify his own name.

**12.28b. A voice came from heaven:** This is the first time in John that the Father speaks from heaven.

**12.28c. I have glorified it, and I will glorify it again:** This refers to Jesus' previous works, the events unfolding and his future exaltation.

**12.29. Thunder . . . An angel:** Both were signs of a message from God in the ancient world (Genesis 19.1; 2 Chronicles 32.21; Acts 12.7–11, 23; Revelation 6.1; 10.3–4; 14.2; 19.6).

**12.30a. This voice has come for your sake:** The crowd has not understood the voice. The voice spoke for their sake, but they have been unable to comprehend even a direct message from the Father himself.

**12.30b. Not for mine:** Jesus' momentary distress had passed even before the Father spoke (12.27–28).

**12.31a. Now is the judgement of the world:** This judgement is about the whole of the created world, not just the judging of individuals.

**12.31b. The ruler of the world will be driven out:** The ruler, who is the devil or Satan (6.70; 7.20; 8.44; Appendix J) will lose authority over this world, but not yet (13.27).

**12.32a. I, when I am lifted up:** This includes both death and glory, and may echo Isaiah 52.13.

**12.32b. Will draw all people:** Jesus repeats the universal dimension of his mission (10.16; 11.52; 12.20).

**12.33. He said this to indicate the kind of death he was to die:** John adds a clear reference to the crucifixion.

**12.34a. We have heard . . . that the Messiah remains for ever:** Jesus' previous remarks meet with opposition: his description of the Messiah does not meet with contemporary expectations based on Scripture. They expect a Messiah who will descend (Daniel 7.13–14), not one who will be lifted up to heaven like Enoch (Genesis 5.24) or Elijah (2 Kings 2.1–12).

**12.34b. How can you say that the Son of Man must be lifted up?:** This means: 'Only you say this' – only Jesus has described the Messiah in this way – and the people think this is worthless compared to the authority of the law.

**12.34c. Who is this Son of Man?:** This is not a challenge to identify the person who is the Son of Man (12.23–26). It is a rhetorical question which refers back to the previous statement about the kind of Messiah who is expected. We might make an extended paraphrase to get the sense of the question: who is this lifted-up Son of Man of whom you speak? The implied answer is: there is no such Son of Man as you describe.

**12.35a. Jesus said to them, 'The light is with you for a little longer. Walk while you have the light, so that the darkness may not overtake**

you': Light and darkness are common metaphors for belief and unbelief (Appendix B; 1.3–9); 'walk' is a metaphor for 'live' (6.66). Jesus warns that the anticipated events will take place soon (7.33; 13.33; 14.19; 16.16).

**12.35b. You do not know where you are going:** Living without right faith implies a lack of direction and moral purpose.

**12.36. While you have the light, believe in the light, so that you may become children of light:** This section concludes with a focus on judgement, on whether people choose darkness over light.

 Interpretation

The Greeks (12.20) indicate this is the beginning of the messianic age (10.16; 12.23; Isaiah 56.6–8). This does not mean that all God's promises in their fullness have now been completed: there is still work to be done. Yet this marks a decisive point in John's inaugurated eschatology (3.2). The promise that the ruler of this world will be driven out (12.31) lies in the future. Satan will enter Judas (13.27), but Jesus says that Satan's activity is ultimately futile. Some later theologians would use this to define a theology of the atonement (the explanation of how Jesus brings about salvation) by describing Jesus as bait on a fish-hook (Rufinus of Aquileia): Satan takes the bait, and kills Jesus thinking that this will secure his power, when, in reality, it will bring about the opposite. Much modern theology uncomfortable with talk of the satanic considers this an historical relic.

At the heart of Jesus' teaching lies a claim about reversal: that things are not what they seem to be. In his analysis, the quest to cling to this life and world is ultimately destructive, and eternal life is found in death and the rejection of what is considered so important. Satan becomes the ultimate spokesman for common sense: we've always done it that way. Jesus challenges this: conventional ways of making sense of the world are to be put aside (see 'The good news according to John', p. 7). Understanding this is to walk (live) in light; failing to understand is darkness. Paul says much the same in 1 Corinthians 1.18–25. This even includes status, honour and shame: belief in Jesus offers the chance of honour and glory from God, which is much better than human conventions (12.26).

This episode includes elements familiar from the Synoptic traditions not yet seen in John. His account of Jesus' baptism (1.33) does not contain a heavenly voice (compare Mark 1.11; Matthew 3.17; Luke 3.22), nor is there a Transfiguration scene (Mark 9.2–8; Matthew 17.1–8; Luke 9.28–36). As in the Synoptics, the heavenly voice follows a prediction of death (Mark 8.31–9.1; Matthew 16.21–28; Luke 9.21–27). If the Transfiguration scenes anticipate the glory of God, John also promises that the Father will be glorified in the future when Jesus is lifted up (12.32). The contrast of past and future is John's way of indicating an inaugurated eschatology (3.2). John's combination of the predictions about death and glorification has strong similarities to the Synoptic Gospels.

John describes Jesus' soul being troubled (12.27). Being free from stress or disturbance was one of the goals of both Stoic and Epicurean philosophers, even if they disagreed on what exactly this meant. The statement that Jesus was troubled might be a sign of weakness, were it not for the fact that his distress is quickly overcome. He is the master, not the victim, of his emotions. Greek philosophers sought ways to live well. From this perspective, John makes Jesus like the great philosophers of the ancient world. They did not always conform readily to the conventions of the communities in which they lived, and made this a sign of honour. Socrates gained a heroic reputation for his unconventionality. Jesus' non-conformism is a sign of honour to John and his audience. The philosophers also gave positive advice on how to live the good life. Often these could be summed up in terse statements which look simple, but require a lot of effort to work out in detail: 'know yourself', 'nothing in excess', and so on. Jesus' constant reference to being at one with the Father suggests that this might be the goal of Christian ethics: easy to say, but difficult to practise.

The passage summarizes points raised previously: it embraces Jesus' claim to be the Messiah, the definition of the Messiah, the authority on which such expectations are based, and concludes with an argument which shows that none of the arguments brought forward by Jesus have changed the minds of his opponents. They conclude that Jesus is someone who is merely voicing his own opinions. His final remarks sum up their position: they do not know as much as they think – enlightenment, true understanding and the opportunity to live life to its fullest are passing them by.

 ## STUDY SUGGESTIONS

### Word study

**1** 'Grain of wheat' (12.24). Do the Synoptic writers use grain imagery to talk about dying and death as John does?

### Review of content

**2** Is 'doing the Father's will' a good summary of Jesus' teaching about ethics? Is there an alternative that you prefer? Why?

### Discussion and application

**3** Are we tempted to reject visionary figures and their new ideas because they do not fit our conventions? What might John teach us about such behaviour?

**4** Should Christians be masters or victims of their emotions?

## 12.36b–50: Peroration

 Introduction

This peroration (final part or climax of a speech or piece of writing) marks the end of the Book of Signs. It gives a summary of key themes and explains why Jesus has not been accepted by many. His rejection is the fulfilment of prophecies from Isaiah (12.36b–43), and represents a failure to trust God (12.44–50).

 Notes and commentary

**12.36. After Jesus had said this, he departed and hid from them:** Jesus vanishes from public view until the time of his arrest.

**12.37. Although he had performed so many signs in their presence, they did not believe in him:** Signs are again shown to be an inadequate basis for faith.

**12.38. This was to fulfil the word spoken by the prophet Isaiah: 'Lord, who has believed our message, and to whom has the arm of the Lord been revealed?':** The quotations from Isaiah show:

- Jesus is part of a divine plan revealed in Scripture, and he is the fulfilment of these words;

- Rejection of Jesus by God's people is to be expected; it does not mark the frustration of God's work (1.10).

These arguments contest the claim made earlier by Jesus' opponents (12.34) that his teaching is not based in the law (Scripture).

The quotation comes from Isaiah 53.1 – part of the longer Suffering Servant passage (Isaiah 52.13—53.12) which describes both the Servant's fate and the unbelief of the people of Israel. The verse links Jesus as Messiah with the Isaiah traditions, and confirms the unbelief of God's people. Such unbelief is seen as part of a longer tradition which begins with Exodus (Deuteronomy 29.2–4) and continues until the time of John. The text is also used this way in Romans 10.16 and 1 Peter 2.22–25.

**12.40. He has blinded their eyes and hardened their heart, so that they might not look with their eyes, and understand with their heart and turn – and I would heal them:** The quotation comes from Isaiah 6.10, which shows that God's way of dealing with his people is unchanging: judgement is a key theme. John's interpretation is closer to the Hebrew text. God ('He') hardens their hearts. John also shifts the focus from hearing to seeing; hearing is better than seeing 'signs' (Appendix C; 2.11, 23–25; 12.37).

**12.42a. Many, even of the authorities, believed in him:** Not even all of those who are powerful and important oppose Jesus; Nicodemus is an example of one who is more sympathetic to Jesus' message (3.1; 7.50–52).

**12.42b. They would be put out of the synagogue:** Many argue that this reflects the later tension between the followers of Jesus and other worshippers at the synagogues (7.35).

**12.43. For they loved human glory more than the glory that comes from God:** The verse is literally translated as: 'For they loved human glory than the glory of God.' The two phrases may mean 'the glory *given by* people [or God]' or 'the glory *due to* people [or God]'. In either case, what is human has taken the place of God.

**12.44. Whoever believes in me believes not in me but in him who sent me:** Belief in Jesus assumes that the believer also has trust in the God who sends him (5.23–24, 30; 6.29, 38–39, 50–51).

**12.45. Whoever sees me sees him who sent me:** Jesus is the way in which God reveals his nature (5.19, 37–38; 6.46).

**12.46. I have come as light into the world:** Light is a symbol for belief and faith (8.12).

**12.47–48. I do not judge anyone who hears my words and does not keep them . . . on the last day the word that I have spoken will serve as judge:** These verses repeat earlier teaching about salvation and judgement (3.16–18).

**12.49. I have not spoken on my own, but the Father who sent me has himself given me a commandment about what to say and what to speak:** This repeats the earlier theme that Jesus' words are identical to the Father's (7.16–18; 8.26, 28).

**12.50. His commandment is eternal life:** Hearing and responding to God's word is the source of eternal life (3.15).

 Interpretation

If 12.35–36 focuses on the choice to walk in darkness or light, 12.44–50 provides a summary of who is to be judged. As in 3.16–18, the word which Jesus speaks acts as a catalyst, prompting judgement. Jesus' focus is on saving the world (12.47).

The citations from Isaiah repeat a question which has already been asked (3.19; 8.37, 44; 9.38): how can God's rule or sovereignty be reconciled with human responsibility? John has seen this tension: how can people have any moral responsibility or choice if God's rule is all-powerful and all-directing? He resolves the two by saying that a new beginning is possible (3.5). This new beginning is given by a positive response to Jesus, and is connected to the principle that people condemn themselves, and that Jesus is the focus of salvation or eternal life. The second Isaiah citation, in John's hand, is not a general statement about God, but a statement about Jesus: he is the one who makes these things happen. Condemnation comes not because God has planned it, but from a failure to recognize Jesus and so accept what he offers; people prefer the things of the world to the things of God (12.43).

This section warns about crude generalizations. The crowd is a mixed bunch, which includes those who believe in Jesus (12.42). John even includes authority figures in this group (12.42). John is an astute psychologist and gives a number of reasons why people who believe may fall away. Fear of expulsion is not confined to the ancient world. Even in today's world, believing in Christ may mean expulsion from family or clan, and lead to victimization. Mission strategies which focus on converting individuals do not always reckon with the power that family or peer pressure may have (4.43–54), or even the relentless pressure which some societies and cultures put on their members to conform. John does not stop there. He does not see those who deny Jesus as victims; he is acutely aware that, for some, it is their own hopes and aspirations ('they loved human glory', 12.43) which prevent them from believing and living properly. John uses these realities to encourage his audience; they are meant to be an antisociety which has a different set of foundations from the spirit of the age.

The point of 12.43 appears very similar to 12.26, in which Jesus has already made promises about honour. It can refer to either concerns with one's own honour (like 12.26) or giving glory to someone else. The fundamental problem raised by Jesus includes both of these. The end result is the same in either case: those who deny Jesus are really concerned with human affairs rather than the things of God. Elsewhere, the Scriptures call this idolatry. This is not just the worship of graven images (Exodus 20.4), but what happens when any person, object, ideology or worldview takes the place which properly belongs to God in shaping our beliefs and actions. Idols are not just bad or evil entities – even good things can become idols when given the focus which properly belongs to God, even churches, religious institutions, or a particular interpretation of the Bible. Some extreme cults show clearly the danger of the first, like David Koresh and the Branch Davidians at Waco, and phenomena like apartheid, the second. However, they can also appear in more subtle forms in mainline churches and ideologies.

# STUDY SUGGESTIONS

## Word study

**1** Compare the texts of Isaiah 53.1 and 6.10 with John's versions. Are they exactly the same?

## Review of content

**2** Write your own summary of the Book of Signs (chapters 1—12).

## Discussion and application

**3** Are Christians in our societies under the same pressures as the believers mentioned by John (12.42–43)? Do these pressures come from others, or are they of our own making?

**4** Does our religious life concentrate on human issues and lose sight of God's glory?

# Theological essay 2
## Signs in John's Gospel

VOON CHOON KHING

A sign is something that points to a reality beyond itself. In and of itself, it is not the whole truth, but a visible, tangible means to the end purpose for which it exists. In John's Gospel, the miraculous 'signs' (*semeia*) are meant to point people to see Jesus for *who* he really is – the Christ – by *what* he does. Generally, the purpose of 'signs and wonders' in the Gospels is to signal the in-breaking of God's kingdom as inaugurated by the coming of Jesus Christ into the world.

Before we can apply our theological knowledge about signs to our local contexts, we need to understand how John weaves this theme into his Gospel. In this essay I hope to shed light on John's textual movements between the 'I am' sayings or *words*, and the *works* of Jesus.

As we reflect about the meaning of signs, honest and truthful interpretation of the Scriptures is critical, particularly in my own country of Malaysia. Like many Asian contexts, it is a melting pot for religious and cultural pluralism. Claims of miraculous signs and wonders are commonplace in Malaysian society, where folk religions, traditional faith healings, occultism and spiritual power encounters have permeated

165

every sphere of life: social, medical, economic, political, educational and commercial, as well as the field of entertainment. They are not just confined to explicitly religious activities. Being functional and pragmatic people, even Christians have unwittingly adopted these elements into their faith. For example, they may read horoscopes for guidance, consult traditional faith-healers for healing and exorcism of haunted places, and use Christian symbols as amulets in their cars. Being situated in a multi-cultural, multiracial and multi-religious nation, the churches in Malaysia are not immune to the impact of pluralistic culture. Malaysian Christians also face the challenges of the New Age movement, the impact of electronic culture, and the syncretistic elements in mainstream religions. In order to discern the signs of our times in our local contexts, with a view to moving towards greater faithfulness to the gospel of our Lord Jesus Christ, let us glean from John's Gospel the meaning and purpose of signs in God's economy.

## Seven signs and seven 'I am' sayings of Jesus

The clue to understanding the signs in John's Gospel is found in his Prologue and in his concluding remarks: 'In the beginning was the Word (*Logos*), and the Word was with God, and the Word was God' (1.1). Our Creator wants to communicate with his children. God not only wants to communicate with *word*, but also with *works* through Jesus, because word must be confirmed with concrete actions to authenticate Jesus' true identity. 'Jesus did many other signs in the presence of his disciples . . . But these are written so that you may come to believe that Jesus is the Messiah, the Son of God, and that through believing you may have life in his name' (20.30–31). In other words, the panoramic introduction with the grandeur of God's glory as manifested in the Word made flesh (1.14) leaves us with the question of discernment: how many can see this glory as the Gospel unfolds before us?

Word and works must go together as demonstrated in John's Gospel, where the seven signs alternate with the seven 'I am' sayings of Jesus to validate his claim of divine origin. The greatest sign in John's Gospel is the Word become flesh, but the darkness in the world veils our recognition of Jesus as the Son of God. No matter how spectacular and awesome the sign of Emmanuel was as the fulfilment to the prophecy in Isaiah 7.14, not all will believe. Therefore, the seven signs are to help people to gradually discern and recognize Jesus as the Saviour of the world as the Gospel unfolds. Unlike us, who have never met the human Jesus, the people in Jesus' generation knew him as an ordinary son of a poor carpenter. How could he be the long-awaited Messiah who would deliver them from their enemies? Understandably, they had a hard time discerning and believing Jesus' claim that he was the Son of God. Even his cousin, John the Baptist, wondered whether Jesus really was the Messiah or whether he should wait for another. Jesus pointed to his signs and wonders as evidence of his divine origin and mission (Matthew 11.2–5).

A recurrent imagery in John's Gospel is light, and such words as 'see', 'know' and 'believe' convey the idea of receptivity, perception, understanding, personal acceptance and response to God's self-revelation as the divine drama unfolds on our human stage. The implication is that not all who see will necessarily know and believe. Signs are subject to interpretation, and may evoke all kinds of reaction as is the case with Jesus, however powerful his signs were. Let us examine each of the signs and notice their outcome.

## The first sign: turning water into wine at Cana (2.1–11)

The purpose of Jesus' first miraculous sign was to reveal his glory, and the impact on the disciples was to put their faith in Jesus. Many others also did so, except those who challenged Jesus to prove his authority for his outrageous act in chiding the religious authority for using the Temple for corrupted trading. Miraculous signs indicate that God is with the miracle worker, and Jesus introduced Nicodemus to the real miracle of being born again into the kingdom of God (3.1–8).

Most Christians in Malaysia are first-generation believers who were brought up in diverse religious backgrounds. The real miracle of being born again into the kingdom of God to reveal God's glory is most visible in our transformed life and characters. Like the first Christians, we face many challenges in a pluralistic cultural society, such as participation in religious social customs and rites at weddings or funerals. There is no magical solution of changing water into wine when confronted with corruption, injustice, or the seductive temptations of money, sex and power in a developing nation. We can only put our faith in Jesus for him to change the water of our broken humanity into the wine of the Holy Spirit, so that his glory can be revealed in and through us in the marketplace.

## The second sign: the healing of the royal official's son in Cana (4.46–54)

Jesus knew that unless people saw miraculous signs and wonders, they would not believe. It is also a common belief today that seeing is believing. In this second miraculous sign of healing, Jesus only spoke the word from a distance (4.50, 53). This sign confirms the power of Jesus' word in restoring wholeness in the same way that God, by his spoken word, brought about the original Creation out of nothing. Likewise, I witness the power of God's word in healing and restoring lives in the ministry of pastoral counselling among our seminarians.

With the advance of modern medical investigative tools, Western-trained doctors are able to detect, diagnose and treat many diseases. However, not all Malaysians trust the efficacy of Western medicine, for either physical or psychological disorders. Many still resort to traditional medicine or faith healing with promises of a cure, especially in cases of terminal disease. Unscrupulous practitioners have exploited the situation and cheated many of their life-savings. Christians can also be gullible to such deception when we are undiscerning, and ignorant of the biblical understanding of healing as salvation, *shalom* and eternal life. Many claims to miraculous healing are not subjected to the scrutiny of medical scientific verification. When a miraculous healing is genuinely a work of God to reveal his glory, the medical profession are able to confirm it, and this is not a sign of lacking faith in God. That was true in my former work with the mentally ill. The psychiatrists could see and affirm their patients' improvement and reduce their medications accordingly.

## The third sign: the healing of the paralysed man (5.1–18)

Jesus knew that the man by the Pool of Bethesda had been paralysed for 38 years, yet he still asked him a very curious question: 'Do you want to be made well?' (5.5, 6). Any of us who has worked with the chronically sick would appreciate the wisdom of Jesus' question. A deep sense of helplessness, futility, despondence, hopelessness and despair can erode a sufferer's dignity and paralyse his or her will to live. It is so easy for the chronically sick to become angry and bitter, and to adopt a victim mentality. If that man had lost his will to live, even Jesus could not have performed the third sign of healing, because Jesus wanted to restore his whole person. Jesus commanded him: 'Stand up, take your mat and walk' (5.8). If one has been sick for 38 years, the challenge to get going and be responsible for one's own life could be overwhelmingly insurmountable. Understandably, many would choose to stay paralysed physically, emotionally and mentally to justifiably resume a lifestyle dependent on charity.

There is more to Jesus' third sign than healing the paralysed man, as is evident in the consequent murderous plot by the Pharisees. Because Jesus healed, they tried all the harder to kill him; not only was he breaking the Sabbath, but he was even calling God his own Father, making himself equal with God (5.18). For Jesus, this third sign was part of doing his Father's work which testified that the Father had sent him (5.36–38) and thus authenticated his identity as the Messiah, the Christ, the Sent One. In other words, his work was his testimony about his divine origin. However powerful and impressive his miraculous signs were, Jesus also knew that not all would accept and believe that he was the long-awaited Messiah, because he knew that not all had the love of God in their hearts (5.41–42). That did not deter Jesus from continuing his messianic mission on earth, because he lived in total submission to his Father's will, in tune with the Father's ways and timing.

In our diverse religious and cultural Malaysian society, there are many effective agencies of mercy and charity. The motives are rather mixed and not readily discernible. All social agencies are vulnerable to the pitfalls of financial gain, mismanagement, pseudo-spirituality or ethical malpractice. Unless Christian agencies are motivated by the same Holy Spirit with discernment in embodying the gospel of our Lord Jesus Christ, our pastoral care and ministry will be gullible to these pitfalls, and unsustainable as authentic witness in the face of opposition or persecution. The reality is that the people in the street care primarily about their basic needs for food and shelter, as seen in the next miracle of feeding the 5,000.

## The fourth sign: the feeding of the 5,000 (6.1–15)

Although the miraculous signs created curiosity among the people about Jesus as the messianic prophet, and they intended to forcefully make him king, Jesus knew that the crowd looked for him because of the loaves, and not because of the miraculous signs (6.15, 26). That became an occasion for Jesus to teach them to work for food that lasts to eternal life, which he gave by simply believing that God the Father had sent him. Unconvinced, they demanded an equivalent of the heavenly manna received through Moses. So Jesus pointed them to himself as the true bread from heaven (6.32, 35) – the first 'I am' saying.

Malaysia is blessed with diverse culinary gastronomic delights from its rich multiracial heritage, not to mention the cosmopolitan fast-food culture. One Western visitor commented that Malaysians eat only one meal a day – continuously throughout the day! The god of the belly has truly captivated the devotion of the populace. The rise in lifestyle diseases like diabetes, cardio-vascular and digestive disorders is the sign of our times. Simultaneously, there is also the phenomenal increase in health-food outlets, as well as a huge market for fitness and massage centres. Humans are pragmatic in our attempts to secure satisfaction for life materially, while missing out on the eternal life that Jesus brings. The challenge for the Malaysian Church is to be a living sign for Christ, pointing people to the true, living Bread. When churches are united in holistic ministry, providing food for the homeless on the streets of our cities, health care for the poor, tuition for school dropouts, rehabilitation for drug or gambling addicts, and a hospitable place to worship together across social boundaries, many come to know that true, living Bread.

## The fifth sign: the storm on the lake and Jesus walking on water (6.19–21)

While his disciples were still reeling from the excitement of the feeding miracle, Jesus sprang a surprise on them, demonstrating his power over Creation. After all, it is through the Word that all things were made (1.3).

Faced with the complexity of personal, national and global changes, we can only learn to discern the living Word in the midst of the overwhelming storms of life. As a developing nation, Malaysia is confronted with many challenges and pitfalls. The current economic and political climate signals a gathering storm that threatens to break out at the instigation of unscrupulous characters through racial or religious unrest. Being in the minority, Malaysian Christians are discerning the coming of Christ with courage and faith. The Christian Federation of Malaysia urged the government, in the spirit of the latest theme of '1 Malaysia', to resolve issues like corruption, seditious political statements with racial overtones, and sectarian religious values that discriminate and destroy the unity in diversity of our nation (Press Statement, Merdeka and Malaysia Day, 27 August 2010). Ironically, it takes a catastrophic tragedy to unite nations of all faiths in prayer, as we saw when flight MH370, a Malaysian national airliner, disappeared mysteriously on 8 March 2014, and when another Malaysian passenger plane, flight MH17, was shot down over Ukraine on 17 July 2014.

## The sixth sign: the healing of the blind man (9.1–41)

The miracle of healing a man blind from birth confirms Jesus as the Son of Man who originated from God. The arrogance of the Pharisees blinded them so that they could not see the truth about Jesus. Many in the crowd believed, while others had divided opinions because of Jesus (7.3–5, 21–22, 31, 43). Against such a background, Jesus proclaimed, 'I am the light of the world' (9.5), followed by 'I am the gate' (10.7) and 'I am the good shepherd' (10.11, 14).

Spiritual blindness is not so easy to detect, given the plethora of multiple religious choices in Malaysia. At one end of the spectrum are the diverse religious rites and festivals of pious devotees, performed as social customs for personal blessings of wealth and health. At the other end are the religious fanatics who champion violence in defence of religion. Religious sensitivity is a reality that people live with in Malaysia. In December 2007, the Internal Security Ministry forbade the editors of the Catholic weekly *The Herald* to use the word *Allah* for God, as a condition of renewing its publishing permit, for fear of confusing Muslims. *The Herald* filed a lawsuit against the government. On 31 December 2009, the Malaysia High Court overturned the ban, ruling that the Catholic Church has a constitutional right to publish the word *Allah* in *The Herald*. In the wake of the court decision there were arson attacks on nine Christian churches, a convent and a Sikh temple. The government appealed against the court's decision, and the final verdict from the Federal Court on 23 June 2014 was to ban *The Herald* from using *Allah*. It is into this situation that members of the Malaysian Church are called to live as signs pointing to Jesus the Christ by our forgiving, non-retaliating response to the attacks.

## The seventh sign: the raising of Lazarus from death (11.1–53)

The last and seventh sign, that of raising Lazarus from the dead, validated Jesus' claim: 'I am the resurrection and the life' (11.25–26). As Jesus' ministry coupled with his claim to divine origin gained momentum, so did the intensity of opposition and hostility from the religious authorities, as they moved towards exterminating him (11.53). Their hard-core unbelief fulfilled Isaiah's prophecy as an indictment against them (12.37–38). This is the fallacy of 'seeing is believing', whereas to believe is a matter of choice, an act of the will. Indeed the 'seed' of God's word takes root in a person's heart depending on how the heart receives it, as in the parable of the sower.

Living in the midst of religious pluralism in Malaysia, Christian converts from ancestral religious traditions are accustomed to the challenges of 'proving' the uniqueness of Jesus Christ. This last sign points to the ultimate sign of Jesus' own death and resurrection – the distinctive feature of Christianity that demonstrates that Jesus is not just a way, a truth and a life among many religious systems, but *the* Way, *the* Truth, and *the* Life by which we know God as Father. Only through Jesus Christ can we have such a relationship of love with God as our Father. Both the sayings and the miracles of Jesus point to his divine origin as the Son of God and the Son of Man, being one with the Father. Therefore, Jesus' last saying: 'I am the true vine' (15.1, 5), reiterates our essential need to nurture this love relationship with the Father through him and in the community of believers who love one another across racial boundaries. How else can the resurrection and life of Christ be visible in any local church if not in the transforming power of God's love in and through us? It is this transforming power of our risen Lord in our lives that has brought many elderly parents to see that Christianity is not a Western religion that turns their children away from filial piety, but rather leads their sons and daughters to honour them. Moreover, Jesus Christ can deliver them from their fear of death into eternal life.

The primary purpose of the miraculous signs is that we may believe that Jesus is the Messiah, the Son of God, and so have life in his name (20.30–31). Now, our Lord Jesus Christ has left us as his sign in the world, wherever we are, so that people can discern God in and with us, through our word and work.

# Part 2

## The Book of Glory

The teaching of Jesus in chapters 1—12 has shown that two themes are key to God's plan: death and glory. In chapters 13—20, this teaching is lived out by Jesus. In chapters 13—17, he teaches his disciples in detail about the demands and blessings of obedience to the Father. In his Passion and death (chapters 18—19), he shows the ultimate example of such obedience. Chapter 20 shows the ultimate reversal; obedience ends not in death, but eternal life. 'Lifting up' is exploited for a double meaning: death by crucifixion, which demands being lifted up on the cross, and being glorified. Who is glorified? The short answer is: everyone on whom Jesus' death has a positive impact: the Father, who is given glory by Jesus as he does the Father's will; Jesus, through his obedience to the Father's will; and all who respond positively by believing in Jesus (12.26).

Printed and bound by CPI Group (UK) Ltd, Croydon, CR0 4YY

14/04/2025

14656910-0001

# John 13.1—17.26

# The Last Meal and farewell speeches

 Summary

Jesus, like other great thinkers of the ancient world, passes on his teaching to his disciples at a meal. After enacting a parable of discipleship and service (13.1–19), he will predict the tragic events which are to take place (13.20–37). In the farewell speeches which follow, Jesus will outline the blessings of being a disciple (14.1–30), the relationship between disciples and God, and the gift of the Spirit (15.1—16.33). He finishes by commending his disciples to the Father in prayer (17.1–26).

## 13.1–20: Washing the disciples' feet

 Introduction

Jesus takes an action which was part of meal practice and hospitality (12.3; 13.5) and invests it with new meaning for his disciples.

 Notes and commentary

**13.1a. Before the festival of the Passover:** The meal takes place before the Passover begins and cannot be the Passover *Seder* (meal).

**13.1b. His hour:** This term often refers to the Passion (2.4; 4.21; 7.6, 8, 30; 12.23; 17.1).

**13.1c. Depart from this world:** This means to leave the time and place of human activity. 'World' has no moral dimension here (1.4).

**13.1d. To the end:** This means all of the following: 'to the end of his life', 'beyond what is imaginable', 'perfectly'.

**13.2. The devil had already put it into the heart of Judas son of Simon Iscariot to betray him:** The devil has decided to use Judas as the means to destroy Jesus (1 Samuel 29.10; Job 22.22; Appendix J). Judas has already been introduced as a close disciple who will betray Jesus (6.71).

**13.3. Jesus, knowing that the Father had given all things into his hands, and that he had come from God and was going to God:** Jesus is confident about his fate. The stress of 12.27 has passed.

**13.5. He poured water into a basin and began to wash the disciples' feet and to wipe them with the towel that was tied around him:** For footwashing, see 12.3. Jesus now performs the most menial task of service as a sign for the disciples. It includes a number of possible ideas:

- an act of humility to prepare for the cross, which the disciples must live out in their own lives;
- purification as preparation to receive forgiveness;
- a ritual comparable to baptism which gives an identity to the disciples;
- an act which welcomes the disciples into God's household.

**13.7. You do not know now what I am doing, but later you will understand:** The events which follow help to explain Jesus' actions (2.22; 12.16, 23).

**13.8. Peter said to him, 'You will never wash my feet.' Jesus answered, 'Unless I wash you, you have no share with me':** Peter refuses Jesus' ministry, probably because he thinks the action is inappropriate: a teacher would not usually wash his pupils' feet. Jesus' reply challenges Peter's thinking.

**13.9. Lord, not my feet only but also my hands and my head!:** Peter makes an impulsive and extravagant reply. He will do this again later (13.37).

**13.10a. One who has bathed does not need to wash:** Some think that 'bathed' means 'participated in total immersion and baptism', which indicates complete forgiveness. Others argue that 'wash' is simply an alternative for 'bathe', and there is no significant difference in meaning. In that case, the verse may not be about baptism.

**13.10b. Except for the feet:** This phrase is missing from some ancient manuscripts. If the words were added later, they suggest that sins committed after baptism could be forgiven. Alternatively, if these words were removed later, it meant that Christians who took them out thought that sins committed after baptism could not be forgiven.

**13.10c. You are clean:** This may imply that the disciples have undergone purification rituals demanded by Passover practice. The word 'cleansing' is used of ritual purification (2.6; 3.25; 15.2–3).

**13.11. For he knew who was to betray him; for this reason he said, 'Not all of you are clean'**: See 6.70 for an earlier prediction.

**13.13. You call me Teacher and Lord**: 'Teacher' was an honorific title (1.38). 'Lord' was a title with a number of meanings (4.10–11): it may be translated 'master', implying superiority, or 'Lord', implying that Jesus is God.

**13.14. So if I, your Lord and Teacher, have washed your feet, you also ought to wash one another's feet**: The disciples are to copy Jesus' behaviour. This is a *qal-wahômer* argument (3.12; 7.23; 10.34).

**13.15. For I have set you an example**: The word 'example' is used for models of humility (Hebrews 4.11; 8.6; 9.23; James 5.10; 2 Peter 2.6) and for the deaths of martyrs (2 Maccabees 6.28; 4 Maccabees 17.22–23; Sirach 44.16).

**13.16. Very truly, I tell you, servants are not greater than their master, nor are messengers greater than the one who sent them**: For the phrase 'very truly', see 1.51. This verse, which has the feel of a proverb, warns that Jesus is not superior to the Father, and that church leaders are not superior to Jesus (15.15, 20). It also warns that they may well be treated as he is treated (15.18–26).

**13.17. If you know these things, you are blessed if you do them**: Blessing relates to eternal life (3.15; 10.10).

**13.18. To fulfil the scripture, 'The one who ate my bread has lifted his heel against me'**: The quotation comes from Psalm 41.9. Eating together was a sign of loyalty (2 Samuel 9.7–13; 1 Kings 18.19; 2 Kings 25.29). The rabbis took the psalm to refer to Ahitophel's conspiracy (2 Samuel 15.12). The word used here is the same as in 6.54–55, and may refer back to that passage and the Eucharist. On the other hand, it might simply be a synonym (13.10) with no such cross-reference.

The quotation shows that Jesus is already aware of Judas' treachery, which is intensified by their intimacy. Jesus has been placed in the messianic tradition of David because he is opposed by enemies and friends (Psalm 41.9).

**13.19. I tell you this now, before it occurs, so that when it does occur, you may believe that I am he**: The literal translation reads: 'I say this to you now before it happens, so that, when it happens, you may believe that I am.' This suggests that Jesus' divinity is to be revealed (8.58).

Foreknowledge (knowing what will happen before it takes place) is a characteristic of God (Ezekiel 24.24; Isaiah 41.26; 43.10; 46.10; 48.3, 5–6).

**13.20. Whoever receives me receives him who sent me**: This statement repeats the theme of unity between Jesus and the Father (12.44–49).

Interpretation

The timing of the Last Supper (13.1–2) provokes a major debate about historical accuracy. John presents Jesus' final meal with his disciples before the Passover feast starts, while the Synoptics (Mark 14.12; Matthew 26.17–18; Luke 22.7–8) describe the Passover meal or *Seder*. For many, the Synoptic date is the historically correct one. John's date is shaped by his theology (19.31). However, a number of reputable scholars think John is more accurate. Their arguments include:

- Paul connects Jesus' death with the Passover, not the *Seder* (1 Corinthians 5.7; 11.23–30; 15.20).

- Chronological references do not refer to the Passover lamb symbolism: they are historical rather than theological. The timing and the lamb references would be linked if they were theological.

- The Synoptic date depends on hypothetical Aramaic texts, not the Greek ones we possess.

- Locating the whole interrogation and execution within the Passover feast is unlikely.

- Barabbas would be more likely to be freed before the Passover.

- Mark's account would make it unlikely for Jesus to celebrate his meal in the house of someone holding his own celebration.

'John versus Synoptics' is too simple. The traditions used by the Gospel writers were themselves divided: Matthew 26.17, Mark 14.12 and Luke 22.15 all include material which does not fit precisely with the dating of 14 Nisan (Eve of Passover: Day of Preparation) and 15 Nisan (the date of the Passover, Numbers 28.17), but are closer to John's chronology. So the dates given in the Synoptics are muddled. The date was a problem even in the early Church; the Quartodeciman controversy is an early example (see the Introduction). A firm or clear record would not permit such a dispute.

Nor can the debate be presented as 'Synoptic historicism versus Johannine theologizing'. John has historical interests within his narrative, and the Synoptic association of the meal with the *Seder* is not 'pure history', but is also a theological interpretation.

Some suggest that different calendars are the root of the problem. Such theories share a common weakness: it is impossible to say that Jesus used a different solar calendar from the lunar calendar used for the feast, as did other sectarians (for example, the Qumran communities). His presence in Jerusalem itself distances him from their rejection of the Temple cult and calendar. Others have suggested an 'illegal' Passover, but there is neither evidence nor criticism of Jesus doing so. A better solution suggests

Passover is not a precise date: Josephus can use Passover to describe the period leading up to Passover, 14 Nisan, the Passover itself, *and* the feast of Unleavened Bread (*Jewish War* 2.10; also Leviticus 23.5–8; Numbers 28.16–18; Deuteronomy 16.4). We might compare this to how Christmas is used in English: to mean 25 December or the holiday season.

Where does this leave us? It means we cannot accept as completely accurate the timing given by either John or the Synoptics, but it does allow us to say that all four Gospels locate Jesus' last meal and death at the time of the Passover season. They are not alone in this; Paul makes the same claim in 1 Corinthians 5.7.

The Passover, in John, focuses on the death of Jesus on the Day of Preparation, which means there is no historical connection to the Passover meal. John gives no description of the meal which Jesus celebrates with his disciples, beyond some incidental details. For John, the significant meal celebrated by Jesus is the feeding of John 6.1–15, not the *Seder*.

There is no need to make a choice between the Synoptic focus on the *Seder* or the Johannine messianic banquet. It is a case of 'both . . . and . . .' rather than 'either . . . or . . .'. This has been seen in 6.4: John invests the feeding miracle with the significance of the Passover by setting it at that point in time.

John uses the setting of the meal in a way typical of much philosophical and rhetorical writing of the time. The discourses which follow function as a farewell address (13—17) in which the dying hero leaves a significant message for his followers. Examples are found in both Jewish (*The Testaments of the Twelve Patriarchs*) and Greek literature, and include:

- predictions about death;

- warnings of future persecution;

- encouragement for ideal behaviour;

- a final commissioning;

- a guarantee of faithfulness (often from God);

- a doxology.

Jesus' address starts with a series of predictions (13.21–38), and then a number of discourses. The first are interrupted by the disciples (Appendix H).

From Plato's *Symposium* and Xenophon's *Memorabilia* to Plutarch's *Moralia* and Athenaeus' *Deipnosophistae*, a meal or banquet provided the setting for expositions of the school's core values. Behaviour and conversation at the banquet exemplify the beliefs and practices of the school. John uses the meal in precisely this way: what really matters is the behaviour and teaching described. Here, the washing of the disciples' feet exemplifies the teaching about service (12.26).

The Farewell Discourse presented in these chapters does not record the exact words (*ipsissima verba*) of Jesus himself. The Supper Narratives in the

Synoptics are significantly different. Yet the discourse is not completely invented: it shares many themes with the Synoptic traditions. Here, this material has been put together in an idealized form which allows, so to speak, the historical Jesus to speak directly to John's audience – and us.

The footwashing also has a familiar shape, including a misunderstanding (Appendix H). Peter persists in arguing with Jesus (13.8). Given this form, the episode is not simply a discussion of hygiene (13.9).

The washing and its commentary (13.14–16) provide an acted alternative to words spoken by Jesus at the Last Meal in Luke 22.24–27. Both Gospel writers see Jesus' behaviour as something to be copied by the disciples. In terms of honour and shame, Jesus is spelling out a radical departure from the conventions of society, and inverting the usual codes. He does this by invoking the practice of reciprocity: that what he (the patron) does for his clients (disciples) demands some service from them in return.

The washing narrative is sometimes said to refer to baptism, but others would reject this. Often scholars may be importing what is important to them. To see what John might have meant we need to look at the points which come out of the story itself:

- Washing will only be understood in light of events to come (13.7).

- Washing is necessary for discipleship (13.8).

- The disciples are those who have bathed (13.10).

- Bathing has not guaranteed cleanliness for all (13.10).

- Judas is the model for the one who is unclean (13.10–11).

- Those who claim Jesus as Lord and teacher (13.13) are right.

- They need to follow his example (13.14–15).

- Discipleship is not to be a source of pride (13.16).

- To live out such beliefs will make a positive difference to the disciple (13.17).

- What is about to happen will confirm what Jesus has just done and said (13.18–19).

Those who argue that the washing is a reference to baptism note that 'bathe' is frequently used of baptism in the NT (1 Corinthians 6.11; Acts 22.16; Ephesians 5.26; Titus 3.5; Hebrews 10.22; Revelation 1.5). However, modern linguistics warns us that words are not like bricks which can be joined in various combinations and always have the same meaning. Where and how the word is used (2.6) contributes to the meaning. It is not possible to say that 'bathe' must always mean 'baptize'.

We do not need to interpret the passage as referring to baptism. John offers a middle way between two extremes. He rejects the views of those who would claim that, since they have accepted Jesus' offer, they are perfect now (1 Corinthians 4.8) through Jesus' death and are thus free from any ethical commands; this is sometimes called libertarianism. He also rejects the views of those who believe that all sin committed by those who have accepted Christ's offer is unpardonable. John is realistic: even those who have faith can sin again, but sin can still be forgiven as long as those who have fallen maintain their faith. In the text as we have it, there is still pardon for future sins, and a need for an ethic or rule of life and behaviour (13.12–17).

A final word about the meaning of 'clean'. What does Judas do that makes him unclean? Christians have wrestled with this problem in a number of related arguments, but they boil down to this: is there any sin that cannot be forgiven? Scripture seems to suggest that there is: the sin against the Holy Spirit (Mark 3.29; Matthew 12.32; Luke 12.10). Hebrews 6.1–8 and 12.14–28 explore the question. Read superficially, these verses suggest that any sin may be unforgivable. In reality, they are only talking about what is called apostasy, that is, the wilful turning away from Christ. Apostasy allows no forgiveness because the one who turns away separates himself from the one who gives salvation. It is a commonplace of theology that we are saved by Christ (Acts 4.12), not by our own works or faith. Someone who keeps faith in Christ still is able to receive what has been promised. Only those who freely choose to distance themselves from Christ separate themselves from his salvation (3.16–18). This is the tragedy of Judas; he rejects Jesus for Satan (13.2), and so distances himself from the only Saviour.

Jesus is depicted as a hero approaching death. He has anticipated his death, shown his knowledge of what has gone on, imparted advice about the future to his disciples, warned of the likelihood of their being treated as he is, and given guarantees that will confirm his foreknowledge and his own identity.

 STUDY SUGGESTIONS

## Word study

1 Read 13.10. Do you think 'except for the feet' is more likely to have been added or removed?

2 Compare the literal translation of 13.19 given above with your usual translations. Does the literal translation give the verse a different sense?

## Review of content

3 Do you think the washing refers to baptism?

4 Do you agree that apostasy is the only unforgivable sin?

## Discussion and application

**5** Do Christians live out Jesus' teaching about service? Is service a visible sign of church life and structures, or is there a concern with power and greatness?

**6** Do Christians ever forget that they are not greater than their Master? How?

---

## 13.21–38: Predictions to the disciples

 Introduction

Jesus gives the disciples hard news about his own fate and their reactions to what will happen.

 Notes and commentary

**13.21a. Jesus was troubled:** The word suggests stress or emotional turmoil (11.33; 12.27). This may echo Psalm 42.12.

**13.21b. In spirit:** This may indicate the depth of Jesus' feeling. Some think this is better translated 'by the Spirit', to suggest it drives him on, but this does not fit the picture of Jesus controlling his own destiny (12.27).

**13.21c. And declared, 'Very truly':** 'Declared' is literally 'bore witness': the formality of a legal witness or a solemn declaration as well as frank speaking (Appendix I). This is confirmed by the introductory phrase, 'Very truly . . .' (1.51).

**13.21d. One of you will betray me:** Judas' role has already been introduced (6.64).

**13.23. One of his disciples – the one whom Jesus loved – was reclining next to him:** The place next to Jesus would imply a privileged position according to ancient conventions: he has a better place than Simon Peter (13.24) who is placed further away. This position may stress the authority of the Beloved Disciple as a reliable source. Some scholars, notably Jeremias, have suggested that 'reclining' indicates the *Seder*. However, this might be a posture for a ceremonial or formal meal (Luke 24.30; Mark 16.14), and is even used of an ordinary meal (Luke 17.7). John is not talking about the *Seder*.

**13.26. 'It is the one to whom I give this piece of bread when I have dipped it in the dish.' So when he had dipped the piece of bread, he**

**gave it to Judas son of Simon Iscariot:** Jesus' identification of his betrayer fulfils the Scripture quoted in 13.18. The phrase translated 'piece of bread' (NRSV) need not include bread. The giving of such a piece of food by the host was a sign of favour and, therefore, highlights the seriousness of Judas' betrayal (compare the kiss of Judas in Mark 14.45; Matthew 26.48–49; Luke 22.47–48).

**13.27a. After he received the piece of bread:** Judas' role as a disciple has already been made clear (6.70; 12.4–7; 13.11).

**13.27b. Satan:** The term 'Satan' (original meaning: 'accuser', Zechariah 3.1–2; 1 Chronicles 21.1) is only used here; elsewhere 'the devil' is used. See Appendix J.

**13.27c. Entered into him:** Compare Luke 22.3. The Synoptic writers use the phrase for demonic possession (Mark 5.12; Luke 8.30). Judas has abandoned Jesus and his authority or patronage.

**13.27d. Jesus said to him, 'Do quickly what you are going to do':** Jesus remains in control (6.15; 7.6, 8; 8.20; 12.27), despite Satan manipulating Judas.

**13.29. Some thought that, because Judas had the common purse, Jesus was telling him, 'Buy what we need for the festival':** Judas holds the common purse for the group around Jesus (12.6). The verse shows the gap between Jesus' knowledge and the disciples' thoughts.

**13.30a. He immediately went out:** The dramatic pace of the story is speeding up.

**13.30b. And it was night:** This comment may include both timing and symbolism: night stands for evil, ignorance and unbelief.

**13.31a. Son of Man:** This is a complex Aramaic phrase which sometimes functioned as a title (1.51).

**13.31b–32. God has been glorified in him. If God has been glorified in him, God will also glorify him in himself and will glorify him at once:** The clause 'If God has been glorified in him' is missing in some early manuscripts, but is retained by most commentators. If retained, the tenses reflect John's inaugurated eschatology (3.3): the glorifying has happened and will also happen in the future. Glory is revealed both in the public ministry and in Jesus' Passion, death and resurrection (7.39; 12.16, 28).

**13.33a. A little longer:** The events Jesus is about to foretell will happen soon (7.33; 12.35; 14.19; 16.16).

**13.33b. You will look for me; and as I said to the Jews so now I say to you, 'Where I am going, you cannot come':** The idea that Jesus will go away, and others will not be able to follow, has already been discussed in the Book of Signs (7.34; 8.21). Peter will recognize that this is about discipleship (13.36–37), not just geography.

**13.34. I give you a new commandment, that you love one another. Just as I have loved you, you also should love one another:** This is a typical command found in farewell addresses and banquet talks (13.1–17).

**13.36. Peter said to him, 'Lord, where are you going?' Jesus answered, 'Where I am going, you cannot follow me now; but you will follow afterwards':** The meaning of 'follow' may include martyrdom.

**13.37–38a. Peter said to him, '. . . I will lay down my life for you.' Jesus answered, 'Will you lay down your life for me?':** The phrase 'lay down' is used when referring to the Good Shepherd (10.11), and is similar to Caiaphas' expression (11.50). It has an overtone of sacrificial death or martyrdom.

**13.38b. Before the cock crows, you will have denied me three times:** This detail is found in the Synoptics (Mark 14.30–31, 72; Matthew 26.33–35, 74–75; Luke 22.31–34, 60–62). The Romans counted cock-crow between 12 midnight and 3 a.m.

 ## Interpretation

Jesus' dealings with Judas show that Jesus is the master of his own destiny. Even if Judas is possessed (13.27), it is still Jesus who is in control of the sequence of events which will take place. He also knows exactly what is going on: Psalm 41 (13.18) refers to events already passed (6.1–15, 70) as well as this meal (13.27). This is immediately contrasted with the disciples' (wrong) interpretations of what is happening (13.28): they have no clue of what Judas is about to do. Jesus' status as a leader, as one who knows his own (10.14), is confirmed by his superior knowledge.

The association of Judas and Satan rings differently for Christians from various cultures. For some, Satan is a redundant figure: they do not believe in such an entity. Others may strip him of personal characteristics and acknowledge the way in which evil takes up an existence and power of its own – a psychological fact. Others will accept the existence of such a person as self-evident. What happens when one speaks with a person whose views are very different from one's own, and for whom such issues may be hugely disturbing? To dismiss the other's belief as wrong, especially if it is deeply held, simply is ineffective. Also, it is more important to focus on dealing with the effects of such belief on a person than to argue metaphysics. The passage here is a reminder of God's ultimate control of what happens in the world, and that freedom from oppression or malevolent influences is found in God and Jesus, whatever one's worldview.

If Satan is the one who drives Judas, is he (Judas) absolved from responsibility or culpability for his actions? Is 'The devil made me do it' any more of an excuse in cultures which recognize the supernatural than 'I can't help it – I'm an addict' or 'It's part of my genetic make-up' in cultures with medical or psychological worldviews? The role of Judas suggests that it is not. If such excuses were justified, there could theoretically be people who stood in no need of God's love or a saviour's work, purely and simply because they could say in all honesty that they have done nothing wrong. In John, all people stand in need of God's help because they are not perfect, but they are never beyond the love of God. Everyone is loved and lovable in the divine economy; no one is unloved or unlovable.

The commandment to love asks the disciples to live out that kind of love in their dealings with one another. It tells them to take up the work of God himself (3.16–18). It makes behaviour a primary way to recognize God and his people. Love is the defining characteristic of the people of God. There is a warning for us in the narrative: Peter ignores completely Jesus' words about love, and focuses on martyrdom (Appendix H). Nevertheless, this has a positive dimension: Peter has understood that Jesus is talking about discipleship (indicated by 'follow', 1.37, 38–39, 43; 13.36) rather than geography, despite his opening remarks (13.35). However, Jesus knows Peter better than he knows himself, and is aware that Peter does not yet have the qualities necessary for the kind of discipleship demanded. Peter's boast will prove to be vain (18.15–18, 25–27). Only later will Peter understand the kind of love which leads to death (21.15–19).

 STUDY SUGGESTIONS

### Word study

1 Read 13.23 and check the references to reclining. Is it right to criticize the view that reclining must mean the *Seder*?

2 Compare 13.38 with the Synoptic accounts of Peter's betrayal. Are the differences important?

### Review of content

3 How do you understand 13.27? What does this say about Judas' actions?

4 Read Mark 12.28–34; Matthew 5.43–48; 22.34–39; Luke 6.27–36; 10.25–37. Does their teaching make the love ethic as significant as it is in John?

### Discussion and application

5 Have Christians made love the characteristic that best defines them? Does your church build its identity on other forms of behaviour?

6 Would our neighbours know we are Christians by the way we love one another?

## 14.1–31: Farewell Speech 1

 Introduction

Earlier scholars thought that these speeches were originally spoken word for word by Jesus. Increasingly they are seen as a Farewell Speech, like that given by Socrates and other famous people in the ancient world: they reflect Jesus' teaching but were really composed by the author of the Gospel. This does not make them any less important. William Temple called the speeches 'the most sacred passage even in the four gospels' (*Readings in St John's Gospel*, vol. 2, p. 307). In this first part of the speech, Jesus stresses again his relationship with the Father, and promises the gift of the Spirit.

 Notes and commentary

**14.1a. Do not . . . be troubled:** See 11.33; 12.27; 13.21.

**14.1b. Believe in God, believe also in me:** The Father and Jesus have equal status. For 'believe', see Appendix B.

**14.2. Many dwelling places:** The word translated 'dwelling place' may mean a temporary resting place for the righteous until the day of judgement (*1 Enoch* 22.1–6), but it is also used for their dwellings after the final judgement (*1 Enoch* 39.1–14). The word shares the same root as 'stay' (1.32, 38, 39; 7.27; 8.31, 35; 9.41; 12.34, 46) and suggests a permanent state of affairs. 'Many', which may be correctly translated as 'all', challenges conventional ideas about limited good or blessings which might allow only room for a few in the afterlife.

**14.3. If I go and prepare a place for you, I will come again and will take you to myself, so that where I am, there you may be also:** This verse contains a promise that the disciples will be with Jesus in the future, but not after the resurrection (16.16–22).

**14.4. You know the way to the place where I am going:** This suggests that Jesus will depart and return (indicating an inaugurated eschatology, 3.3). Elsewhere, the idea of his continuing presence is stronger (3.15, 16, 36; 4.14, 36; 5.24–25; 6.27, 35, 47, 56, 63; 10.10, 28; 11.25–26; 12.50).

**14.5. Thomas said to him, 'Lord, we do not know where you are going. How can we know the way?':** Thomas' question repeats the previous confusion about Jesus' destination (11.16).

**14.6. I am the way, and the truth and the life:** This is a construction which both describes who Jesus is, and also suggests that he is God, by using 'I am'; for this construction, see 6.35. 'Truth' (1.14) and 'life' (eternal life, 3.15) explain 'way' (Mark 12.14). Other Jewish groups might call themselves 'the way', notably in the Dead Sea Scrolls (1QS 8.12–16; 9.17–18; CD 1.3). This may have shaped emerging Christianity's view of itself (Acts 9.2; 19.9, 23; 22.4; 24.14, 22). 'Truth' indicates that Jesus gives people freedom from their fears and weaknesses – a positive outcome of judgement (3.16–18).

**14.7. If you know me, you will know my Father also. From now on you do know him and have seen him:** This verse repeats the shared identity of Jesus and the Father (8.19, 38, 58; 10.31, 39).

**14.8–9a. Philip said to him, 'Lord, show us the Father, and we will be satisfied.' Jesus said to him, 'Have I been with you all this time, Philip, and you still do not know me?':** Philip was one of the first disciples (1.43; 12.21). Jesus reminds him of what he should know already.

**14.9b–11. Whoever has seen me has seen the Father . . . Do you not believe that I am in the Father and the Father is in me? . . . Believe me that I am in the Father and the Father is in me:** This passage repeats the claim that the Father is recognized by seeing Jesus (5.19–38).

**14.12. The one who believes in me will also do the works that I do and, in fact, will do greater works than these, because I am going to the Father:** Jesus promises that the disciples will do greater work after he has gone: his work will not stop because he is elsewhere. The promise may give encouragement to John's audience in difficult times.

**14.16a. Another Advocate:** While the primary meaning of the Greek here is 'advocate', others include concepts like intercessor, an angelic being (Qumran) or a consoler (Job 16.2; Isaiah 40.1). The word suggests a legal trial or court, with advocates for God's people pitted against an accuser (13.27). The use of 'another' indicates that the Spirit is the second Advocate – the first is Jesus (14.13–14; 1 John 2.1).

**14.16b. To be with you for ever:** This second Advocate will be with the disciples in Jesus' absence.

**14.17a. The Spirit of truth:** The Spirit communicates truth (1.14) and is God's continued presence in the world. He is related to Jesus who is 'the truth' (14.6).

**14.17b. He abides with you, and he will be in you:** The original Greek is difficult and three different interpretations are given:

1 Jesus is with the disciples, and the other Advocate will be with them after his departure.

2 The Spirit abides in the disciples and is present within them.

3 The Spirit abides in the community and will be present within the individual believer.

We do not need to choose one of these, because they can be combined. We should think of the work of the Advocate as shared by Jesus and the other Advocate, just as they share truth: the Spirit-Advocate carries on the work of the earthly Jesus. Raymond Brown's summary is worth quoting:

> the Spirit of Truth is a Paraclete precisely because he carries on the earthly work of Jesus. The Paraclete/Spirit will differ from Jesus the Paraclete in that the Spirit is not corporeally visible and his presence will only be by indwelling in the disciples. The OT theme of 'God with us' (the Immanuel of Isa vii 14) is now to be realized in the Paraclete/Spirit who remains with the disciples forever.
>
> (*The Death of the Messiah*, vol. 2, p. 644)

**14.18. I will not leave you orphaned; I am coming to you:** The giving of the Advocate and the return of Jesus (14.16) means that the disciples will never be left apart from God ('orphaned').

**14.19a. In a little while:** This refers to Jesus' imminent death (12.35; 13.33; 16.16).

**14.19b. The world will no longer see me, but you will see me:** The world does not see Jesus and the Advocate, but the disciples recognize them (14.17). Through them the disciples have life (i.e. eternal life, 3.15).

**14.19c. Because I live, you also will live:** This statement repeats that Jesus is the source of life (3.15).

**14.20. On that day you will know that I am in my Father, and you in me, and I in you:** This verse repeats the promise that Jesus and the Advocate will stay with the disciples (14.17).

**14.21. They who have my commandments and keep them are those who love me; and those who love me will be loved by my Father, and I will love them and reveal myself to them:** The disciples need to follow Jesus' example to ensure the continued presence of Jesus and the Advocate (14.15).

**14.22. Judas:** This individual is not Judas Iscariot (6.70), who has already left (13.31). Several candidates have been suggested:

1 Judas/Jude, the brother of Jesus (Mark 6.3; Matthew 13.55; for 'brother' see 2.12);

2 Judas (son) of James (Luke 6.16; Acts 1.13), sometimes identified as Thaddeus (Mark 3.18; Matthew 10.3), but not found in Luke's list of the twelve.

3 Simon from Cana (Mark 1.18; Matthew 10.4); this suggestion imports an unknown character from the Synoptic traditions;

4 Thomas/Didymus (11.16).

No choice can be made between these different characters: most scholars leave the question open.

**14.23. Those who love me will keep my word, and my Father will love them, and we will come to them and make our home with them:** Love is the guarantee of a continued relationship with God, and is based on obedience.

**14.24. Whoever does not love me does not keep my words; and the word that you hear is not mine, but is from the Father who sent me:** This verse repeats the claim that not keeping Jesus' words means rejecting the Father.

**14.25. I have said these things to you while I am still with you:** Jesus is the source of this teaching.

**14.26. The Advocate, the Holy Spirit, whom the Father will send in my name, will teach you everything, and remind you of all that I have said to you:** This statement stresses the continuity of Jesus' teaching and the witness of the Advocate (14.15). Jesus and the Advocate both share the same status: both are sent by the Father.

**14.27. Peace I leave with you; my peace I give to you. I do not give to you as the world gives. Do not let your hearts be troubled, and do not let them be afraid:** Peace is the opposite of being 'troubled' (11.33; 12.27; 13.21; 14.1; also below). It is also a Hebrew greeting (*shalom*). It includes all of the following meanings:

- peace and restfulness;
- reconciliation with God;
- salvation – an eschatological peace.

**14.28a. You heard me say to you, 'I am going away':** This repeats the theme of Jesus' departure (13.33; 14.4, 18), and so emphasizes that this will happen.

**14.28b. And I am coming to you. If you loved me, you would rejoice that I am going to the Father:** What is normally an occasion for sadness becomes a joyful event.

**14.28c. The Father is greater than I:** Some later interpreters understood subordinationism here (5.1–47). The phrase 'greater than I' only means that Jesus makes himself subject to the Father's authority.

**14.29. I have told you this before it occurs, so that when it does occur, you may believe:** These predictions will confirm the truth of what follows.

**14.30. The ruler of this world:** This is identified with the devil or Satan (12.31; 16.11; Appendix J).

**14.31. Rise, let us be on our way:** Jesus tells the disciples to leave the room where supper has been eaten. A number of commentators think this the end of an original short farewell discourse and that chapters 15—17 were added to later versions of the Gospel.

 Interpretation

When Jesus tells his disciples not to be distressed, he addresses themes familiar to Greek philosophy, notably Epicureanism. Epicureanism made death and the gods two of the main causes of fear. Jesus here will address both. Death will hold no fear because it offers only positive benefits, given to his followers. Furthermore, there is no room for doubt, worry or fear here because God is good. If Christians sometimes sum up Christ's work in the statement, 'By his death he has destroyed death', we might say here 'By his distress, he has destroyed distress.' Christ's gift of himself reverses the usual pattern of life.

The interruptions by the disciples (Appendix H) allow Jesus to clarify his meaning. He is not simply a guide, but is also both the way and means of salvation. He replaces whatever has previously been considered the means of salvation. As the Way, he exemplifies right behaviour. His claims further point to him as the only way to the Father: his function is unique.

This worries theologians who see it diminishing other faith traditions. However, even inclusive claims which would deny this and say that all faiths are equal are arrogant. For in making such claims, those who think this way say that they know the ultimate truth about all faiths. The famous picture that all religions are like different paths leading to the same mountain top demands that one puts oneself in a superior position above the mountain, looking down on everyone else.

There is a second consideration. Jesus himself is the true revelation and means of salvation, and we must be careful not to confuse him with what we believe, and make that the means of salvation. It is who he is and what he did that are the grounds of our salvation, not our faith or understanding of him. Our faith is always inadequate: we are saved through grace, through God's gift of Jesus to us.

There is also a need for honesty: people rarely, unless forced by circumstances, subscribe to a set of beliefs or a particular faith when they believe another is better. We believe that ours is the best. To pretend otherwise is a kind of hypocrisy. What is critical is that such attitudes do not become a source of arrogance, pride or prejudice which damage our relationships with people of other faiths.

Jesus' answers to Thomas and Philip may suggest that Jesus will do anything that is asked for in his name (14.14). This needs to be qualified. Answers to unjust or selfish prayers are contrary to the name of Jesus. Whatever is asked for must ultimately be for the glory of God (Appendix D) and therefore embrace and reveal what is valuable to God. Asking for what is harmful or contrary to the glorifying of God will be answered in an unexpected way so that God is still glorified. Jesus' prayer in Gethsemane sets a benchmark for intercessory prayer (Mark 14.36). Significantly, John has Jesus follow his remark about prayer with a word about love: prayer will be shaped by love, in harmony with the values and ethics taught and shown by Jesus himself. Asking for anything contrary to his commandments will not get an answer.

We need to take care when describing the Advocate. It would be very easy to think that John has a full theology of the Trinity. We need to read John's Gospel on its own terms, not through later doctrines. Function and status, not metaphysics, are at work. The introductory statement about 'another Advocate' shows this advocate has the same status and function as Jesus himself – the first Advocate. This second Advocate is linked to the Father, just like Jesus.

This section exhibits signs of parallelism: themes raised in the first segment (14.15–17) are repeated in the second (14.18–21). The two sections share related themes typical of farewell addresses: predictions about death (14.18), encouragement for ideal behaviour (14.15, 21), and a guarantee of faithfulness (14.18, 19). John's purpose is, in part, directed to the situation of his audience. John uses these farewell remarks to say that the first generation of believers had no special privileges: the promise of the presence of the Spirit of truth ('another Advocate') guarantees experiences equal to living with the earthly Jesus. This presence of Jesus is linked to baptism (3.3–5) and the Eucharist (6.51–58) for John's audience. An even bolder claim is made: they may even be able to accomplish greater things than that first generation (14.12), and are in no way inferior believers (20.24–29).

In 14.25–31 Jesus revisits earlier themes. The Advocate is mentioned again, as a teacher and aid to memory, thus guaranteeing continuity with the earthly Jesus. This is also a claim for the reliability of the tradition and witness which John's audience receives and passes on. A further promise is made: peace which is superior to worldly peace. The love ethic described by Jesus brings three significant advantages:

1 *High status*: Those who keep the love ethic are loved by God, and he shares a home with them (14.23). This is a higher status than any earthly patron could give.

2 *The desirable goal of peace*: This is a wide-ranging term. It includes freedom from worry (14.1, 27), but also political and social peace and stability. The period of the early Roman empire was described as the *Pax Romana* (the Roman peace). Historians date this period from roughly 27 BCE (the accession of Augustus) until 180 CE (the death of Marcus Aurelius). During this period the Roman Empire was largely free from external threats, piracy and civil strife. However, it was a peace brought at a price. The ancient Roman historian Tacitus, in the *Agricola* (98 CE), puts the following description of Roman rule on the lips of an enemy chieftain: 'To ravage, slaughter and rape is a false name for "empire":

they make a desert, and call it peace.' Even today, peace and prosperity may be achieved through the suppression of dissent, freedom of speech and even the curtailing of human rights. The *Pax Romana* was a less than perfect peace, and this would have been particularly clear to those living at the time the Gospel was composed. Jesus offers a better kind of peace to his disciples.

3 *A superior understanding of God and the world ('truth')*: Ancient religion attempted to understand how the world works and to discern the powers that shape it – through philosophical insight, the use of drugs, altered states of consciousness like dreams, or through religious ritual. In contrast to such mystical states, Jesus' love ethic is made the launching point for superior understanding. It is worth asking whether Christian traditions which have made mystical experience or phenomena like glossolalia (speaking in tongues) the basis for claims of heightened spiritual awareness have neglected the value of love and behaviour as the way to understand God and life.

This section expands themes already identified, such as the unity between the Father and the Son (5.19–31; 10.30, 38). Here that unity is expanded to include believers, and is based not just on knowledge of God (1.14, 9–13, 19–51; 2.1—4.54), but on love (14.15, 21, 23–24). This echoes the general picture of faith given in the NT (Appendix B): it must include both mind and behaviour. Later patristic theologians would develop theologies such as *perichoresis* (the mutual indwelling of members of the Trinity) and *theosis* (divinization, as a way of understanding salvation) to explain the believer's union with God. The germ of such ideas is found here. There is a flip side: those who do not follow Jesus' commands are effectively rejecting God. John is not a universalist: people can condemn themselves (3.16–18).

 STUDY SUGGESTIONS

### Word study

1 Write a description of 'love' based on this section.

2 What does John mean by 'peace'?

3 Does the translation 'Advocate' change your understanding of the Spirit?

### Review of content

4 How can Jesus and the Spirit of truth both be described as an advocate? Try to avoid using later Trinitarian language like 'person'.

5 Read 1 Corinthians 12.1—14.25. Do you think that Paul would agree with John about the place of love?

**6** Read Mark 13.11 and Luke 11.13. Compare their teaching with what John says about the Spirit.

### Discussion and application

**7** Does your current Christian practice give due place to the love ethic as the basis for right living and faith? Has it made some other behaviour more important?

**8** Does your society provide peace or prosperity at a cost to human dignity? Is this really *peace*?

## 15.1—16.33: Farewell Speech 2

 Introduction

In what may be a later addition to a short original speech (ending at 14.31), Jesus gives his disciples further teaching about the demands and privileges of discipleship, including the gift of the Spirit.

 Notes and commentary

**15.1. I am the true vine, and my Father is the vine-grower:** For the 'I am' construction, see 6.35. This is the only time it is followed by equivalent statements like 'my Father is' and 'you are' (15.5).

The word 'true' indicates that Jesus (with those who follow him) is claimed as superior to other forms of Judaism. The OT uses the vineyard as a symbol for Israel (Isaiah 5.1–7; 27.2–6; Jeremiah 5.10; 6.9; 12.10–11; Ezekiel 15.1–6; 17.5–10; 19.10–14; Psalm 80.9–20; Hosea 10.1; 14.8), as do the Synoptic Gospels (Mark 12.1–12; Matthew 20.1–16; 21.28–32, 33–46; Luke 13.6–9; 20.9–19).

**15.2. He removes every branch in me that bears no fruit. Every branch that bears fruit he prunes to make it bear more fruit:** Here is a warning that the community based on Jesus contains both fruitful and barren members. If a commentary, it may contrast Judas Iscariot, Nicodemus and Peter. The verb 'prune' indicates that additional action is needed for disciples to stay clean, as in 13.4–11.

**15.3–4. You have already been cleansed by the word that I have spoken to you. Abide in me as I abide in you. Just as the branch cannot bear fruit by itself unless it abides in the vine, neither can you unless you abide in me:** The branches are sustained by being joined to the vine.

Disciples need to maintain a relationship with Jesus. The NRSV uses 'cleansed' (for 'pruned'), which may refer back to 13.10. It is a reminder that Jesus is a source of purity, a major concern of Jewish piety. 'Abide' is the same word as in 1.38–39; 14.2. It stresses the need to remain in relationship with Jesus. The image of bearing fruit includes both fulfilling one's potential, and carrying out mission to others.

**15.5. I am the vine, you are the branches. Those who abide in me and I in them bear much fruit, because apart from me you can do nothing:** This verse repeats the need to be in right relationship with Jesus (14.6).

**15.6. Whoever does not abide in me is thrown away like a branch and withers; such branches are gathered, thrown into the fire, and burned:** The image of dead and withered branches shows the emptiness and futility of life without Jesus.

**15.7. If you abide in me, and my words abide in you, ask for whatever you wish, and it will be done for you:** Jesus repeats and confirms the promise that God will answer the prayers of his people (14.14).

**15.8. My Father is glorified by this, that you bear much fruit and become my disciples:** The Father is glorified by the actions of Jesus' disciples (Appendix D).

**15.9. As the Father has loved me, so I have loved you; abide in my love:** Encouragement to love Jesus comes from the certainty that Jesus is loved by the Father.

**15.10. If you keep my commandments, you will abide in my love, just as I have kept my Father's commandments and abide in his love:** The link between love and the love ethic of Jesus is repeated (14.21).

**15.11. I have said these things to you so that my joy may be in you, and that your joy may be complete:** Jesus' teaching gives confidence in the future. 'Joy' was a Greek greeting (14.27); joy is one of the results of keeping Jesus' commandments and remaining in the Father's love. It is linked to the completion of Jesus' ministry.

**15.12. This is my commandment, that you love one another as I have loved:** This verse repeats the theme of love and service seen in 13.15.

**15.13. No one has greater love than this, to lay down one's life for one's friends:** This repeats the theme of self-sacrifice found in the Good Shepherd image (10.11). By using the word 'friends' Jesus promises his disciples a higher quality of relationship than those of a superior and inferior (master–slave; teacher–pupil).

**15.14. You are my friends if you do what I command you:** Friendship with Jesus is based on obeying his commands.

**15.15. I do not call you servants any longer, because the servant does not know what the master is doing; but I have called you friends, because**

**I have made known to you everything that I have heard from my Father:** Friendship involves recognizing who Jesus is and understanding what he is doing, as well as obedience. The new status is also based on understanding what has been revealed by Jesus.

**15.16a. You did not choose me but I chose you:** Jesus is shown to be in charge of choosing and sending disciples (6.70; 13.19–20).

**15.16b. I appointed you to go and bear fruit, fruit that will last:** The assistance of Jesus makes the disciples effective.

**15.16c. The Father will give you whatever you ask him in my name:** This repeats the promise that God answers prayers already seen in 14.13–14; 15.7. Asking should be for the glory of God, in keeping with his plans and values, not for selfish ends.

**15.17. I am giving you these commands so that you may love one another:** Jesus' advice concludes with a reminder of the love ethic (13.15).

**15.18. If the world hates you, be aware that it hated me before it hated you:** Love is now compared to its opposite: hate (Appendix B). 'World' here has a negative moral value; it is not just a physical location (1.10; 13.1).

**15.19. If you belonged to the world, the world would love you as its own. Because you do not belong to the world, but I have chosen you out of the world – therefore the world hates you:** Rejection by the world comes from being loved by Jesus: it is a the mark of Jesus' disciples as an antisociety (see 'The good news according to John', p. 7).

**15.20. Remember the word that I said to you, 'Servants are not greater than their master.' If they persecuted me, they will persecute you; if they kept my word, they will keep yours also:** Jesus repeats the warning of 13.16: his disciples will be treated as badly as he was.

**15.21. But they will do all these things to you on account of my name, because they do not know him who sent me:** Jesus blames ill-treatment of his followers on ignorance, rather than deliberate malice.

**15.22. If I had not come and spoken to them, they would not have sin; but now they have no excuse for their sin:** This idea repeats that of 3.16–18. Jesus' teaching has given everyone the ability to make right choices and decisions.

**15.23. Whoever hates me hates my Father also:** The individual's reaction to Jesus indicates his or her reaction to the Father. Love for Jesus implies love for the Father; hating him implies rejecting the Father. The unity between Father and Son is repeated (5.19–31).

**15.24. If I had not done among them the works that no one else did, they would not have sin. But now they have seen and hated both me**

**and my Father:** Rejection of the Father is linked to the rejection of Jesus' public ministry. John prefers to describe Jesus' public ministry as 'works' rather than 'signs' (5.36).

**15.25. To fulfil the word that is written in their law, 'They hated me without a cause':** The text comes from Psalm 35.19 or 69.4. If from Psalm 69.4 (which is not clear), it means that this psalm may have gained messianic significance (19.28–29). Both refer to a righteous person suffering. The accusations which have been made are groundless: the accusers are driven by false motives or ignorance (15.21; 19.28–29).

**15.26. When the Advocate comes, whom I will send to you from the Father, the Spirit of truth who comes from the Father, he will testify on my behalf:** Jesus re-emphasizes the teaching role of the Spirit (14.26).

**15.27a. You also are to testify:** God's people are witnesses in the end times (Isaiah 43.10–12; 44.8).

**15.27b. You have been with me from the beginning:** This refers to the beginning of Jesus' ministry.

**16.1. To keep you from stumbling:** This could also be translated: 'to keep you from being scandalized' (6.61). Scandal causes the disciple to give up faith in Jesus, leave the community of disciples, or commit sin (6.61; Matthew 16.23; Matthew 26.31 for the disciples' desertion of Jesus). Christ crucified and the cross were also obstacles to faith (1 Corinthians 1.23; Galatians 5.11) for people who thought crucifixion (19.6) was a particularly shameful death (Deuteronomy 21.23; Galatians 3.13) or who rejected a suffering Messiah.

**16.2a. They will put you out of the synagogues:** While the focus here is expulsion from synagogues (7.35), expulsion from family groups and kinship systems was also possible for followers of Jesus (7.5; Mark 13.9–13; Luke 21.12–19).

**16.2b. Those who kill you:** This is a rhetorical figure of speech to suggest the depth of feelings involved, as no historical event can be connected to this warning. Some have thought it might refer to persecutions by the Romans, but this does not tally with expulsion from synagogues.

**16.2c. Offering worship to God:** Worship includes both personal worship of God, and civic duty or public works which benefit the community.

**16.4. I did not say these things to you from the beginning:** Jesus is now telling his disciples things they have not heard before, despite being with him for some time (15.27).

**16.5. None of you asks me, 'Where are you going?':** This seems odd as Peter has already asked the question (13.36) and Jesus has given explanations which stress that he is talking about a departure which is more than physical death (14.1–3). The verse means that the disciples are not thinking the right way, but are confused. Grief has clouded their understanding. Jesus understands their emotions.

**16.6. Sorrow has filled your hearts:** The disciples are thinking only in terms of physical death or loss, but Jesus wants them to reflect more widely. Greek thought was divided about grief or sorrow, and viewed it either as something painful, a necessary opposite to pleasure, or as wrong emotion. Here, grief is viewed negatively as the opposite of joy (3.29; 15.11; 16.20), but it will not last (16.20).

**16.7a. I tell you the truth: it is to your advantage that I go away:** The focus on 'truth' suggests that events should not be considered only as loss and grief.

**16.7b. The Advocate:** The verse reintroduces the Spirit (14.16–17, 26). The Spirit sheds light on three matters (16.9–11).

**16.9. Sin:** This has already been described (1.29; 15.21). Here sin is related directly to a failure to believe in Jesus (3.16–21).

**16.10a. Righteousness:** This term is used only here by John. It implies justice as much as righteousness. Righteousness or justice should not be defined by our contemporary understandings, but rather seen as an expression of God's character – the fairness or treatment of people demanded by love. The verse condemns the world's failure to be just towards Jesus. His return to the Father proves his righteousness and the injustice of the world.

**16.10b. You will see me no longer:** This is a repetition of the idea of a separation from Jesus (7.33–34; 8.21). While Jesus himself will no longer be visible, the Advocate makes belief possible.

**16.11a. Judgement:** The world is made to judge itself and finds itself inadequate (3.17; 12.31).

**16.11b. The ruler of the world:** This phrase refers to Satan or the devil (12.31). Judgement involves the transformation of the whole of Creation, not just the salvation of individuals (Appendix J).

**16.11c. Has been condemned:** The condemnation of the devil has already taken place according to John's inaugurated eschatology (3.3).

**16.12. I still have many things to say to you, but you cannot bear them now:** This verse means that the disciples have yet understand fully everything which has been said. The coming of the Advocate clarifies what has already been revealed.

**16.13. The Spirit of truth:** This is the Advocate or Spirit who has already been introduced (14.17).

**16.14a. He will glorify me:** To glorify is to give recognition of the proper place which God, Jesus and the world all have (Appendix D).

**16.14b. He will take what is mine and declare it to you:** The Advocate will repeat what has already been declared or announced for additional emphasis.

**16.15. All that the Father has is mine:** This repeats the theme of the unity of the Father and Jesus (5.19–31; 14.7, 10–11).

**16.16. A little while, and you will no longer see me, and again a little while, and you will see me:** Already used in 13.33, here the phrase 'a little while' describes two periods of time:

1 *a little while*: the period between Jesus' death and resurrection;

2 *again a little while*: the period up to the resurrection experiences.
The OT prophets used a similar expression for God's purposes (Isaiah 10.25; 26.10; Jeremiah 51.33; Hosea 1.4; Haggai 2.6).

**16.20. Your pain will turn into joy:** Transforming pain into joy was an action typical of God in the OT (Isaiah 61.1–3; Jeremiah 22.10; 31.13; 2 Esdras 2.27; for the feast of *Purim*: Esther 9.22; 1 Maccabees 7.49; 2 Maccabees 15.36).

**16.21. A woman . . . in labour:** This was a common figure in OT prophecy (Isaiah 13.8; 21.3; 42.14; 66.7–13; Jeremiah 4.31; 6.24; 13.21; 22.23; 30.6; 49.22–24; 50.43; Micah 4.9–10), often of the salvation to be brought by the Messiah. It may be linked to resurrection (Isaiah 26.16–21).

**16.23. On that day you will ask nothing of me:** This means that Jesus will have answered any questions the disciples could ask about what is happening: 'you will not ask me anything on that day' (14.13–14; 15.16–17). It is not about intercessions.

**16.24. Until now you have not asked for anything in my name. Ask and you will receive, so that your joy may be complete:** Jesus shows that the previous verse is not about intercessions by promising that prayers of that kind will be answered.

**16.25a. Figures of speech:** These may include parables (10.1, 6, 7; Appendix G).

**16.25b. I . . . will tell you plainly:** Plain speech is considered superior to figurative language (Appendix I).

**16.26. On that day you will ask in my name. I do not say to you that I will ask the Father on your behalf:** There is no further need for Jesus as an intermediary between the disciple and the Father. The right relationship with Jesus has guaranteed direct access to the Father.

**16.29. His disciples said, 'Yes, now you are speaking plainly, not in any figure of speech! Now we know that you know all things':** The disciples are overconfident in their claim, sharing the same weakness as Peter

(13.36–38): they think they know everything and are perfect disciples. Full explanations come with the sending of the Advocate (14.26).

**16.30. You do not need to have anyone question you:** The disciples say that they do not need to ask questions any more to make up for their earlier failure to ask the right questions themselves (16.5).

**16.31–32. Do you now believe? The hour is coming . . . when you will be scattered, each one to his home, and you will leave me alone:** Jesus dismisses the disciples' confidence by telling them how they are going to fail, just as he told Peter (13.38; 16.25). 'The hour is coming' here refers only to the scattering of the disciples (unlike 12.23; 13.1; and 17.1). Scattering is not mentioned directly in the events which follow, but has already been indicated (10.13). The verse may refer to Zechariah 13.7 (see also Matthew 26.31, 56). While the OT image usually refers to the scattering of God's people (Isaiah 53.6; Jeremiah 23.1; 50.17; Ezekiel 34.6, 12, 21), here it refers to Jesus being deserted as his disciples flee. As 17.1–26 is addressed to the Father, these are the last words spoken to the disciples (except 18.11 – to Peter). As the only words which Jesus spoke 'plainly' to the disciples (16.25), they contain a bitter prediction of the disciples' impending failure. The phrase 'each one to his home' is a possible reference to 1 Kings 22.17. It may refer to the disciples' lodgings in Jerusalem (19.27) rather than to Galilee (21.2).

**16.33a. In me you may have peace:** This refers to the eschatological peace as the final point in God's work (14.27).

**16.33b. I have conquered:** These words are used only here in the Gospel, but more in other Johannine writings (1 John 2.13–14; 4.4; 5.4; and frequently in Revelation). Used in Psalm 50.6 (LXX) of God as conqueror.

 ## Interpretation

The metaphor of the vine in 15.1–6 is used to describe the relationship of Jesus and his disciples. It is more likely that the OT and Judaism provide this imagery rather than the more mythical Gnostic and Mandaean (originally Jewish Gnostic) writings which do not refer to 'branches'.

John uses the vine image to describe Jesus, not Israel. This is a further example of using terminology about Israel to make Jesus 'the new Israel', using the Temple and Jewish feasts. Not all John's imagery comes from the OT texts: none use the vine as a source of life (15.4). Possible bridges between the OT and John may come from wisdom literature (Sirach 24.17–21). Even so, John has developed the imagery in a new way to suit his purposes.

The idea of the vine as life-giving may refer to the Eucharist. Even if the Last Supper is not described in detail in John, it nonetheless provides a background, and possible eucharistic layer of meaning. The following are possible points of contact:

1  15.13 and sacrificial death;

2  comparisons between 6.51–58 and 15.1–17; 15.5 and 6.56; 15.4 and 6.57; 15.13 and 6.51;

3  6.51 and 15.1 echo the eucharistic pairing: 'This is my body' . . . 'This is my blood'.

While the vine imagery stresses the importance of 'abiding' in Jesus, these cross-references make the Eucharist the way to achieve this.

Keeping the love ethic and 'abiding' give high status. Instead of a superior–inferior relationship (15.15), friendship becomes the primary mode of relating to Jesus (15.14). This is a radical departure from many of the social patterns experienced in the cultures of the time: client–patron, pupil–teacher and slave–master. All involved a ranking or hierarchical structure. Friendship flattens out this structure. We do not always grasp this in our Christian life and often place ourselves 'under' God. To an extent this is right and proper, but it does fail to acknowledge the gift given to us: to be called 'friends'. Do we accept God's wish to be close to us, or do we keep ourselves distant from him through excessive humility? If we do, the virtue of humility has become an obstacle to our closeness to God and must be rejected, no matter how good it seems. The new antisociety (see 'The good news according to John', p. 7) proposed here by Jesus offers a new close relationship with God which is alien to the world.

This new relationship comes from the love ethic and abiding. The new antisociety is 'hated' by the 'world'. Two radically different orders are presented to John's audience:

| Discipleship | World |
| --- | --- |
| Abiding | (Distance) |
| Love | Hate |
| Knowledge | Ignorance |
| Right behaviour | Sin |
| Close to Father | Absent from Father |
| Obedience | Persecution |
| Vision | (Blindness) |

Some of these pairs are clearly stated; others are implied (the ones in brackets). The difference between the world and discipleship is centred on the response given to Jesus ('on account of my name', 15.21). John's audience is left in no doubt that discipleship is better, but also that discipleship is not an easy option. The section repeats the previous claim: there can be no closeness to the Father which does not involve Jesus. Such a claim is completely opposed to the hopes of Jesus' opponents (8.41), and reflects the polemic style of debate (5.1–47; 8.39–59) and plain speaking (Appendix I).

While Jesus' judgement may seem harsh, the world is primarily seen as unknowing or ignorant. This echoes Luke 23.34: 'Father, forgive them;

for they do not know what they are doing', which also claims Jesus' opponents are acting out of ignorance, not deliberate sin. This picks up Numbers 15.22–31, which separated intentional and unintentional sin arising from ignorance. Traditions had emerged from this text and its parallels, which viewed unintentional or involuntary sin as able to be forgiven, unlike intentional sin. This pattern is seen in Christian texts (9.41; Mark 4.12; Luke 12.47; Acts 3.17; 23.5; 2 Corinthians 4.4). Even if one must take the blame for unintentional sin (Acts 3.17), it is a lesser offence. Jesus accuses the world of sin coming from ignorance, not deliberate malice. Even when Jesus reveals sins (3.16–18; 15.24), and the world can no longer claim innocence or deny its sinfulness (15.22), God will continue to look mercifully on the world because of its ignorance (15.21). This does not, however, mean automatic pardon or a universalist understanding of salvation and judgement (3.1–21). Such a perspective is significant: it demands that the reactions of Christ's followers to their opponents must be tempered by an understanding that they act from ignorance.

Chapter 16 repeats themes already introduced in 14—15, including the work of the Advocate (16.8–11). This is done through a series of reversals. Normally persecution and the loss of a leader would be seen as monumental setbacks to the hopes and life of a group like the disciples. Instead, John's Jesus shows that every reversal is a benefit:

1 It is good to be expelled from the synagogue, because this is a sign of being a true worshipper of God (knowing the Father, 16.1–3).

2 It is good that he (Jesus – the leader or hero) leaves, because the Advocate will come (16.7–12);

3 Mourning for the leader will turn to joy (16.16–24).

4 Figurative speech will be replaced by plain speaking: a sign of increased intimacy (16.25–30).

5 Desertion by the disciples will become victory (16.31–33).

This anticipation of Jesus' Passion is completely at odds with conventional wisdom. This message is intended not just for the disciples, but for John's audience, and ourselves as readers. While we are prepared to live in hope that Jesus' death conquers death, we often, when faced with the crises of life, resort to conventional reactions to loss and difficulty. In many countries, particularly those identified as the Global North or the West, the Church is in decline. Do we react to such crises and situations of loss as John has suggested? More often than not, we resort to the wisdom of the world, and ignore the message of reversal seen here. The pattern of reversal outlined here asks Christians whether they have really embraced the fullness of eternal life offered by Jesus, or whether they still live by the values and expectations of the world.

Jesus' compassion in talking to the disciples (16.6, 12) shows an understanding of how emotions confuse and paralyse, possibly heightened by his own recent experience (12.27). Insights like this surface in writing on spiritual guidance. Ignatius of Loyola (1491–1556 CE) advised that the process of discernment (making choices in line with the will of God) should never be undertaken during times of desolation (stress or anxiety) because the activity of the emotions and senses can obscure the prompting of the Spirit. This is what has happened to the disciples: their grief and stress has made it impossible for them to understand Jesus' teaching. This is not the only psychological point made: the disciples swing from sorrow-induced paralysis to a rash overconfidence (16.29–30) which will turn out to be completely inadequate.

 ## STUDY SUGGESTIONS

### Word study

1 What view of the 'world' is given here? Does it match how the term is used elsewhere in the Gospel (for example, 1.10)? What does this tell us about words and their meanings? (Clue: see 2.6.)

2 Outline John's view of the Spirit (16.7–15) without using technical theological language.

3 What are the two kinds of sin found in Jewish theology? What is the difference between them?

### Review of content

4 How does John's use of vine imagery compare to that of the Synoptic Gospels?

5 Does the vine imagery refer to the Eucharist? Do you find the points made to support such a claim convincing?

6 Compare 15.18–26 with Matthew 5.11; 10.24–25; Luke 6.22. Do you think the Gospel writers share common views about the relationships between Jesus, his disciples and the world? Consider especially factors like honour, shame and the expulsion of the followers of Jesus from the synagogues.

7 Read Hebrews 4.15. Does this support the idea that Jesus is able to empathize with the disciples from his own experience (12.27; 16.6, 12, 29–30)?

### Discussion and application

8 Have we experienced the pattern of reversal which separates the hopes and values of the disciples from those of the world? Do we live as though this pattern of reversal is God's gift to us?

9  Where might the followers of Jesus experience rejection in your context? What message might they hear from John's Jesus in such circumstances?

10  Should we attempt to make decisions in times of desolation, either as individuals or as communities?

11  Which 'scandals' cause people to fall away from Christ in your context, or make it difficult for them to accept Christ?

## 17.1–26: Farewell Speech 3 – the prayer of Jesus

 Introduction

Jesus completes his farewell address with a prayer directed to the Father.

 Notes and commentary

**17.1a. Jesus . . . looked up to heaven:** This indicates speech directed towards God (11.41). 'Heaven' may just mean 'sky'.

**17.1b. Father:** The repeated address of the Father as 'you' throughout this chapter (17.5, 11, 21, 24, 25) shows that this part of the speech is addressed primarily to God, not the disciples.

**17.1c. The hour has come:** This is a phrase which refers usually to the Passion and death of Jesus (2.4; 4.21; 7.6, 8, 30; 12.23; 13.1).

**17.1d. Glorify your Son:** The verse does not mean that Jesus has lost his glory (Appendix D) by becoming human, but that his glory includes the fact that he was sent by God and completed this work. Jesus' ministry and death are as important as the act of creation (1.2–3). Jesus refers to himself as 'Son'. A first glorification has happened in the public ministry; more will follow in the Passion.

**17.2. Since you have given him authority:** Jesus' authority has been given directly by God, not human authority. Glory is linked to the nature and purpose of Jesus' work.

**17.3. This is eternal life, that they may know you, the only true God, and Jesus Christ whom you have sent:** The hopes of the disciples are connected with knowing the Father and Jesus (3.15, 16–21).

**17.4. I glorified you on earth by finishing the work that you gave me to do:** 'Finishing' includes both (a) completing and (b) bringing to perfection (18.30).

**17.5. So now, Father, glorify me in your own presence with the glory that I had in your presence before the world existed:** Jesus resumes the status which he previously had; 'glory' refers to Jesus' pre-existence with the Father (1.1).

**17.6a. I have made your name known:** Jesus has not spoken for his own advantage, but to make the Father known. For 'name', see 8.24, 28, 54; 13.19; 18.5.

**17.6b. You gave them to me:** This point stresses that discipleship is a gift from God, not a human choice (6.65; 10.29).

**17.6c. They have kept your word:** Jesus praises his disciples; this acknowledgement also includes John's readers.

**17.9. I am not asking on behalf of the world:** Jesus will not pray for the world, that is, approve and work for what it holds valuable. That would contradict the whole point of his mission and work (14.1–31, esp. 14.14). 'World' here has a negative moral value.

**17.10. I have been glorified in them:** The actions of the disciples give glory (Appendix D) to God.

**17.11. In your name:** This phrase includes the sense: 'with your authority' (6.27). Jesus' behaviour has been approved by the Father: he is not using God's name falsely.

**17.12a. While I was with them, I protected them in your name that you have given me. I guarded them, and not one of them was lost:** Jesus has acted as promised (6.37–9; 10.28). God rejects no one. Those who are lost choose to leave him.

**17.12b. The one destined to be lost:** This is literally, 'son of loss [or destruction]', and includes a pun on the verb 'lost' (NRSV). Here Judas is meant; elsewhere the phrase refers to a character destined to appear before the Last Days (2 Thessalonians 2.3).

**17.12c. So that the scripture might be fulfilled:** This most likely refers to Proverbs 24.22a (the son keeping the word will be spared from destruction). That verse is more concerned with the fact that most people are saved, rather than that one is lost ('the one destined to be lost').

**17.13. I speak these things . . . so that they may have my joy:** Joy is a sign of blessings received from God (15.11).

**17.14. I have given them your word, and the world has hated them because they do not belong to the world, just as I do not belong to the world:** This verse repeats ideas already seen in 15.18–25. Here 'world' has a negative sense (17.9).

**17.15a. I am not asking you to take them out of the world, but I ask you to protect them:** Jesus' prayer asks for protection for the disciples, not escape or avoidance of problems (being 'taken out of the world').

**17.15b. The evil one:** See 3.19. This phrase could be translated either 'the evil one' or 'evil' (Matthew 6.13). Other Johannine texts (3.19; 1 John 2.13–14; 3.12; 5.18–19) suggest a reference to the devil (Appendix J).

**17.16. They do not belong to the world, just as I do not belong to the world:** The repetition (17.14) stresses the separation of the disciples from the world and its values.

**17.17a. Sanctify them in the truth; your word is truth:** Jesus asks the Father to make the disciples share characteristics which belong to both of them: truth and holiness (see 'Holy Father', 17.11).

**17.17b. In the truth:** This phrase may function grammatically as an instrumental, meaning 'by the power of the truth' or 'by means of the truth'.

**17.18. As you have sent me . . . so I have sent them into the world:** Jesus' sending is the source of the disciples' sending. Again, this is a source of encouragement to the disciples and John's readers. 'I have sent' is open to different interpretations as there has been no sending in John's Gospel (unlike the Synoptic tradition: Mark 6.7–13; Matthew 10.5; Luke 9.1–6; 10.1–20). Some have seen this as a reference to 4.38; others think this might be a saying which really belongs after the resurrection, but has been inserted here. A third is that 'have sent' indicates that everything is prepared for this to happen soon.

**17.19a. I sanctify myself:** The Father has previously consecrated (10.36), but this verse shows that Jesus shares the same powers (6.27). The verse does not make clear how and when the sanctification takes place, but several interpreters see it as referring to Jesus' death. What Jesus does becomes the basis for what will happen to the disciples.

**17.19b. So that they also may be sanctified in truth:** This may involve another instrumental (17.17): 'by the power of truth' or 'by means of truth'.

**17.20a. I ask not only on behalf of these, but also on behalf of those who will believe in me:** What has been given to the disciples is now promised to future believers, including John's audience.

**17.20b. Through their word:** The verses which follow are directed to those who have believed because of the testimony passed on to them: not only John's audience, but, by extension, today's readers.

**17.21. They may all be one . . . so that the world may believe:** Unity demands both a vertical dimension (with God) and a horizontal dimension (with other believers, 13.34–35; 15.12, 17). The intimacy which unites the Father and Jesus is the model for the relationships which will be shared by believers. The need for the horizontal element is stressed by the words 'so that the world may believe': something needs to be seen or perceived that will let this happen. Both 10.16 and 15.5–6 anticipate this. While earlier scholarship identified the positive value of unity (the One) with Greek philosophy or Gnosticism, the Dead Sea Scrolls show a group living by an agreed rule of life, anticipating the day when they will be joined with God. This may be a Jewish idea. 'The world' should respond by rejecting its own values.

**17.22. The glory that you have given me I have given them:** The promises here are spoken in the past tense, although Jesus has not yet completed his work. This promise is really directed to John's audience (17.21), and so refers to actions which, by their time, had already been accomplished.

**17.23. I in them, and you in me:** These words imply both the horizontal and vertical aspects of being 'one', repeating and emphasizing the importance of 17.21. The believers' relationship will match the intimate relationship that Jesus has with the Father. Such intimacy and status come from adopting the values of Jesus and the Father.

**17.24. I desire that those also . . . may be with me where I am, to see my glory:** Intimacy is expressed in spatial terms, which allows Jesus' followers to see his true glory (17.5).

**17.25. Righteous Father:** Holiness, justice and righteousness are all linked and all are best seen in the character of God. 'Righteous' fits the theme of judgement, linked to love and knowing (3.16–21).

**17.26. I made your name known to them, and I will make it known, so that the love with which you have loved me may be in them, and I in them:** Jesus concludes the prayer by repeating themes of love and knowing (14.15–24; 15.9–15; 16.12–15; 17.6–9).

 ## Interpretation

It was not uncommon for farewell speeches to include material which might be classified as a prayer or devotional (Deuteronomy 32.43). Although shaped like a prayer, this part of the farewell speech really contains important messages for the disciples:

- The love between the Father and the Son will be realized in the lives of the disciples.

- Those who are bereaved will not be separated or left desolate. Farewell addresses often stress that the family of the person who is dying will not be broken by their loss. The fictive family (7.1–13) of disciples will survive.

As the climax of the Farewell Speech, the prayer shows that Jesus gives a number of benefits to those who believe in him. A good way to think of liberation (being made 'free', 8.32) is the answering of one's hopes, needs and expectations. John would add that true liberation is found when these hopes match up with the values of God (17.9). Here, the gifts of knowledge (17.3), protection (17.11), joy (synonymous with peace, 3.29; 14.27; 15.11; 17.13), sanctification (including righteousness, 17.11, 25) through the truth (17.19), unity (17.21), glory (Appendix D; 17.22) and an enduring or long-lasting presence with their leader (17.24) would all be viewed as attractive across a broad spectrum of philosophical traditions.

The prayer is also divided into three parts applied to different groups:

- Jesus prays for himself (17.1–6a);

- Jesus prays for the disciples (17.6b–19);

- Jesus prays for those who believe because of the disciples (17.20–26).

Each section repeats a number of themes:

- *Giving* (17.2, 6, 7, 8, 9, 11, 12, 14, 22, 24). This is a characteristic of God linked to his nature: grace, or generosity (1.14).

- *The relationship of Jesus to the world* (17.11, 14, 16, 18). This involves two distinct ideas: the world as the place where Jesus is sent to perform his saving work, and the world as Jesus' opponent. The first is the object of God's love; the second, an opponent considered hostile to God and all that he represents. The hostile world is condemned by Jesus (3.16–18), and he will not compromise with it, even if it means that he and his disciples must endure its hostility before they triumph over it (16.31).

- *Being sent* (17.3, 8, 18, 21, 23, 25). This means to be given a task by God and the ability to perform that task.

- *Unity* (17.11, 21, 22, 23). This includes both unity with God and unity with other disciples.

This pattern guarantees continuity for generations of believers. The argument flows like this:

- The Father engages with Jesus (presented as a fact);

- The Father through Jesus engages with the disciples (again, presented as fact);

- The Father, through Jesus and the disciples, engages with fresh generations of believers (a hope grounded in the facts);

- The audience or readers thus may have a confident hope based on the facts.

The final section, with its plea for visible unity, is central to ecumenical work which brings different churches and Christian traditions closer together. It does not say that Christians must all worship or live in one way. The NT reveals many varying Christian beliefs and practices which might be better described as 'unity in diversity'. Nevertheless, it asks two things:

1 Our dealings with other Christians must be seen to be *loving and respectful*. As such, these verses are a corrective to the anger and intolerance which has often characterized the relations between Christians of different traditions. Ecumenical dialogue is not just about the issues discussed, but about the ways in which Christians meet and treat one another. The quality of relationships between Christians must match that of the relationship between the Father and the Son.

2 Christians must be seen to work *for unity*. We cannot hide behind claims of some invisible mystical unity in the face of visible quarrelling and animosity. Such visible living is part of the task of mission left to the Church by Jesus.

The speech ends by repeating that love, knowledge and faith go hand in hand. The final promise is meant to overcome grief and loss: there is no separation from Jesus for the believer, but a promise to be together with him. The farewell is no farewell; it is a promise of greater intimacy. It is the first flowering of the great Orthodox tradition of *theosis*: 'God became man so that man might become a god' (St Athanasius, *On the Incarnation* 54.3; see also 14.11–31).

 STUDY SUGGESTIONS

### Word study

1 Explain what the 'hour' is in two different ways: (a) using theological language and (b) without using technical language.

2 Do you think it is right to link holiness with righteousness (17.11, 25), and joy (17.11) with peace? How does this change your understanding of holiness and joy?

### Review of content

3 Is the work performed by Jesus in his public ministry and death as important as the work of creation?

4 Look at the list of promises which come from Jesus' prayer. How many of these would be desirable to people in your context who (a) share the Christian faith or (b) do not?

5 Do you think that St Athanasius' words exceed the promises of John 17?

## Discussion and application

**6** Does the way Christians of different churches talk about and relate to one another fall short of Jesus' demands?

**7** What is your reaction to the idea of *theosis*? Why does it make some people feel uncomfortable?

---

# Theological essay 3

## The 'I am' sayings of Jesus in John's Gospel

SAMUEL OTIENO SUDHE

## Introduction

This essay intends to analyse the 'I am' sayings of Jesus in the Gospel of John in the context of African Christianity. The seven 'I am' sayings can be described simply as the self-descriptions of Jesus. Jesus, the Word of God, comes to the earth from heaven and has to use limited ordinary human language to communicate eternal heavenly truths: 'Very truly, I tell you, before Abraham was, I am' (8.58). For that reason the sayings of Jesus are presented in figurative language:

1 'I am the bread of life' (6.41, 48, 51);

2 'I am the light of the world' (8.12; 9.5);

3 'I am the gate' (10.7, 9);

4 'I am the good shepherd' (10.11, 14);

5 'I am the resurrection and the life' (11.25);

6 'I am the way, and the truth, and the life' (14.6);

7 'I am the true vine' (15.1, 5).

As the following brief analysis shows, Jesus uses ordinary examples from everyday life to convey vivid pictures of his relationship to the world now and in the future:

- Jesus picks an example from the dining room: the most basic ingredient on the table – bread. He connects this very ordinary basic nutritional ingredient to eternal life. Jesus is the bread that gives life.

- He takes the significance of light in the cosmos to relay his vital role as the light of the world. Jesus lights the way for the world. 'Walk while you have the light' (12.35).

209

- A door (or gate), as the way of entry into the complexities and beauty of the interior of a house or garden, is a vivid example. It also lends credence to the other 'I am' saying in which Jesus is the way, the truth and the life. Jesus is the opening to the mysteries of God.

- Jesus borrows from the OT symbolic understanding of the shepherd as the royal caretaker of God's people (cf. Psalm 23; Ezekiel 34.11–16). Jesus is the promised Good Shepherd, the Messiah (Ezekiel 34.23).

- Jesus, picking up on the dreaded finality impending for all life forms, demonstrates that he has power over death (11.25). Jesus is life and he has the capacity to restore to life the dead. Therefore, death will never triumph over believers: 'Everyone who lives and believes in me will never die' (11.26).

- Jesus draws examples from the world of agriculture. Jesus is not only the vine but he is the true vine growing under the husbandry of the Father (15.1). Jesus says that, as branches on the vine, human beings have to accept the pruning by the vinedresser in order to increase their yield: 'Those who abide in me and I in them bear much fruit' (15.5b).

The 'I am' sayings point to a relationship between Jesus and his immediate listeners. These sayings, analysed from the perspective of African philosophy, bring out a sense of community in the relationship between Jesus and those around him. Jesus as a sage knew the wisdom and tradition of his people, the Jewish community, and using divine wisdom he brought the best from this tradition. He lived every facet of the Jewish culture, and his life was determined by the norms, values and belief system of the Jewish community of the first century CE. He, however, challenged the same cultural structures, laws and beliefs, and this forms the basis for understanding the 'I am' sayings in the Gospel of John. Jesus was indeed divine as well human. He united humanity and divinity in such a way that challenged and transformed the human relationship to God the Creator.

In Jesus, all things were created, and the fullness of God – Father, Son and Spirit – is revealed. God is indeed three persons in one communion; therefore community existence derives from God. This is best expressed by a proverb of the Maasai of Kenya: *Erisio imaasai we Enkai*, 'The community is like God.' The idea of community that stems from the Trinitarian communion is significant in the African context. Africans recognize life as being complete only in relationship within a community. Africans are communitarian people as is captured in the Kikuyu proverb *Andu nio indu*, 'Peoplehood is wealth.' Evidently every person's life is geared towards the well-being of the community. A Swahili saying, *Mtu ni Watu*, 'A person is people', shows that individuals discover their personalities in the sum total of the relationships that provide the unique identity of each community. Community life in African societies can be said to be an expression of the extended family. Togetherness of purpose is envisaged in the mutuality and reciprocity of all the communal undertakings; the individual members are bound like the strands of a rope. The traditional values of participation, consensus and solidarity form the core of an African community.

Among the Luo people of Kenya there is a proverb that expresses this economy of affection: *Agwony ngei igwony ngea*, translated roughly, 'As I scratch your back, you scratch my back.' This proverb implies that we need our fellow human beings to help scratch those parts of our backs we cannot reach. Yet another proverb with such great moral teachings on the centrality of togetherness is: 'Life is when you are with others; alone you are like an animal.'

From this intricate relationship arise many 'I am' African proverbs that provide a summary picture of what it entails to belong to a community. These 'I am' sayings are accompanied by 'we are' sayings: 'I am because we are; and since we are, therefore I am'; 'We are our relationships. I belong; therefore I am.' Within this kind of framework a relationship that is right and harmonious is created and sustained.

The cultural context in which this relationship is continued finds expression in well-structured and thoroughly defined means of communication. Life in the African context rests on the methods of communication employed (both interpersonal and group interaction). In Africa, although communication helps a lot in establishing relationships, it is on many occasions accompanied by doing actions. Communicating through meaning stories, myths, proverbs, sayings and riddles helps to concretize the African experience.

When this African everyday experience is used as the basis for understanding the 'I am' sayings of Jesus then their deep theological meaning becomes easily evident. Jesus' sayings, which are pictures of real-life situations, bring out community interrelatedness. God's grace is abundantly evident in the rich African cultures, and the gospel illuminates this rich endowment. To understand the context from which Jesus is communicating these sayings is to understand their significance. The 'I am' sayings convey the need for a mutually interdependent relationship where every individual Christian acts as a cog in the wheel that moves forward the kingdom of God as the body of Christ is built: 'Abide in me as I abide in you' (15.4). One of the fruits of intimacy with Christ is an abiding presence with him: 'It is no longer I who live, but it is Christ who lives in me' (Galatians 2.20).

## 'I am the bread of life' (6.41, 48, 51)

*Jesus said to them, 'I am the bread of life. Whoever comes to me will never be hungry.'*

Jesus declares himself to be the sustenance that nourishes the spiritual life. One must feed on his flesh and blood to get eternal life. Jesus came to satisfy earthly hunger. 'Bread of life' primarily means the bread that gives life and secondarily the living bread.

Jesus, in declaring himself as nourishment, is extending an invitation to all. This invitation by Jesus expresses the deep African understanding of hospitality that manifests itself in love, peace and reconciliation. In the African context a meal is a communal affair as is depicted in the Luo proverb *Chamgiwadu*, which means sharing or eating with your brother or sister. Being offered food was a clear sign of being welcomed and accepted to share in the life of a particular community. A meal, especially when it is offered and shared with a visitor, remains the most basic symbol of friendship, love and unity in hospitality. This is strongly depicted in an African proverb that says, 'Relationship is in the eating together: a meal will build community and trust.' Community progress and prosperity was founded in this selfless sharing as is emphasized in the Kikuyu proverb *Muria wiki ndegunega*, which means 'He who eats alone will never prosper.' It was very unusual for Africans to eat by themselves. Jesus, the bread of God, came down from heaven to give life to the world (vv. 33, 50). Those who partake of this bread 'abide in me, and I in them' (v. 56) and will remain a living community.

## 'I am the light of the world' (8.12; 9.5)

*Again Jesus spoke to them, saying, 'I am the light of the world.'*

Jesus identifies himself as the light of the world. In the Gospel of Matthew Jesus identifies his followers as the light of the world (Matthew 5.14). The followers of Jesus are likened to a city built on a hill that cannot be hid or to a lamp placed on a lampstand that lights the house, providing light to all in the house. In the Prologue of John's Gospel Jesus is associated with both light and life (1.4). To have light means to have Jesus (see John 12.35: 'Walk while you have the light'). Jesus' followers will not stumble because with them is the light of life (8.12).

For Africans, fire was not only a source of light and heat but a symbol of unity. In every family the fireplace was an evening gathering-point where the values, norms and belief systems were handed down by the authorities in the community. The fire became a symbol of communion and sharing. A traveller moving across the African hills and plains at night was advised to carry a fire brand to light his paths and also to ward off the wild animals. Because of problems with the sources of ignition, the family fire was not supposed to go out. The fire was to be shared. When the fire had been lit in one home then all the other homes in the neighbourhood could get their fire from this one home. A Malawian saying connects fire with life: 'As long as there is a fire burning in the village, so long God will give us life.' In every village where the fire remains burning, there is always light available for all.

When the Word of God, Jesus Christ, remains the 'lamp to my feet' and the 'light to my path', then walking in the night is as secure and safe as walking during the daylight (Psalm 119.105). The East African Revival Fellowship uses the expression 'walking in the light' to mean sharing one's plans, and also as a confession of sin among fellow Christians. A community that 'walks in the light' does not have any fears because its members do everything in the open. Being a light in the world is to bring out the good works in us and, in so doing, give glory to God (Matthew 5.16).

## 'I am the gate' (10.7, 9)

*Very truly, I tell you, I am the gate for the sheep . . . Whoever enters by me will be saved.*

When Jesus refers to himself as the gate (or door), he is referring to that opening that leads in or out of an enclosure or building. In this particular case he makes a qualification by saying that whoever goes through this gate will ultimately find salvation. The saying that Jesus is the gate connects well with that in John 14 where Jesus says that he is the way, and the truth and the life, and that he is the way to the Father. Jesus is truly the only way that leads humanity back to that harmonious relationship with the Father. Here again the openness of Jesus' invitation to commune with the triune God is evident. Jesus' openness is best captured in the great invitation in Matthew 11.28: 'Come to me, all you that are weary and are carrying heavy burdens, and I will give you rest.' Through Jesus the believers are relieved of their burdens. Through Jesus the sheep find satisfying pasture – the provision of all material and spiritual needs (here equated with salvation). That Jesus is indeed the way to salvation is demonstrated by the depth of his conviction that anyone who comes to him will not be driven away (John 6.37).

Africans have a deep sense of welcome and openness in their culture. In African culture, hospitality is deeply rooted. The householder always uses the Swahili word *Karibu* ('Welcome' or 'Come close'), which is an invitation made with open hands.

A Swazi saying goes: 'It is through people that we are people.' The way to the understanding of an individual is through the community that he or she is reflecting. For an African, the way to understand an individual is through the family's values.

## 'I am the good shepherd' (10.11, 14)

*I am the good shepherd. The good shepherd lays down his life for the sheep.*

In this scenario of a community, the Gospel writer paints a picture of intimacy and sincerity. Jesus the good shepherd has knowledge of the sheep – he understands their needs. His great desire is a perfect, harmonious, cordial and peaceable relationship with the flock. This relationship with the flock is modelled on the relationship between Jesus and God the Father. Jesus and the Father are in perfect harmony. The purpose for which he came down from the Father is to perfectly accomplish the will of him who sent him. The twin purpose of a shepherd lies in the provision of nourishment to the sheep and protection from would-be predators. Jesus' understanding and love for the welfare, development and growth of the sheep ensures the accomplishment of this dual role.

The sheep and the shepherd know each other; the sheep are obedient, and know their roles in that relationship. Jesus is the 'good shepherd' as contrasted with a hired worker and a thief. The thief has a three-pronged destruction agenda for the life of the sheep; that is, to steal, to kill and to destroy. The hired worker will forsake the sheep at the point of danger. Jesus the good shepherd, who knows the sheep intimately, leads them out to the best pasture, which is referred to as abundant life. Jesus' shepherding binds the sheep into a community, a community that has life. Jesus as the shepherd in the African context brings a picture of the village elder, who as the sage was the centre that held, controlled and moved the village life. Each and every member, to maintain harmony, adhered to the rules and norms prescribed by the community. A Maasai proverb helps in understanding this: *Mikiwa enatalaikinote olosho*, 'One who isolates himself from the community will die.' Within a community is shelter, hope and life; outside is loneliness and desperation.

## 'I am the resurrection and the life' (11.25)

*I am the resurrection and the life. Those who believe in me . . . will live.*

Jesus' greatest miracle and most powerful act is the demonstration that he has power over death. Jesus brought back Lazarus from the dead and, further, he himself triumphed over death. Given the superstitious nature of many African beliefs connected to death, Christ's victory over death is convincingly powerful and is a clear indication that he has power over all evil, even that of witches and witchcraft. Jesus is the Medicine of life because he has the medicine of death and of immortality. Because of his triumph over death Jesus is therefore best referred to as *Mganga wa Waganga*, the Healer of Healers. Jesus in the African context becomes the Chief Diviner-Healer, Chief Medicine-Man. Jesus is the all-powerful Saviour who can free people from all forms of fears and oppression. A powerful African proverb gives a clear summary of what Jesus did for all humanity at Calvary: 'The powerful hero is a single person, but all kill the lion.' In a hunting expedition villagers could track a lion, but eventually a single brave warrior would spear the lion. Jesus our ancestor overcame death, but all Christians are conquerors because of his great triumph over death.

## 'I am the way, and the truth, and the life' (14.6)

*I am the way, and the truth, and the life. No one comes to the Father except through me.*

In this saying Jesus puts a strong claim to be the one and only way to God. The context of this saying affirms that Jesus has a mission to prepare places for the believers in his Father's house. Jesus stands for truth. Knowledge of Jesus leads to knowledge of the Father, and this leads to eternal life. Knowing Jesus means coming to the full knowledge of God's salvific plans for humankind. Faith believes that Jesus and the Father are one (John 14.11).

The Akan saying has a similar teaching: 'When you follow in the path of your father, you learn to walk like him. The child resembles the father but he has a clan.' Christ indeed walked the path of his Father just as he requires of his followers to follow on this very path. Here again the claim that Jesus is the gate is appropriate, for as Jesus says: 'No one comes to the Father except through me.'

## 'I am the true vine' (15.1, 5)

*I am the true vine, and my Father is the vine-grower.*

When Jesus uses the agricultural example of the vine, the gardener and pruning, he is actually appealing to the people's understanding of optimum production in an agricultural enterprise. The gardener has the responsibility of insuring the cleanliness of the vine so that production can be maximized. It is imperative that people remain on the vine if they are to be of value to the community. Minus Christ, our productivity remains in jeopardy.

Many African proverbs point to the foundational concept of unity and interconnectedness. The health of the community and the height of the success of its members depends fully on how integrated the community is. The Luo proverb that a community is like many beads threaded on one thread is indeed very appropriate in describing the unity and interconnectedness in a community: we belong together, we are interconnected, we are all valuable, as seen in the aesthetic enhancement that individual beads provide to a multi-coloured necklace. These beautiful items portray the fact that right and harmonious relationships are of great value in African society: 'I am because we are; we are because I am. I belong by blood relationship, therefore I am.'

A key African value is that any individual is always at the service of the community. African society has prescribed roles and a specified mode of behaviour in every situation.

For an African, the centre of life is not achievement but participation. The worst evil in an African community was to be cut off from the community. Any offence that would lead the individual to be ostracized was the height of alienation and was not encouraged among the Africans. So the African understanding of solidarity can be compared to what Jesus means when he says, 'Abide in me as I abide in you' (15.4).

## Conclusion

Reading the 'I am' sayings in an African context conveys a deep sense of belonging, of fellowship and participation. They show the values of Jesus Christ and indicate who 'we are' as Christians. Jesus to a community of believers is the embodiment of who God is and what his purposes for the fallen humanity are: 'You are from below, I am from above; you are of this world, I am not of this world . . . [but] If you continue in my word, you are truly my disciples; and you will know the truth, and the truth will make you free' (John 8.23, 31). As Christians we are sent to propagate these values as we proclaim the gospel of Jesus in our words and deeds (John 17.18). The realization of this fellowship is the familial relationship where every believer regards the other as a brother or a sister as we pool our resources for the mutual development of the Christian community (Acts 2.42–47).

In the African Church, this is best seen in the Small Christian Communities (cell groups) where every believer becomes Christ for others. The basic human needs of every member are met and the spiritual nourishment of each member is enhanced. They point one another to Jesus who is the way, the truth and the life. Jesus walked this path and is walking the path with believers today. Jesus remains the light of this community that he shepherds and feeds, as he leads us through abundance now to life eternal in the future. Jesus the eternal Word of God is the true vine, and every Christian is that branch that has been pruned by the Father to perform every good work.

As we study the 'I am' sayings, we see that Christianity illuminates African cultures, and African cultures challenge the Christian faith to be truly universal. The good news has to be good news to all in all cultures. This mutual challenge and enrichment gives Christianity a deeper meaning and shows the universal value of African philosophies. African proverbs reflect the values and aspirations of the community that has created them, and through them the community may look at itself and bring itself to the knowledge of others.

# John 18.1—19.42

# From Jesus' arrest to his death and burial

 Summary

What is often called the Passion Narrative now begins. It includes Jesus' arrest (18.1–11), an informal hearing before the Jerusalem authorities (18.12–27), his interrogation by Pilate (18.28—19.16), and then his execution and burial (19.16–42).

## 18.1–11: The arrest of Jesus

 Introduction

Jesus and his disciples leave the site of his last meal, and go out of the city. They are met by a group of soldiers and police who arrest Jesus after he is pointed out by Judas. Jesus is taken to the house of the high priest, and his disciples scatter.

 Notes and commentary

**18.1a. Jesus . . . went out with his disciples across the Kidron valley:** This valley separated Jerusalem from the Mount of Olives on the south-east of the city. Jesus' action may echo David's flight from the city (2 Samuel 15.23).

**18.1b. To a place where there was a garden:** Some of the Church Fathers read this as symbolic of the Garden of Eden (Genesis 2.8) and the restoration of paradise, but John does not. The Synoptics identify the place of Jesus' arrest with Gethsemane (Mark 12.32; Matthew 26.36) or the Mount of Olives (Luke 22.39).

**18.2a. Judas . . . also knew the place:** John does not mention the fate of Judas (6.71; 12.4–6; 13.26–30), perhaps because it might contradict 18.9 (compare Matthew 27.3–10; Acts 1.16–20).

**18.2b. Jesus often met there with his disciples:** This detail is known to John, but has not been mentioned in the Gospel.

**18.3a. A detachment of soldiers:** This was a cohort: a tenth part of a legion with a maximum size of 600 soldiers, often about 480 active troops. It is unlikely that such a large body of soldiers would have been sent to arrest Jesus, so this is not a precise number.

**18.3b. Police from the chief priests:** Their role has been described already (7.32).

**18.3c. They came . . . with lanterns and torches and weapons:** Their lights and weapons are contrasted with the light of the world (8.12) who rejects violence (18.11; Luke 22.38).

**18.4. Knowing what was going to happen to him:** Jesus' superior knowledge of his own fate is repeated.

**18.5a. They answered, 'Jesus of Nazareth':** The term translated 'of Nazareth' may mean either 'from Nazareth' or 'the Nazorean' (holy man).

**18.5b. Jesus replied, 'I am he':** The Greek reads 'I am', which may imply he is God as well as answering the question: 'Yes' (4.26; 8.58).

**18.6. They . . . fell to the ground:** If Jesus' reply (18.5) includes a claim to be God, his opponents ironically respond with this action, which is a sign of worship (Job 1.20), defeat (Psalm 27.2; 35.4; 56.10) or a reaction to a revelation (Daniel 2.46; 8.18; Revelation 1.17).

**18.7–8. Again he asked them, 'For whom are you looking?' And they said, 'Jesus of Nazareth.' Jesus answered, 'I told you that I am he':** This is an emphatic repetition of the previous question and answer.

**18.9. To fulfil the word that he had spoken, 'I did not lose a single one of those whom you gave me':** There is no reference to Judas as lost. This would echo 17.12 with its focus on those who are saved.

**18.10a. Simon Peter . . . had a sword:** John's chronology means that the carrying of the sword does not break regulations for the feast, which has yet to start, unlike in the Synoptic traditions. Only John identifies Peter as the sword-bearer, giving no explanation of where he obtained the sword, what kind it was, or how he carried it. Only Luke explains the sword as a misunderstanding of Jesus' words (Luke 22.38): Jesus really meant that they should forget all talk of weapons.

**18.10b. Cut off his right ear:** This detail is also found in Luke 22.50.

**18.10c. The slave's name was Malchus:** This was a common name. The detail may be historical, or provide a fictitious named character. If historical, this detail may indicate that John or his sources were part of the high priest's circle (see 'The identity of John', p. 4).

**18.11. Am I not to drink the cup that the Father has given me?:** The 'cup' and the 'Father' echo the Synoptics (Mark 14.29 (also 10.38); Matthew 26.39; Luke 22.42). John has already raised the kind of question placed here by the Synoptics (12.27), showing Jesus praying at the Last Meal (17.1–26), rather than just before his arrest.

 ## Interpretation

The Passion Narratives are unlike contemporary ancient literature, although they share some common features with stories of the death of famous historical and mythical figures.

The arrest of Jesus marks a return to material which is more obviously parallel to the Synoptic Gospels. As in the Synoptics, the arrest follows quickly after the departure of Jesus and his disciples from the place of the meal (John 13). John's account is much more abrupt: there is no lengthy prayer in the garden, and no dialogue with the disciples.

All the accounts agree that Judas identifies Jesus to his persecutors. John makes no mention of any kiss; Judas leads the armed detachment to a place frequented by Jesus and the disciples. John's Gospel makes clear that Jesus' death is not solely due to Jewish opponents: the detachment of soldiers would most likely be from the Roman garrison, under Roman orders. This is the first appearance of Roman figures hostile to Jesus within the Gospel. It indicates that opposition to Jesus is not confined to elements within Judaism, and also anticipates the wider opposition of the world to John's audience.

Jesus is the most powerful person in the episode. First, his knowledge of the events unfolding is superior to the rest of those involved. Second, although he is vastly outnumbered, his identification of himself is a manifestation of his true nature and power; his opponents fall before him. Jesus is not powerless, but allows himself to be taken prisoner; this will resurface in his discussion with Pilate (18.36–37). This picture adds to John's depiction of Jesus' Messiahship. John distances Jesus from violence. His opponents come to arrest him by force, but are overawed by Jesus' word. Later, Peter, who resorts to violence, is told to put away his sword. Jesus' weapon is his word, which has already overcome his opponents (18.6). Their reaction is a sign that conventional understandings of force, violence and the Messiah are subverted by Jesus, confirming his words to Peter that his disciples are not to rely on such methods. Jesus is identified as a Spirit-filled Messiah whose word brings judgement (3.16–18) and thus separates the just and unjust. While this is often presented in spiritual language (the world belongs to the devil), it includes a strong social and political element. Jesus' opponents, both Jewish and Roman, are increasingly identified as unrighteous, because they cannot accept the truth spoken by Jesus, which tests the powers of this world, finds them flawed and corrupt, and demands their reform. Both the spiritual oppression caused by the devil, and the social and political oppression which comes from worldly powers, are being overturned by Jesus.

# STUDY SUGGESTIONS

## Word study

1 Who are Jesus' enemies in this account?

2 If 'I am' is a claim to be divine, what does 'fell to the ground' imply?

## Review of content

3 What do the elements of light and dark add to the account?

4 What is John's version of Judas' betrayal? How does it differ from the Synoptic accounts?

## Discussion and application

5 What does this story tell Christians about the use of force and violence?

# 18.12–27: At the house of the high priest

 Introduction

Jesus is taken to the house of Annas where an informal interrogation takes place. In the final scene, Peter denies knowing Jesus.

 Notes and commentary

**18.13a. First they took him to Annas:** Only John records this detail: in the Synoptics the high priest remains unnamed (Mark 15.53; Matthew 26.57; Luke 22.54).

Annas was high priest from 6 CE until his dismissal by the Roman procurator Gratus in 15 CE. As high priests were appointed for life he might well have been called by this title even though Caiaphas was holding office that year.

**18.13b. The father-in-law of Caiaphas, the high priest that year:** Caiaphas (11.49) served as high priest from 18 to 36 CE, and was son-in-law of Annas (Josephus, *Antiquities* 18.34; 20.198). All the other high priests who served until 63 CE were sons of Annas. The family was known for its links to the Roman authorities.

Details about the high priests may point either to sources familiar with Jerusalem, or suggest that John was a part of Jerusalem society.

**18.14. Caiaphas was the one who had advised the Jews that it was better to have one person die for the people:** This episode is recorded in 11.50.

**18.15a. Another disciple:** This disciple accompanies Peter, and persuades the staff of the high priest's house to admit them (18.16). This suggests that this disciple is well known, and warns against simply assuming that all Jesus' followers came from the lowest strata of society. His presence with Peter and possible identification with the Beloved Disciple (see 'The identity of John', p. 4) indicate that his Gospel carries the same weight as the Petrine traditions, or even greater. In the Synoptics, Peter follows alone and has no difficulty entering the high priest's house (Mark 14.54; Matthew 25.58; Luke 22.54).

**18.15b. Of the high priest:** While Caiaphas was the serving high priest, it is more likely that this refers to Annas (18.13).

**18.16. The woman who guarded the gate:** Doorkeepers were one of the lowest ranks of servants or slaves, often women. Doorkeepers would ask guests their identity before admitting them.

**18.17. I am not:** Here is Peter's first denial. His 'I am not' stands in contrast to Jesus' 'I am' (18.5). That Peter denies Jesus to a woman may further indicate his weakness: men were expected to be stronger than women.

**18.18. The slaves and the police had made a charcoal fire . . . and they were . . . warming themselves. Peter also was standing with them and warming himself:** Peter's defection from Jesus is indicated by the way he shares the false warmth and light of Jesus' opponents: he becomes more interested in his own comfort and security.

**18.19. Then the high priest questioned Jesus about his disciples and about his teaching:** The story of Peter is now interrupted by a brief cross-examination of Jesus which contrasts their strength and integrity. No specific charge is given here, unlike Mark 14.55–65; Matthew 26.59–68; 27.1; Luke 22.66–71.

**18.20. Jesus answered, 'I have spoken openly to the world; I have always taught in synagogues and in the temple . . . I have said nothing in secret':** No case is to be answered because the charges made against Jesus earlier in this Gospel have been shown to be baseless (Mark 14.49; Matthew 26.55; Luke 22.53).

**18.22. One of the police . . . standing nearby struck Jesus on the face:** The act of violence shows this is not a fair and properly conducted trial (Mark 14.65; Matthew 26.68; Luke 22.63–65). Strictly, the slapping of an innocent man is itself an offence. To strike someone with the hand is a sign of rejection as much as a violent response.

**18.25. Simon Peter was standing and warming himself. They asked him, 'You are not also one of his disciples, are you?' He denied it and said, 'I am not':** The prophecies of 13.38 are coming to pass. This continues the story of Peter from 18.18. Peter denies Jesus a second time. Again Peter is shown as weak in the face of a low-status group, those who are not part of the hearing.

**18.26. One of the slaves of the high priest, a relative of the man whose ear Peter had cut off, asked, 'Did I not see you in the garden with him?':** Peter denies Jesus to a relative of Malchus (18.10); he is now weaker than he was in the garden. His violence and threats have collapsed. Again, Peter denies Jesus to a low-status opponent, a slave of the high priest. This is not just the third denial of being a follower of Jesus (13.38; 18.17, 25), but a denial of what Peter himself has done (18.10): he stands revealed as a false witness. The pattern of three related claims will appear again (21.15–17).

**18.27. At that moment the cock crowed:** This was a confirmation of Jesus' earlier prediction (13.38). The event may serve as a bad omen (Petronius, *Satyricon* 74) and as an indication that it was time to bring Jesus before other authorities as the working day began.

 ## Interpretation

This section contrasts Peter's denial of Jesus (18.15–17, 25–27) with the cross-examination of Jesus. This is a technique often found in Mark's Gospel, known as intercalation: a narrative is split into two parts, and a second narrative is inserted between them. Here it gives the impression that the two events occur simultaneously. The intercalation highlights the difference between Jesus' courage and moral victory in the face of the powerful, and Peter's weakness and denials before the insignificant. The answers given by Peter are also contrasted with Jesus' in Gethsemane. Peter's denials are all the more ironic since Jesus is asking his interrogators to supply witnesses (18.23) – and outside stands his disciple, bearing false witness about himself. A quotation from the Roman orator and politician, Cicero, may also shed light on Peter's repeated denials: 'Any man can make mistakes, but only an idiot persists in his error.' John's Gospel does not deny or underplay Peter's desertion of Jesus. It is so serious that it is emphasized by the threefold denial and by his identification as a disciple of Jesus from the beginning of his ministry (1.40–41). However, even if Peter fails badly, he is also forgiven, restored and learns from his failure. Critics might point out Peter's weakness, but Christianity is not a perfectionist faith. Jesus has, at the heart of his teaching, not a call to be perfect, but a call to admit weakness and the need to change. Peter exemplifies this; his experience gives us hope that we can become better, rather than despairing that we are doomed because we are flawed. He also shows that high rank or status (in his case, as a disciple) within the community does not, in itself, guarantee faithfulness. Furthermore, Peter's weakness shows why disciples are right to depend on Jesus' strength, as they are unable on their own to show such courage and resolve.

The questioning in 18.19–24 is not a proper legal trial. There are a number of factors which reveal it was not: the location, its date on the eve of a feast (*Sanhedrin* 4.1), the timing at night (*Sanhedrin* 4.1 demands daytime for capital cases), the lack of formal charges, appeals for clemency and process for the witnesses (*Sanhedrin* 4.1; 5; *Tosefta* 7.5), and a single judge (*Pirke Abot* 4.8). John's Gospel, which dates this event to the night leading into the Day of Preparation, does not face the additional problem in the Synoptics: a 'trial' during Passover.

It is similar to the Synoptic Gospels, yet very different from them. The date is different, but all say the trial happens at night. More significantly, the Synoptic accounts all point towards a hearing with a specific charge of blasphemy levelled at Jesus. There is no such charge in John at this point because this material already surfaced (5.1–47; 7.14–31). John has already shown that Jesus has no charge to answer, is innocent of the charges of blasphemy (because of his real identity), and that his accusers' case has been weakened by their own poor handling of the case. The short conversation which appears here shows that there has been no change. No fresh evidence is available, and there has been no improvement in his treatment: the threats and intimidation which have accompanied previous dialogues are now laid bare (7.44; 8.59; 10.31, 39; 11.53, 57; 18.22).

The location is also significant. Annas did not hold the office of high priest at that time, but remained a power behind the scenes as his son-in-law and sons held the office throughout this period. This is a scenario familiar in many places. The public office-bearers and those who ostensibly hold power are often figureheads: real power is held by those who operate behind the scenes. Jesus is now in the hands of people of this type. John shows that Jesus' opponents are a small but powerful group.

In this scene:

- Jesus is portrayed as the model and inspiration for disciples who face persecution;

- the true nature of the world and its justice, as opposed to the judgements which come as a result of God's love (3.16–21), are revealed.

The audience will assume that Jesus has spoken the truth (18.23) and therefore that he is innocent of making false claims about his own identity.

# STUDY SUGGESTIONS

## Word study

1 Compare this account to Mark 14.53–72; Matthew 26.57–75; Luke 22.47–71. Identify the points shared by one or more of the accounts

and those which are unique. Hint: see if there are points of contact between details which initially appear different.

### Review of content

**2** Read 2 Corinthians 4.7. Do you think the description of Peter in this Gospel sends a similar message?

**3** Compare the stories of Jesus and Peter. How is Jesus' strength compared to Peter's weakness?

**4** Many cultures have proverbs or wisdom teaching which suggests that a mistake may be made only once. How does this affect their reading of Peter's denial?

### Discussion and application

**5** Do we grow as a result of our failures, or do we despair? What message are we being given here?

**6** What message does Jesus' treatment offer to those who are also the victims of systems of 'justice' which employ corrupt practice and intimidation?

---

## 18.28—19.16a: At the headquarters of Pilate

 Introduction

The preliminary interrogation before the high priest has been completed. In the early morning, after cock-crow, Jesus' opponents take him to the headquarters of the Roman governor, Pontius Pilate, for further questioning, in the hope of declaring him a criminal in the eyes of the Roman authorities.

 Notes and commentary

**18.28a. Then they took Jesus from Caiaphas:** See 11.49; 18.14. No details are given of any happening which occurs before Caiaphas. John has focused on Annas (18.13), who is the significant leader. Such a relationship between Annas (father-in-law) and Caiaphas (son-in-law) may be contrasted with the relationship which exists between the Father and Jesus.

**18.28b. To Pilate's headquarters:** Pontius Pilate was appointed prefect of Judaea by Tiberius in 26 CE; his title later seems to have been procurator. As procurator he was allowed to take his wife with him (Matthew 27.19).

He had full control of the army garrisoned in Judaea, and powers of life and death (18.31). He also appointed high priests for the Temple and had control of its governance and finances. Tacitus mentions him only in a text associated with the death of Jesus (*Annals* 15.44). Jewish writers were more critical: Philo considered his governorship harsh and corrupt (*Embassy to Gaius* 301). Josephus records a number of incidents in which Pilate upset the people of Judaea. A massacre of the Samaritans led to his recall to Rome in 37 CE. The verdict of his trial is unknown, but he appears to have committed suicide during the reign of Gaius (Caligula, 37–41 CE).

The headquarters were the official residence of the governor. Two sites are possible, but the old palace of Herod the Great is more likely than the Fortress Antonia with its Roman garrison near the Temple. This official site may be contrasted with the unofficial hearing before Annas (18.13).

**18.28c. To avoid ritual defilement:** Entering any non-Jewish household would have made a Jewish visitor impure. Concerns about ritual impurity contrast with the Jewish leaders' contempt for justice (18.23). John has this meeting in the morning of the Day of Preparation, the Synoptics after the beginning of the Passover (Appendix A; 13.1–20).

**18.28d. It was early in the morning:** This is a similar detail to that given in 18.27. Clients tended to approach their patrons in the early morning (Horace, *Satires* 1.1.9–10; Martial, *Epigrams* 3.36.1–3).

**18.29. What accusation do you bring against this man?:** Pilate's question anticipates a formal charge.

**18.30. If this man were not a criminal, we would not have handed him over to you:** No formal charge is made. Pilate either has to agree with those who have brought Jesus, or cause them to lose face. Jesus' opponents seem to dare Pilate to disagree with them.

**18.31a. Take him yourselves and judge him according to your law:** Pilate avoids causing offence: they should judge Jesus themselves.

**18.31b. We are not permitted to put anyone to death:** Jesus' opponents imply that Jesus is guilty of a charge deserving death, but that they depend on Pilate to impose this penalty. They force him to become involved again.

The claim is not strictly accurate. The Roman governor had authority which included the death sentence. Later Jewish tradition claims Jewish authorities lost this right in about 30 CE, though some suggest this occurred at the founding of the Roman province (6 CE). However, it appears that the Jewish authorities could carry out a capital sentence with Roman permission (Josephus, *Jewish War* 6.2.4). When Roman permission was not given, the Romans might punish those who had carried out the sentence (Josephus, *Jewish War* 6.6.2). In this case, the opponents of Jesus ensure that they are keeping strictly to established protocols by demanding that Pilate approves the sentence. The comparison between the irregular hearing (18.19–24) and the insistence that Pilate now follows due process to the letter is ironic.

**18.32. The kind of death:** This phrase refers to crucifixion. Stoning was the preferred method for punishment in Judaism, especially for blasphemy (5.18). Death by crucifixion demands Roman involvement. Any attempt to blame only Jewish opponents for Jesus' death fails to take this into account.

**18.33. Are you the King of the Jews?:** Pilate does not use technical terms like 'Messiah' or 'Christ'. The question suggests that, despite his apparent ignorance, he has some idea of what is going on (12.13–15). His question fits better with his Roman and political background. In its early history, Rome had suffered under tyrannical monarchy which had been overthrown to form the republic. The end of the republic had brought the empire, but the language of kingship and monarchy was never used to describe the emperors. Royal language was often used in political debate and polemic to criticize opponents and to imply they would be tyrants. Roman laws on treason could have been used to accuse Jesus of sedition.

**18.34. Do you ask this on your own, or did others tell you about me?:** Jesus' question challenges Pilate to admit whether he is really relying on his own knowledge or that of others. It suggests he is depending on the opinions of his inferiors.

**18.35a. I am not a Jew, am I?:** Pilate attempts to avoid Jesus' question. He may be implying that, as a Roman, he is superior to the Jews. The irony is that his claim also reveals his ignorance.

**18.35b. Your own nation and the chief priests have handed you over to me:** Pilate may be claiming that to be handed over by one's own people and leaders is a mark of the seriousness of the charge. Again, it may be ironic: Pilate is being revealed as a leader who is not in control of events. The same word, 'handed over', is used to describe Judas' actions (6.64). The action of the Jewish leaders is not a betrayal because they are not claiming to be disciples of Jesus.

**18.35c. What have you done?:** Pilate appears to have no knowledge of the charges (18.29–32).

**18.36a. My kingdom is not from this world:** Jesus has already distanced himself from 'this world' and criticized it (17.6–19), rejecting attempts to make him king in any conventional sense (6.15; 12.13). As in 18.20, the charge has already been shown false.

**18.36b. If my kingdom were from this world, my followers would be fighting to keep me from being handed over to the Jews. But as it is, my kingdom is not from here:** Jesus' kingdom is different from what Pilate expects. Two factors make this clear: that Jesus' disciples do not fight to defend his kingdom, and that it is 'not from here' (3.3).

**18.37a. Pilate asked him, 'So you are a king?' Jesus answered, 'You say that I am a king. For this I was born, and for this I came into the world,**

**to testify to the truth':** Pilate attempts to obtain an admission that Jesus is a king, and therefore guilty either of treason (a king without the approval of the Roman authorities) or of false witness (because he is not a king). In reply, Jesus answers that his primary concern is 'truth' (Appendix E), and ignores any question about kingship. Talk about kingship is attributed only to Pilate ('You say').

**18.37b. Everyone who belongs to the truth listens to my voice:** Jesus' statement repeats themes from the description of the Good Shepherd (10.3–4, 8, 16).

**18.38a. What is truth?:** Pilate attempts to win the discussion by rejecting truth as useful.

**18.38b. I find no case:** Pilate is unable to find Jesus guilty of perjury or treason. He may be asserting his superiority: he finds no case against someone accused by his inferiors (18.30, 35).

**18.39a. But you have a custom that I release someone for you at the Passover:** To release Jesus may be a false favour, because Jesus is innocent. However, Roman law allowed for pardon when a prisoner was acquitted before a trial. No firm evidence supports the practice of such a 'custom' in Judaea, but this was not an unusual power for Roman officials. Mark 15.6 and Matthew 27.15 imply it was Pilate's custom.

**18.39b. Do you want me to release for you the King of the Jews?:** If this is a play on Jewish hopes to win Jesus' freedom, it backfires. Pilate does not understand the significance of what Jesus has said, and does not understand what is going on. Note the difference from the choice given in Matthew 27.17: here Pilate seems to offer only freedom for Jesus. The crowd's demand for a different person to be set free, not Pilate's choice, may again indicate his lack of control over the unfolding events.

**18.40. Barabbas was a bandit:** Bandits were the opposite of the Good Shepherd (10.1). There are two additional ironies:

- The name Barabbas means 'son of a father'.

- The activities of people like Barabbas would lead to the civil war and destruction of Jerusalem in 70 CE. Condemning an innocent man (11.50) will not save the nation, but end in disaster.

**19.1. Pilate took Jesus and had him flogged:** Flogging was a part of Roman punishment: even an innocent man could be flogged (Josephus, *Jewish War* 6.304–5). Here, it may indicate a warning, rather than a scourging before execution (Mark 15.15; Matthew 27.26); the show of brutality may cause his opponents to back off, enabling Jesus to be set free. Jesus might have been beaten with either a whip or rods while lashed to a post. Punishments like this were a cause of shame as well as physical pain: they showed the power of the authorities.

**19.2a. The soldiers wove a crown of thorns and put it on his head:** Crowns were prizes for triumphant generals or victors in athletic contests (1 Corinthians 9.25). Jesus is mocked using symbols of authority.

**19.2b. They dressed him in a purple robe:** Purple clothing, usually coloured with a dye made from shellfish, was expensive, and signified power and authority.

**19.3. They kept . . . striking him on the face:** Blows to the face were considered especially shameful (Matthew 5.39).

**19.4. I find no case:** Pilate says for the second time that he can find no case against Jesus.

**19.5. Here is the man:** Some suggest that this is a title: the Samaritan text *Memar Marqah* uses 'man' to describe the Messiah. Others point out that the same words describe Israel's first king (1 Samuel 9.17). Jesus is being mocked (19.14), but these words may point to his true identity.

**19.6a. The chief priests and the police . . . shouted, 'Crucify him':** Only Jesus' opponents demand his crucifixion, unlike in the Synoptics where the whole people (crowd) assents to his death (Mark 15.11–15; Matthew 27.15–23; Luke 23.13–25). The call for crucifixion implies either a Roman penalty for a Roman crime (19.12), or Pilate's involvement. Crucifixion was a Roman punishment, but also was practised elsewhere. Even Roman historians saw it as a barbarous method of execution. The victim was nailed to a wooden stake, with nails through the wrists and the ankles. It is not clear whether cross-beams were used on some occasions: victims were crucified in a variety of postures. Death was often slow (19.33) and could take several days. Some Roman writers viewed suicide as preferable. As the victim grew more and more tired, the increasing weight of their body caused death by asphyxiation; shock, loss of blood and other factors also were involved. Crucifixion might be preceded with torture. It was the most severe Roman punishment and considered so shameful that it was restricted at times to lower orders of society, especially slaves. It was used as punishment for rebellion, violent crime and robbery.

**19.6b. I find no case:** Pilate's third denial of any charge against Jesus compares with Peter's three denials. Pilate hands Jesus over to his opponents, giving up his place both as judge and executioner. Even if Pilate surrenders his responsibilities, Roman soldiers will still carry out the sentence (19.23).

**19.7. We have a law, and according to that law he ought to die because he has claimed to be the Son of God:** The offence might lie in claiming to be the Messiah or making a statement which should be uttered only by God (5.1–47). The title 'Son of God' has been used already in 1.34 (Appendix F).

**19.8. When Pilate heard this, he was more afraid than ever:** Pilate is portrayed as fearing the supernatural. Such fears are found in contemporary Graeco-Roman culture, but this may be John's description rather than historical accuracy. Fear is a sign of weakness according to shame–honour systems (12.20–36a). Pilate's character is being questioned.

**19.9a. Where are you from?:** Pilate's question repeats the theme of origins seen at several points (1.43–51; 8.12–20, 39–59; 10.31–39; 17.6–19).

**19.9b. Jesus gave him no answer:** As in previous trials, Jesus does not give a detailed defence. This question has already been addressed: there is no basis for any charge against him (18.20).

**19.10. Power to release you . . . power to crucify you:** Pilate reminds Jesus of the earthly power which he possesses (18.32).

**19.11a. You would have no power over me unless it had been given from above:** Jesus denies Pilate's claim to absolute power, repeating that God and Jesus are always ultimately in control (2.4; 7.6; 10.18; 13.3, 27; 18.11), and anticipating Pilate's fear of the emperor (19.12–13). 'From above' indicates a superior authority (3.3, 7, 31; 8.23). The courage of Jesus is a marked contrast to the fear which motivates Pilate.

**19.11b. The one who handed me over:** The verb 'handed over' has been used of both Jesus' opponents (18.35) and Judas (6.64). The singular noun ('the one') may indicate Judas rather than a group of opponents.

**19.11c. A greater sin:** This may simply mean a greater mistake or error. 'Greater' nevertheless suggests that Pilate, as well as the Jewish leaders, has made an error or mistake of some kind.

**19.12a. Pilate tried to release him:** Pilate's ineffectiveness is stressed: he is powerless in the face of his subjects.

**19.12b. You are no friend of the emperor:** The governor was appointed by the emperor (18.34). Jesus' opponents play on Pilate's insecurity or fear of Tiberius who ruthlessly got rid of potential political rivals. The language here is political, not theological.

**19.12c. Everyone who claims to be king:** Jesus' opponents play on Pilate's fear: if he does not eliminate Jesus, he too will be seen as a traitor.

**19.13a. When Pilate heard these words, he brought Jesus outside:** Pilate gives in to the demands of Jesus' opponents. His fear of the emperor outweighs his fear of Jesus (19.8). He has again been outplayed by his subjects.

**19.13b. And sat on the judge's bench:** The location was more likely to be outside the palace of Herod rather than the pavement at the Fortress Antonia (18.28), which dates from the time of Hadrian (117–138 CE). If this marks the formal verdict, Jesus' scourging may have been presented as a judicial warning (19.1).

**19.13c. A place called The Stone Pavement, or in Hebrew Gabbatha:** See 1.38 for John's custom of giving translations. The detail may indicate the historical accuracy of this account.

**19.14a. It was the day of Preparation for the Passover:** Jesus is condemned to death before the beginning of the Passover feast (13.1–20).

**19.14b. It was about noon:** According to some Passover regulations, this was when any leavened bread would be removed from the house. It was also the time when lambs were taken to the Temple for the afternoon sacrifice. The Synoptics record different times for the crucifixion: 9 a.m. (Mark 15.25) and before noon (Matthew 27.45; Luke 23.44).

**19.14c. Here is your King:** Pilate voices an ironic prophecy about Jesus' identity (19.5).

**19.15a. Shall I crucify your King?:** Pilate compounds his previous failure to exercise power properly, and remains complicit in Jesus' death.

**19.15b. We have no king but the emperor:** This statement continues the theme of loyalty (19.12). It shows how far Jesus' opponents have departed from the traditions they claim to preserve: the emperor, not God, is their king. There is a particular irony: the *Hallel* prayer sung at the Passover states that Israel has no king but God.

 Interpretation

In 18.28–40, Pilate has two conversations: with Jesus' opponents (18.28–32, 38b–40) and with Jesus himself (18.33–38a). The passage in 19.1–16 describes a series of events which culminate in a formal verdict (19.13) being brought against Jesus by Pilate.

This first section (18.28–40) must raise questions about the accuracy of the events portrayed, not because they are historically impossible, but because of how they were witnessed. While 'another disciple' (18.1) might have been in the delegation or heard from those who were present (18.28–32, 38b–40), the text itself gives no such evidence. Even more difficult is the conversation between Jesus and Pilate (18.33–38): no witnesses are mentioned. These accounts are likely to be John's idea of what really went on. They confirm that the Romans were involved in the death of Jesus. Limiting historical blame for Jesus' death to the Jewish people or leaders is wrong.

In 18.28–32, the argument focuses on who should condemn Jesus. His opponents seek to involve Pilate in the judicial process, despite their own failure to observe correct legal methods. In 18.33–38a, Pilate's discussions with Jesus reveal a misunderstanding (Appendix H) about Jesus' kingship and truth.

While some commentators say John downplays Pilate's role in order to show that Christianity is no threat to the Roman Empire, reading these scenes as examples of a contest about honour and shame suggests a very different picture. Consider Pilate's talk with Jesus' opponents: his political subjects and inferiors effectively manipulate him to get the outcome that they wish. Pilate is neither a strong leader nor a skilled diplomat.

His meeting with Jesus is no better. He reveals that he cannot judge this case (18.35), and then fails to understand Jesus' words about kingship. He does not understand that Jesus' kingship is 'not from this world' (18.36) and is ignorant of what John's audience knows: that Jesus' kingship is superior to the Roman Empire. Pilate then does not know how the world really works, and has no grasp of 'truth' (18.37–38a): modern philosophers might call this a 'category mistake'. Pilate's concept of 'kingdom' is of a completely different order (category) from Jesus'. To compare them is impossible. Pilate ultimately is portrayed as a failure: as leader, judge and philosopher.

Our worldview is increasingly described as pluralist (there is no single truth, but many truths) or postmodern (lacking any of the certainties which science claimed to have found). For some philosophers, there is a lack of certainty about what constitutes truth. The ancient Graeco-Roman world also knew a vast variety of worldviews, philosophies and beliefs, all in competition with one another. Because of people like Socrates and Plato, what were claimed to be certainties – the nature of bravery, for example – were revealed as flawed definitions. In the hands of the truly wise this can be a helpful method to gain knowledge, unlearning what is false. In the hands of those who are unscrupulous, it becomes a simple trick which leaves everything open to question: old certainties are removed and nothing is put in their place. This fits Pilate to a remarkable degree: a man of power and privilege who uses word-games to dodge his responsibilities and, in so doing, condemns an innocent man to death. He typifies what happens when a hollow ideology is put into practice by those who hold real power, and when a political regime ceases to care for those who live under its authority. This encounter also lays bare the bankruptcy of Roman rule by comparing it unfavourably with the Father and Jesus. They offer a radically different understanding of truth: an imitation of God, and a way of life which does not leave the vulnerable exposed to yet more degradation, but loved, valued and liberated. This scene lays bare the flawed political structures of the Roman Empire while avoiding direct criticism or confrontation. The Johannine antisociety (see 'The good news according to John', p. 7) claims to be better than the *Pax Romana* (14.1–31), and to know what truth is (8.32; 17.17).

Pilate states three times that he can find no case against Jesus (18.38; 19.4, 6). This echoes Peter's three denials of Jesus. Pilate does not protect the one whom he believes to be innocent. Jesus, at this point, has been let down by a friend who will not stand up for him (Peter 18.15–18, 25–27) and by a legal and political system that will not protect the innocent.

The later conversations highlight the weakness of Pilate as a leader. Despite his cynicism (18.38), even he is aware of the unfolding miscarriage of justice. However, he does not use his power to do what is right. He is involved in a power struggle with the opponents of Jesus. Perhaps he hopes they will back down when they see Jesus scourged and mocked (19.1–5). It is a further indictment of the legal system that torturing an innocent man is a way to win an argument.

He is also easily moved by the arguments of Jesus' opponents. The weakness of his position becomes clearer: he is driven by fear (19.8). This is itself a sign of weakness, but it is heightened when he surrenders further to his opponents. Pilate is portrayed as one who is rightly fearful, because he seems to fear the Son of God (19.7), but his real motivation is fear of the emperor. There is a further insult to Pilate in this section. John portrays him not only as a failure as a judge, but as someone who gives up his power as executioner (19.6). He has surrendered all his power to his inferiors.

The final verses show how pathetic the power games have been. Pilate, despite all his protests, cannot escape involvement in the final condemnation of Jesus. Jesus' opponents ultimately end up betraying all that they should represent (19.15). Only Jesus emerges with any honour from this travesty of justice. Neither Roman imperial power nor the Jerusalem hierarchy has escaped John's criticism.

 # STUDY SUGGESTIONS

## Word study

1 What are the differences between Jesus' and Pilate's understanding of 'truth'? Refer back to the texts mentioned in the notes to find your answer.

## Review of content

2 Write your own description of Pontius Pilate's role in these events, based on John's portrayal of him.

3 What evidence is there to show that the Romans were complicit in the death of Jesus?

4 Why did some people in the ancient world see Jesus' death as an obstacle to believing in him?

## Discussion and application

5 Does the criticism of Pilate resemble political realities in today's world?

6 Do we base our understanding of truth on Jesus, or on the values of the world in its different philosophies, ideologies and worldviews?

7 Have truth and justice become the victims of ideological and philosophical posturing in your context? Have vulnerable people in your community suffered as a result?

## 19.16b–42: The crucifixion and death of Jesus

 Introduction

Jesus is taken to the place of execution, Golgotha. The story of his final hours includes a number of dialogues with those at the scene.

 Notes and commentary

**19.16b. So they took Jesus:** 'They' refers to Jesus' opponents (also 19.6). Pilate's troops are involved in the carrying out of the crucifixion (19.23).

**19.17a. Carrying the cross by himself:** John shows that no one else suffers because of Jesus and his firmness of purpose (12.27). The Synoptics include assistance given by Simon of Cyrene (Mark 15.20–21b; Matthew 27.31b–32; Luke 23.26–32). The 'cross' means a cross-piece carried by the prisoner to a post (Plautus, *The Braggart Captain* 2.4.7).

**19.17b. The Place of the Skull . . . Golgotha:** The name may refer to a place of execution, to skulls at an execution site, or a graveyard. It appears to be situated outside the city walls (19.20; Hebrews 13.12). The exact site remains disputed, and the traditional site was later located within the walls of the city as developed by Hadrian.

**19.18a. There they crucified him:** See 19.6. John omits the offer of wine, which might have been offered as sedative (Mark 15.23; Matthew 27.34).

**19.18b. And with him two others:** The Synoptics give more information: these were robbers (Mark 15.27; Matthew 27.38; see 10.1) or evildoers – criminals (Luke 23.33–34). John also omits any dialogue between them (Mark 15.27–32a; Matthew 27.38–43; Luke 23.35–38).

**19.19a. Pilate also had an inscription written and put on the cross:** A member of the execution squad might carry a tablet detailing the crime (Suetonius, *Caligula* 32.2; *Domitian* 10.1). The original Greek says that Pilate wrote the inscription and put it on the cross. It more likely means that Pilate's staff did this.

**19.19b. It read, 'Jesus of Nazareth, the King of the Jews':** All the Gospels record different wordings (Mark 15.26; Matthew 27.37; Luke 23.38). For 'of Nazareth', see the previous discussion in 18.5.

**19.20. This inscription . . . was written in Hebrew, in Latin, and in Greek:** Only John records this detail. For Hebrew, see 1.38; 19.13. Public writings, like funerary inscriptions, were often written in several languages. Some think this indicates Jesus' universality (12.20–26) and how he died for the world (3.16).

**19.21. Do not write 'The King of the Jews', but, 'This man said, I am King of the Jews':** Only John records this controversy. Despite the charge, Jesus' opponents appear unwilling to see the title 'King of the Jews' made public. Their wording may attempt to shift the charge away from the claim that he is the king of the Jews to his fault in making such a proclamation (8.59).

**19.22. What I have written, I have written:** The writing may have been ordered, rather than written by Pilate (19.19). Pilate has not given into his subjects, but this cannot reverse the injustice being done. Pilate's declaration may show Jesus' identity and innocence, like the sayings attributed to the centurion (Mark 15.40; Matthew 27.54; Luke 23.47).

**19.23. When the soldiers had crucified Jesus, they took his clothes and divided them into four parts, one for each soldier. They also took his tunic; now the tunic was seamless, woven in one piece from the top:** John records more details than the Synoptics (Mark 15.24–26; Matthew 27.35–36; Luke 23.34). Goods such as clothes could be taken from the condemned (Sallust, *The War with Catiline* 51.43; 52.14), and nakedness was typical (Polybius 11.30.1–2). This would add additional shame (Juvenal, *Satires* 1.70). Only John records the detail that Jesus' robe was divided into four parts. The basic number of a small Roman military unit was eight soldiers who shared a tent; half might be used for a task like crucifixion.

A 'tunic' was a long tight-fitting undergarment usually made from two pieces of fabric, such as wool, linen or leather. A 'seamless' garment made from one piece of material would fit better at the neck, have short sleeves, and be more valuable. Because it was 'woven', some see a reference to the garments of the high priest (Exodus 28.6; 39.3, 5, 8, 22, 27), but the word 'tunic' is absent from those descriptions. Josephus describes the high priest's blue vestment as a seamless garment (*Antiquities* 3.161); this was an outer garment rather than a tunic (Exodus 39).

**19.24. So they said . . . 'Let us not tear it, but cast lots for it to see who will get it.' This was to fulfil what the scripture says, 'They divided my garments among themselves, and for my clothing they cast lots':** The incident is historically likely (19.23). If so, John uses it to confirm a prophecy in Psalm 22.18. It is the first of a series of quotations considered to fulfil Scripture (19.28, 36–37).

**19.25a. And that is what the soldiers did:** Psalm 22 functions as prophecy: what is happening is not controlled by the soldiers, but part of God's plan.

**19.25b. His mother, and his mother's sister, Mary the wife of Clopas, and Mary Magdalene:** Four women are described as present. It is more likely that the 'mother's sister' and 'Mary wife of Clopas' refer to two people rather than an aunt also called Mary. The Synoptic lists differ (Mark 15.40; Matthew 27.55; Luke 23.49); none has the mother of Jesus present. Her presence later is recorded in Acts 1.14. Instead of 'Clopas', some early manuscripts read 'Cleopas' (Luke 24.18). The names were distinct: Clopas is Semitic; Cleopas is Greek.

Mary Magdalene is commonly identified with Mary of Bethany (11.1, 28–37; 12.1–8). The strongest evidence for this is the perfume associated with Jesus' burial (12.3–7), but it is Nicodemus who supplies the spices for the burial (19.39). Luke knows her as one from whom seven devils were cast out (Luke 7.2). The common understanding that Mary Magdalene is the one who anoints Jesus, is the sister of Lazarus and also is present at the crucifixion and resurrection is actually a composite picture made by compiling scenes from different Gospels which may originally relate to two or three different characters. Magdala is her place of origin, on the north-west shore of the Sea of Galilee.

**19.26a. The disciple whom he loved:** This is the Beloved Disciple (see 'The identity of John', p. 4).

**19.26b. Woman:** This is not an insulting form of address (2.4).

**19.26c. Here is your son:** The Beloved Disciple is given responsibilities usually associated with a close relative (Exodus 20.12; Ruth 3.23–24).

**19.27a. Here is your mother:** This is a complementary remark indicating the relationship which will exist between Mary and the Beloved Disciple.

**19.27b. And from that hour:** The immediacy of the disciple's response indicates the high regard he gives to Jesus' request, fulfilling it immediately. It need not imply that he and the mother of Jesus leave, even if 'hour' refers to Jesus' departure to the Father (19.35).

**19.27c. Into his own home:** The Greek is literally, 'to his own': Mary and the Beloved Disciple were not necessarily living in the same house, but he was responsible for her well-being.

**19.28a. Jesus knew:** Jesus has full knowledge of what is happening, implying his control and assent to God's plan.

**19.28b. 'I am thirsty':** This saying is said to be a further fulfilment of a scriptural prophecy (19.24). No direct text from the OT is identifiable. Some see a further reference to Psalm 22.15, which does not include this exact phrase. Others link to Psalm 69.21 (LXX), which shares more vocabulary (19.29). This phrase also underlines the true humanity of Jesus: he endures genuine physical suffering. This may counter Docetism (see the Introduction; 1.14; 6.35; 11.35).

**19.29a. Sour wine:** This is also mentioned in Psalm 69.21: a further fulfilment of a Scripture. Without the addition of myrrh (Mark 15.23; Matthew 27.34), this drink would only quench thirst, not reduce pain. The Synoptics link the offering of wine to the coming of Elijah (Mark 15.36; Matthew 27.48).

**19.29b. On a branch of hyssop:** This is one of a family of herbs with an aroma like mint. It may have a reference to the Passover lamb, as hyssop was used to daub the doorposts of the houses protected by God (Exodus 12.22). The symbolism may suggest that Jesus' blood, and sacrifice of himself, offers protection to his disciples. Psalm 51.7 uses hyssop to symbolize purification and forgiveness. John's timing of the death of Jesus also supports his identification with the Passover lamb (see 1.29 for 'lamb'; 13.1; 18.28; 19.14, 31 for timing). The Synoptics use the phrase 'on a reed', which lacks this symbolism (Mark 15.36; Matthew 27.48).

**19.30a. 'It is finished':** This expression includes all of these meanings: 'It is finished/completed/made perfect.' None of the Synoptics have this saying (Mark 15.35, 37; Matthew 27.46, 50; Luke 23.46). Some see a reference to the creation story in which God completed the work on the seventh day (Genesis 2.2 (LXX)). A new creation or age has been completed.

**19.30b. He . . . gave up his spirit:** 'Gave up' is the same Greek word as 'betray' (6.71; 18.30). Used of a thing rather than a person, it simply means 'hand on' or 'hand over'. 'Spirit' signifies life or soul, but also may have a divine element. The Synoptics use different phrases: 'breathed out [his last]', 'died' (Mark 15.37; Luke 23.46) or 'sent out his spirit [or breath]' (Matthew 27.49). Jesus is in control: it is he who hands over the Spirit, not his opponents or the authorities.

**19.31a. Since it was the day of Preparation, the Jews did not want the bodies left on the cross during the sabbath, especially because that sabbath was a day of great solemnity:** The Synoptic Gospels share these two details about the date (Mark 15.42; Matthew 27.62; Luke 23.54) which clashes with their depiction of the Last Supper as the Passover *Seder*. Evidence for Jesus' death on the Day of Preparation is also found in some of their sources, not just in John. The combination of Passover and the Sabbath made for a particularly sacred day. Jewish writers note that the Romans sometimes made concessions to Jewish sensitivities (Philo, *Flaccus* 83; Josephus, *Jewish War* 4.317). The opponents of Jesus are concerned about both Passover (18.38) and Sabbath (5.9–12) observance, but not a miscarriage of justice.

**19.31b. They asked Pilate to have the legs of the crucified men broken:** An iron club might be used. Breaking the legs would speed up the onset of death by asphyxiation as the weight of the crucified person would be supported only by the arms (19.6). As the legs of the Passover lamb were not broken (Exodus 12.46; Numbers 9.12), Jesus is being identified with it.

**19.33. Jesus . . . was already dead:** This detail is added perhaps to counter claims that Jesus did not die on the cross.

**19.34a. One of the soldiers pierced his side:** Historical parallels to this action are debatable, and may refer only to being nailed to the cross (Quintilian, *Declamatio Maior* 6.9). Whether historical or not, John is using it to interpret Jesus' death.

**19.34b. Blood and water came out:** The Gospel writer is stressing the reality of Jesus' death, especially by placing 'blood' first. Medical studies show that a substance like water might issue from the pericardial sac. A number of other allusions are possible, but none is agreed to be present by all commentators:

1 *Passover tradition*: Lambs were hung up and flayed, and their blood was sprinkled on the altar. This, however, does not include 'water'.

2 *Temple imagery*: Jesus dies as the blood from the lambs flows from the Temple. Water is a major symbol in the Gospel. Jesus is the eschatological temple from which the water of life flows (7.37–39; Revelation 22.1, 17).

3 *Sacramental significance*: Blood symbolizes the Eucharist (6.53–56); water symbolizes baptism (3.5).

**19.35. He who saw this has testified so that you also may believe. His testimony is true, and he knows that he tells the truth:** This comment implies that the Gospel comes from an authoritative eyewitness account.

**19.36. 'None of his bones shall be broken':** This quotation combines Psalm 34.19–20, Exodus 12.46 and Numbers 9.12. The event is described as a fulfilment of Scripture. Some Pharisaic traditions stress that a person was resurrected in the same state as that of their death (20.24–29).

**19.37. 'They will look on the one whom they have pierced':** This is a quotation from Zechariah 12.10 (compare 19.36) which some rabbis interpreted as referring to the Messiah. The verse originally referred to the wound inflicted on God by his people and his gift of the Spirit to them; both would fit here.

**19.38a. Joseph of Arimathea:** All the Gospels identify Joseph as asking for Jesus' body (Mark 15.43; Matthew 27.57; Luke 23.26). John does not identify him as a rich man (Matthew 27.57), but as a follower of Jesus and friend of Nicodemus. He appears to have been a member of the Sanhedrin (11.47), but his status as a disciple is unclear. Several facts suggest that he was already connected to Jesus:

1 He is trusted to assist in the burial, even though he comes from a group associated with Jesus' opponents.

2 He has a likely connection to Nicodemus.

3 He is described as a 'secret disciple'.

Joseph presents a positive role model: he boldly declares himself a follower of Jesus in asking for the body. Although Jewish traditions were respectful even of the dishonourable dead, Roman custom prohibited the burial of the executed (Tacitus, *Annals* 6.29), though they might be given over to friends or relatives. Pilate's permission to bury the body of a traitor might signify one of two things:

1 He did not really believe the charge.

2 He is less powerful than Joseph. This makes a claim about the relative power of disciples in relation to the state: Pilate cannot refuse them justice.

Scholars cannot decide which is the right reason.

**19.38b. A disciple of Jesus, though a secret one:** Joseph offers a model of service which the 'real' disciples have failed to give (20.19).

**19.38c. Fear of the Jews:** The exact fear is not stated, but it stopped people from becoming disciples of Jesus (8.13, 34). It may also echo the fear of expulsion known to John's audience (9.22; 12.42), and provide an example of courage in the face of such threats. 'Jews' here is likely to mean Jesus' opponents (1.19).

**19.38d. Pilate gave him permission:** The Roman governor is still the dominant figure of authority involved in deciding Jesus' fate (18.28—19.16, esp. 18.28). Mark 15.44 describes Pilate getting confirmation of Jesus' death from the centurion.

**19.39a. Nicodemus:** This individual has already been seen in 3.1; 7.50. He does not figure in the Synoptic accounts, but here is a second witness (8.4) to the removal and burial of Jesus' body. Respect for the dead indicates a degree of conventional piety, which demanded burial by sunset (Deuteronomy 21.23; Josephus, *Jewish War* 4.317), and even burial for those who were foreigners (Josephus, *Against Apion* 2.211) or who had died dishonourable deaths (Josephus, *Antiquities* 4.202, 264–265). Such conventions meant that even Jesus' opponents would be unlikely to oppose his burial. The appearance of Nicodemus suggests the number of disciples was growing.

**19.39b. A mixture of myrrh and aloes:** This was used to both reduce the smell of the corpse and pay respects (12.1–8). The action here takes place at night; in Mark 16.1, anointing is delayed until the Sabbath is over.

**19.39c. Weighing about a hundred pounds:** The exact weight may be between 75 to 100 pounds (35–45 kilogrammes): a vast amount worth as much as 30,000 denarii (12.5). Some see this quantity as indicating a royal burial (Josephus, *Jewish War* 1.673; *Antiquities* 17.199) or echoing Jesus' own generosity (2.6; 6.11–13; 21.11).

**19.40a. They took the body of Jesus and wrapped it . . . in linen cloths:** This treatment of the body was a traditional part of Jewish burial custom, particularly for the righteous (*Testament of Abraham* 10.20; *Apocalypse of Moses* 40.1–3).

**19.40b. According to the burial custom of the Jews:** This refers to Jewish tradition in general (2.6).

**19.41a. There was a garden in the place where he was crucified:** The reference to a garden has made some think this is a reference to Eden

(Genesis 2.15; 3.22), indicating a return to the kind of life which God planned for his people at the beginning of creation. If this refers to Eden, the words John uses are found only in the Septuagint text of Ezekiel 36.35, which declares that the restored land is 'like Eden'.

**19.41b. In the garden there was a new tomb:** Matthew 27.60 identifies the tomb as that of Joseph's own family, and makes it into a fulfilment of Isaiah 53.12. 'New' is meant to reduce any possible confusion about Jesus' corpse with others. Some tombs might hold a number of corpses.

**19.42. It was the Jewish day of Preparation:** John makes a final reference to the day on which these events took place to fix the date in the minds of the audience.

 Interpretation

John's record of the crucifixion focuses on the following elements:

- the crucifixion(19.16–18);
- the inscription (19.19–22);
- the division of garments (19.23–25);
- the adoption of Jesus' mother (19.26–27);
- wine and thirst (19.28–29);
- completion of Jesus' task (19.30);
- the removal of Jesus' body (19.31–38).

The Synoptics share the following:

- the crucifixion;
- the inscription (note, however, the different wordings);
- the division of garments;
- the presence of women at the foot of the cross;
- wine (at a different point);
- last words (but note the differences in content);
- the removal of the body.

John omits:

- the conversation Jesus has with those crucified beside him;
- supernatural elements: the darkening of the skies (Mark 15.33; Matthew 27.45; Luke 23.44), the tearing of the veil of the Temple (Mark 15.33;

Matthew 27.51; Luke 23.45), the earthquake and opening of tombs (Matthew 27.51–53);

- the declaration of the centurion (Mark 15.40; Matthew 27.54; Luke 23.47), but claims about Jesus' identity and innocence, and their proclamation by the Roman establishment, have already been placed on the lips of Pilate (18.31, 38; 19.6, 22).

Scholars consider the inscription, in spite of the variations in wording, to be a significant element. The argument here (19.19–22) marks a clash between Jesus' accusers and Pilate. The accusers do not wish to identify Jesus as king. Their proposed alteration to the wording focuses on making this claim rather than whether it is true. The Roman authorities would have not have been concerned with such niceties. Any claim to be a king, whether legitimate or not, would still challenge their authority. However, the change may also indicate an attempt to conform the charge against Jesus to one of blasphemy (8.59; 19.19, 21).

From John's perspective, such quibbling is irrelevant: Jesus is the king of the Jews (though not as conventionally understood) and God. The Jewish accusers and the Roman establishment have not understood who Jesus really is. John's use of misunderstanding (Appendix H) is particularly pointed: such people, unlike the disciples, are shown to be incapable of moving beyond misunderstanding to understanding. Instead they continue to argue about what is irrelevant and insignificant.

John focuses on the division of Jesus' garments. The events portrayed all fulfil Scripture, showing that Jesus' death is not an accident. It is part of a plan long anticipated by God and revealed in Scripture. The theme of God's control is being stressed. Other layers of meaning also surface:

- *The footwashing* (13.4). The symbolic action when Jesus removed his clothes is now a reality.

- *The unity of Jesus' kingdom.* Tearing a cloth stands for political division or loss in the OT (1 Kings 11.29–31; 1 Samuel 15.27–28; 24), continuing the theme of unity (10.16; 11.51–52; 12.32). If the Gospel is written in the period 70–100 CE, this invites a critical comparison of Jesus' kingdom (18.36) with the Roman Empire, split by civil wars and insurrections.

- *The high priesthood.* The seamless garment indicates a reference to the garments of the high priest. This is less likely: the vocabulary used need not have that significance, nor does John develop a priestly resonance.

- *The Messiah.* Psalm 22 is sometimes described as messianic. The quotation is therefore seen as a fulfilment of a messianic prophecy. However, there are no references to Judaic messianic readings of the psalm in this period. It is more likely that this line of interpretation has been developed as a result of how John has used the verse.

None of these has received universal support, but the first two appear more likely. The echo of 13.4 is part of a common pattern in which prophetic words and actions of Jesus become realities, and the idea of unity finds further support when the Beloved Disciple adopts Jesus' mother (19.25–27).

The encounter between the mother of Jesus and the Beloved Disciple is unique – not least because he is the only male disciple credited with being at the foot of the cross. Doubts have been raised about the historical likelihood of this exchange, given that Jesus has other family members (7.5) who could take care of their mother. We can also query the claims that the adoption is symbolic of the Johannine community rather than an historic action: the Gospel does not usually portray the Beloved Disciple as a symbolic character, but as a participant in key events of Jesus' life.

However, either separation from the family – who might be expected to be in Galilee rather than Jerusalem – or the hard fact that families do not always look after their own might explain these actions. Scripture repeatedly demands correct treatment for widows and so points to a real abuse. If so, John may echo other NT documents in a concern for widows (Acts 6.1–3; 1 Timothy 5.1–10). Irrespective of such conjectures, the handing over of a parent by a dying man fulfils a number of social roles. It reveals Jesus as a pious and devoted son in accordance with the Judaic custom of the time. Roman traditions also reveal the practice of entrusting relatives to close family friends (Virgil, *Aeneid* 9.297). The exchange highlights Jesus' care for his mother, and his closeness to the Beloved Disciple. It also shows:

1 Jesus making his disciples into a community which will function as a fictive family (7.1–13);

2 shared faith as a social bond rather than blood and affinity (1.13);

3 the care and devotion that disciples should have to Jesus and his legacy.

'I am thirsty' is presented as a fulfilment of Scripture, but is not a direct quotation. Citations from Scripture were not limited to direct quotations of verses. The shared vocabulary suggests a fulfilment of Psalm 69, making Jesus a righteous man made to suffer. In its original context the psalm may refer to the suffering of David. Here, using 'correspondence in history' (see the Introduction), it refers to the suffering of Jesus. As with Psalm 21, a messianic reading of the psalm is not found within Judaism: messianic interpretation seems to originate with John (15.25) and Paul (Romans 15.3; Psalm 69.9). Acts 1.20 also uses Psalm 69.25 to describe the fate of Judas as the fulfilment of a scriptural prophecy.

Christian exegetes must not assume that verses used as messianic proofs by the NT writers always had such an interpretation throughout Second Temple Judaism. These may be texts which had not previously been considered messianic, but now appear to be so, based on the experience and understanding of Jesus.

Jesus' pronouncement, 'It is finished', announces the completion of the work given to him by the Father (3.16–21). His pronouncement again signifies that he is in control of events. He alone can make this statement. Jesus is also saying that all has been made perfect. Greek philosophies often had a *telos*, an end point, which was the perfect outcome for their beliefs. Jesus is declaring that perfection has been attained: the world is now loved perfectly.

The English idiom, 'giving up the ghost [one's spirit]' – a euphemism for death – has obscured 19.30. John stresses the reality of Jesus' death (19.31–37), but John 19.30 says more. Jesus has already spoken of the Spirit (3.5–8; 14.15–17, 25–30; 16.7–15). The death of Jesus is the beginning of a new era: the age of the Spirit, passed on by Jesus as he dies. This will be confirmed by the gifting of the Spirit to the disciples after the resurrection (20.22–23). By this reckoning, the lowest point of Jesus' wretched death became the high point, the moment of his glorification (7.39): the values of the world have been turned upside down. Note that this verse does not indicate the exact moment at which the Spirit is handed on: it stresses the fact that Jesus gives his Spirit to his followers, as does 20.22.

The verses which follow stress the reality of Jesus' death. John was well aware of arguments that Jesus did not really die. As a result, not only is the eyewitness testimony stressed, but so are the roles of the Roman soldiers, experts in the business of death and torture, and unlikely to make a mistake and let someone escape. Pilate makes an official pronouncement in letting the body go for burial. Again, this is presented not just as an unfolding of events, but as part of a plan revealed by Scripture. Ultimately God is cited as a witness to the truth of Jesus' death.

Witnessing to the reality of Jesus' death continues in the burial. Two reliable witnesses, Joseph of Arimathea and Nicodemus, dress and bury the corpse. Their courage suggests that the disciples of Jesus are beginning to regain their shattered confidence. Such actions will allow the growth of the new family (19.25–27).

The new tomb also becomes a witness: it means that there can be no confusion in what will follow. This is a pristine tomb. There is no confusion about whose body is in it, or whether it has been tampered with, or that there are signs of entrance and exit which might be misread; all such traces can be identified with the activities of Joseph and Nicodemus. Just as he stressed the reality of Jesus' death (19.31–37), John is ruling out alternative explanations for the absence of Jesus' physical remains.

 # STUDY SUGGESTIONS

## Word study

1 Compare the different versions of the inscription (Mark 15.26; Matthew 27.37; Luke 23.38; John 19.19). Are the differences significant?

2 Read John 11.1, 28–37; 12.1–8; Mark 14.1–11; Matthew 26.1–14; Luke 7.36–49; 8.3. Do these passages refer to Mary Magdalene? Give evidence from the texts (not from your church tradition) to support your view.

## Review of content

3 Read John 19.34–35. Is it possible to identify sections of the text as 'pure history' or 'pure theology'?

4 Read Zechariah 12.10. Why does John apply this Scripture to Jesus? What are the implications of such a reading?

5 Is it right to call Jesus a victim?

## Discussion and application

6 Does experience or history reveal 'secret disciples' who are often more courageous in their service than professed Christian or church members?

7 Would it matter to you if this account was not based on historical events?

8 How has the above reading of Jesus' death altered your understanding of these events?

9 Have Christian piety and devotion taken the shock and horror out of Jesus' death by crucifixion?

# John 20.1–31

# The resurrection appearances

 Summary

The resurrection narratives consist of two sections, each of two scenes:

1 *Events in the garden*:

   (a) Mary Magdalene and the two disciples (20.1–10);
   (b) Mary Magdalene and Jesus (20.11–18).

2 *The disciples indoors*:

   (a) The disciples and Jesus (20.19–23);
   (b) Thomas and Jesus (20.24–29).

The section finishes with a set of concluding remarks which appear to mark the end of the Gospel (20.30–31). The two main sections share a similar pattern. In both, a character uninvolved in the first subsection (Mary and Thomas) gains an understanding which surpasses his or her colleagues. The effect is that belief in the resurrection is escalated by a series of actions.

## 20.1–10: Mary Magdalene and the two disciples

 Introduction

Early the next morning, Mary Magdalene, and then Peter and the Beloved Disciple, find that the tomb is empty.

 Notes and commentary

**20.1a. Early on the first day of the week:** Mark 16.2 shares the tradition that followers of Jesus went early to the tomb. Matthew 28.1 and Luke 24.1 place the event at dawn.

That it was the first day of the week is a detail shared with the Synoptics (Mark 16.2; Matthew 28.1; Luke 24.1). Matthew and Mark add a reference to the Sabbath (19.31). 'First' may indicate the beginning of something new.

**20.1b. While it was still dark:** Darkness may signify a state of confusion or unbelief (19.12).

**20.1c. Mary Magdalene came to the tomb:** Mary has been mentioned already in the Passion Narrative (19.25). Mary appears to go alone; no reason is given for her visit. Unlike the Synoptic accounts, the body has already been anointed (19.39). She may have come to weep (11.31; 20.11).

**20.1d. The stone had been removed:** John has not mentioned this detail; the Synoptics share it (Mark 16.3–4; Matthew 28.2; Luke 24.2). Tombs were not dug into soft earth, but might be mausoleums or caves. A stone would be used to seal the entrance, if needed.

**20.2a. So she ran and went to Simon Peter:** Peter is a disciple from the beginning of the public ministry who becomes increasingly important (1.40–42; 6.68; 13.6–11, 24, 36–38; 18.10–11, 15–18, 25–27). Mary does not figure again in this episode.

**20.2b. The other disciple, the one whom Jesus loved:** The two phrases 'other disciple' (18.15–16) and 'whom Jesus loved' (13.23–26; 19.25–27) are combined: they refer to the same person.

**20.2c. They have taken the Lord:** 'They' are not identified, but contrasted with the followers of Jesus ('we'). Several possibilities are suggested:

1 *The unidentified owners of the tomb* (19.41): However, why would they remove a body if permission had been given to bury it? There is no evidence of an illegal burial, and it would not fit with the other careful (and expensive) measures taken to bury Jesus (19.39).

2 *Tomb robbers*: Sometimes a body might be stolen to be used for magic (Apollonius Rhodius 4.51–53; Lucan, *Civil War* 6.538–68; Ovid, *Herodes* 6.90).

3 *The disciples*: Matthew 28.11–15 suggests that such a story circulated. Yet given their failure to protect Jesus when he was alive, why would they become brave enough to steal his corpse? They would be unlikely to fake a resurrection if no one was expecting such a phenomenon.

4 *The opponents of Jesus*: But why would they want his body?

There is no agreement about which is the best answer. Mary's words may only show her confusion: someone (unknown to her) must have done this. Some commentators believe that the 'them–us' language reflects a later situation, in which followers of Jesus were opposed by other sectarians.

'Lord' was a title with a range of meanings (4.11–12). It need not have a high meaning (as 9.38) here.

**20.2d. We do not know:** As Mary is on her own (20.1), 'we' may be:

- the preservation of an earlier tradition in which Mary was not alone (perhaps as in the Synoptics);

- a Semitism (as English sometimes uses 'we/us' for 'I/me').

- 'interfigurality' – Mary of Bethany's experience (11.1–46; 12.1–8) is used to understand Mary Magdalene: she is growing in faith through her encounter with death and Jesus.

There is no agreement about a right answer.

**20.4. The other disciple outran Peter and reached the tomb first:** The speed of the other disciple is compared positively with Peter, indicating he is more eager.

**20.5a. He bent down to look in:** Tombs were not dug in the ground, but were formed from caves or built into hillsides. Low doors provided access and were more secure against tomb robbers.

**20.5b. Linen wrappings:** These were part of Jewish funeral practice (11.44; 19.40).

**20.5c. But he did not go in:** The other disciple waits outside the tomb. No reason is given.

**20.6. Simon Peter . . . went into the tomb:** Peter is first to enter.

**20.7a. The cloth that had been on Jesus' head:** Some contrast this with Moses' veil (Exodus 34.33–35; 2 Corinthians 3.7–18), but John has used a different word, so this is not obvious. The parallel only becomes clear through the Aramaic commentaries on Exodus 34 (*Targum Pseudo-Jonathan and Targum Yerushalmi* (Codex Neofiti 1)).

**20.7b. Not lying with the linen wrappings:** Lazarus still wore his grave clothes (11.44). Jesus no longer bears the marks of death.

**20.7c. Rolled up in a place by itself:** This indicates the activity of God, and rules out the theft of the body: thieves would not be this neat.

**20.8a. Then the other disciple . . . also went in:** The other disciple now follows Peter into the tomb.

**20.8b. He saw and believed:** The other disciple achieves a degree of belief. No indication is given of Peter's belief. Seeing and believing indicates a degree of partial faith, superior to belief governed by self-interest (6.26), but inferior to belief which is not based simply on experience (20.29).

If the previous verses show a degree of competition between Peter and the other disciple, they conclude with the other disciple considered superior in belief to Peter. Some have suggested rivalry between different groups in the emerging Christianity, but there is no evidence of conflict between Peter and John to match that of Peter and Paul (Galatians 2).

**20.9. They did not understand the scripture, that he must rise from the dead:** The Scripture here is identified with either:

1 John's own writing, implying Christian Scripture not in circulation at the first Easter, but available to John's audience;

2 Jewish Scriptures. No texts are clearly identified: some suggest Psalm 16.10.

Both answers are possible.

**20.10. The disciples returned to their homes:** This may suggest returning to their old way of life (16.32; 19.27) or that they are slipping back in faith. It may simply mean that they do not stay by the tomb.

 ## Interpretation

All four Gospels share a significant amount of detail about the first visit to the tomb: early, just before dawn, on the first day of the week. All have the empty tomb first witnessed by women, either Mary Magdalene or a group. This may be a historically significant detail. Previous sections have already shown that women would have been less credible witnesses (5.31; 8.17): female witnesses would not have had the authority of males, and are less likely to have been invented.

A number of commentators have seen Peter and the other disciple as symbolic. They are made to represent pastoral and prophetic ministries, or official and contemplative churches. Claims that Peter represents Jewish Christian traditions, while John represents Gentile Christian traditions, are also problematic. We should not read into their characters more than is possible. Their presence simply reflects their importance as witnesses within emerging Christianity.

The account of the tomb is meant to rule out reasons for it being empty, specifically that:

1 Jesus' body is still in the tomb;

2 the tomb has been robbed: the clothes would either have been taken or left in a mess;

3 Jesus has escaped. He would be unlikely to leave naked. The theory that Jesus might only have seemed to have died is contrary to experience: people did not readily recover from crucifixion, even with medical attention (Josephus, *Life* 75).

Some have suggested that the grave clothes represent leaving behind Jewish culture. Such ideas fit better with Paul's use of Exodus 34.29–35 in 2 Corinthians 3.12. Paul's theology should not be imported, as it makes this text depend on an alien tradition. There is no guarantee that Paul and John shared the same theological concerns. The Pauline passage has no reference to the events of Jesus' resurrection. Furthermore, the concept of a revelation of Jesus, and thus of the Father, arising only after the events of the resurrection is alien to John's theology: it contradicts Jesus' earlier remarks to the disciples (14.8–12; 16.9) and the Prologue (1.14). Importing Moses' veil does not stand up to scrutiny; it is rather an example of parallelomania (the excessive desire to find parallels between various parts of Scripture) to be rejected because of differences in both vocabulary and ideology. The grave clothes do not represent a rejection of Jewish culture.

This also means rejecting claims that Judaism should be 'left buried in the tomb' because 'it has been judged and proved to be shallow' (in *The African Bible*, p. 1821), an influential presentation of Scripture. Any idea that Judaism is rejected and shallow is alien to this Gospel. John's Jesus does not reject the Temple (2.13–22) or the feasts, but perfects or fulfils all they stand for (7.37; 8.12). The core hopes of Judaism are not rejected, but perfected in Jesus. It is not Judaism which is rejected, but the idea that the Gospel supports any such claims. John is far more subtle than such critics have allowed; their reading should be placed in the dustbin of history, and serve as a warning of how easy it is to fall back into the stereotypes of the past.

The section concludes on a note of mystery: Jesus has not escaped, and his tomb has not been robbed. John's audience may feel a sense of smugness or satisfaction: they know more than the disciples.

##  STUDY SUGGESTIONS

### Word study

**1** Describe Jewish burial customs.

### Review of content

**2** Does Christian faith need an empty tomb? Why?

**3** Describe John's understanding of the risen Jesus. What explanations has he ruled out?

### Discussion and application

**4** Give a reply to someone who tells you that the resurrection stories in this section mean that Judaism is to be rejected as valueless.

## 20.11–18: Mary Magdalene and Jesus

 Introduction

Mary stays at the tomb, and has a conversation with the risen Jesus.

 Notes and commentary

**20.11a. Mary stood weeping outside the tomb:** Mary returns to the story, and is back in the garden (20.2). Her tears (11.33) suggest that Peter and the other disciple have not spoken with her: she continues to mourn (20.13).

**20.11b. She bent over to look:** She is bending into the entrance to the tomb (20.5). The Greek does not contain 'to look'. It is implied by 20.12. Mary does not enter the tomb. The conversation takes place outside it.

**20.12a. Two angels in white:** White symbolizes the heavenly world (*1 Enoch* 71.1; Revelation 4.4). The descriptions of clothes indicate heavenly beings, even if they seem human (Mark 16.5; Matthew 28.2–3; Luke 24.4).

**20.12b. Sitting where the body of Jesus had been lying, one at the head and the other at the feet:** The angels are unlikely to sit on Jesus' body; this detail confirms the tomb is empty.

**20.13a. Woman, why are you weeping?:** The greeting, 'Woman', is not disrespectful (2.4; 19.26).

**20.13b. They have taken away my Lord:** Again, 'they' are not clearly identified (20.2).

**20.13c. I do not know:** Mary speaks only of her own ignorance here, unlike the 'we' in 20.2.

**20.14a. She turned around and saw Jesus standing there:** 'Standing' confirms that Jesus is not dead; corpses rarely stand.

**20.14b. But she did not know:** This is a misunderstanding (Appendix H), because Mary does not recognize the risen Jesus.

**20.15a. Woman, why are you weeping?:** This verse repeats 20.13.

**20.15b. Supposing him to be the gardener:** Some early Jewish reports claimed Jesus' body was taken by a gardener (Tertullian, *On the Games* 30). There are two possible references which may be added, but John does not develop them:

- a cross-reference to the vine (15.1), but there is no pruning here;

- a new Creation (19.41), identifying Jesus with God.

**20.15c. Sir:** Mary uses a greeting with a number of possible meanings (4.11–12; 9.38; 20.2). Here it is only a polite greeting, because Mary has not recognized Jesus.

**20.15d. If you have carried him away:** Mary confuses Jesus with 'they' (20.2, 13).

**20.16a. Jesus said to her, 'Mary':** Jesus calls her by name, revealing himself as the Good Shepherd (10.3).

**20.16b. She said to him in Hebrew, 'Rabbouni' (which means Teacher):** For 'rabbi', see 1.38. Mary recognizes Jesus by his voice – a further echo of the Good Shepherd (10.4–5). The suffix *-ouni* shows intimacy or a close relationship: 'my teacher'. John translates terms for an audience who may not know Aramaic (1.38).

**20.17a. Do not hold on to me:** Mary is touching Jesus, and he is asking her to stop. A number of fanciful interpretations have been given to suggest why this command is given:

- She was showing a lack of respect;
- She was making him impure because of her sinful past;
- It was inappropriate for a woman to touch a man;
- The text should read: 'Don't be afraid.' There is no manuscript evidence for this, and it imports ideas from the Synoptics (Matthew 28.10).

The simplest answer is that Jesus wishes Mary to let go of him so that she may go to the disciples.

**20.17b. I have not yet ascended:** This suggests that the final stages of Jesus' work have started, but it is not completed.

**20.17c. Go to my brothers:** Jesus identifies the believers as a fictive family (7.1–13; 19.26, 38). This will continue in 20.18.

**20.17d. I am ascending:** Mary is to tell the disciples that this process is taking place.

**20.17e. To my Father and your Father, my God and your God:** The stress on 'my' and 'your' makes clear that Jesus has made it possible for his disciples to share the same relationship with God that he has, described in terms of sonship (1.12; 10.34–38). This confirms their description as 'brothers'.

**20.18a. The disciples:** These need not be the twelve apostles of the Synoptic tradition.

**20.18b. I have seen the Lord:** Only John gives a direct quotation as Mary's report to the disciples. Some see echoes of Psalm 22.23, implying Jesus' divinity, and that Mary has grown in faith.

**20.18c. She told them he had said these things to her:** John's account is traced back to Mary's own experience.

 Interpretation

Events unfold in two encounters:

1 with angels who are seen inside the tomb;

2 with the risen Jesus.

Both are misunderstandings (Appendix H). In the first, Mary cannot grasp that Jesus' body has been taken away. The second repeats this misunderstanding, and adds a failure to recognize Jesus. Mary will only recognize Jesus when he speaks (10.3–5). This suggests growth in faith, but not full faith (3.1–21; 4.16–26).

The angels indicate that the risen Jesus is clearly not like them, an angel. Acts 23.8 allowed for resurrection as an angel; John does not. If anything, Jesus is confused with an ordinary person, the gardener (20.15). Most of the Mediterranean cultures of the period embraced beliefs of some kind about life after death. However, none can readily be cited as a source for bodily resurrection:

- Appearances of the dead, such as that of Apollonius of Tyana, may occur even if the physical remains are buried;

- Stories about magical resuscitations do not imply bodily immortality;

- The clearest parallels to resurrection in the mystery cults come from a period after the Christian writings, suggesting that Christian beliefs influenced the mystery cults, not the other way;

- Many Graeco-Roman accounts of life after death concern the immortality of the soul, which does not include any reference to the body;

- Belief in bodily resurrection was a Jewish belief (Psalms of Solomon 3.12; 15.12–13; 1 *Enoch* 22.13; Daniel 12.2), but not universal: the Sadducees rejected such beliefs (Acts 23.8).

Jesus' appearance as an apparently human gardener indicates a bodily resurrection and has potential origins within Judaic thought. The later appearances (20.19–29) will add more detail.

John does not have an Ascension narrative like the Synoptics (Mark 16.19–20; Luke 24.50–51; Acts 1.6–11). Rather than focus on the exact moment of the Ascension, John talks of the short period in which Jesus appears to his followers after the resurrection and his permanent presence through the Spirit. The events described here mark the fulfilment of earlier prophecies (6.62; 16.7) which imply that the Spirit is given after immediately after his death (20.17, 22). The Ascension is when Jesus is fully glorified and when humanity becomes the children of God. This has an important consequence. Jesus' disciples receive the Spirit while they are still on earth: the gifts of God to his people should never, in John's view, be restricted to a time after death or to the heavenly realm.

## STUDY SUGGESTIONS

### Word study

**1** Why did Mary 'weep' (20.11, 13, 15)? Compare her actions at the tomb with Mary of Bethany and Jesus at Lazarus' tomb (11.33, 35).

**2** What might 'garden' and 'gardener' symbolize?

**3** What is the best explanation of 'Do not hold on to me'?

### Review of content

**4** How does John show that Mary is still growing in faith?

**5** Was Mary a close friend of Jesus? Refer to this and earlier passages.

### Discussion and application

**6** Does preaching about the resurrection talk of the immortality of the soul? How should preaching stress bodily resurrection?

**7** If we were told 'Do not hold on to me' by Jesus, what might this mean?

## 20.19–23: The disciples and Jesus

 Introduction

Jesus appears to the disciples and makes a formal gift of the Spirit to them.

 Notes and commentary

**20.19a. When it was evening on that day, the first day of the week:** 'Evening' may indicate a time of fear or doubt (Appendix B). It is the late afternoon, before twilight, on the same day as Mary has met the risen Jesus in the garden.

**20.19b. The doors of the house were locked:** A normal entry to the room would not be possible.

**20.19c. Fear of the Jews:** This refers to both the historical fear of the disciples and the current fears of John's audience (20.28). 'Jews' here are Jesus' opponents (1.19).

**20.19d. Jesus . . . stood:** His posture shows that Jesus is not dead (20.14).

**20.19e. Peace be with you:** Peace was promised earlier as a gift to the disciples (14.27). The words seem to echo a liturgical formula. John may be using a form familiar to his audience from their own worship, and may even be suggesting that this is the origin of the phrase.

**20.20a. His hands and his side:** These had the wounds that Jesus had received on the cross (19.18, 34).

**20.20b. The disciples rejoiced:** The disciples' reaction shows that they have received the promised gift of joy (3.29; 15.11; 16.20).

**20.21a. Jesus said to them again, 'Peace be with you':** Such repetition stresses the significance of what is being said, and the authority of Jesus.

**20.21b. As the Father has sent me, so I send you:** The disciples are given the same high status (that of being sent) as Jesus (1.1, 18; 5.26–27; 6.27) as well as the status of brothers (20.17).

**20.22a. He breathed on them:** The action of breathing is used in the LXX (Genesis 2.7; Ezekiel 37.9–10; Wisdom 15.11) to describe God's act of creation. Some consider this the only gift of the Spirit (19.30): it allows the disciples to overcome their fear.

**20.22b. Receive the Holy Spirit:** Some argue that this is the moment when the disciples receive the Spirit breathed out in 19.30. Passing on (19.30) and receiving are the two complementary acts in passing on a tradition or gift (1 Corinthians 11.23). The Spirit has already been promised to the disciples (14.25–26; 16.4–33).

**20.23. If you forgive the sins of any, they are forgiven them; if you retain the sins of any, they are retained:** This is most likely a different tradition from Matthew 16.19; 18.18. All come from Isaiah 22.22: Matthew as 'binding–loosing', John as 'retaining–forgiving'.

 ## Interpretation

The passage in 20.19–23 marks an advance over the vision given to Mary Magdalene. The disciples have seen the risen Jesus, and received the 'other

Advocate' (20.22), promised by Jesus (14.16, 26; 16.7, 13) and passed on at his departure (19.30).

Fear of the Jews explains why the disciples were in a safe place, presumably locked from the inside so that entry was restricted. The risen Jesus bypasses this and appears with them. Thus the location gives information about the nature of the risen body: it has life without physical limitations.

The contrast of the disciples' fear with their joy (20.20) at seeing Jesus indicates a reversal of fortunes, and includes peace (20.21). It would be attractive to those schools of philosophy which stressed that positive emotions were important for living the good life. The influence of these schools extended far beyond the philosophical elites to people in many strata of society, and many readers would see this change as a positive outcome. Those familiar with Jewish traditions about the end times would consider this an indicator of the last age in which God finally solves the world's problems. John has linked such hopes to the gift of the Spirit, available now to believers, not at some vague point in the future.

Members of the Church share the high status of Jesus, indicated by titles, gifts and functions:

- brothers (20.17);

- 'my Father and your Father' (20.17);

- 'my God and your God' (20.17);

- peace (20.19, 21);

- joy (20.20);

- the Spirit (20.22);

- forgiveness of sins (20.23).

John has set out the boundaries which will mark a new community whose members share the very status of God.

This account performs two functions: it provides a record of what happened historically, and spells out the theological implications of these events. It describes both the post-resurrection events and Jesus' permanent presence through the Spirit. The use of 'disciples' has already bridged this gap: it does not restrict the giving of the Spirit to a clearly named historical group, but is able to include the members of John's audience who may well, like their predecessors, be in fear. The giving of the Spirit ensures that the work of the Spirit is not to be considered as a gift only made to the few who were present at Jesus' death (19.30), but enables all his followers to live in the world as he did (20.22). There is much to be said for the view that Jesus gives the Spirit (19.30) but it is not immediately received by the disciples (20.23): an act of 'passing on' really demands the two linked actions of giving and receiving. The action begun in 19.30 is not completed until 20.23.

In keeping with John's earlier views that people pass judgement on themselves, the community of believers is not described as having powers of judgement (3.19). Rather they have powers to forgive or retain sins. This reiterates the high status of the Church. The Synoptic Gospels make clear that the claim to forgive sins was central to the hostility which Jesus provoked (Matthew 9.6; Mark 2.10; Luke 5.24). Jesus entrusted this same power to his disciples (Matthew 16.19; Peter 18.18 (the disciples)). The Church receives this power as a gift from God, the work of the Spirit who now lives in it (14.18–21), not as a result of its own goodness, virtues or abilities. If the Church has any connection to judgement, according to John's thinking, it should be that its presence in the world continues to hold up a mirror to the world by which it judges itself, rather than claiming to be prosecutor, judge and jury (3.16–21).

 ## STUDY SUGGESTIONS

### Word study

1 What is the significance of the disciples' 'rejoicing' (20.20)?

2 Read John 19.30; 20.23. Do you think these signify one or two gifts of the Spirit?

3 Read Isaiah 22.22; Matthew 16.19; 18.18; John 20.23. Do these have themes in common?

### Review of content

4 Does Christian faith need an empty tomb? Why?

5 When do believers receive the gifts of the Spirit: now, or in the future? Give an explanation based on John's writing.

6 Write an outline of John's understanding of the new community of believers based on the meetings of the risen Jesus with his followers.

7 What hope does 20.19–23 offer to a persecuted Church?

### Discussion and application

8 Read 20.20. Try to rewrite Christian hopes using everyday or 'street' language. Avoid even simple church language like 'blessing'. Do you think this makes it easier for outsiders to grasp the advantages given by faith?

9 Do we act as though we have received or are waiting to receive the gifts of the Spirit?

## 20.24–29: Thomas and Jesus

 Introduction

Jesus appears to Thomas and the other disciples. Thomas has not believed the accounts given by his colleagues that Jesus is risen.

 Notes and commentary

**20.24. Thomas . . . one of the twelve:** Thomas has already appeared in the Gospel (11.16; 14.5).

**20.25. Unless I see the mark of the nails in his hands . . . in his side:** The nails used in crucifixion would have been put through the wrists. Thomas refers also to the mark where Jesus was pierced with a spear (19.34).

**20.26a. A week later:** This means it was the same day of the week as the previous meeting (20.19). The eighth day was known to early Christians as the 'day of the Lord', as opposed to the significant days of Judaism.

**20.26b. The doors were shut:** This is the same phrase as 20.19, but without any mention of 'fear'. This may give confidence to John's audience: if the disciples lost their fear through a meeting with Jesus, so should they. The detail stresses the supernatural quality of the risen Jesus.

**20.26c. Peace be with you:** This saying repeats the fact that Jesus' promise of peace has been fulfilled (14.27; 20.21).

**20.27. Put your finger here and see my hands. Reach out your hand and put it in my side:** The risen Jesus responds to Thomas' challenge (20.25). The account does not say whether Thomas did as asked.

**20.28. My Lord and my God:** This phrase is the clearest indication of Jesus' identity and status: it affirms that he is God. Some think that the phrase may be a response to claims by the Roman emperor Domitian to be Lord and God (Suetonius, *Domitian* 13). This is only possible if the Gospel, and in particular this phrase, originates after Domitian's claim. Otherwise, it is a similarity rather than a source.

**20.29a. Have you believed because you have seen me?:** Jesus' words here may be translated as a statement: 'You have believed because you have seen me.'

**20.29b. Blessed are those:** This form of makarism (blessing) is familiar from the Sermon on the Mount (Matthew 5.3–11) and its parallels (Luke 6.20). All the emphasis is placed on believing without seeing.

**20.29c. Who have not seen and yet have come to believe:** Future generations of disciples share the belief of the other disciple (20.8) who has already believed without seeing. This Beloved Disciple (see 'The identity of John', p. 4) is the source or writer of this Gospel.

 ## Interpretation

The passage in 20.24–29 concludes with Jesus' revelation of himself to Thomas: the crucified and risen Jesus, identified by his wounds, is the one who has passed on the Spirit. The section confirms the humanity of Jesus and the reality of his death. It also leaves the audience in a still more privileged position. The risen Jesus has left a prophecy which they have now received: they are blessed because they have believed without seeing.

Much ink has been spilled over the question of whether Thomas received the Holy Spirit as he was absent from the first meeting of Jesus with the disciples. There really can be no doubt that he too receives the Spirit. Any reading which sees the Spirit only gifted to those in the locked room denies the gift of the Spirit to all future generations, not just Thomas.

Both Thomas and Mary Magdalene recognize Jesus in ways that do not depend on his appearance. Mary hears his voice (20.16); Thomas recognizes him by his wounds (20.27–29). This has serious implications for Christian identity. Often in its history the Church has been recognized by its power and its grandeur, and has sought power and influence. It should be recognized by its suffering for being faithful to God. Faith reveals triumph over adversity more than earthly power and might.

The physicality of the encounter rejects the Docetic theology that Jesus only appeared to be flesh or only appeared to die. These verses stress the reality of both his Incarnation and suffering, as his risen body has a tangible physical quality. Resurrection is not just about the post-mortem existence of the soul, but the transformation of the whole person (mind, body and soul – if such distinctions are made). In 1 Corinthians 15.44 Paul rejects Graeco-Roman thinking which limits such new life to only the soul or spirit. His 'spiritual body' denies such divisions of person which deny any place to the physical, the 'body', by putting together two terms – 'spirit' and 'body' – which were thought to be distinct. John makes the same point in the encounter between Jesus and Thomas. Both John and Paul draw on Jewish ideas of resurrection rather than Graeco-Roman thinking about the immortality of the soul (which has no physical dimension).

The section finishes with a climax which focuses on blessing given to the audience. What form does this blessing take? They receive the good gifts promised by Jesus in the Farewell Discourses (13.1—17.26), which are already given to the disciples (20.1–29) and are now theirs (20.31).

STUDY SUGGESTIONS

**Word study**

1 Write a description of Thomas based on the information seen here and earlier in the Gospel.

**Review of content**

2 What do the marks on the body of the risen Jesus tell about him?

3 What is the best kind of belief or faith?

**Discussion and application**

4 'We have drifted away from the joyful burden of the wooden cross, to the proud glory of the golden cross' (Geevarghese Mar Osthathios; Poster No. 86, USPG/Ikon Productions, 1972–1987). Is this true of the Church in your place and time?

## 20.30–31: Concluding remarks

 Introduction

John explains why the Gospel has been written.

 Notes and commentary

**20.30a. Jesus did many other signs:** These include events during Jesus' public life and after the resurrection (Appendix C).

**20.30b. Which are not written:** The Gospel provides a selection of material about what Jesus did; it is not a full account.

**20.30c. In this book:** Early copies of the Gospel might have been in the form of a scroll or a codex (a book with pages).

**20.31a. These are written:** The events recorded in the Gospel serve a specific purpose, of bringing the believer to eternal life (3.15). This formula suggests that Scripture (20.9) includes this document.

**20.31b. The Messiah:** Jesus' claim to this title has been frequently disputed throughout the Gospel (1.41; Appendix K).

**20.31c. The Son of God:** For this title, see 1.31–32; Appendix F.

**20.31d. Life in his name:** 'Life' means eternal life (3.15). The 'name' stands for the reality and power of the one who bears it (1.12; 14.14).

 Interpretation

These verses place the audience on centre stage. All these things have been recorded so that they may believe and have life. There are two positive outcomes:

1 being fully aware of who Jesus is, and so understanding the nature of God;

2 receiving the benefits of (eternal) life.

What has been written is not an exhaustive account of all that Jesus did, but rather is a selection of events considered to be particularly important by John. John's work has given future believers all that they need in order to know the meaning of life, the nature of God, and the right way of living.

In 20.31, John explains why he wrote the book. It will:

1 provide evidence which will bring his readers to the belief that Jesus is the Messiah;

2 give material which will allow that faith to grow so that believers will be able to partake in eternal life (3.15).

 STUDY SUGGESTIONS

**Word study**

1 Write a definition of a Gospel based on John's description of his 'book'.

**Review of content**

2 Where might we find the 'many other signs . . . which are not written in this book'?

**Discussion and application**

3 Has our reading of the Gospel brought the results which John describes?

# Part 3

## The Epilogue

The last chapter of John is called an epilogue because it seems to be added on after what looks like the end of the Gospel (20.30–31). This chapter has always been part of the written forms of the Gospel. It is called an epilogue here because it seems to be connected to what has gone before, like the feeding miracle (6.1–15), and Peter's denials (18.15–18, 25–27). Scholars who think it is less well linked to the rest of the Gospel sometimes call it an appendix.

This final chapter breaks into three parts:

1 Jesus at the Sea of Tiberias (21.1–14);

2 Jesus, Peter and the Beloved Disciple (21.15–23);

3 The Afterword (21.24–25).

# John 21.1–14

## Jesus at the Sea of Tiberias

 Introduction

The scene shifts to the Sea of Tiberias, where Jesus appears to some disciples who have returned to their home area.

 Notes and commentary

**21.1a. After these things Jesus showed himself again:** This appearance follows the events of chapter 20. No precise timing is given, unlike 20.19, 26.

**21.1b. By the Sea of Tiberias:** This is the Sea of Galilee (6.1, 16). No precise location on the shore is given.

**21.2a. Gathered there together were Simon Peter, Thomas called the Twin, Nathanael of Cana in Galilee:** Simon Peter was a person close to Jesus from the beginning of his public ministry (1.40–42; 6.68; 13.6–11, 24, 36–38; 18.10–11, 15–18, 25–27; 20.2). Thomas has already appeared in the story (11.16; 14.5; 20.24). Nathanael of Cana was one of the first to meet Jesus (1.45–51). Only here is Nathanael identified as coming from Cana.

**21.2b. The sons of Zebedee:** This is the first time these men are mentioned in the Gospel (unlike Mark 1.19–20; 3.17; Matthew 4.21–22; 10.2; Luke 5.10; 6.14). This late appearance, together with the previous focus on Jerusalem, is seen as evidence that John, the son of Zebedee, is not John, the source or writer of the Gospel.

**21.2c. Two others of his disciples:** One of these anonymous disciples may be the Beloved Disciple (see 'The identity of John', p. 4; 20.2; 21.7, 20).

**21.3a. Simon Peter said to them, 'I am going fishing'. They said to him, 'We will go with you':** This action marks a return to the disciples' former way of life, although this is only mentioned in the Synoptics (Mark 1.16; Matthew 4.18; Luke 5.3–11). Commentators offer a number of explanations:

1 the mental state of the disciples;

2 Peter's symbolic role as leader of the disciples;

3 aimless disorientation;

4 apostasy (renouncing their faith).

All are problematic: points 1, 3 and 4 suggest that the events of 20.19–29 have been forgotten; point 2 gives Peter a dominant role which is more familiar from the Synoptics (Mark 5.37; 9.2; 14.33), where he acts as spokesman (Mark 1.36; 8.29; 9.5; 10.28; 11.21; 14.29; Matthew 15.18; 18.21; Luke 5.5; 12.41) and holds a special commission (Matthew 16.18), but this role is not seen in this Gospel. None of these answers is accepted by all commentators.

**21.3b. That night:** The timing may be symbolic (Appendix B) or simply a time reference (20.19).

**21.3c. They caught nothing:** The disciples' independent efforts will be contrasted with their success when following Jesus' advice.

**21.4. Just after daybreak:** The coming of light may indicate hope, a change for the better, or a new beginning.

**21.5. Children, you have no fish, have you?:** 'Children' might be translated as 'Lads'. It shows a close relationship between Jesus and the disciples. The question is rhetorical – Jesus knows they have caught nothing.

**21.6. 'Cast the net to the right side . . . and you will find some.' So they cast it:** The command asserts Jesus' authority over nature (2.1–11; 6.1–15, 16–21) and the disciples. Jesus' power and authority is the same in both his public ministry and the post-Easter period. The men's wordless response may be based on previous experience (6.16–20).

**21.7a. That disciple whom Jesus loved:** For this phrase, see 21.2. His presence suggests links to Galilee as well as Jerusalem (18.15).

**21.7b. It is the Lord:** The Beloved Disciple is the first to recognize the risen Jesus. This may indicate a claim about his value as a witness.

**21.7c. When Simon Peter heard:** Peter only acts after he hears what the Beloved Disciple says.

**21.7d. He put on some clothes:** This is better translated as: 'He tucked up his clothes.' Peter tucks up his long outer garment (wrapping it around his waist and between his legs) to move better in the water, and avoid being naked. The original text reads: 'He tucked up his garment (for he would have been naked) and jumped into the sea.'

**21.9. A charcoal fire there, with fish on it, and bread:** Both fish and bread were the food used for the feeding miracle (6.9).

**21.11a. Simon Peter went aboard:** To 'go aboard' often means 'get out of the water'. Peter may be getting out of the water, dragging the net on his own. The others have already gone ashore (21.9).

**21.11b. Large fish, a hundred and fifty three of them . . . the net was not torn:** The number is unusually precise. A number of possible interpretations have been suggested:

1 The number means all the fish in the sea. This would echo some Greek scientists who said there were 153 types of fish, and also echoes Matthew 13.47. It may symbolize the mission to all people.

2 Augustine notes that 153 is the sum of all numbers from 1 to 17 added together; 17 is the sum of the 10 Commandments and the 7 gifts of the Spirit (*Homilies on the Gospel of John*, Tractate 122.8). This symbolism is later, and not biblical.

3 A triangle with 17 dots on each side will contain a total of 153, indicating perfection. John has shown no interest in such number patterns.

4 In the Jewish system of *gematria*, a number stands for a word value; for example, 666 equals Nero (Revelation 13.18). John has no visible interest in *gematria*, nor do any of the proposals find endorsement elsewhere in the Gospel.

5 17 is the total of 5 and 12, representing the 5 loaves and 12 baskets in the feeding miracle (6.13). As none of the fragments of bread were lost (6.12–13), so none of the catch is lost: the 'net was not torn'.

The last of these seems most likely if the audience could make the connection. However, the significance of the number may simply not be recoverable.

**21.13. Jesus took the bread and gave it to them:** The actions and vocabulary are shared with 6.11, which also includes a thanksgiving.

**21.14. This was now the third time that Jesus appeared to the disciples after he was raised from the dead:** If 20.1–18 is included, this would be the fourth appearance.

 Interpretation

This section is markedly different from the rest of the Gospel. The location in Galilee is not new, but marks a return to the earliest stages of Jesus' public ministry (chapters 1—2). The passage also explores the relationship between the Beloved Disciple and Peter, already seen in chapter 20. In many ways Peter is seen as the dominant leader of the group (21.3, 7, 11), but there are indications that the Beloved Disciple is considered to be at least his equal, if not his superior (21.7).

Luke 5.1–11 may be helpful in explaining some of the meaning of the passage: fishing symbolizes mission. John 20.21 includes a sending of the disciples; this passage expresses that commission through the symbolism of fishing. If this link holds up, the results are also significant. Left to their own devices, the disciples can catch nothing (20.3). However, when they follow Jesus' advice (20.6), the results are spectacular (20.8, 11). Being sent is not, in itself, a guarantee of success. That only comes when those who are sent do what Jesus says.

However, we should be careful when we use Luke to interpret John. We should not say that this meal is the Eucharist simply because it resembles Luke 24. The meal does not serve to reveal Jesus to the disciples (compare Luke 24.30–31) because they have already recognized him before they eat (20.12). There is no need to look to Luke for a eucharistic interpretation. The echoes of John 6, particularly the miracle of 6.1–15 (21.1, 9, 13), all point to the Eucharist. The miracle of 6.1–15 provides parallels in location (21.1), language (20.9) and actions (21.9, 13). In both scenes, Jesus is the focus of the action, feeding those who have come to him: the crowd (6.5) and the disciples (21.12). The most significant feature of the meal (and so of the Eucharist) is the idea of commensality (eating together).

Commensality is a sociological term: what you eat, how you eat, and with whom you eat define who you are. The disciples are the community which eats with the risen Lord. John's audience are being told the same thing: they also eat with the risen Lord. In a ritual setting like the Eucharist, commensality sends a message that those who eat together are united by social, religious or ethical bonds, and are accepted by one another. In 1 Corinthians, Paul sees such meals as symbolic of the allegiance or loyalty which one has to a divinity (1 Corinthians 10.14–22).

This passage reminds both the disciples in the story and John's audience that they eat with the risen Jesus. If it causes them to remember Jesus' last meal (13.1—17.26), they will remember the demand he made for them to be united as he and the Father are one. As in 20.19–24, the disciples' experience is used to describe a relationship which continues to be enjoyed by those who come after the event. This section makes John's audience remember:

- their missionary vocation;

- the status of the Beloved Disciple;

- the significance of the Eucharist as a meal shared with the risen Jesus.

Its focus is much more on the identity of the audience as a community of believers than the person of Jesus – a significant departure from chapters 1—20.

STUDY SUGGESTIONS

## Word study

**1** Look at the translations suggested in 21.7, 11. Do they make sense to you?

**2** Identify the features which link this passage with John 6.1–15.

**3** Does it matter if we cannot interpret '153' (21.11)?

**4** Is Peter as important in John as in the Synoptic Gospels? Use the references given in 21.3 to assist your answer.

## Review of content

**5** Read Luke 5.1–11. What features are shared with this passage?

**6** Which elements of this section are new?

## Discussion and application

**7** Does sharing the Eucharist bring your faith community closer together?

# John 21.15–23

# Jesus, Peter and the
# Beloved Disciple

 Introduction

After the meal, conversations between Jesus and Peter indicate what lies ahead for both Peter and the Beloved Disciple.

 Notes and commentary

**21.15a. When they had finished breakfast:** The dialogue follows the meal by the shore. It is possible that the two sections, 21.1–14 and 21.15–24, were originally separate; this phrase links them together.

**21.15b. Simon son of John:** Simon Peter is called this only in John's Gospel. Simon is sometimes called 'bar Jonas' (Matthew 16.17).

**21.15c. Do you love me more than these?:** This question may be translated a number of ways:

1  Do you love me more than these others love me?

2  Do you love me more than you love these other people?

3  Do you love me more than these things (fishing)?

The focus on the action of love suggests that option 1 is the most likely.

**21.15d. Yes, Lord; you know that I love you:** For 'Lord', see 4.11; here it is probably used as a title.

**21.15e. Feed my lambs:** 'Lambs' is most likely a synonym for 'sheep'.

**21.16a. 'Do you love me?' . . . 'Yes, Lord; you know that I love you':** Two different words are used for love in this context, but they are synonyms, and no greater significance should be read into them (5.20; 21.15).

**21.16b. Tend my sheep:** The 'sheep' are the same people as indicated by lambs (21.15).

**21.17a. He said to him the third time:** This matches Peter's third denial (18.27).

**21.17b. Peter felt hurt:** Jesus' questioning causes Peter to feel a harmful emotion (12.27; 14.1–31).

**21.17c. 'Do you love me?' . . . 'Lord . . . you know that I love you':** For 'love', see 5.20; 21.15.

**21.17d. Feed my sheep:** The use of 'shepherd' to mean a pastor is seen throughout the NT (Ephesians 4.11; Acts 20.28; 1 Peter 5.2–4).

**21.18a. Very truly:** This phrase indicates that Jesus is saying something very significant (Appendix I; 1.51).

**21.18b. When you were younger, you used . . . to go wherever you wished:** Jesus comments on Peter's own previous freedom (possibly including 18.10, 15–17, 25–27).

**21.18c. When you grow old . . . someone else will . . . take you where you do not wish to go:** Peter no longer has his freedom. His loss of freedom comes from following Jesus.

**21.19a. He said this to indicate the kind of death:** An editorial remark explains Jesus' words as a prophecy about Peter's martyrdom (compare 12.33).

**21.19b. By which he would glorify God:** Peter's work will serve the same purposes as Jesus': it will reveal God to the world and give him glory (13.31–34; 15.8; 17.4). Suffering may be seen as glorifying God (1 Peter 4.16).

**21.19c. Follow me:** This refers to literal physical following, but also to an unwavering pattern of discipleship. For 'follow', see 1.35.

**21.20a. The disciple whom Jesus loved:** This phrase most likely refers to the Beloved Disciple (20.2; see 'The identity of John', p. 4).

**21.20b. The one who had reclined next to Jesus at the supper:** People reclined to eat; this refers specifically to Jesus' last meal before his death (13.23–25).

**21.21. Lord, what about him?:** 'Lord' was a title with a variety of possible meanings. Here, it is likely to include Jesus as God (21.15). Peter's question gives an opportunity for a prophecy about the Beloved Disciple.

**21.22a. If it is my will that he remain until I come:** The Beloved Disciple may live to see Jesus' coming. This verse suggests a belief in the second coming, which is different from the resurrection appearances (20.19–24).

**21.22b. What is that to you?:** Peter's question about the fate of the Beloved Disciple is not something with which he should concern himself.

**21.22c. Follow me:** 'Following' means discipleship (1.35; 21.19).

**21.23a. So the rumour spread:** There is no other record of this rumour.

**21.23b. In the community:** This can be translated 'among the brothers'. This need not mean that Jesus' followers were all men: Greek may use the masculine to include both men and women.

**21.23c. He would not die:** The rumour suggests that some thought the Beloved Disciple would not die before the second coming. The following explanation may have been written either because he had died, or because he might be about to die, and so it was necessary to break this rumour. The question is never answered, but considered irrelevant: the answer given to Peter applies to the audience (21.22). The death of the Beloved Disciple does not indicate the closeness of the second coming.

 Interpretation

This section is characterized by three misunderstandings (Appendix H):

1 *An emotional reaction* (21.17): Peter feels upset because Jesus repeats his question. While it is always difficult to analyse a character psychologically, it is not unreasonable to suggest that Peter thinks Jesus is questioning his sincerity. He has misunderstood that the questions are a form of healing and renewal rather than criticism.

2 *A distraction*: Jesus has asked Peter to follow him (21.19). Peter looks back, sees the Beloved Disciple and asks about his future. Jesus tells Peter to mind his own business and concentrate on his own discipleship, repeating the call to follow (21.21).

3 *A tradition about the Beloved Disciple* (21.22).

These three misunderstandings prompt three warnings:

1 Failure to understand Jesus can take away the benefits he offers: joy (3.29; 15.1; 16.20; 20.20) and peace (14.27; 20.26).

2 Disciples should focus on their own discipleship, not other people's.

3 Misunderstanding is still a reality (21.23). There is a continued need for authoritative teaching (21.24). This is not confined to the historical disciples, but can be minimized by embracing the authoritative teaching found in the Gospel.

The dialogue between Jesus and Peter involves three questions. Older commentaries claimed a difference between two Greek words for love. Modern scholarship sees two synonyms, as Augustine also did (*Homilies on the Gospel of John*, Tractate 123.5). Attempts to grade the different words used for love as representing different qualities of love which are more or less spiritual or physical are increasingly frustrated by careful studies of the use of these different terms in both ancient literature and pottery: they are used more interchangeably than the theories would like. Christian distinctions of the different 'love' words come later. The three commands are all basically the same, asking Peter to take on the work of the Good Shepherd. These three questions cancel out the three denials (18.15–18, 25–27). This passage indicates a reversal of fortunes, in which Peter is reinstated and a prophecy is made (21.18–19). This prophecy is most likely a saying made after the event: even the earliest dating of the Gospel would place it after Peter's martyrdom (see 'The date of the Gospel', p. 5).

Nothing here supports any claim to a superior hierarchical role for Peter. Such claims derive from Matthew 16.17–19, and should not be read into this text (see 'John and the Synoptic Gospels', p. 6). Claims that there is some kind of power struggle between Peter and the Beloved Disciple should be treated with caution, and certainly not read as if they were the struggles of Peter and Paul (Galatians 2), the split between East and West which culminated in the great Schism of 1054 CE, or the Reformation. The Beloved Disciple is thought to be a leader of at least equal stature to Peter within the Church. This has already been seen in:

1 the Last Meal, where he occupied a place of honour (13.23);

2 his proximity to the interrogation of Jesus (18.15);

3 his place at the foot of the cross (19.26–27);

4 his presence at the empty tomb (20.2–10);

5 his witness to the Tiberias experience (21.7).

Points 1, 2, 4 and 5 pair him with Peter. It appears that the Beloved Disciple needs to be presented as comparable with Peter because of later events.

The Gospel of Mark was based on the witness of Peter, according to Papias (see 'The identity of John', p. 4). Peter, and the tradition which followed him, also gained authority because of his martyrdom. In contrast, the Beloved Disciple appears less spectacular. If John was not a martyr (see 'The identity of John'), the Gospel offers an apology for this lack, without rubbishing Peter. John may not have been a martyr, but he is still an authoritative witness.

His legacy is also a reminder that low-key, even anonymous, living out of faith is important. Christians do this in living ordinary, day-to-day lives. What matters is that they live in obedience to God, not that their discipleship is marked by spectacular events. Almost 2,000 years later, the fact that this Gospel is still widely read, loved and influential bears witness to that reality.

# ? STUDY SUGGESTIONS

## Word study

1 Is there any significance in the variety of words used for 'love'?

2 Is 'What is that to you?' the main point of 21.21–23?

## Review of content

3 Compare Matthew 16.17–19 and 21.15–19.

4 How does the warning of Luke 9.62 compare to 21.20–22?

5 Why did the Beloved Disciple need to defend his authority?

## Discussion and application

6 Do we stress adequately the pastoral dimensions of commissioning and leadership?

7 Consider 21.17. Should Christians react badly to constructive criticism or questioning?

8 Do we overlook the ordinary when we experience spectacular examples of Christian witness? Should we?

# John 21.24–25

# The Afterword

 Introduction

This short section is a formal conclusion to the Gospel.

 Notes and commentary

**21.24a. These things:** This phrase refers to the whole substance of the Gospel.

**21.24b. Has written them:** This need not mean that the author has written all the Gospel, but rather he has caused it to be written (19.22): the Beloved Disciple is responsible for this Gospel.

**21.24c. We know that his testimony is true:** This may mean:

- a group of Christians bears witness to the authority of the Gospel;
- the writer is using an editorial 'we'.

The first option is more likely, even if one figure stands behind the whole editorial process which has produced the Gospel. More than one witness stands behind this testimony (5.31), and thus it is more reliable. It is not just the work of one person, but has been 'signed off' by many. It is possible that this statement puts in written form what might have happened in a public reading of the Gospel: an affirmation of what it says by those who have heard.

**21.25. There are also many other things that Jesus did; if every one of them were written down, I suppose that the world itself could not contain the books that would be written:** Verses of this kind were conventional in the ancient world (20.31; Ecclesiastes 12.9–12; Philo, *Special Laws* 4.238).

## Interpretation

The Afterword lets the writer conclude the work, and vouch for its authority. The final verse makes clear that the Gospel is not meant to be exhaustive or comprehensive (20.30). It pre-empts any criticism that the writer has said everything about Jesus. By implication, it admits that this is a structured and selective account of Jesus' life.

## Theological essay 4
## Discipleship in John's Gospel

KWA KIEM-KIOK

### Introduction

My husband and I are Christians living and working in Singapore, and we lead busy lives. We both work and so are out of our home for many hours each day. He is a pastor and has meetings at night, and is often in church on Saturdays and Sundays, whereas my work teaching at a seminary occupies my weekdays. We have duties to our elderly parents who do not live with us but whom we visit each week. We try to maintain a healthy lifestyle with regular exercise and eating well. Each year, we try to go away for a short holiday. Singaporeans enjoy a high standard of living, but that comes at the cost of dual-career families with children brought up by foreign domestic helpers or grandparents. Singapore is one of the most globalized cities in the world, and therefore vulnerable to global economic forces and movements. Hence there is a constant striving for higher growth and productivity so as to overcome those forces; but at the cost of stressful lives. Singapore is also a multiracial society in which various religions are practised: Buddhists and Taoists are the majority of the population at about 51 per cent; Muslims make up about 15 per cent and Christians about 18 per cent of the population.

This then is the context for Singapore Christians. The two issues which Christians face are, first, living as disciples in a fast-paced globalized urban setting which is materialistic and driven by the primacy of economics, and second, living with and being witnesses to people of other world religions.

The Gospel of John can be especially meaningful for Christians today because it is about life. The author himself writes that the purpose of the Gospel is that, 'these [things] are written so that you may come to believe that Jesus is the Messiah, the Son of God, and that through believing you may have life in his name' (John 20.31). As Christians, we seek to live the 'life' in Jesus every day. John's Gospel explicates and expounds that life in Jesus.

Let us keep in mind that life in Christ is necessary both for discipleship and for witness. That is, the life well lived, which glorifies God, will also draw all people to God himself (John 12.32). When Jesus is lifted up, people will be drawn to him. For example, Christians who show joy and peace in difficult times witness to the reality of God in their lives and can testify about that to family and friends. The apostle Peter makes a similar point in his letter to 'God's elect, strangers in the world' (1 Peter 1.1 NIV) when he urges believers to 'Live such good lives among the pagans that, though they accuse you of doing wrong, they may see your good deeds and glorify God on the day he visits us' (1 Peter 2.12 NIV). Therefore, discipleship is not just about being good Christians to ensure rewards in heaven. Discipleship should also attract non-believers to the light of Christ.

In this essay we shall explore the sayings of Jesus around the theme of 'life' as found in John's Gospel. There is some overlap since the Gospel is one seamless whole and we are drawing apart these themes:

1 life in Jesus, the light for all people;

2 eternal life and resurrection life;

3 the bread of life and rivers of living water;

4 life to the full;

5 Jesus: the way, the truth and the life.

## 1. Life in Jesus, the light for all people

In the profound Prologue to his Gospel, John starts, like the book of Genesis, 'in the beginning'. He introduces the Greek word *logos*, the 'Word', as one who was there even when the world began. He expounds on this Word, and equates him with God. Already there in the beginning of time, the Word was involved in the creation of the world. God created humanity in his image and with this wonderful capacity to multiply and create life. When we create something, we give it life. Thus a child is created by the joining of husband and wife; they have given this child life. The life that humanity receives in God is a spiritual life, and born of the will of God, not human will (John 1.13). God graciously makes it possible for people to become his children by first reaching out and drawing us to himself, by sending Jesus into the world. It is Jesus' death on the cross which makes it possible for us to have life.

This life was also special because it is also light (John 1.4–5). Light here is a symbol of goodness, truth, grace and even God himself. The light of Jesus shines in the dark world as a beacon of the hope and truth of God. However, there is no hint here of universalism; that is, that all religious paths lead to the same end, because John says that 'the darkness has not understood it' (1.5 NIV) and 'the world did not know him' (1.10). The darkness did not understand the light, and even rejects the light. Here, at the beginning of the Gospel, the writer makes it clear that Jesus is the true light, yet this truth is not and will not be universally accepted. Although this light is for all people, not everyone will want to be embraced by this light. Some people prefer walking in the dark.

Jesus as the light of the world is significant for discipleship because his light shines on the dark areas of sin in our life. Christians live in that light, seeking to live according to God's ways and purposes, even when those ways are demanding or counter-cultural.

## 2. Eternal life and resurrection life

Nicodemus the Pharisee went to see Jesus at night to find out more about the kingdom of God, and Jesus challenged him to be born again (John 3). By being born again, a person will have eternal life. This is often the message of hope given at Christian funerals.

In other religions, death is seen as the end of life. There is mourning and wailing at funerals. In the Chinese religion, houses or luxury cars made of paper are burned during the funeral ritual so that the deceased will have these comforts in the netherworld. Other world religions believe in the endless cycle of reincarnation and rebirth, with little hope of breaking out. The Christian message of eternal life in the presence of God stands in stark contrast to these beliefs. While tears are shed at funerals, there is also the conviction that there will be a reunion with the loved one in the presence of God, and so Christian funerals can be occasions of hope.

But eternal life is also life experienced here and now. This is shown by Nicodemus himself after the crucifixion of Jesus. Together with Joseph of Arimathea, Nicodemus asks for Jesus' body (John 19.38–42). Although the Gospel does not say so explicitly, that early encounter with Jesus must have influenced Nicodemus. By burying the body of Jesus, they put themselves at personal risk since both he and Joseph were members of the Sanhedrin which had sentenced Jesus to death.

Christian disciples today should also show that same courage. There may be situations when it is difficult to be a witness for God, yet, like Nicodemus, Christians can stand up for what they believe because they have experienced life in Christ here and now and have the hope of life eternal.

## 3. The bread of life and rivers of living water

Food and water are basic necessities for life. Without them humans cannot survive for more than a couple of days. Globalization has affected the supply of both food and water. Global warming has affected weather patterns and so influenced the growth of crops; for example, in some places because of drought or floods, crop production has been severely diminished. Drought also affects water supply. Furthermore, in some instances, land and water resources are polluted by careless industries, and whole communities suffer.

In Jesus' day, bread and water were also precious. In the semi-desert conditions, water had to be brought from wells, and wheat had to be cultivated to make flour and bread. The Samaritan woman in John 4 had to trek to the well each day to get water. In the familiar story of the feeding of the 5,000 Philip exclaims that it would take eight months' wages to feed the crowd (John 6.7). Today, in some economies, feeding the family can take the bulk of one's wages.

Hence it is especially meaningful that Jesus says he is both the bread of life (John 6.35) and that the water that he gives means that one will never thirst again (John 4.14). Indeed, that water will be a spring of water 'welling up' (NIV) or 'gushing up' (NRSV) into eternal life. That sounds like such an astonishing promise – no wonder the Samaritan woman wants it. In the semi-arid conditions of those days such water was a wonderful gift. This metaphor of Jesus as both bread of life and living water continues to be significant for Christians today. Food and water are basic to human life and so are meaningful pictures for discipleship.

Disciples of Christ are people who have springs of water gushing out of them. This could mean that their demeanour is such that others feel refreshed in their presence. There are some people who are emotionally demanding, because they demand a lot of our time and energy. Other people are a real joy to be with because they encourage and affirm. Disciples of Christ should be like the latter. Springs of water also connote a continuous flow of water rather than a stagnant pool. A spring of water is running water and suggests a connection to a source. The disciple must be constantly connected to God. There can be no Christian life without that deep, ongoing relationship with God.

A disciple is also one who feeds daily on Jesus the Word of God and living Bread. Such a person will live for ever (John 6.51). This feeding also comes from the sacrament of Holy Communion where Christians gather to remember and feed on the bread that is Jesus' body which has been broken. This ritual is an important reminder of the unity of all Christians who love the Lord Jesus Christ. Unity is an important factor in witness because that reflects the very nature of God. Jesus prays that disciples

> *may all be one. As you, Father, are in me and I am in you, may they also be in us, so that the world may believe that you have sent me. The glory that you have given me I have given them, so that they may be one, as we are one. I in them and you in me . . .*

(John 17.21–23)

## 4. Life to the full

As I look around nature, whether at the intricacies of a flower, the antics of animals or the splendour of the mountains, I marvel at the beauty and variety that God has created. I also particularly enjoy classical music, and every now and then my husband and I attend a concert. There are people in my church community who are passionate cyclists and cooks. I recently met a man in his early fifties who is preparing to run a marathon in a year's time. Music, food and running are all part of life.

Jesus came to give us life, and life to the full (John 10.10). In the context of this passage, Jesus says he is the shepherd who takes care of his sheep. He is also the gate who protects the sheep from the thieves and robbers who seek to destroy life. When the sheep are safe in the sheepfold, they feel secure.

Fullness of life in God must surely include enjoying and appreciating all the good things that God has created. Disciples are those who live to the full despite the difficulties and adversities they face, and help others to do likewise. Sometimes Christians can seem narrow-minded because they are only interested in 'spiritual' things. This is also partly because Christians are so busy with church activities they neglect other aspects of life.

The ability to enjoy the various aspects of life comes to Christians because they are secure in their relationship with the Shepherd. They know that there are aspects of life which are out of their control, for example that they may lose their jobs when the factory they are working in moves to another country. But disciples do not need to be anxious. An attitude of security in the Lord in the vicissitudes of life can be a witness to those who do not know this Shepherd. When disciples also display a zest for life and show an interest in many areas apart from 'churchy' concerns, they witness to the work and presence of God in all areas of life.

## 5. Jesus: the way, the truth and the life

These days Singaporeans seem to be more religious. That is, more Singaporeans are going to places of worship and participating in religious services. On a small island, such behaviour means that there needs to be sensitivity to people of other faiths, while at the same time clear boundaries need to be laid down so that Buddhists, Muslims, Hindus and Christians can relate courteously in public. Since Christianity is an exclusive and an evangelizing faith, that is, Christians believe that theirs is the one true faith and seek to convert others, they must be particularly sensitive to these trends in society. In this context, Jesus' claim that he is the way, the truth and the life (John 14.6) sounds intolerant. However, this is not the first time in the Gospel that the author refers to the exclusive nature of Jesus. This has already been mentioned in the Prologue.

This exclusive claim of Jesus was a challenge to the early believers. In the multi-religious context of the Graeco-Roman world, the early Christians also had to defend these exclusive claims. They were mocked and ridiculed as they brought the message of Jesus Christ as Lord and Saviour. Christians today can expect no less a reception as they present the same message. Since such absolute claims are perceived as narrow-minded today, there are some Christians who choose to leave out these claims and concentrate on the love and grace of God. Such an approach waters down the message of the gospel to such an extent that the good news loses its meaning.

Christians who live as salt and light in their communities must consider how they can continue to hold fast to the unique message of Jesus in today's religious climate. While it may have been permissible in the 1980s for Christians to launch public campaigns and to stop people on the streets to engage them in conversation, those methods are no longer appropriate. Today's more hostile audience requires that Christians need to be gracious and loving to their neighbours in order to gain an opportunity to give a reason for the hope that they have, doing so with gentleness and respect (1 Peter 3.15). This conduct has an impact on discipleship and how, for example, apologetics, or defending the Christian faith, is taught. Rather than just marshalling arguments, today all the more we need to consider how to build bridges and show hospitality to others. As disciples, Christians need to be winsome in their speech and conduct and be attractive, and point the way to Christ who gives them hope and life.

## Conclusion

John reminds us that Christians should lift up Jesus in their daily lives, individually and corporately, and in this way be bold witnesses. This Gospel also tells us how Jesus stooped down to wash the disciples' feet and therefore showed humility and servanthood, and exhorted his disciples to follow this example (John 13.12–15). As Christian disciples today, we can do no better than our Master who is the Word made flesh, full of grace and truth (John 1.14).

# Appendices

## A: Chronology

The Gospel differs significantly from the Synoptic Gospels both in the events described and in the sequence of those which they have in common.

The Gospel is our only source for incidents such as the miracle at Cana (2.1–11), the dialogue with the Samaritan woman (4.1–42) and the raising of Lazarus (1.11–44). It also omits any account of the Last Supper beyond the washing of the disciples' feet, and incidental details. We hear nothing of the command to share bread and wine in memory of Jesus in John's version.

There are differences in timing. The Gospel places the cleansing of the Temple right at the beginning of Jesus' ministry (2.13–22), and the date of the Last Supper is the day before Passover (13.1–2; 18.28; 19.31). While many scholars in the past thought that the Synoptic Gospels preserved a more accurate record of events, and that John's chronology was shaped by his theological interests rather than an interest in history, an increasing number now consider that John may preserve more accurate historical details than the Synoptics, and that his chronology cannot simply be dismissed as a theological invention. We will look at these different claims in our study of the events.

## B: Dualism

The Gospel uses a technique called dualism, using contrasting pairs of ideas (often opposites) to make its points, and to make a decision or a choice. This dualist language shapes the identity of those who wish to follow Jesus. To do this, John describes a worldview which embraces personal identity, ethics, and church or community. The result is a split between the faithful people of God and the ordinary world and its values. Hearing the Gospel does not simply give information about the values of this community based on Jesus. The act of hearing encourages those who might be unsure or wavering to increase their commitment to, or deepen their identification with, the community. John hopes that the hearer or reader of the Gospel will make a choice for Jesus and the community which follows him. The pairs which focus such decision-making include:

- *Belonging to God or the devil.* The devil is not presented as a second god, but is nonetheless a figure who claims loyalty which should be offered to God.

- *From above–from below; heaven–earth.* Heaven and its values (above) is favourably contrasted to this world (below).

- *Of this world–not of this world.* These compare to 'below' and 'above'.

- *Spirit–flesh.* Knowledge or experience associated with the spirit is of a higher quality than that associated with the flesh. Note that John does not reject or deny the flesh as many later Gnostic or puritan movements did. They followed Greek thinking which viewed flesh and matter as corrupt. John uses flesh and spirit in a different way, following Judaic ideas that it is the spirit which gives life to the flesh, and can even re-store life to the dead (Ezekiel 36.25–27).

- *Believing–not believing.* Believing implies a belief according to what God wants as opposed to not believing, which is more a failure to believe correctly rather than a lack of any kind of belief. Belief in the New Tes-tament includes two activities: trust or 'believing in' (in the context of relationships), and 'believing that' (performing a mental activity).

- *Seeing–not seeing.* Seeing is a quality of belief too reliant on visible phenomena or signs; it is, therefore, inferior or of a lower quality. John will constantly stress the superior faith of those who believe without seeing.

- *Death–life.* A correct belief, response or relationship to God leads to life (the continued existence of a person) rather than death (when that person ceases to exist).

- *Light–darkness.* To be in the light is to know the truth and live according to it. To live in darkness or shade is to be unaware of the truth and un-able to live by it.

- *Love–hate.* Love is to be in agreement with God; hate is to follow one's own desires, or someone who is wrongly put in the place of God. In the language of a former age, we might call hate self-centredness or idolatry – where another entity is given the respect and loyalty which really be-long to God alone.

- *Truth–falsehood.* This is like light–darkness.

It is clear that a choice to follow Jesus includes acceptance of the positive rather than the negative of each pair. The exception to this general rule is the pair about 'being chosen/choosing for oneself' which serves to remind the hearer or reader that they need to be part of the process of making a choice, but such choices should agree with the will of God.

## C: Signs

Chapters 1—12 are sometimes known as the Book of Signs after the 'signs' used to describe the miracles which Jesus performs; the Synoptic Gospels call these works 'acts of power'. For John, these signs are ambiguous: they may encourage either belief or disbelief. In John, faith is ultimately to be based on something more positive and less confusing than signs; believers need to base their faith on something more reliable than miraculous events.

## D: Glory

Chapters 13—20 are sometimes known as the Book of Glory. 'Glory' is a theme which appears earlier in the Gospel (for example, 1.14; 8.54).

'Glory' primarily refers to value, what something is worth. It has a positive meaning. Something or someone who is glorious has a great positive value: beautiful, true, worth acquiring, life-enhancing, and/or good. 'Glory' means that something is recognized and acknowledged as valuable and worthwhile in this way. Giving 'glory to God' means that God is recognized as good, true, etc. The Latin translation 'clear'/'make clear' used in the Vulgate to translate 'glorious'/'glorify' (17.1, 4, 5, 10, 22) brings out this layer of meaning.

'Giving glory' or 'glorifying' thus means recognizing and acknowledging someone or something's value and its power as a force for good. Wrongly used, it becomes only lip-service or words used in worship. 'Glorifying God' thus means not simply to utter prayers and praise, but to live in agreement with the values revealed by God. 'Glorifying God' should mean making intentional choices to live in a way which is filled with the values seen in God. It thus also challenges the norms of honour and shame which societies hold, suggesting that honour is what is pleasing to God, not humanity.

In John's Gospel, this means a life lived in love, which is what best describes both who God is and how he acts (3.16–18) and how those who recognize and acknowledge his glory should also live (13.34–35). This is why the last chapters are called the Book of Glory: Jesus both teaches and lives out those values, showing how positive and important they are, and giving his followers an example on which to base their own lifestyles.

## E: Truth

Truth first appears in the Prologue (1.14), but becomes a central theme of the Gospel in the Book of Glory (13—20). It is identified as a characteristic of the Father (1.14) and Jesus (14.6). John's reflections on truth will climax in Jesus' interrogation by Pilate (18.38).

Truth is a broad concept in John. It includes ideas of revelation: the word literally means 'not hidden'. Truth is a description of how things really are.

Its connection to the Way (14.6) as a description of Jesus makes an important point. Truth is not a pot of meaning to be quarried out and found: it is a journey, a process, a way of living. Truth and behaviour are intimately linked. Truth is to be lived, not dissected.

The idea of 'not hidden' implies that truth is marked by openness and transparency. This is significant in personal and psychological terms. The English word 'person' is also the word for a mask: living in truth means living without masks, without putting on a show or pretending to be something else. Many people do this to hide what they are ashamed of or embarrassed about concerning themselves, their lifestyle or their circumstances. In doing this, they become trapped by their sins. The idea of truth as something which reveals how things really are breaks the cycle of hiding and deceit, and allows for healing, not hiding, to begin. Throughout the Gospel, Jesus is shown to be someone who knows what people are really like (2.25; 4.17; 6.70; 10.3; 13.21–30, 38; 16.32) but nonetheless still loves them. Truth does not lead to condemnation, but to salvation for those who continue to believe in Jesus.

## F: Pre-existence

From its opening verses, John's Gospel suggests that there is more to Jesus than simply being born a human. Both in the Prologue (1.1–4) and at other points in the Gospel (3.17, 31–32; 5.36–37; 6.62; 8.38, 58; 17.5, 24), Jesus is claimed to have existed before the time of his public life and ministry. The technical name for this is pre-existence. The possible sources or origins for a belief in pre-existence have been disputed. These theories face several difficulties.

First, much of the literature used to support both claims often comes from the time after the Gospel was written. In such circumstances, we cannot simply assume that the ideas found in them necessarily existed in the earlier forms at the time of the Gospel. The date of a supposed source or influence must always be carefully checked. So must its geographical location: an idea which is found, say, only in Spain is unlikely to have influenced another found mainly in the eastern Mediterranean.

Second, they raise the possibility that these ideas may have been formed by the Gospel rather than the other way around: the cross-fertilization of ideas is rarely a one-way process.

Third, increasingly, study of Jewish materials reveals that these ideas were found within Second Temple Judaism. Terms like wisdom, word (1.1) and name of God (4.26; 6.35; 8.58), angels (1.32) and Messiah indicate interest in pre-existence. Even more significant is the description of the Messiah in 1 Enoch 48.5: 'For this reason he was chosen and hidden in his presence before the world began.'

Scholars like Daniel Boyarin and Margaret Barker suggest that traditions like this stretch right back to the earliest Judaism. They appear to combine two claims: of a heavenly Redeemer who becomes human (most famously in Daniel 7) and of a human becoming divine (*apotheosis*, 1.51). Reflections like this attempt to answer the question of how God may appear remote and other (transcendent), yet also close to his people (immanent).

That said, none of these provides a fully developed understanding of pre-existence, which was adopted wholesale by Christian theologians:

there was no existing pattern which could be used to describe Jesus. Traditions about angels, exalted righteous ancestors or even a Messiah would not be acceptable if they effectively made creatures equal with God. The idea of a pre-existent Messiah seems to make 'Spirit-inspired' equal to 'pre-existent'; it is not certain that this was so. Early Christian theologians used existing language to develop their theories of pre-existence, particularly the phrase 'Son of Man' (1.51).

All this suggests that pre-existence is more likely to come from a Judaic context. Given the Jewishness of Jesus, it suggests a greater chance of continuity with the tradition based on what he said and did, not simply distortions imported from an alien cultural system by later writers.

## G: The content of Jesus' teaching

The way in which Jesus speaks is significantly different from the Synoptic Gospels.

The 'I am' sayings exemplify this. These are John's parables and they are Jewish in form and function. Jewish parables functioned differently from their Greek counterparts: they provide commentaries on the actions which unfold in the narrative of the Gospel. They are not 'stand-alone' moral stories.

Jesus also talks much more directly about the Father and their relationship. It is almost as if this language of relationship has replaced the Synoptic focus on the kingdom, and *Abba*. In John, Jesus repeatedly stresses the unity he has with the Father. This unity is seen at work in the two actions which characterize their relationship: love and sending.

## H: Dialogue and misunderstanding

A recurring feature of the Gospel is the dialogue form in which Jesus converses with all kinds of people. It starts with a sign, or a statement by Jesus, or his explanation of a sign. In reply to Jesus, the other party makes a comment which shows misunderstanding. This remark becomes an opportunity to explain the real significance of what has happened. This process may result in either agreement with Jesus or increased hostility to him.

## I: *Parrhēsia*

Frank or plain speaking (Gk, *parrhēsia*) stresses that the speaker is giving a firmly held opinion, free from rhetorical flourishes. It concerns the truth, in part, revealed by the courage of the speaker in making such claims and taking a risk – by challenging authority figures or others viewed as superior. It often contains criticism either of the speakers or the ones to whom they speak. Speakers are motivated by a desire for truth and moral duty. Frank speaking also is intended to affect how people live: in their community life (the church), in public life (the world) and personal relationships.

In John, this pattern of speech will be seen when people speak boldly to one another, especially authority figures. Introductory phrases like 'Very truly' (1.51) are often indicators of plain speaking.

In Numbers 12.8 Moses claims that he speaks with God face to face and not 'in riddles' (see also 1 Corinthians 13.12; for more on face-to-face encounters, see 1.18). This may mean that God speaks plainly to Moses. If this is right, plain speaking also implies a close and open relationship with God.

## J: The devil

John gives a satanic dimension to his description of Jesus' opposition. His portrayal of the devil has the following features:

1 Jesus' opponents are charged with belonging to the devil (8.38, 41, 44).

2 The devil is identified as a murderer. This is more likely to refer to the fall of Adam (Genesis 3) than the story of Cain and Abel (Genesis 4.1–16).

3 He is identified as the 'father of lies' (Genesis 3; 2 Corinthians 11.3).

4 Jesus is portrayed as aware of the devil's involvement in what is happening to him (6.70; 13.27).

5 The devil is portrayed as ruler of this world (12.31; 14.30; 16.11; 17.15). Human beings who do not obey God put themselves under the devil's authority. Blaming the devil is not a means of abrogating responsibility for one's own actions: he has authority because it has been given to him voluntarily.

6 Whatever power has been given to the devil is limited and inferior to the power wielded by Jesus (13.27).

7 Whatever power has been given to the devil is broken by Jesus, whose death on the cross breaks the authority which has been handed over to him (12.31–32).

## K: The Messiah

A key figure in Jewish thought at the time of Jesus and John was the Messiah (Hebrew), Christ (Greek) or Anointed One (English): a heavenly figure, an agent of God who would intervene decisively and procure freedom for Israel. There were a number of different views about this Messiah. Hopes that the Messiah would appear were common at the time: Josephus details a number of messianic claimants at about the time of Jesus (*Antiquities* 17.271–84; 18.85–9; *Jewish War* 2.433–4, 444; 4.510; 6.300–9). As late as the 130s CE the Bar-Kochba revolt against the Romans in the time of Hadrian was driven by messianic hopes.

Some thought the Messiah was divine, others a heavenly or angelic figure; there is much debate about whether a figure called Metatron who appears in Second Temple literature and is often portrayed like the Messiah was considered to be God, or a supernatural being of some lesser kind, like an angel. Some thought the Messiah would be a prophetic figure like Moses (Deuteronomy 18.15; Exodus 20.17), while others expected a warrior-king in the style of David (Psalm 110.1). While warlike language was often used, it was not necessarily meant to be read literally. So there were beliefs in a teacher-Messiah imbued with the Spirit and wisdom, often drawn from Isaiah 11 and 42 (*Psalms of Solomon* 17—18; Dead Sea Scrolls, 1Q28b; 4Q161; 4Q534; 4Q175; *Similitudes of Enoch* (*1 Enoch* 37—71), *4 Ezra* (*2 Esdras* 3—14)). Such a Messiah would come to separate the righteous from the unrighteous. Sometimes, as in the Qumran writings, the righteous were identified as a group within Israel, which, as a nation, also included corrupt and unrighteous elements which would be weeded out. Some texts, for example the *Gabriel Revelation*, written in the late first century BCE, even seem to show a belief in a Messiah who would suffer, die and rise again.

Messianic thinking was not limited to conventional Judaism. The 'prophet-king like Moses' was a view of the Messiah particularly held by the Samaritans, who called him the *Taheb* ('one who returns/restores'). Judaic messianic thinking may even have penetrated Roman thinking: the Roman poet Virgil, in his *Fourth Eclogue*, describes the birth of a special child who will usher in a golden age.

## L: The Jews

'Jews' is a difficult word throughout this Gospel. It covers a variety of meanings: sometimes referring to Jesus' opponents, sometimes not (2.6; 4.9).

Verses like 2.6 suggest that the term refers to Judaism and Jews in general. Other information may qualify or limit the term (5.21). On the other hand, some scholars suggest it might be better translated 'Judaeans', following the usage of writers like Josephus, and refer to a distinct sub-group within Israel. Israel also included Galileans and Pereans. The Synoptic Gospels prefer to identify the particular schools or groups in conflict with Jesus by name; this is a more accurate way of reporting the various debates and conflicts.

John's usage also may well reflect the situation in which he wrote, when there was increased tension between the early Christians and adherents of Judaism. Christians must, however, be aware that John's wording has been used by some to legitimize anti-Semitism. Any reading which attempts to do this must be rejected as false. It is a source of regret that John's wording has been used to justify ethnic or racial propaganda. Above all, our modern understandings of 'Jew' or 'Jewishness' are not appropriate and we must be careful not to use them anachronistically.

## M: The kingdom

The kingdom/the kingdom of God/kingdom of heaven is central to Jesus' teaching in the NT. In the Synoptics, the kingdom refers to the rule of God in which he judges and purifies the world to cleanse it from corruption; it is often described as a place which the faithful hope to enter. Different traditions in the Gospels see the kingdom as having already come (realized eschatology) or going to come (future eschatology). Attempts to reconcile these two different timings point to a consensus that the kingdom has come in part (as witnessed in the Jesus of history) but not completely (and so will be seen in its fully perfect form in the future): sometimes called 'yes/already . . . but not yet'. In John's Gospel, the kingdom is effectively replaced by talk of eternal life (3.15), and scholars talk of this 'yes . . . but not yet' view as *inaugurated* or *complementary eschatology*. It is possible that these remaining traces of the kingdom may point back to speeches originating with Jesus himself, even if John has edited them and translated them for his readers, who might have been less familiar with Judaic expressions like this.

# Index

*1 Enoch* 46, 159, 186, 249, 251, 284, 287
1 and 2 Corinthians 45, 62, 84, 89, 90, 113, 126, 158, 160, 178, 179, 180, 181, 192, 196, 201, 224, 228, 246, 247, 253, 257, 266, 286
1 and 2 Kings 19, 20, 23, 39, 48, 51, 55, 75, 102, 122, 143, 150, 156, 159, 177, 199, 240
1 and 2 Peter 62, 117, 135, 162, 177, 269, 275, 279
1 and 2 Samuel 21, 61, 85, 132, 147, 176, 177, 217, 228, 240
1, 2 and 4 Maccabees 20, 23, 32, 138, 143, 147, 177, 198

abiding 21, 22, 50, 86, 130, 136, 186, 187, 188, 193–4, 211–12, 215, 216; *see also* dwelling
*'Abot see Pirke Abot*
Abraham 41, 112–15, 117–19, 209
Acts, book of 21, 22, 54, 59, 61, 85, 99, 102, 135, 141, 143, 144, 152, 159, 180, 181, 187, 188, 201, 216, 217, 235, 241, 251, 269
*ad hominem* (philosophy) 65, 66, 110, 115, 116, 126
addiction 43
adoptionism 21
Advocate (Holy Spirit) 187–9, 191, 192, 196, 197–8, 201, 253–4; as angelic being 187; *see also* Holy Spirit
*African Bible, The* 248
*agōn* (contest) 98
Alexandria (possible location for John's Gospel) 2, 4
*anagnōrisis* (recognition of Jesus) 134

Andersen, Hans Christian ('Emperor's New Clothes' story) 113–14
Andrew (apostle) 5; comes to Jesus 22; finds boy with loaves and fishes 75; introduces Greeks to Jesus 158
angels 22, 24, 51, 59, 69, 159, 284, 285; angels at empty tomb 249, 251
Annas 220–1, 223, 224
anointing: after death 238, 245; of Jesus at Bethany 143, 153–4, 156, 235; of the Messiah 97, 286
Antioch 2, 4
anti-Semitism 157
*Apocalypse of Moses* 238
*apotheosis* (a human becoming divine) 284
Aramaic 4, 22, 26, 37, 58, 158, 178, 183, 246, 250
Asia Minor 2, 4–5, 21
Asklepios (Greek god of healing) 144
Athanasius (*On the Incarnation*) 208
Athenaeus (*Deipnosophistae*) 179
Augustine of Hippo 91, 265, 270
Augustus (emperor) 191

baptism 38, 39, 41, 191, 237; by Jesus 44; of Jesus 160; by John the Baptist 21; as opposed to bathing 176, 180, 181
Bar-Kochba revolt 110, 287
Barabbas 178, 227
Barker, Margaret 284
Baruch, book of (Apocrypha) 94; *2 Baruch* (Old Testament Pseudepigrapha) 51, 84
belief 29, 30, 35–6, 39, 42, 46, 53, 56, 61–2, 63–4, 66–8, 69, 70,

80, 82, 88, 91, 95, 110, 125, 139, 145, 148, 149, 160, 163, 164, 167, 184, 190, 197, 208, 214, 231; in the resurrection of Jesus 245–59, 263–7

Beloved Disciple: adopts Jesus' mother 235, 241; authority as reliable source 182; goes to empty tomb 244; goes to high priest's house 221; with Jesus and Peter at Sea of Tiberias 261, 263–4, 265, 266, 268–70, 272; possible author of John's Gospel 4–5, 257, 273; possible identity with John the Evangelist 143; stands at foot of the cross 271

*Beth ha Midrash* 118

Bethany (across the Jordan) 20, 22

Bethany (Jerusalem) 138, 143, 144, 148, 152, 153

Bethesda 58, 168

Bethsaida 22

betrayal of Jesus: by Judas 88–9, 153, 154, 176, 177, 182–3, 226; Peter's denial 185, 221, 222, 224

blasphemy 60, 64, 118; Jesus accused of 138–42, 150, 223, 226, 240

blindness: physical 121–9, 148, 170; spiritual 121, 133

blood 29; at the death of Jesus 236, 237; of Jesus 71, 85–7; link with Eucharist 90–2, 200

Booths, Festival of 93–120, 122, 133, 138, 155; *see also Sukkoth*

born from above (born again) 37–8, 41, 43, 51, 167, 276

Boyarin, Daniel 284

bread 177, 182–3; breakfast after the resurrection 264–6, 281; feeding of five thousand 74–7, 79–87, 169; Jesus as bread of life 80, 81–4, 209, 211–12, 275, 276–7; lack of, a crying evil in parts of today's world 70; link with Eucharist 84–6, 90–2; link

with manna in wilderness 80; *see also* Passover

Brodie, Thomas 91

Caesarea Philippi 109, 134, 149; *peripeteia* (change of fortune, reversal) 143

Caiaphas *see* high priest

Caligula, Gaius (emperor) 225, 233

Cana, wedding feast at 13, 19, 26–30, 281

*chiasmus*, in Prologue 18

children of God 15, 17, 116, 118, 252

Christ *see* Jesus

Church: accused of cover-up 126, 127; African Church cell groups 216; challenges of today 166, 169–71, 182, 278; dangers of idolatry 164; dangers of power-seeking 257–8; in decline today in Global North and West 201; early Church formulates canon of Scripture 141; ecumenical work 207–8, 209; functions as family led by God 95; as group of God's people 8, 53; mission of Church 71, 136, 137, 169; 'prosperity churches' 135–6; relationship with Christ 45, 254, 255; seen as judgemental 42, 43

cleansing 181, 193; cleansing of the Temple 6, 31–5, 281

community: of believers 171, 196; church as alternative or new 5, 7–9, 254–5, 281, 285; containing fruitful and barren members 193; of disciples 193–9, 266–270; Holy Spirit in 187; importance of in African societies 210–16

creation: 'creation mandate' as part of Church's mission 135, 136, 169; gift of sight as new creation 121–3, 129; Jesus as link between God and his creation 67, 69, 70; judgement's transforming of 197; link with sabbath 59, 239, 249, 253; as part of God's plan of salvation 7, 13, 14, 67; role of Logos in 17, 18, 167, 275; role of Spirit in 21; and through his ministry and death 203, 208, 236

cross 50, 176, 233, 236, 253, 258; analogy with bronze serpent 39, 42; displays suffering of God 123; inscription on Jesus' cross 233, 239, 240, 242; John portrays cross as glory 71, 72, 173; obstacle to faith 196; question by Nicodemus 40

crucifixion 111, 159, 173, 196, 256, 276; death by, demands Roman involvement 226, 228; Jesus crucified at Golgotha 233–43; Synoptics record different times for 230

Daniel, book of 22, 23, 24, 54, 61, 62, 80, 104, 105, 138, 143, 159, 218, 251, 284

dark/darkness 2, 14–15, 18, 19, 24, 37, 42, 77, 107, 143, 159, 160, 163, 166, 220, 239, 245, 275, 276, 282

David 85, 98, 101, 130, 139, 164, 177, 217, 241, 287

Dead Sea Scrolls 2, 46, 91, 119, 187, 205, 287

death: conquered 39, 61, 210, 214; death of Jesus gives us life 276; of Jesus 1, 27, 67, 71, 72, 85, 225–43, 254; Jesus predicts his own death 109–11, 132–4, 188, 190, 191, 197, 198, 203; link with Eucharist 90–1, 200; reasons for 34, 52, 142–61; *see also* resurrection

Dedication, Festival of 133, 138–51

Deuteronomy, book of 16, 20, 22, 29, 31, 32, 58, 59, 62, 82, 85, 94, 97, 102, 104, 105, 116, 122, 132, 162, 179, 196, 206, 238, 287

devil 88, 116, 118, 119, 120, 159, 176, 183, 184, 189, 197, 205, 219, 235, 281, 286

Diaspora 99, 100, 125

*Didascalia Apostolorum* (relating to woman taken in adultery) 105

disciple(s)/discipleship: 4, 5, 13, 16, 19, 22, 23, 25–9, 31–6, 39, 44, 47, 48, 50–2, 67–9, 74, 75, 78, 79, 85–90, 94, 95, 109, 112, 114, 121, 125, 129, 135–6, 142, 143, 144, 149, 151, 153, 155, 158, 166, 167, 169, 173; after the resurrection 253–5; essay on in John's Gospel 274–9; farewell speeches to disciples at the Last Meal 175–207; with Jesus before his arrest 217–23; *see also individual disciples by name*

Docetism 1, 15, 85, 146, 158, 235, 257

Donne, John 56

Donovan, Vincent 56

dualism 2, 14, 91, 281–2

dwelling 86, 186, 188, 192

earth/heaven 1, 13, 15, 16, 17, 19, 21–9, 38, 45–6, 68–9, 72, 79–85, 91, 117, 131, 159, 160, 169, 203, 209, 211, 212, 229, 240, 245, 249, 252, 257, 275, 282, 284–8

Easter 1, 150, 247, 264

Ecclesiastes, book of 23, 84, 273

Eden, Garden of 82, 217, 238–9

Elijah 19–20, 21, 25, 97, 102, 125, 159, 235

Enlightenment, effect on European scholarship 76

Ephesians, letter to 45, 64, 135, 180, 269

Ephesus 2, 4
Epicurus/Epicureanism 59, 158, 161, 190
Epilogue (John 21) 263–79
eschatology 41, 53; future 81, 288; inaugurated 51, 65, 101, 119, 160, 183, 186, 197; realized 39, 288
Eucharist 29, 39, 79, 85, 87, 90–2, 177, 191, 199, 200, 202, 237, 266, 267
Eusebius of Caesarea (*Ecclesiastical History*) 105
exaltation 1, 21, 72, 111, 159, 285; *see also* Jesus, 'lifted up'
exodus (event) 15, 16, 18, 20, 21, 22, 29, 31–3, 48, 50, 54, 58, 59, 63, 75, 78, 80–2, 84, 94, 97, 101, 105, 110, 112, 114, 116, 122, 124, 125, 126, 133, 135, 155, 162, 164, 234–7, 246–7, 287
*Exodus Rabbah* 60
Ezekiel, book of 16, 38, 45, 49, 94, 101, 104, 110, 115, 122, 126, 130–2, 177, 193, 199, 210, 239, 253, 282
Ezra, book of 48, 125, 134, 136, 287

farewell speeches (of Jesus) 175–208
Father (God) *see* God the Father
father (human relation) 16, 23, 27, 28, 55, 65, 110, 115–19, 220, 224, 227, 286
feet, washing of 176–7, 180, 181, 240
flesh 15, 18, 38, 45, 71, 84–7, 90, 107, 141, 166, 211, 257, 279, 282
flogging (of Jesus) 227
following 5, 8, 13, 19, 22–3, 25, 27, 29, 38, 40, 51, 55, 60, 63, 69, 74, 80, 82, 87, 89, 100, 103, 107, 109, 112, 118, 125, 131, 132, 139, 157, 158, 180, 188, 193, 215, 246, 266, 269, 270, 279, 281, 282; part of discipleship 183–5
friendship 29, 36, 45, 48, 66, 143, 146, 177, 194–5, 229, 235, 237, 241, 252, 275

Gabbatha (Pavement) 230
*Gabriel Revelation* 287
Galatians, letter to 114, 135, 196, 211, 246, 271
Galilee 19, 23, 26, 27, 37, 41, 54, 55, 74, 101, 102, 199, 241, 263, 264, 265
Galilee, Sea of 22, 28, 74, 77–9, 235, 263; *see also* sea, symbolism of
Geevarghese Mar Osthathius (saying) 258
*gematria* 265
Genesis, book of 13–14, 16–17, 18, 21, 22, 23, 24, 27, 29, 38, 39, 42, 47, 48, 59, 60, 61, 77, 81, 82, 85, 97, 110, 112, 115, 116, 117, 122, 130, 135, 159, 217, 236, 239, 253, 275, 286
*Genesis Rabbah* 60
Gerizim, Mount *see* Samaritans
Gethsemane 158, 217–18, 222; Jesus' prayer in 191
glory 24, 26, 125, 158–9, 160, 166, 190, 269, 277, 283; attained through suffering 71–3; demonstrated in Gospel through the 'seven signs' 165–71; Jesus as glory of God 107, 146, 150, 156; linked with Passion of Jesus 101; received from God alone 63, 96, 116, 123; Shekinah 16; shown at wedding at Cana 28, 29
Glory, Book of 173–259
glossolalia (speaking in tongues) 192
Gnostics 1, 17, 199, 205, 282
God the Father 7, 16, 17, 32, 45, 50, 51, 60, 61–72, 80–2, 84, 86, 88, 95, 96, 100, 107–13, 115–17, 118, 119, 123, 132, 139, 140,

142, 146, 158-61, 163, 168-9,
171, 173, 175-7, 186-210,
213-19, 224, 231, 235, 241, 250,
253, 254, 266, 277, 283, 285
Good Shepherd 121, 130-3, 136,
139, 142, 145, 147, 148, 150,
151, 153, 155, 170, 184, 194,
209, 210, 213-14, 227, 250, 271
goodness: contrasted with evil 14,
40, 42, 62, 164; goodness of God
190; goodness of Jesus 95, 134,
139; light as symbolic of 275
grace 16, 19, 191, 207, 211, 275,
278, 279
Greek (language) xiii, xiv, 4, 13,
15, 22, 23, 24, 29, 35, 37, 39,
44, 47, 49, 50, 54, 55, 61, 85,
88, 90, 101, 117, 128, 134, 144,
146, 157, 178, 187, 194, 218,
233, 235, 236, 249, 269, 270,
275, 286
Greeks 2, 5, 14, 17-18, 23, 37, 41,
51, 52, 85, 100, 110, 134, 144,
157-8, 160, 161, 179, 190, 197,
205, 242, 265, 282, 285

Hadrian (emperor) 229, 283, 287
Haggadah see Passover
Hallel (Psalms 113—118) 100, 155,
230
heart: hardening of 162-3; hearts
not to be troubled 189; not all
have God's love in their hearts
168; 'seed' of God's word in 171;
where a person's heart lies 135
heaven 1, 13-30, 38, 45, 46, 68,
69, 72, 79, 80-7, 91, 117, 131,
159, 160, 169, 203, 209, 212,
249, 252, 275, 282, 284, 286-7
Hebrew (language) 4, 18, 22, 26,
39, 50, 58, 85, 131, 155, 162,
189, 230, 233, 250, 286
Herod the Great 225
high priest (Caiaphas) 6, 147, 153,
154, 217-18, 220-5, 234, 240
HIV and AIDS x, 42
Holy Spirit 7, 8, 38, 39, 40, 41,

43, 44, 45, 46, 49-50, 65, 87-8,
101, 167, 168, 175, 181, 187,
202, 210, 237, 242; as a dove 21;
gifted to disciples 252-5, 257; as
Paraclete 7, 8, 188
honour/shame 6, 18, 25, 27, 28,
45, 46, 47, 54, 61, 65, 72, 81,
101, 116, 146, 152, 158, 160-1,
164, 171, 180, 202, 229, 231,
232, 238, 271, 283; see also status
Horace (Satires) 225
Hosea, book of 22, 27, 33, 45, 115,
193, 198
hour: in terms of Passion and
death of Jesus 27, 29, 62, 98,
158, 175, 199, 203, 208, 233
hymn see Prologue

'I am' (sayings of Jesus) 50, 110,
111, 117, 220, 275-8, 285; bread
of life 81-3, 85; essay on John's
view of 'I am' words, and works
165-71; gate 131; Good Shepherd 132; Light of the World
122-3; resurrection and the life
145; theological essay on each
'I am' saying 209-16; true vine
193-4; the way, the truth and
the life 186-7
immortality of the soul 251, 252,
257
Incarnation (of Jesus) 14, 257;
theological issues about 141,
208
Isaac 16, 42, 112, 117
Isaiah, book of 13, 14, 20, 21, 23,
24, 27, 31, 38, 39, 45, 46, 49,
51, 54, 75, 76, 77, 80, 81, 82,
94, 97, 101, 110, 116, 126, 130,
132, 136, 144, 147, 156, 159,
160, 162, 164-6, 170, 177, 187,
193, 196, 198, 199, 239, 253,
255, 287

Jacob 23-4
Jacob's well, Jesus at 47-54
James, letter of 177

James, son of Zebedee 4
Jamnia, Council of 99–100, 132
Jeremiah, book of 16, 21, 27, 32, 45, 49, 51, 82, 105, 116, 122, 130, 132, 135, 147, 193, 198, 199
Jerusalem 4, 5, 19, 20, 34, 54, 58, 74, 124, 132, 136, 138, 143, 155–7, 178, 199, 217, 221, 227, 232, 241; Festival of Booths held in 93, 94, 96–9; pool of Siloam in 122
Jerusalem Temple *see* Temple
Jesus 135, 140, 164, 165, 166, 168–71, 181, 190, 196, 201, 203, 211, 212, 214, 215, 216, 226, 275, 276–8, 286; cleanses Temple 31–5, 45, 46, 68, 70, 114; heals blind man 122–5; in heaven and on earth 13–30; as Lamb of God 13, 20–1, 236, 237; leads to controversy 124–9; 'lifted up' 279; as Logos 7, 13–16, 166, 275; *Taheb* 48, 49, 50, 51, 287; *see also* Logos; Messiah; tomb of Jesus
Jewish culture and society 15, 48, 51, 52, 60, 61, 64, 65, 69, 75, 76, 80, 83, 85, 88, 91, 93–4, 99, 100, 102, 110, 112, 113, 114, 117, 119, 122, 132, 138, 140, 143, 144, 146–7, 150, 152, 156, 157, 158, 179, 187, 194, 199, 202, 206, 210, 219, 225, 236, 237–9, 246–8, 249, 251, 254, 257, 265, 284–6
Jewish Diaspora *see* Diaspora
Jews (opponents of Jesus) 19, 20, 26, 32, 37, 44, 58–62, 65, 72, 74, 81, 85, 93–6, 99, 102, 110, 113, 117, 125, 139, 146, 148, 183, 219, 221, 226, 234, 238, 240, 253, 287
Job, book of 22, 122–3, 126, 176, 187, 218, 278
John, son of Zebedee 4
John of Ephesus 4, 5

John the Baptist 5, 6, 13, 15, 18, 19, 25, 26, 31, 44, 52, 99, 166
John the Evangelist 4–5, 92
Jonah, book of 33, 102, 147
Jordan 20, 22, 44, 140
Joseph (earthly father of Jesus), 23, 81
*Joseph and Aseneth* 91
Joseph of Arimathea 237, 242, 276
Josephus (historian), 25, 32, 225, 247, 287; *Against Apion* 119, 238; *Antiquities* 25, 54, 102, 138, 220, 234, 238, 286; *Jewish War* 102, 110, 138, 147, 179, 225, 227, 236, 238, 286
joy 45, 117, 189, 194, 197, 198, 201, 204, 207–8, 253–4, 258, 270, 275, 277
*Jubilees* 60, 117, 141
Judas, son of James 188
Judas Iscariot 6, 88, 152–4, 160, 176, 177, 180–5, 188, 193, 204, 217–20, 226, 229, 241
judge (verb or action) 36, 39, 52, 53, 61–3, 97, 98, 102, 107–8, 127, 130, 163, 197, 225, 231, 248, 255, 288; judgement 39, 42–3, 46, 48, 51, 60–3, 80, 97, 98, 107–9, 159, 160, 162, 186, 187, 197, 200–1, 206, 219, 223, 255
Judges, book of 16, 21, 38

Kidron Valley 104, 217
king 24–5, 32, 48, 51, 54, 76, 79, 139, 141–2, 150, 155, 156, 169, 226–34, 240, 287
kingdom of God 39, 40–1, 45, 131, 165, 167, 211, 226, 240, 276, 285, 288

lamb: 'Feed my lambs' 268; paschal lamb 21; Passover lamb 31–2, 178, 230, 237; symbolic of Suffering Servant (Isaiah) 20–1

last day 38, 45, 81, 84, 86, 93, 108, 144, 158, 163, 204; *see also* resurrection
Last Supper 29, 90, 178, 199, 236, 281
Latin (language) 233, 283
law (Torah) 16, 23, 48, 59, 60, 64, 70, 75, 80, 81, 83–5, 90, 96–7, 102, 104, 107, 108, 112, 113, 124, 139, 150, 159, 162, 196, 210, 225, 228
Lazarus 4, 6, 133, 138; death of 142–56; raising to life 170, 246, 281
*Letter of Aristeas* 60
Levites 19
Leviticus, book of 21, 27, 31, 45, 59, 60, 85, 94, 97, 104, 179
libertarianism, 181
life 1, 6, 7, 8, 14, 15, 17, 19, 38, 39, 41, 49, 61–3, 65, 67, 68, 70–3, 80–3, 85–8, 91, 97, 111, 116, 132, 134–6, 139, 142, 145, 147–51, 158, 160–1, 165–71, 181, 182, 184, 186–8, 190, 192, 194, 199–201, 206, 209–16, 220, 225, 231, 236, 237, 239, 241, 247, 251, 257, 258–9, 263, 274–9, 282–5; eternal life 6, 39, 42, 43, 45–6, 49, 51, 53, 61, 63, 65, 79, 80–2, 85–8, 132, 136, 139, 150, 158, 163, 164, 168, 169, 173, 177, 186–8, 203, 209–12, 214, 258–9, 275–9, 288
lift up *see* exaltation; Jesus, 'lifted up'
light 14–15, 18–19, 21, 37, 38–40, 63, 71, 94, 107, 114, 143, 157, 159–60, 163, 165, 167, 216, 220–2, 264, 275, 279, 282; *see also qal-wahômer*
Light of the World 93, 95, 107, 109, 119, 122, 143, 163, 170, 209, 212–13, 218, 275–6
Logos 7, 13–15, 17–18, 166, 275
love 7, 16, 18, 39, 40, 42–3, 45, 61, 63, 67–8, 70–3, 103, 132, 133, 143, 146, 151, 158, 163,

164, 168, 171, 182, 184–5, 188–9, 191–7, 200, 206–8, 212, 213, 221, 223, 231, 235, 268–72, 277, 278, 282–5
Luke, Gospel of 6, 20, 21, 22, 26, 27, 32–5, 40, 44–6, 51–2, 54, 57, 59, 60, 64, 66, 75, 77, 91, 95, 97, 101, 104, 105, 109, 117, 122, 124, 130–4, 143, 148, 149, 151, 153, 155, 156, 158, 160, 178, 180–5, 188, 193, 196, 200–2, 205, 217–21, 223, 228, 230, 233–7, 239–40, 243–5, 249, 251, 255, 261, 263–7, 272

Maasai 56, 210, 214
McKnight, Scot (*Who Do My Opponents Say that I Am?*) 150
magic 121–4, 167, 245, 251
makarism (blessing) 256
Malachi, book of 14, 17, 20
Malchus 218, 222
Mandaean writings 199
manna 80, 82, 84, 90, 91, 169
Marcion 141
Marcus Aurelius 191
Mark, Gospel of 6, 16, 20–2, 26, 28, 29, 32, 35, 44, 45, 51, 52, 54, 55, 59, 60, 64, 66, 74–5, 77, 78, 88, 91, 94, 95, 97, 104, 105, 108, 109, 117, 120, 122, 130, 131, 134, 138, 143, 148, 149, 151, 153–6, 158, 160, 178, 181–5, 187–8, 191, 193, 196, 201, 205, 217, 219–23, 227, 228, 230, 233–40, 243–5, 249, 251, 255, 263, 264, 271
Martha 4, 142–53
Martial (*Epigrams*) 225
martyrdom 149, 184, 185, 269, 271
Mary (mother of Jesus) 27–9, 234, 235, 241
Mary (sister of Martha and Lazarus) 6, 142–51
Mary (wife of Clopas) 234
Mary of Magdala 4, 67, 131, 152–4, 234–5, 244–53, 257

Matthew, Gospel of 6, 19–22, 26–7, 32, 34, 35, 44–6, 51, 54–5, 57, 59, 60, 63, 64, 66, 74, 75, 77, 78, 83, 91, 95, 97, 101, 104, 105, 109, 124, 128, 129, 131, 132, 134, 135, 148, 149, 151, 153–8, 160, 166, 178, 181, 183–5, 188, 193, 196, 199, 202, 205, 212, 213, 217, 219, 220, 221, 223, 224, 227, 228, 230, 233–43, 244, 245, 249, 250, 253, 255, 256, 263–5, 268, 271–2
Matthias (apostle) 4
Melchizedek (king and priest of Salem) 42
Messiah 14, 19, 20, 23, 24, 25, 27, 32, 40, 44, 45, 50, 51, 52, 54, 56, 76, 82, 90, 95–8, 100–3, 109, 117–19, 125, 131–3, 135, 138, 139, 141, 142, 155–62, 166, 168, 171, 188, 196, 198, 210, 219, 226, 228, 237, 240, 258, 259, 274, 284–7; *see also* Jesus
Micah, book of 23, 24, 98, 126, 130, 131, 132, 135, 144, 198
Midrash 80
Midrash Rabbah on Ecclesiastes 23
miracles 19, 23, 26, 29, 30, 35, 36, 54, 55, 59, 74–9, 85, 86, 90, 92, 122, 124, 125, 140, 150, 167, 169, 170, 171, 179, 214, 261, 264–6, 281, 282
Mishnah, *Shabbat* 59, 97
misunderstandings 25, 28, 33, 83, 98–101, 111, 113, 118, 144, 149, 180, 218, 230, 240, 249, 251, 270, 285
Modica, Joseph (*Who Do My Opponents Say that I Am?*) 150
*modus tollens* (a denial) 115, 116, 118, 120
Montanism 1
Moses 16, 18, 20, 23, 38, 58, 63–6, 72, 75, 79, 80–4, 90, 96, 97, 104, 125, 126, 169, 246, 248,

286, 287; and bronze serpent 39, 72
mysteries (in Greek and Roman religions) 5, 41, 251
mysticism 1, 192, 208

name of the Lord 64, 155
Nathanael 19, 23–4, 26–8, 52, 65, 263
Nazareth 23, 25, 27, 97, 101, 218, 233
Nazorean, meaning of 218
Nehemiah, book of 58, 80, 134, 136
Nero (emperor) 265
Nicodemus 31, 37–49, 65, 102, 103, 153, 163, 167, 193, 235, 237, 238, 242, 276
Noah 21, 77
Numbers, book of 16, 21, 29, 31, 39, 59, 62, 74, 75, 82, 117, 122, 125, 131, 132, 147, 149, 152, 178, 179, 201, 236, 237, 286

Olives, Mount of 104, 217
ontology (nature of being) 64, 141
Ovid (*Herodes*) 245

Papias, Bishop of Hierapolis 4, 271
Papyrus 52 (Gospel fragment) 2, 5
parables 6, 16, 52, 83, 131, 134, 136, 139, 148, 151, 155, 171, 175, 198, 285
Paraclete *see* Holy Spirit
*parrhēsia* (plain speaking) 285, 286
Passion, the 27, 33, 34, 49, 50, 87, 99, 101, 136, 150, 158, 173, 175, 183, 201, 203, 217, 219, 245
Passover: calendar 11, 178; *Haggadah* (telling) 31–2
Passover meal (*Seder*) 11, 21, 29, 31–58, 74–89, 152–63, 175, 176, 178, 179, 223, 225, 227, 230, 236, 237, 281

Paul (apostle) 64, 89, 114, 126, 160, 178, 179, 192, 241, 246, 247, 257, 266, 271
*Pax Romana* 191, 192, 231
peace 23, 135, 189, 191, 192, 193, 199, 207, 208, 212, 213, 253, 254, 256, 270, 275
Pentateuch (five books of Moses) 48
Peter (Simon/Cephas) 5, 6, 22, 23, 62, 88, 109, 149, 176, 180, 182–5, 193, 196, 198, 199, 218, 219, 220–4, 228, 231, 244, 245, 246, 247, 249, 261, 263–71
Petronius (*Satyricon*) 222
Pharisees 20, 29, 37, 40, 47, 59, 61, 68, 99, 102, 104, 108, 110, 115, 121, 124–30, 133, 134, 136, 139, 145, 146, 147, 152, 156, 168, 170
Philip (apostle) 19, 22, 23, 25, 68, 75, 109, 158, 187, 190, 277
Philippians, letter to 3, 17
Philo Judaeus 2, 17, 18, 60, 83, 107, 117, 119, 141, 147, 225, 236, 273
Pilate, Pontius 6, 37, 217, 219, 224–38, 240, 242, 283
*Pirke Abot* 82, 112, 223
Plato 45, 52, 179, 231
Plautus (*The Braggart Captain*) 233
Plutarch (*Moralia*) 179
Polybius (*Histories*) 234
pre-existence 2, 21, 84, 87, 98, 110, 117, 141, 204, 284–5
priests 19, 94, 99, 102, 147, 152, 153, 218, 220, 221, 225, 226, 228
Prologue (John 1) 11, 13–19, 21, 46, 72, 166, 212, 248, 275, 278, 283, 284
prophets 14, 19, 20, 21, 23, 33, 48, 49, 50, 54, 76, 79, 82, 101, 102, 116, 117, 123, 125, 131, 132, 147, 150, 154, 158, 162, 169, 198, 241, 247, 287
prosperity gospel 135, 136

psalms 13, 18, 22, 49, 100, 107, 126, 131, 141, 155
*Psalms of Solomon* 251, 287
purification 28, 46, 91, 122, 176, 236
Purim, Festival of 198

*qal-wahômer* (light and heavy) 38, 97, 98, 99, 139, 150, 177
Quartodecimanism 1, 178
Quintilian (*Declamatio Maior*) 236
Qumran 6, 178, 187, 287

rabbi 22, 23, 24, 37, 38, 44, 45, 50, 52, 59, 60, 79, 82, 121, 125, 143, 156, 177, 237, 250
Rebekah 48
Reformation, the 34, 56, 271
remaining *see* abiding
resurrection 27, 31, 33, 34, 35, 61, 62, 67, 72, 86, 108, 133, 142, 144, 145, 149, 150, 151, 158, 170, 171, 183, 186, 198, 205, 209, 214, 235, 242, 244–59, 269, 275, 276; as opposed to resuscitation 61, 150, 151, 251
revelation 1, 16, 18, 20, 24, 46, 61, 67, 68, 69, 112, 117, 147, 167, 190, 218, 237, 248, 257, 283
Revelation, book of 4, 17, 20, 23, 27, 45, 48, 49, 75, 131, 141, 143, 159, 180, 199, 218, 237, 249, 265
Roman Catholicism 34, 170
Roman Empire 191, 230, 231, 240
Romans, letter to 39, 64, 135, 162, 241
Rufinus of Aquileia 160
Ruth, book of 136

Sabbath 27, 58–66, 70, 93, 97, 121–38, 168, 236, 238, 245
sacrament/sacramentals 29, 42, 86, 90, 91, 92, 114, 237, 277
sacrifice 21, 32, 100, 194, 230, 236
Sallust (*The War with Cataline*) 234
salvation 5, 27, 41, 42, 44, 50, 54, 67, 68, 69, 70–3, 88, 89, 114,

132, 134, 135, 144, 155, 160, 163, 164, 168, 181, 189, 201; Jesus himself the true means of 190–2, 213; truth leads to 284

Samaritans 2, 31, 32, 44, 47, 48, 50–5, 116, 225, 228, 277, 281, 287; Mount Gerizim 32, 48

Samaritan woman 48–50, 52; *see also* Jacob's well, Jesus at

Sanhedrin 147, 237, 276

*Sanhedrin* (rabbinic text) 110, 223

Satan 153, 159, 160, 181, 183, 184, 189, 197, 286; *see also* devil

saviour 51, 52, 53, 135, 166, 181, 185, 214, 278

sea, symbolism of 77

seal 45, 80, 245

Second Temple Judaism (Synoptic Gospels: Mark, Matthew, Luke) 2, 61, 90, 91, 141, 241, 284, 287

*Seder see* Passover meal

seeing (in relation to belief) 29, 82, 130, 163, 167, 170, 187, 246, 256, 257, 282

self-testimony 62, 65, 107, 109, 125

sending: of disciples 51, 195, 205, 253, 265; of Jesus, 7, 39, 42, 61, 65, 72, 108, 163, 189, 196, 199, 275, 285

Septuagint (LXX) 23, 54, 239

Sermon on the Mount 6, 256

Sermon on the Plain 6

serpent: analogy 41–2; Hebrew word for 39; *see also* Moses

service (discipleship) 158, 175, 176, 179, 180, 182, 194, 215, 238, 243

'seventy', the (disciples) 44, 51

sheep 32, 58, 121, 131–4, 136, 139, 145, 153, 213–14, 268–9, 278

Sheep Gate 58

*Shekinah* 16

shepherds 131, 132, 134, 136, 139; identification of Jesus with 133, 278; imagery 130, 133, 210, 269; *see also* Good Shepherd

*Sifre Leviticus* 112

*Sifre Numbers* 112

sign(s) 13, 26, 28–30, 35–7, 40, 41, 46, 63, 74, 79, 83, 92, 98, 103, 124–5, 126, 154, 158, 159, 162, 163, 165–71, 183, 191, 196, 242, 258, 259, 282–3; and wonders 54, 56, 57, 165–7

Signs, Book of 13–174; peroration (climax of speech or writing) 11, 162–4

Siloam, pool of 122

Simon of Cana 188

Simon of Cyrene 233

sin 20, 21, 41, 43, 60–1, 64, 105, 109–10, 113, 116, 121–6, 130, 136, 143, 176, 181, 195–8, 200–2, 212, 229, 250, 253–5, 276, 284; intentional/ unintentional 201

Sinai, Mount 20, 82

Sirach, book of 29, 48, 49, 81, 82, 130, 156, 177, 199

slaves 6, 20, 41, 112–14, 194, 200, 218, 221, 222, 228

Socrates 161, 186, 231

Son of God 21–2, 24, 40, 62, 66, 67, 69, 71, 118, 140, 143, 166, 171, 228, 232, 258, 274

Son of Man 24, 26, 34, 38, 62, 66, 69, 71, 72, 80, 85–7, 111, 128, 158, 159, 170, 171, 183, 285

Song of Songs, book of 27, 45, 153

status 14, 16, 18, 21, 23, 25, 27, 34, 37, 41, 46, 53, 55, 64, 65, 70, 81, 82, 101, 112, 113, 116, 134, 145, 160, 191, 200, 204, 222, 253, 254–6; *see also* honour/shame

staying *see* abiding

Stoics/Stoicism 14, 45, 161

subordinationism 65, 189

Suetonius: *Caligula* 233; *Domitian* 233, 256; *Tiberius* 131

Suffering Servant 20, 162

*Sukkoth* 96–9, 100–4, 107–9, 122, 138; *see also* Booths, Festival of

Susanna, story of 23, 62, 104, 105
Sychar (Samaritan city) 47, 48
synagogue 99, 125, 127, 163, 196, 201, 202, 221
Syria 2, 4, 5

*Ta'an* (Babylonian Talmud) 60
Tacitus (*Annals*) 191, 225, 237
*Taheb see* Jesus
Temple 2, 6, 11, 16, 19, 21, 31–5, 38, 48, 59, 61, 77, 90, 91, 93, 94, 99, 101, 102, 104, 107, 121, 138, 141, 147, 167, 170, 178, 199, 221, 225, 230, 237, 239, 241, 248, 281, 284, 287; treasury 108
Tertullian (*On the Games*) 249
*Testament of Abraham* 238
*Testaments of the Twelve Patriarchs* 141, 179
Thaddeus (disciple) 188
theodicy 123
theosis 192, 208, 209
Thomas (Didymus, apostle) 144, 186, 188, 190, 244, 256–8, 263
Tiberias, Sea of 55, 74, 79, 261, 263–7, 271; *see also* Galilee, Sea of
Tiberius (emperor) 131, 136–7, 224, 229
tithes/tithing 135–6
tomb of Jesus 142, 144–6, 239, 240, 242, 244, 245–9, 251, 252, 255, 271
Torah *see* law
*Tosefta* 122, 223
Transfiguration, the 160
Trinitarian communion 210
Trinitarian debates 64
Trinitarian language 192
Trinity, doctrine of 16, 191, 192; *perichoresis* (mutual indwelling of members of) 192
trust (related to belief) 15, 35–7, 42, 134, 136, 145, 150, 154, 162, 163, 212, 237, 282
truth 7, 16, 33, 34, 36, 41, 42, 43, 45, 46, 50, 52, 53, 62, 63, 71, 76, 85, 90, 91, 96, 103, 112, 113, 115, 116, 118, 127, 135, 165, 170, 171, 186–92, 196, 197, 205, 207, 209, 210, 213, 214, 216, 219, 223, 227, 230–2, 237, 242, 275, 276, 278, 279, 282–5
Tutu, Desmond 150
'twelve', the (apostles) 22, 44, 88–9, 121, 188, 256
typology 41

Valentinus 2
Virgil: *Aeneid* 241; *Fourth Eclogue* 287
vine 69, 171, 193–4, 199–200, 202, 209–10, 215–16, 249

Waco, Texas 164
water 13, 19, 20, 21, 27, 28, 38, 44, 48, 49, 55, 59, 64, 74, 77, 78, 85, 94, 101, 122, 124, 167, 169, 176, 237, 264, 276–8; living water 39, 49, 53, 95, 101–5, 109, 119, 275–7
Water Gate 94
way 171, 186–7, 190, 209–10, 213–14, 216, 275, 278, 283
wedding at Cana 26–9
weddings 167
wheat 158, 161, 277
wine 13, 19, 28, 29, 55, 85, 86, 167, 233, 235, 239, 281
wisdom 14, 17, 41, 49, 61, 80, 81, 83, 84, 86, 90, 91, 94, 125, 127, 141, 168, 199, 201, 210, 224, 253, 284, 287
works 25, 39, 56, 61, 63, 64, 68, 69, 80, 90, 94, 99, 122, 123, 134, 139, 140, 159, 165, 166, 181, 187, 192, 195, 196, 213, 231, 282
world 1, 2, 5, 7, 8, 13–15, 17–21, 27–9, 33, 37, 39, 41–3, 45, 51–3, 56, 67–73, 77, 79, 80, 83, 85, 88, 89, 93–5, 97, 103, 106, 107, 109–12, 119, 122, 123, 129, 135, 143, 147, 154, 156,

158–61, 163–6, 170, 171, 175, 184, 186–9, 191, 192, 195, 197, 200–2, 204–7, 209, 210, 212, 213, 215, 218, 219, 221, 223, 226, 231–3, 242, 249, 254, 255, 269, 273–8, 281, 282, 284, 285, 286, 288

worship 5, 19, 30, 32, 34, 48, 49, 50, 53, 59, 65, 68, 70, 94, 98, 99, 100, 110, 126, 128, 129, 163, 164, 169, 196, 201, 207, 218, 253, 278, 283

Xenophon (*Memorabilia*) 179

Zechariah, book of 23, 24, 94, 97, 101, 126, 130, 132, 155, 156, 157, 183, 199, 237, 243
Zephaniah, book of 132
Zion, Mount 75, 76, 155